The Laṅkāvatāra Sūtra

The present translation of D.T. Suzuki is based upon the Sanskrit edition of Bunyu Nanjo (1923).

The Laṅkāvatāra Sūtra reflects those fundamental themes of Buddhism which the Mahāyāna in general cherishes and upholds. It looks at existence from the absolute and relative realms, and thinks that suffering will be experienced so long as one confines oneself to the realm of the relative. Since the relative cannot be ultimately realm, it has to be seen as nothing more than a projection of the mind. As to how to realize the ultimate truth of unity the text resorts to general Mahāyāna theory of Buddhalogy in which the Buddha is seen as the ultimate ontological principle. In order to realize unity with this ontic principle, we have to make use of such methods which, though relative, terminate in the realization of Enlightenment. These methods are spoken of as Skilful Means. As a spiritual manual, the text points out as to how the Bodhisattvas, on account of their unlimited compassion for sentient beings, work for the salvation of all. While delineating on the theme of Bodhisattvas, the text thereby speaks about the ten vows of a Bodhisattva. It is in incarnating these vows within that a real turn-about or spiritual transformation occurs, and thereby are uprooted the roots of ignorance. The text, thus, offers a spiritual banquet to those who want to taste the bliss eternal.

Bodhidharma
By Sesshu (1420-1506)

The Laṅkāvatāra Sūtra

A Mahāyāna Text

Translated for the first time from the original Sanskrit by
DAISETZ TEITARO SUZUKI

Foreword by
MOTI LAL PANDIT

Munshiram Manoharlal
Publishers Pvt. Ltd.

ISBN 81-215-0925-4
First Indian edition 1999
Originally published in 1932

© 1999, Munshiram Manoharlal Publishers Pvt. Ltd., New Delhi

All rights reserved. No part of this book may be reproduced, stored in a retrieval system, or transmitted, in any form, or by any means, electronic, mechanical, photocopying, recording or otherwise, without the written permission of the publisher.

Printed and published by
Munshiram Manoharlal Publishers Pvt. Ltd.,
Post Box 5715, 54 Rani Jhansi Road, New Delhi 110 055.

CONTENTS

Bodhidharma by Sesshū (1420-1506) *Frontispiece*

Foreword ix
Preface xii c
Introduction xiii

CHAPTER ONE. RAVANA, LORD OF LANKA, ASKS FOR INSTRUCTION 3

CHAPTER TWO. COLLECTION OF ALL THE DHARMAS .. 22

§ I.	Mahāmati Praises the Buddha with Verses	22
§ II.	Mahāmati's "One Hundred and Eight Questions"	23
§ III.	"The One Hundred and Eight Negations"	31
§ IV.	Concerning the Vijñānas	33
§ V.	Seven Kinds of Self-nature (*svabhāva*)	35
§ VI.	Seven Kinds of First Principle (*paramārtha*), and the Philosophers' Wrong Views regarding the Mind Rejected	35
§ VII.	Erroneous Views held by Some Brahmans and Śramanas Concerning Causation, Continuation, etc.; The Buddhist Views Concerning Such Subjects as Alayavijñāna, Nirvana, Mind-only, etc.; Attainments of the Bodhisattva	36
§ VIII.	The Bodhisattva's Disciplining himself in Self-realisation	39
§ IX.	The Evolution and Function of the Vijñānas; The Spiritual Discipline of the Bodhisattva; Verses on the Alaya-ocean and Vijñāna-waves	39
§ X.	The Bodhisattva is to Understand the Signification of Mind-only	44
§ XI(a).	The Three Aspects of Noble Wisdom (*āryajñāna*)	44
§ XI(b).	The Attainment of the Tathāgatakāya	45
§ XII.	Logic on the Hare's Horns	46
§ XIII.	Verses on the Alayavijñāna and Mind-only	49
§ XIV.	Purification of the Outflows, Instantaneous and Gradual	49
§ XV.	Nishyanda-Buddha, Dharmatā-Buddha, and Nirmāṇa-Buddha	51
§ XVI.	The Śrāvaka's Realisation and Attachment to the Notion of Self-nature	52
§ XVII.	The Eternal-Unthinkable	53
§ XVIII.	Nirvana and Alayavijñāna	55
§ XIX.	All Things are Unborn	55
§ XX.	The Five Classes of Spiritual Insight	56
§ XXI.	Verses on the Triple Vehicle	58

§ XXII.	Two Classes of the Icchantika	58
§ XXIII.	The Three Forms of Svabhāva	59
§ XXIV.	The Twofold Egolessness (*nairātmyadvaya-lakshaṇa*)	60
§ XXV.	Assertion and Refutation (*samāropāpavāda*)	62
§ XXVI.	The Bodhisattva Assumes Various Personalities	64
§ XXVII.	On Emptiness (*śūnyatā*), No-birth, and Non-duality	65
§ XXVIII.	The Tathāgata-Garbha and the Ego-soul	68
§ XXIX.	A Verse on the Philosophers' Discriminations	70
§ XXX.	The Four Things Needed for the Constitution of Bodhisattvahood	70
§ XXXI.	On Causation (Six Kinds), and the Rise of Existence	72
§ XXXII.	Four Forms of Word-discrimination	75
§ XXXIII.	On Word and Discrimination and the Highest Reality	76
§ XXXIV.	Verses on Reality and its Representations	77
§ XXXV.	Mind-only, Multitudinousness, and Analogies, with an Interpolation on the Dualistic Notion of Existence	78
§ XXXVI.	The Teaching (*dharmadeśanā*) of the Tathagatas	84
§ XXXVII.	Four Kinds of Dhyāna	85
§ XXXVIII.	On Nirvana	86
§ XXXIX.	Two Characteristics of Self-nature	87
§ XL.	Two Kinds of the Buddha's Sustaining Power (*adhishṭhāna*)	87
§ XLI.	On the Chain of Causation (*pratityasamutpāda*)	90
§ XLII.	Words (*abhilāpa*) and Realities (*bhāva*)	91
§ XLIII.	On Eternality of Sound (*nityaśabda*), the Nature of Error (*bhrānta*), and Perversion (*viparyāsa*)	63
§ XLIV.	On the Nature of Māyā	95
§ XLV.	That All Things are Unborn	96
§ XLVI.	On Name, Sentence, Syllable, and Their Meaning	97
§ XLVII.	On Inexplicable Statements (*vyākṛitāni*)	98
§ XLVIII.	All Things are and are not (Verses on Four Forms of Explanation)	99
§ XLIX.	On the Śrāvakas, Srotaāpanna, Sakṛidāgāmin, Anāgāmin, and Arhat; on the Three Knots (*samyojāni*)	100
§ L.	The Intellect (*buddhi*), Examining and Discriminating	105
§ LI.	The Elements, Primary and Secondary	106
§ LII.	The Five Skandhas	107
§ LIII.	Four Kinds of Nirvana and the Eight Vijñānas	108
§ LIV.	The False Imagination Regarding Twelve Subjects	110

CONTENTS

§ LV.	Verses on the Citta, Parikalpita, Paratantra, and Parinishpanna	112
§ LVI.	The One Vehicle and the Triple Vehicle	114

CHAPTER THREE. ON IMPERMANENCY 118

§ LVII.	Three Forms of the Will-body (*manomayakāya*)	118
§ LVIII.	The Five Immediacies (*pañcānantaryāṇi*); Desire as Mother and Ignorance as Father	120
§ LIX.	The Buddha-nature (*buddhatā*)	122
§ LX.	The Identity (*samatā*) of Buddhahood and its Four Aspects	122
§ LXI.	Not a Word Uttered by the Buddha; Self-realisation and an Eternally-abiding Reality	123
§ LXII.	On Being and Non-Being; Realism and Nihilism	125
§ LXIII.	Realisation and Word-teaching	127
§ LXIV.	Discrimination, an External World, Dualism, and Attachment	129
§ LXV.	The Relation between Words (*ruta*) and Meaning (*artha*)	133
§ LXVI.	On Knowledge, Absolute (*jñāna*) and Relative (*vijñāna*)	135
§ LXVII.	Nine Transformations (*pariṇāma*)	137
§ LXVIII.	The Deep-seated Attachment to Existence	138
§ LXIX.	Self-nature, Reality, Imagination, Truth of Solitude, etc.	141
§ LXX.	The Thesis of No-birth	144
§ LXXI.	True Knowledge and Ignorance	146
§ LXXII.	Self-realisation and the Discoursing on it	148
§ LXXIII.	On the Lokāyatika	149
§ LXXIV.	Various Views of Nirvana	157
§ LXXV.	Is Tathagatahood Something Made? Its Relation to the Skandhas, to Emancipation, to Knowledge	161
§ LXXVI.	The Tathagata Variously Designated; Relation Between Words and Meaning; Not a Word Uttered by the Buddha	164
§ LXXVII.	Causation, No-birth, Self-mind, Nirvana	170
§ LXXVIII.	Verses on No-birth and Causation	172
§ LXXIX.	Various Views of Impermanency	176

CHAPTER FOUR. ON INTUITIVE UNDERSTANDING 182

§ LXXX.	Perfect Tranquillisation Attained by Śrāvakas, Pratyekabuddhas, and Bodhisattvas; Stages of Bodhisattvahood	182

CHAPTER FIVE. ON THE DEDUCTION OF THE PERMANENCY OF TATHAGATAHOOD 187

§ LXXXI.	Permanency of Tathagatahood	187

CHAPTER SIX. ON MOMENTARINESS 190

§ LXXXII.	The Tathāgata-garbha and the Alayavijñāna	190

§ LXXXIII. The Five Dharmas, and Their Relation to the
            Three Svabhāvas 193
§ LXXXIV. The Five Dharmas 197
§ LXXXV. Tathagata and Sands of the Gangā 198
§ LXXXVI. Momentariness; the Eight Vijñānas 202
§ LXXXVII. Three Kinds of the Pāramitās 204
§ LXXXVIII. Views on Momentariness; Discrimination 206

CHAPTER SEVEN. ON TRANSFORMATION 207
§ LXXXIX. On Transformation 207

CHAPTER EIGHT. ON MEAT-EATING 211

CHAPTER NINE. THE DHĀRANĪS 223

SAGĀTHAKAM 226

Appendix   297

FOREWORD

Prior to explaining as to what is constitutive of the *Laṅkāvatāra* text, we shall direct our attention to the evolution of the Tathāgatagarbha School so that the link between the contents of the latter could be established with the contents of the former. It is a historical fact that the Tathāgatagarbha School is closely allied in its philosophic orientation to the Yogācāra-vijñānavāda School. It speaks of Reality as being identical with the Womb of Thatness or Suchness (*tathāgatagarbha*), and as such is considered to the basis of that which is manifest, or which is termed as being phenomenal. The manifest world, which we experience cognitively and of which we think ourselves to be a part, has, if we may say so, its ontic basis in what is called the *buddhadhātu*, which is non-different from the *tathāgatagrabha*. Since the world, as a manifest category, is but the self-extension of Reality, so it cannot be accorded with any ontic significance in itself. We can think of it only as being apparent or non-real. It is at this apparent level that the so-called birth and death, or emergence or destruction, of beings and entities occurs within the Womb (*garbha*) of Reality (*tathata*). Within this Womb, thus, both the real and the apparent coincide, which means that the *tathāgatagarbha* is equally the source of *saṃsāra*, of the Buddha, of the Dharma, and of the Saṃgha.

The historical evolution of the Tathāgatagarbha School seems to have gone through three historical phases or periods. The first phase of development is characterized by the interaction between the ontological frameworks of *tathāgatagarbha* and *ālayavijñāna*. As the principle of subjectivity, *ālayavijñāna* is considered as the basis of everything that is either phenomenal or non-phenomenal. The *tathāgatagarbha*, considered conceptually objective, is like the *brahman* of the Upaniṣads, whereas the *ālaya* may be linked to the *ātman*. It is within this ontological framework that the manifest world is considered as the expression of the Womb of Tathāgata. It is during this first phase of development that such texts as, for example, the *Tathāgatagarbhasūtra* and the *Anuttarāśrayasūtra* were produced. The latter text, in particular, delineates such Mahāyāna doctrines as the conception of the *triple body* (*trikāya*) of the Buddha, the five spiritual lineages, and the idea that the sinners are potentially as much of the nature of the Buddha as are the men of high moral conduct. This idea of non-difference between a sinner and non-sinner would ultimately result in the eradication of difference that occurs, at the relative level of existence, between good and evil. As everything would be ontically seen as being identical, so the conceptual differences of the relative realm will be seen as being relatively, and not ultimately, real. Also to this phase belong the composition of such texts as the *Śrīmālāsimhanādasūtra*, the *Mahāparinirvāṇasūtra*, and the *Aṅgulimālikasūtra*. The date of composition of the texts of this phase may be assigned to AD 300-400.

In the second phase of development the ontological concepts of *tathāgatagarbha* and the *ālayavijñāna* seem to have been worked out separately. This may be inferred from the fact that the texts of this period do not at all explain as to whether any kind of links exists between the two concepts. The main texts that were composed during this phase of development are the *Mahāyānasūtrālamkāra* and the commentaries upon the *Mahāyānasamparigrahasūtra*.

Finally, we have the third phase of development in which the dependent co-arising (*pratītya-samutpāda*) is explained as having its source in the Womb of Thathāgata, which denotes that the phenomenal has its source in the Transcendent. The projection of the Transcendent as the phenomenal occurs through the *ālayavijñāna*, or the *storehouse consciousness*. It would mean that which is objective is nothing but the mode of the subjective. It is during this period that the important texts were composed, and some of them are the *Laṅkāvatārasūtra*, *Gaṇḍavyūhasūtra*, which is the last section of the *Avataṁsaka* and the *Mahāyānaśraddhā-utpādaśāstra*.

FOREWORD

The *Laṅkāvatāra* is the most important text, and is equally respected by the Tathāgatagarbha School and by the Yogācāravijñānavāda School. The text is also held in high esteem by the Cha'n or Zen School of Meditation. The text, so we are informed, was, for the first time, translated in Chinese by Dharmarakṣa between AD 412-33. This translation, however, is no more extant. The earliest translation of the text that is available is that of Guṇabhadra (AD 433). The original Sanskrit composition is believed to have taken place somewhere between AD 300-350. The text, however, does not seem to be earlier than the *Śrīmālādevīsiṁhānādasūtra,* as there are many quotations of the latter work to be found in the former.

The text of the *Laṅkāvatārasūtra* repeats the basic idealistic idea that one finds scattered in the *Avataṁsaka,* namely, the nature of the Real is nothing else but the Mind-only (*cittamātra*). While the Yogācāra treats the mind as the basis of subjectivity, the *Laṅkāvatāra,* on the contrary, thinks of it as being Transcendent, i.e., beyond the categories of thought and that which intellectual reflection entails. The understanding of the *Laṅkāvatāra* concerning the "mind" would mean that it is to be seen the substratum not only of subjectivity, but equally of objectivity. The Yogācāra as a pure idealistic school thinks of the objective as being non-existent apart from the mind. The phenomena as events that we experience are viewed as being the modes of our subjectivity. While differing in its interpretation concerning the mind from the Yogācāra, the *Laṅkāvatāra* thus is in a position to say that the Four Noble Truths have their source in the transcendent Mind. Similar, if not identical, thoughts are to be found in the Sāṁkhya system as well as in the *Yogavasiṣṭha.*

In addition to looking at the Mind as the basis of the subjective and of the objective, the *Laṅkāvatāra* may also be treated as a manual on spiritual discipline. It speaks of spiritual regeneration in terms of what it calls the total "turn-about" (*parāvṛtti*). The complete turn-about would entail practical death to that which is defiling, and thereby the cause of saṁsāric becoming. Upon the renunciation or abandonment of that which gives rise to *saṁsāra*, there occurs in the individual a spiritual awakening, which, if described in classical terms, would mean that one, as it were, is reborn supernaturally upon the negation of categories, whether mental or physical, that are defiling or cause the Real to be concealed. In actual terms this death would denote transcending our basic human nature. And this death to human nature, so it is asserted, results in an inner transformation whereby one's essential nature of Buddhahood is realized. For the *Laṅkāvatāra* the knowledge the one's essential nature is non-different from Buddhahood is equivalent to the knowledge of Reality as being Tathāgatagarbha. The revelation of the Tathāgatagarbha as being identical with the Real denotes at the same time the attainment of the state of Enlightenment.

The result of the spiritual turn-about, on the one hand, signifies complete inner transformation, which ultimately terminates in the attainment of Enlightenment, and as a consequence of this Enlightenment, on the other hand, results in the abandonment of views or standpoints that are false. False views are given rise to on account of imagined consciousness (*parikalpita*) and dependent consciousness (*paratantra*). It is upon the destruction of false views, and thereby also of the above two forms of consciousness, that the emergence of perfect consciousness (*pariniṣpanna*) is facilitated. What is the nature, it may be asked, of perfect consciousness? The perfect consciousness reflects the non-discriminative nature of wisdom, and so its nature is said to be unitive. To attain the unitive vision of Enlightenment through perfect consciousness means the realization of complete freedom from the subject-object dichotomy of ordinary consciousness. Rightly, therefore, *Laṅkāvatāra* has been accorded the place of importance on account of it foreshadowing the Yogācāra and Tathāgatagarbha schools.

In translating the text of the *Laṅkāvatāra* into English, D.T. Suzuki thereby has rendered a great service to the cause of Buddhism. To understand the complex thought of the text, Suzuki has written a well thought out Introduction in which the seminal ideas of the Mahāyāna are delineated lucidly. It would help greatly the reader if he also studies the book of this author, namely, *Studies in the Laṅkāvatāra Sūtra,* which was first published in 1930. In reprinting the translation of *Laṅkāvatāra,* Munshiram Manoharlal Publishers as publishers of Indological works have thereby made the text available to those who want to delve deep into the rich heritage of Mahāyāna Buddhism.

MOTI LAL PANDIT

New Delhi
13 July 1999

PREFACE

It is more than seven years now since I began the study of the *Laṅkāvatāra Sūtra* quite seriously, but owing to various interruptions I have not been able to carry out my plan as speedily as I wished. My friends in different fields of life have been kind and generous in various ways, and I now send out to the perusal of the English-reading public this humble work of mine. There are yet many difficu and obscure passages in the Sutra, which I have been unable to unravel to my own satisfaction. All such imperfections are to be corrected by competent scholars. I shall be fully content if I have made the understanding of this signifieant Mahayana text easier than before, even though this may be only to a very slight degree. In China Buddhist scholars profoundly learned and endowed with spiritual insights made three or four attempts extending over a period of about two hundred and fifty years to give an intelligible rendering of the *Laṅkāvatāra*. It goes without saying that these have helped immensely the present translator. May his also prove a stepping board however feeble towards a fuller interpretation of the Sutra!

The present English translation is based on the Sanskrit edition of Bunyu Nanjo's published by the Otani University Press in 1923.

I am most grateful to Mr Dwight Goddard of Thetford, Vermont, U. S. A., who again helped me by typing the entire manuscript of the present book. To assist me in this way was indeed part of the object of his third visit to this side of the Pacific. Says Confucius, "Is it not delightful to have a friend come from afar?" The saying applies most appropriately to this case.

It was fortunate for the writer that he could secure the support and help of the Keimeikwai, a corporation organised to help research work of scholars in various fields of culture; for without it his work might have dragged on yet for some time to come. There is so much to be accomplished before he has to appear at the court of Emma Daiwo, to whom he could say, "Here is my work; humble though it is, I have tried to do my part to the full extent of my power." The writer renders his grateful acknowledgment here to all the advisers of the Society who kindly voted for the speedy culmination of this literary task—a task which he tenderly wishes would do something towards a better appreciation by the West of the sources of Eastern life and culture.

Whatever literary work the present author is able to put before the reader, he cannot pass on without mentioning in it the name of his good, unselfish, public-minded Buddhist friend, Yakichi Ataka, who is always willing to help him in every possible way. If not for him, the author could never have carried out his plans to the extent he has so far accomplished. Materially, no visible results can be expected of this kind of undertaking, and yet a scholar has his worldly needs to meet. Unless we create one of these fine days an ideal community in which every member of it can put forth all his or her natural endowments and moral energies in the direction best fitted to develop them and in the way most useful to all other members generally and individually, many obstacles are sure to bar the passage of those who would attempt things of no commercial value. Until then, Bodhisattvas of all kinds are sorely needed everywhere. And is this not the teaching of the *Laṅkāvatāra Sūtra,* which in its English garb now lies before his friend as well as all other readers?

Thanks are also due to the writer's wife who went over the whole manuscript to give it whatever literary improvement it possesses, to Mr Hokei Idzumi who gave helpful suggestions in the reading of the original text, and to Professor Yenga Teramoto for his ungrudging cooperation along the line of Tibetan knowledge.

DAISETZ TEITARO SUZUKI

Kyoto, November, 1931 (the sixth year of Showa)

INTRODUCTION

For those who have already read my *Studies in the Laṅkāvatāra Sūtra*,[1] no special words are needed here. But to those who are not yet quite familiar with the teachings of Mahayana Buddhism an expository introduction to the principal theses of the *Laṅkā* may be welcome. Without something of preliminary knowledge as to what the Sutra proposes to teach, it will be difficult to comprehend the text intelligently. For thoughts of deep signification are presented in a most unsystematic manner. As I said in my *Studies*, the *Laṅkā* is a memorandum kept by a Mahayana master, in which he put down perhaps all the teachings of importance accepted by the Mahayana followers of his day. He apparently did not try to give them any order, and it is possible that the later redactors were not very careful in keeping faithfully whatever order there was in the beginning, thus giving the text a still more disorderly appearance. The introduction that follows may also serve as one to Mahayana Buddhism generally.

I

The Classification of Beings

From the Mahayana point of view, beings are divisible into two heads: those that are enlightened and those that are ignorant. The former are called Buddhas including also Bodhisattvas, Arhats, and Pratyekabuddhas while the latter comprise all the rest of beings under the general designation of bāla or bālapṛithagjana—*bāla* meaning "undeveloped", "puerile", or "ignorant", and *pṛithagjana* "people different" from the enlightened, that is, the multitudes, or people of ordinary type, whose minds are found engrossed in the

[1] Published by George Routledge and Sons, London. 1930. Pp. xxxii+464.

pursuit of egotistic pleasures and unawakened to the meaning of life. This class is also known as Sarvasattva, "all beings" or sentient beings. The Buddha wants to help the ignorant, hence the Buddhist teaching and discipline.

The Buddha

All the Buddhist teachings unfold themselves around the conception of Buddhahood. When this is adequately grasped, Buddhist philosophy with all its complications and superadditions will become luminous. What is the Buddha?

According to Mahāmati the Bodhisattva-Mahāsattva, who is the interlocutor of the Buddha in the *Laṅkā*, the Buddha is endowed with transcendental knowledge (*prajñā*) and a great compassionate heart (*karuṇā*). With the former he realises that this world of particulars has no reality, is devoid of an ego-substance (*anātman*) and that in this sense it resembles Māyā or a visionary flower in the air. As thus it is above the category of being and non-being, it is declared to be pure (*viśuddha*) and absolute (*vivikta*) and free from conditions (*animitta*). But the Buddha's transcendental wisdom is not always abiding in this high altitude, because being instigated by an irresistible power which innerly pushes him back into a region of birth and death, he comes down among us and lives with us, who are ignorant and lost in the darkness of the passions (*kleśa*). Nirvana is not the ultimate abode of Buddhahood, nor is enlightenment. Love and compassion is what essentially constitutes the self-nature of the All-knowing One (*sarvajña*).

The Buddha as Love

The Buddha's love is not something ego-centered. It is a will-force which desires and acts in the realm of twofold egolessness, it is above the dualism of being and non-being, it rises from a heart of non-discrimination, it manifests itself in the conduct of purposelessness (*anābhogacaryā*). It is the Tathagata's great love (*mahākaruṇā*) of all beings, which never ceases until everyone of them is happily led to the final asylum of Nirvana; for he refuses as long as there is a single unsaved soul to enjoy the bliss of Samādhi to which he is entitled by his long spiritual discipline. The Tathagata is indeed the one who, endowed with a heart of all-embracing love and compassion, regards all beings as if they were his only child. If he himself enters into Nirvana, no work will be done in the world where discrimination (*vikalpa*) goes on and multitudinousness (*vicitratā*) prevails. For this reason, he refuses to leave this world of relativity, all his thoughts are directed towards the ignorant and suffering masses of beings, for whom he is willing to sacrifice his enjoyment of absolute reality and self-absorption (*samādhisukhabhūtakoṭyā vinivārya*).

Skilful Means

The essential nature of love is to devise, to create, to accommodate itself to varying changing circumstances, and to this the Buddha's love is no exception. He is ever devising for the enlightenment and emancipation of all sentient beings. This is technically known as the working of Skilful Means (*upāyakauśalya*). Upāya is the outcome of Prajñā and Karuṇā. When Love worries itself over the destiny of the ignorant, Wisdom, so to speak, weaves a net of Skilful Means whereby to catch them up from the depths of the ocean called Birth-and-Death (*samsāra*). By Upāya thus the oneness of reality wherein the Buddha's enlightened mind abides transforms itself into the manifoldness of particular existences.

There is a gem known as Maṇi which is perfectly transparent and colourless in itself, and just because of this characteristic it reflects in it varieties of colours (*vicitrarūpa*). In the same way the Buddha is conceived by beings; in the same way his teaching is interpreted by them; that is, each one recognises the Buddha and his teaching according to his disposition (*āśaya*), understanding (*citta*), prejudice (*anuśaya*), propensity (*adhimukti*), and circumstance (*gati*). Again, the Buddha treats his fellow-beings as an expert physician treats his patients suffering from various forms of illness. The ultimate aim is to cure them, but as ailments differ medicines and treatments cannot be the same. For this reason it is said that the Buddha speaks one language of enlightenment, which reverberates in the ears of his hearers in all possible sounds. Upāya may thus be considered in a way due to the infinite differentiation of individual characters rather than to the deliberate contrivance of transcendental wisdom on the part of the Buddha.

One Buddha with Many Names

All the Buddhas are of one essence, they are the same as far as their inner enlightenment, their Dharmakāya, and their being furnished with the thirty-two major and the eighty minor marks of excellence are concerned. But when they wish to train beings according to their characters, they assume varieties of forms appearing differently to different beings, and thus there are many titles and appellations of the Buddha as to be beyond calculation (*asaṁkhyeya*).

One noteworthy fact about this—the Buddha's assuming so many names, is that he is not only known in various personal names but also given a number of abstract titles such as No-birth, Emptiness, Suchness, Reality, Nirvana, Eternity, Sameness, Trueness, Cessation, etc. The Buddha is thus personal as well as metaphysical.

The *Laṅkā* here does not forget to add that though the Buddha is known by so many different names, he is thereby neither fattened nor emaciated, as he is like the moon in water neither immersed nor emerging. This simile is generally regarded as best describing the relation of unity and multiplicity, of one absolute reality and this world of names and forms.

Transformation-bodies of the Buddha

While the Trikāya dogma is not yet fully developed in the *Laṅkā*, each member of the trinity is treaceable in such ideas as Dharmatā-buddha, Vipāka-buddha, and Nirmāṇa-buddha. The notion of the transformation-body inevitably follows from the Buddha's desire to save the ignorant whose minds are not enlightened enough to see straightway into the essence of Buddhahood. As they are not clear-sighted, something is to be devised to lead them to the right path, and this something must be in accord with their mentalities. If not, they are sure to go astray farther and farther. If they are not capable of grasping Buddhatā as it is, let them have something of it and gradually be developed. The theory of Upāya (skilful means) is also the theory of Manomayakāya, will-body. As the incarnation of a great compassionate heart, the Buddha ought to be able to take any form he wishes when he sees the sufferings of sentient beings. The will-body is a part of the Buddha's plan of world-salvation. This is one of the reasons why Buddhism is often regarded as polytheistic and at the same time pantheistic.

The Bodhisattva and His Ten Vows

In Mahayana Buddhism the Buddha is not the only agent who is engaged in the work of enlightening or saving the world. While he is able to transform himself into as many forms as are required by sentient beings, he is also assisted by his followers or "sons" (*putra, suta,* or *aurasa*) as they are called in the Mahayana sutras. Bodhisattvas are thus the sons of the Buddha and apply themselves most arduously and most assiduously to the cause of Buddhism. In fact, the actual work of world-salvation, we can say, is carried on by these spiritual soldiers under the leadership of the Buddha. The latter is sometimes felt to be too remote, too serene, too superhuman, and his sight is often lost in the midst of our worldly struggles. But the Bodhisattva is always with us, and ever ready to be our confidant, for he is felt by us to share the same passions, impulses, and aspirations which are such great disturbing, though ennobling too, forces of our human life.

To state the truth, sentient beings are all Bodhisattvas, however ignorant and ready to err they may be. They are all Jinaputras, the sons of the Victorious, and harbour in themselves every possibility of attaining enlightenment. The Bodhisattvas who have gone up successively all the rungs of the Bhūmi ladder, and who are thus capable of extending their help over us, are really our own brethren. Therefore, Mahāmati of the *Laṅkā* opens his questions generally with this: "I and other Bodhisattvas, etc." Mahāmati is our mouthpiece voicing our wants and aspirations.

Thus is not the place to consider historically how the conception evolved in Buddhism whose primitive object seems to have consisted in the realisation of Arhatship. But we can state this that the essence of Bodhisattvahood is an unequivocal affirmation of the social, altruistic nature of humankind. Whatever enlightenment one gains, it must be shared by one's fellow-beings. This idea is classically expressed in the Mahayana by the so-called "Ten Vows of Samantabhadra". The Bodhisattva is a man of "inexhaustible vows" (*daśanishṭhāpāda*). Without these he is not himself. To save the world, to bring all his fellow-beings up to the same level of thought and feeling where he himself is, and not to rest, not to enter into Nirvana until this is accomplished, how infinitely long and how inexpressively arduous the task may be. This is the Bodhisattva. Vowing to save all beings, which is technically known as Pūrvapraṇidhāna in Mahayana terminology, cannot even for a moment be separated from the life of the Bodhisattva.

The Buddha being surrounded by these noble-minded sons cannot fail finally to release all beings from the bondage of karma and ignorance and thirst for life. With this in view, he is always inspiring the Bodhisattvas with his sovereign power (*prabhāva*) and sustaining (*adhishṭhāna*) them in their efforts to bring enlightenment in the whole triple world.

The Ignorant

Life as it is lived by most of us is a painful business, for we have to endure much in various ways. Our desires are thwarted, our wishes are crushed, and the worst is that we do not know how to get out of this whirlpool of greed, anger, and infatuation. We are at the extreme end of existence opposed to that of the Buddha. How can we leap over the abyss and reach the other shore?

INTRODUCTION xix

The Mahayana diagnosis of the conditions in which all sentient beings are placed is that they are all nursed by desire (*trishṇā*) as mother who is accompanied by pleasure (*nandī*) and anger (*rāga*), while ignorance (*avidyā*) is father. To be cured of the disease, therefore, they must put an end to the continuous activities of this dualistic poisoning. When this is done, there is a state called emancipation (*vimoksha*) which is full of bliss. The Buddhist question is thus: "How is emancipation possible?" And here rises the Mahayana system of philosophy.

The Turning back (parāvṛitti)

To this philosophy, a special paragraph is devoted below. I wish here to say a few words concerning the important psychological event known as Parāvṛitti in the *Laṅkā* and other Mahayana literature. *Parāvṛitti* literally means "turning up" or "turning back" or "change"; technically, it is a spiritual change or transformation which takes place in the mind, especially suddenly, and I have called it "revulsion" in my *Studies in the Laṅkāvatāra*, which, it will be seen, somewhat corresponds to what is known as "conversion" among the psychological students of religion.

It is significant that the Mahayana has been insistent to urge its followers to experience this psychological transformation in their practical life. A mere intellectual understanding of the truth is not enough in the life of a Buddhist; the truth must be directly grasped, personally experienced, intuitively penetrated into; for then it will be distilled into life and determine its course.

This Parāvṛitti, according to the *Laṅkā*, takes place in the Ālaya-vijñāna or All-conserving Mind, which is assumed to exist behind our individual empirical consciousnesses. The Ālaya is a metaphysical entity, and no psychological analysis can reach it. What we ordinarily know as the Ālaya is its working through a relative mind. The Mahayana calls this phase of the Ālaya tainted or defiled (*klishṭa*) and tells us to be cleansed of it in order to experience a Parāvṛitti for the attainment of ultimate reality.

Parāvṛitti in another sense, therefore, is purification (*viśuddhi*). In Buddhism terms of colouring are much used, and becoming pure, free from all pigment, means that the Ālaya is thoroughly washed off its dualistic accretion or outflow (*āsrava*), that is, that the Tathagata has effected his work of purification in the mind of a sentient being, which has so far failed to perceive its own oneness and allness. Being pure is to remain in its own selfhood or self-nature (*svabhāva*). While Parāvṛitti is psychological, it still retains its intellectual flavour as most Buddhist terms do.

Self-discipline and the Buddha's Power

As long as Parāvṛitti is an experience and not mere understanding, it is evident that self-discipline plays an important rôle in the Buddhist life. This is insisted upon in the *Laṅkā* as is illustrated in the use of such phrases as "Do not rely on others" (*aparapraṇeya*); "Strive yourselves" (*śikshitavyam*), etc. But at the same time we must not forget the fact that the *Laṅkā* also emphasises the necessity of the Buddha's power being added to the Bodhisattvas, in their upward course of spiritual development and in the accomplishment of their great task of world-salvation. If they were not thus so constantly sustained by the miraculous power of the Buddha, they would speedily fall into the group of the philosophers and Śrāvakas, and they would never be able to attain supreme enlightenment and preach the doctrine of universal emancipation. Indeed, when the Buddha so wishes, even such inanimate objects as mountains, woods, palaces, etc. will resound with the voice of the Buddha; how much more the Bodhisattvas who are his spiritual inheritors!

The doctrine of Adhishṭhāna gains all the more significance when we consider the development of Mahayana Buddhism into the doctrine of salvation by faith alone. The power of a Bodhisattva's original vows may also be judged as being derived from the Buddha. If the possibility of enlightenment is due to the Adhishṭhāna or Prabhāva of the Buddha, all the wonders that are to take place by the strength of the enlightenment must be inferred ultimately to issue from the fountain-head of Buddhahood itself.

At any rate the Mahayana idea of the Buddha being able to impart his power to others marks one of those epoch-making deviations which set off the Mahayana from so-called primitive or original Buddhism. When the Buddha comes to be considered capable of Adhishṭhāna, the next step his devotees are logically led to take would be the idea of vicarious suffering or atonement. Giving power to another is a positive idea while suffering for another may be said to be a negative one. Though this latter is strangely absent in the *Laṅkā*, the *Gaṇḍavyūha* as well as the *Prajñāpāramitā* are quite eloquent in elucidating the doctrine of vicarious suffering. According to this doctrine, whatever suffering one is enduring may be transferred on to another if the latter sincerely desires out of his unselfish and all-embracing love for others, to take these sufferings upon himself so that the real sufferers may not only be relieved of them but escape their evil consequences, thus enabling him to advance more easily and successfully towards the attainment of the blissful life. This goes quite against the idea of individual responsibility. But really religious minds require this vicarious suffering for their spiritual life.

To suffer or atone vicariously is still negative and fails to entirely satisfy our spiritual needs. The latter demand that more good must be done in order to suppress the evils which are found claiming this world for their own glorification. So the Mahayanists accumulate stocks of merit not only for the material of their own enlightenment but for the general cultivation of merit which can be shared equally by their fellow-beings, animate and inanimate. This is the true meaning of Pariṇāmana, that is, turning one's merit over to others for their spiritual interest.

As I said elsewhere, this notion of Pariṇāmana is not at all traceable in the *Laṅkā*, which is strange. The *Laṅkā* cannot be imagined to have been compiled prior to the *Prajñāpāramitā*, nor to the *Gaṇḍavyūha* or *Avataṁsaka*; if so, why this absence? How can this be explained?

Buddha the Enlightened and Sarvasattva the Ignorant

To conclude this section, Buddhism is the story of relationship between the two groups of beings: the one is called Buddha who is the enlightened, the Tathagata, the Arhat, and the other is generally designated as Sarvasattva, literally "all beings", who are ignorant, greedy for worldly things, and therefore in perpetual torment. In spite of their hankering for worldly enjoyments, they are conscious of their condition and not at all satisfied with it; when they reflect they find themselves quite forlorn inwardly, they long for real happiness, for ultimate reality, and blissful enlightenment. They look upwards, where the Buddha sits rapt in his meditation serenely regarding them with his transcendental wisdom. As he looks down at his fellow-beings inexplicably tormented with their greed and ignorance and egotism, he is disturbed, for he feels an inextinguishable feeling of love stirring within himself—the feeling now perfectly purified of all the defilements of selfishness, which embraces the whole world in pity though not attached to it. The Buddha leaves his transcendental abode. He is seen among sentient beings, each one of whom recognises him according to his own light.

Transcendental wisdom (*prajñā*) and a heart of all-embracing love (*mahākaruṇā*) constitute the very reason of Buddhahood, while the desire or thirst for life (*trishṇa*), and ignorance as to the meaning of life (*avidyā*), and deeds (*karma*) following from the blind assertion of life-impulse— these are the factors that enter into the nature of Sarvasattva, all ignorant and infatuated ones. The one who is above, looking downward, extends his arms to help; the other unable to extricate himself from entanglements looks up in despair, and finding the helping arms stretches his own to take hold of them. And from this scene the following narratives psychological, logical, and ontological, unfold themselves to the Buddhist soul.

INTRODUCTION

II

Psychology

What may be termed Buddhist psychology in the *Laṅka* consists in the analysis of mind, that is, in the classification of the Vijñānas. To understand thus the psychology of Buddhism properly the knowledge of these terms is necessary: *citta, manas, vijñāna, manovijñāna,* and *ālayavijñāna.*

To begin with Vijñāna. *Vijñāna* is composed of the prefix *vi*, meaning "to divide", and the root *jñā* which means "to perceive", "to know". Thus, Vijñāna is the faculty of distinguishing or discerning or judging. When an object is presented before the eye, it is perceived and judged as a red apple or a piece of white linen; the faculty of doing this is called eye-vijñāna. In the same way, there are ear-vijñāna for sound, nose-vijñāna for odour, tongue-vijñāna for taste, body-vijñāna for touch, and thought-vijñāna (*manovijñāna*) for ideas—altogether six forms of Vijñāna for distinguishing the various aspects of world external or internal.

Of these six Vijñānas, the Manojivñāna is the most important as it is directly related to an inner faculty known as Manas. Manas roughly corresponds to mind as an organ of thought, but in fact it is more than that, for it is also a strong power of attaching itself to the result of thinking. The latter may even be considered subordinate to this power of attachment. The Manas first wills, then it discriminates to judge; to judge is to divide, and this dividing ends in viewing existence dualistically. Hence the Manas' tenacious attachment to the dualistic interpretation of existence. Willing and thinking are inextricably woven into the texture of Manas.

Citta comes from the root *cit*, "to think", but in the *Laṅkā* the derivation is made from the root *ci*, "to pile up", "to arrange in order". The Citta is thus a storehouse where the seeds of all thoughts and deeds are accumulated and stored up. The Citta, however, has a double sense, general and specific. When it is used in the general sense it means "mind", "mentation", "ideas", including the activities of Manas and Manovijñāna, and also of the Vijñānas; while specifically it is a synonym of Ālayavijñāna in its relative aspects, and distinguishable from all the rest of the mental faculties. When, however, it is used in the form of Citta-mātra, Mind-only, it acquires still another connotation. We can say that Citta appears here in its highest possible sense, for it is then neither simply mentation nor intellection, nor perception as a function of consciousness. It is identifiable with the Ālaya in its absolute aspect. This will become clearer later on.

Ālayavijñāna is *ālaya + vijñāna,* and *ālaya* is a store where things are hoarded for future use. The Citta as a cumulative faculty is thus identified with the Ālayavijñāna. Strictly speaking, the Ālaya is not a Vijñāna, has no discerning power in it; it indiscriminately harbours all that is poured into it through the channel of the Vijñānas. The Ālaya is perfectly neutral, indifferent, and does not offer to give judgments.

Relation Between the Various Functions

Having explained what the various important terms mean and what functions are indicated by them, let us proceed to see in what relationship they stand to one another.

The whole system of mental functions is called in the *Laṅkā* Cittakalāpa or Vijñānakāya; Citta and Vijñāna are here used synonymously. In this mental system eight modes of activity are distinguished: Ālayavijñāna, Manas, Manovijñāna, and the five sense-Vijñānas. When these eight Vijñānas are grouped together under two general heads, the one group is known as Khyāti-Vijñāna (perceiving Vijñānas) and the other as Vastuprativikalpa-vijñāna (object-discriminating Vijñāna). But in fact the Vijñānas are not separable into these two groups, for perceiving is discriminating. When an individual object is perceived as such, that is, as solid, or as coloured, etc., discrimination has already taken place here; indeed without the latter, the former is impossible and conversely. Every Vijñāna performs these two functions simultaneously, which is to say, one functioning is analysable into two ideas, perceiving and discriminating. But it is to be observed that this double activity does not belong to the Ālayavijñāna.

Another way of classifying the Vijñānas is according to their Lakshaṇa or modes of being, of which three are distinguishable as evolving (*pravritti*), as performing deeds (*karma*), and as retaining their own original nature (*jāti*). From this viewpoint, all the Vijñānas are evolving and deed-performing Vijñānas except the Ālaya which always abides in its self-nature. For the Vijñānas may cease from evolving and performing deeds for some reason, but the Ālaya ever remains itself.

The Ālaya, according to the *Laṅkā*, has two aspects: the Ālaya as it is in itself, which is in the Sagāthakam called Pāramālaya-vijñāna, and the Ālaya as mental representation called Vijñaptir Ālaya. These two aspects are also known respectively as the Prabandha (incessant) and the Lakshaṇa (manifested). The Ālaya is incessant because of its uninterrupted existence; it is manifested because of its activity being perceptible by the mind.

From this, we can see that the Ālaya is conceived in the *Laṅkā* as being absolute in one respect and in the other as being subject to "evolution" (*pravritti*). It is this evolving aspect of the Ālaya that lends itself to the treacherous interpretation of Manas. As long as the Ālaya remains in and by itself, it is beyond the grasp of an individual, empirical consciousness, it is almost like Emptiness itself although it ever lies behind all the Vijñāna-activities, for the latter will cease working at once when the Ālaya is taken out of existence.

Manas is conscious of the presence behind itself of the Ālaya and also of the latter's uninterrupted working on the entire system of the Vijñānas. Reflecting on the Ālaya and imagining it to be an ego, Manas clings to it as if it were reality and disposes of the reports of the six Vijñānas accordingly. In other words, Manas is the individual will to live and the principle of discrimination. The notion of an ego-substance is herein established, and also the acceptance of a world external to itself and distinct from itself.

The six Vijñānas function, as it were, mechanically when the conditions are satisfied and are not conscious of their own doings. They have no intelligence outside their respective fields of activity. They are not organised in themselves and have no theory for their existence and doings. What they experience is reported to the headquarters with no comment or interpretation. Manas sits at the headquarters and like a great general gathers up all the information coming from the six Vijñānas. For it is he who shifts and arranges the reports and gives orders again to the reporters according to his own will and intelligence. The orders are then faithfully executed.

The Manas is a double-headed monster, the one face looks towards the Ālaya and the other towards the Vijñānas. He does not understand what the Ālaya really is. Discrimination being one of his fundamental functions, he sees multitudinousness there and clings to it as final. The clinging now binds him to a world of particulars. Thus, desire is mother, and ignorance is father, and this existence takes its rise. But the Manas is also a double-edged sword. When there takes place a "turning-back" (*parāvṛitti*) in it, the entire arrangement of things in the Vijñānakāya or Cittakalāpa changes. With one swing of the sword the pluralities are cut asunder and the Ālaya is seen in its native form (*svalakshaṇa*), that is, as solitary reality (*viviktadharma*), which is from the first beyond discrimination. The Manas is not of course an independent worker, it is always depending on the Ālaya, without which it has no reason of being itself; but at the same time the Ālaya is also depending on the Manas. The Ālaya is absolutely one, but this oneness gains significance only when it is realised by the Manas and recognised as its own supporter (*ālamba*). This relationship is altogether too subtle to be perceived by ordinary minds that are found choked with defilements and false ideas since beginningless time.

The Manas backed by the Ālaya has been the seat of

desire or thirst (*trishṇā*), karma, and ignorance. The seeds grow out of them, and are deposited in the Ālaya. When the waves are stirred up in the Ālaya-ocean by the wind of objectivity—so interpreted by the Manas—these seeds give a constant supply to the uninterrupted flow of the Vijñāna-waters. In this general turmoil in which we sentient beings are all living, the Ālaya is as responsible as the Manas; for if the Ālaya refused to take the seeds in that are sent up from the region of the Vijñāna, Manas may not have opportunities to exercise its two fundamental functions, willing and discriminating. But at the same time it is due to the Ālaya's self-purifying nature that there takes place a great catastrophe in it known as "turning-back". With this "turning-back" in the Ālaya, Manas so intimately in relation with it also experiences a transformation in its fundamental attitude towards the Vijñānas. The latter are no more regarded as reporters of an external world which is characterised with individuality and manifoldness. This position is now abandoned, the external world is no more adhered to as such, that is, as reality; for it is no more than a mere reflection of the Ālaya. The Ālaya has been looking at itself in the Manas' mirror. There has been from the very first nothing other than itself. Hence the doctrine of Mind-only (*cittamātra*), or the Ālaya-only.

The Religious Signification

The necessity of conceiving Ālaya in its double aspect, (1) as absolute reality (*viviktadharma*) and (2) as subject to causation (*hetuka*), comes from the Mahayana idea of Buddhahood (*buddhatā*). If Buddhahood is something absolutely solitary, all the efforts put forward by sentient beings to realise enlightenment would be of no avail whatever. In other words, all that the Tathagata wants to do for sentient beings would never have its opportunity to reach them. There must be something commonly shared by each so that when a note is struck at one end a corresponding one will answer at the other. The Ālaya is thus known on the one hand as Tathāgata-garbha, the womb of Tathagatahood, and on the other hand imagined by the ignorant as an ego-soul (*pudgala* or *ātman*).

The Tathāgata-garbha, therefore, whose psychological name is Ālayavijñāna, is a reservoir of things good and bad, pure and defiled. Expressed differently, the Tathāgata-garbha is originally, in its self-nature, immaculate, but because of its external dirt (*āgantukleśa*) it is soiled, and when soiled—which is the state generally found in all sentient beings—an intuitive penetration (*pratyaksha*) is impossible. When this is impossible as is the case with the philosophers and ignorant masses, the Garbha is believed sometimes to be a creator (*karaṇa*) and sometimes to be an ego-substance (*ātman*). As it is so believed, it allows itself to transmigrate through the six paths of existence. Let there be, however, an intuitive penetration into the primitive purity (*prakṛitipariśuddhi*) of the Tathāgata-garbha, and the whole system of the Vijñānas goes through a revolution. If the Tathāgata-garbha or Ālaya-vijñāna were not a mysterious mixture of purity and defilement, good and evil, this abrupt transformation (*parāvṛitti*) of an entire personality would be an impossibility. That is to say, if the Garbha or the Ālaya while absolutely neutral and colourless in itself did not yet harbour in itself a certain irrationality, no sentient beings would ever be a Buddha, no enlightenment would be experienced by any human beings. Logicalness is to be transcended somewhere and somehow. And as this illogicalness is practically possible, the Mahayana establishes the theory of Mind-only (*cittamātra*).

Ontology and the Twofold Egolessness

In considering the theory of Mind-only, we have to be careful not to understand this term psychologically. Mind (*citta*) here does not mean our individual mind which is subject to the law of causation (*hetupratyaya*). Absolute Citta transcends the dualistic conception of existence, it belongs neither to the Vijñāna-system nor to our objective world (*vishaya*). Therefore, in the *Laṅkā* this Citta is frequently described in ontological terms.

The most significant one is Vastu, which is found coupled with Tathatā in one place (p. 147, line 6)) and with Ārya in another place (p. 164, lines 9 and 10). In the first case, Vastu and Tathatā are synonymously used; what is Tathatā, that is Vastu. Tathatā is to be rendered either "suchness", or "thatness", which is a term most frequently used in the Mahayana texts to designate the highest reality ever approachable by Prajñā, transcendental wisdom; Vastu in Buddhism is usually an individual object regarded as existing externally to the Vijñānas, and so is it in most cases in the *Laṅkā* also. But evidently in this connection where Vastu is Tathatā, it must mean the highest reality.

In the second case in which Ārya is affixed to Vastu, the *ārya* must be a modifier here, that is, this reality is something to be described as *ārya*, "noble", "holy", or "worthy".

The highest reality is also called "something that has been in existence since the very first" (*pūrvadharmasthititā*, p. 241, l. 14), or (*paurāṇasthitidharmatā*, p. 143, ll. 5 and 9). As it is the most ancient reality, its realisation means returning to one's own original abode in which everything one sees around is an old familiar object. In Zen Buddhism, therefore, the experience is compared to the visiting one's native home and quietly getting settled (歸家穩坐, *kuei-chia wen-tso*). The Buddhas, enlightened ones, are all abiding here as gold is embedded in the mine. The ever-enduring reality (*sthititā dharmatā*) is above changes.

To be above changes means to remain in one's own abode, not to move away from it, and for this reason reality is known as "self-abiding" (*svastha*, p. 199, line 4), or "remaining in its own abode" (*svasthāne 'vatishṭhate*, p. 178, l. 15).[1] To keep one's own abode it to be single, solitary, absolute: hence Reality is Viviktadharma, a thing of solitude; *Bhūtakoṭi*, limit of reality, which points to a similar mode of thinking. It is again Ekāgra, the summit of oneness, and this summit or limit (*koṭi*) is at the same time no-summit, no-limit, because this is gained only when one makes a final leap beyond the manifoldness of things.

[1] Cf. p. 124, line 1.

The more ordinary expressions given to the highest reality known as Citta are Tathatā, "suchness" or "thusness", Satyatā, "the state of being true", Bhūtatā, "the state of being real", Dharmadhātu, "realm of truth", Nirvāna, the Permanent (*nitya*), Sameness (*samatā*), the One (*advaya*), Cessation (*nirodha*), the Formless (*animitta*), Emptiness (*śūnyatā*), etc.

From these descriptions it is found natural for Mahayanists psychologically to deny the existence of an ego-soul or ego-substance in the Ālaya, and ontologically to insist that the tragedy of life comes from believing in the substantiality or finality of an individual object. The former is technically called the doctrine of Pudgalanairātmya, egolessness of persons,[1] and the latter that of Dharmanairātmya, egolessness of things; the one denies the reality of an ego-soul and the other the ultimacy of an individual object.

Superficially, this denial of an Ātman in persons and individual objects sounds negative and productive of no moral signification. But when one understands what is ultimately meant by Cittamātra (Mind-only) or by Viviktadharma (the Solitary), the negations are on the plane of relativity and intellection.

The term "the Middle" (*madhyama*), meaning "the Middle Way", does not occur in the *Laṅkā* proper except in its Sagāthakam portion. But the idea that the truth is not found in the dualistic way of interpreting existence, that it is beyond the category of being and non-being, is everywhere emphasised in the *Laṅkā*. In fact, we can say that one of the principal theses of the *Laṅkā* is to establish the Absolute which makes a world of particulars possible but which is not to be grasped by means of being and non-being (*astināstitva*). This Absolute is the Middle Way of the Madhyamaka school.

---

[1] The conception of the Tathāgata-garbha is not to be confused with that of a Pudgala or Ātman. See § XXVIII. For the non-existence of a personal ego-soul and the non-reality of an individual object, see especially pp. 61–62 of this translation.

INTRODUCTION

Unobtainability

This going beyond all forms of dualism, however differently it may be expressed, whether as being and non-being, or as oneness and manyness, or as this and that, or as causation and no-causation, or as form and no-form, or as assertion and negation, or as Saṁsāra and Nirvāṇa, or as ignorance and knowledge, or as work and no-work, or as good and evil, or as purity and defilement, or as ego and non-ego, or as worldly and super-worldly, *ad infinitum*—this going beyond a world of oppositions and contrasts constitutes one of the most significant thoughts of the Mahayana. There is nothing real as long as we remain entangled in the skein of relativity, and our sufferings will never come to an end. We must therefore endeavour to take hold of reality, but this reality is not something altogether solitary. For in this case no one of us will be able to have even a glimpse of it, and if we had, it will turn into something standing in opposition to this world of relativity, which means the loss of solitariness, that is, the solitary now forms part of this world.

Thus, according to Buddhist philosophy, reality must be grasped in this world and by this world, for it is that "Beyond which is also Within". The *Laṅkā* compares it to the moon in water or a flower in a mirror. It is within and yet outside, it is outside and yet within. This aspect of reality is described as "unobtainable" or "unattainable" (*anupalabdha*). And just because it is unobtainable in a world of particulars, the latter from the point of view of reality is like a dream, like a mirage, and so on. The subtlest relation of reality to the world is beyond description, it yields its secrets only to him who has actually realised it in himself by means of noble wisdom (*āryajñāna* or *prajñā*). This realisation is also a kind of knowledge though different from what is generally known by this name.

Epistemology

Without a theory of cognition, therefore, Mahayana philosophy becomes incomprehensible. The *Laṅkā* is quite explicit in assuming two forms of knowledge: the one for grasping the absolute or entering into the realm of Mind-only, and the other for understanding existence in its dualistic aspect in which logic prevails and the Vijñānas are active. The latter is designated Discrimination (*vikalpa*) in the *Laṅkā* and the former transcendental wisdom or knowledge (*prajñā*). To distinguish these two forms of knowledge is most essential in Buddhist philosophy.

The *Laṅkā* is decidedly partial to the use of Āryajñāna instead of Prajñā, although the latter has been in use since the early days of Buddhism. Āryajñāna, noble wisdom, is generally coupled with Pratyātma, inner self, showing that this noble, supreme wisdom is a mental function operating in the depths of our being. As it is concerned with the highest reality or the ultimate truth of things, it is no superficial knowledge dealing with particular objects and their relations. It is an intuitive understanding which, penetrating through the surface of existence, sees into that which is the reason of everything logically and ontologically.

The *Laṅkā* is never tired of impressing upon its readers the importance of this understanding in the attainment of spiritual freedom; for this understanding is a fundamental intuition into the truth of Mind-only and constitutes the Buddhist enlightenment with which truly starts the religious life of a Bodhisattva.

This transcendental Jñāna is variously designated in the *Laṅkā*. It is Pravicayabuddhi, that is, an insight fixed upon the ultimate ground of existence. It is Svabuddhi, innate in oneself; Nirābhāsa, or Anābhāsa (imagelessness), beyond all forms of tangibility; Nirvikalpa, beyond discrimination, meaning direct empirical knowledge before analysis starts in any form whatever; which therefore is not at all expressible by means of words (*vāc* or *ruta*). The awaking of supreme knowledge (*anuttarasamyaksaṁbodhi*) is the theme of the *Prajñāpāramitā-sūtras,* but in the *Laṅkā* the weight of the discourse is placed upon the realisation by means of Āryajñāna of ultimate reality which is Mind-only. This psychological emphasis so distinctive of the *Laṅkā* makes this sutra occupy a unique position in Mahayana literature.

The knowledge that stands contrasted to Prajñā or Āryajñāna is Vikalpabuddhi, or simply Vikalpa, which I have translated "discrimination". It is relative knowledge working on the plane of dualism, it may be called the principle of dichotomy, whereby judgment is made possible. By us existence is always divided into pairs of conception, thesis and antithesis, that is, being and non-being, permanent and impermanent, Nirvana and Samsara, birth and death, creating and created, this and that, Me and not-Me, *ad libitum*. This is due to the working of Vikalpa. The Lakshaṇa (form) of existence thus presented to us is not its real nature, it is our own thought-construction (*vijñapti*); but our Buddhi which seeks after pluralities fails to understand this fact and makes us cling to appearances as realities. As the result, the world in which we now find ourselves living ceases to be what it is in itself; for it is one we have constructed according to our own ignorance and discrimination. Reality escapes us, truth slips off our grasp, false views accumulate, wrong judgments go on adding complexities upon complexities. The habit-energy (*vāsanā*) thus created takes complete hold on the Ālayavijñāna, and Ālaya the Absolute is forever unable to extricate itself from these encumbrances. Eternal transmigration to no purpose must be our destiny.

The Twofold Truth (*satya*)

The distinction between the highest truth (*paramārtha-satya*) and conventional truth (*samvṛiti-satya*) is not explicitly held in the *Laṅkā*, but allusions are occasionally made to them; and it is said that false discrimination belongs to conventionalism (p. 131, l. 3). Another word for conventionalism is Vyavahāra, worldly experience, according to which we talk of things being born and destroyed, and also of the how, what, where, etc. of existence. This kind of knowledge does not help us to have an insight into the depths of being.

The Three Svabhāvas

Another way of classifying knowledge is known as three Svabhāvas in the *Laṅkā*. This is a generally recognised classification in all the schools of Mahayana Buddhism. *Svabhāva* means "self-nature" or "self-reality" or "self-substance", the existence of which in some form is popularly accepted. The first form of knowledge by which the reality of things is assumed is called Parikalpita, "imagined", that is, imagination in its ordinary sense. This is an illusion, for things are imagined to exist really where in fact there are none. It is like seeing a mirage which vanishes as one approaches. Imagined (*parikalpita*) objects have, therefore, no objective reality.

The second form of knowledge by which we examine existence is Paratantra, "depending upon another". This is a kind of scientific knowledge based on analysis. Buddhists make use of this knowledge to disprove the substantiality of individual objects, that is, the *svabhāvatva* of things. According to them, there is nothing self-existing in the world, everything is depending for its existence on something else, things are universally mutually conditioned, endlessly related to one another. Dissect an object considered final, and it dissolves itself into airy nothingness. Modern scientists declare that existence is no more than mathematical formulae. The Mahayanists would say that there is no Svabhāva in anything appealing as such to the Vijñānas when it is examined from the Paratantra point of view.

The imagined view (*parikalpita*) of reality does not give us a true knowledge of it, and the relativity view (*paratantra*) reduces it into nothingness: if so, where does our boat of enlightenment get anchored? The *Laṅkā* tells us that there is a third way of viewing existence, called Parinishpanna, "perfected", which allows us to become truly acquainted with reality as it is. It is this "perfected" knowledge whereby we are enabled to see really into the nature of existence, to perceive rightly what is meant by Svabhāva,

INTRODUCTION

and to declare that there is no Svabhāva as is imagined by the ignorant and that all is empty (*śūnya*).

Perfect or "perfected" knowledge issues from Prajñā, or Āryajñāna, or sometimes simply Jñāna, seeing into the suchness of things. It perceives things as they are, because going beyond the realm of being and non-being which belongs to discrimination, the principle of dichotomisation, it dives into the abyss where there are no shadows (*anābhāsa*). This is called self-realisation (*svasiddhi*). So states the *Laṅkā* that as the wise see reality with their eye of Prajñā, they ascertain definitely what it is, i. e. in its self-nature (*bhāvasvabhāva*) and not as is seen by the ignorant whose eye is never raised beyond the horizon of relativity.

This is again called seeing into the emptiness of things. Emptiness (*śūnyatā*), however, does not mean "relativity", as is thought by some scholars. Relativity-emptiness is on the lower plane of knowledge and does not reveal the real view of existence as it is. Emptiness taught in the Mahayana texts goes far deeper into the matter. It is the object of transcendental knowledge. As long as one stays in the world of relativity where logic rules supreme, one cannot have even the remotest idea of true emptiness or what is designated in the *Prajñāpāramitā* as Mahāśūnyatā. The *Laṅkā* has also this kind of Śūnyatā mentioned as one of the seven Emptinesses (p. 94). Relativity-emptiness so called corresponds to the first of the seven Emptinesses, while the Mahayana Śūnyatā is Paramārtha-āryajñāna-mahāśūnyatā, that is, the great void of noble wisdom which is the highest reality.

The Five Dharmas

Before concluding this section, we must not forget to mention what is known as the Five Dharmas in the *Laṅkā* making up one of the main topics of discourses. The Five Dharmas and the Three Svabhāvas are different ways of classifying the same material. The Five are: Appearances (*nimitta*), Names (*nāma*), Discrimination (*saṁkalpa*), Right Knowledge (*samyagjñāna*), and Suchness (*tathatā*). The first three correspond to the two of the Three Svabhāvas,

Parikalpita and Paratantra, while the last two belong to the Parinishpanna.

Our relative knowledge starts with perceiving Appearances to which Names are given. Names are then thought real and discrimination is carried on. We can say that discrimination has been with us from the first even when what is called perception has not taken place. For naming is impossible without some form of discrimination. Then the worst thing comes upon us as we begin to persuade ourselves and think that by giving Names existence has been successfully disposed of, and feel comfortable about the problems of religion. Although without naming no knowledge is possible, Right Knowledge (*samyagjñāna*) is not to be had here. For this is the inexpressible, the unnamable, it is the meaning (*artha*) not to be grasped by words. In this the *Laṅkā* permits no equivocation, it most emphatically advises us not to attach ourselves to words.

The object of Right Knowledge is Suchness of things as not conditioned by the category of being and non-being. It is in this sense that ultimate reality is said to be like the moon in the water, it is not immersed in it, nor is it outside it. We cannot say that the moon is in water, for it is a mere reflection; but we cannot say that it is not there, for a reflection though it may be it is really before us. Plurality of objects is not real from the point of view of relativity as well as from the point of view of Suchness. If some one declares such reality as maintained by the Mahayana is too ethereal, too phantom-like, too unreal for our religious aspirations, the *Laṅkā* will immediately retort, "You are still on the plane of relativity." When the Āryajñāna is awakened, Tathatā is the most real thing and a term most fittingly applied as far as our power of designation is concerned.

III

The Message of the Laṅkā

There are many other thoughts of interest in the *Laṅkā* which may be discussed in this Introduction. But as I have already given up many pages to it and as the reader who wishes to know more about the Sutra may go to my *Studies in the Laṅkāvatāra*, I will say just a few words about the position of this Sutra among the general Mahayana Buddhist texts.

While we are still in the dark as to how Mahayana Buddhism developed in India, we know that when it was introduced into China by the missionaries from India and central Asia, it was already regarded as directly coming from the Buddha's own golden mouth, and that what must have developed during several hundred years after his death was taken in a wholesale manner for a system fully matured in his life-time extending over a period of about half a century after his Enlightenment. As the sutras were translated into Chinese, the first of which appeared in 68 A.D., they profoundly stirred the Chinese and then the Japanese mind awakening their religious consciousness to its very depths. The following are the most important Mahayana texts that thus served to move the religious feelings of the Far-eastern peoples and are still continuing to do so.

(1) *The Saddharma-puṇḍarīka-sūtra.* One of the main theses of this inspiring scripture is the announcement that the Buddha never died, that he is forever living on the Mount of the HolyVulture and preaching to a group of the Śrāvakas, Pratyekabuddhas, and Bodhisattvas, who are no less beings than ourselves, and that the Buddha has just one vehicle (*yāna*) for all beings. This must have been a revolutionary teaching at the time when the Buddha was thought to be just as transient and mortal as ourselves, and when the only thing that was left behind after his Nirvana was his Dharma, in which his followers were asked to find their Master.

(2) *The Avalokiteśvara-vikurvaṇa-nirdeśa.* This is commonly known as *Kwannon-gyo* in Japan and forms the twenty-fourth chapter of the Sanskrit *Saddharma-puṇḍarīka,* but it will be better to treat it as a separate document as it has quite an independent message and has been so considered though not always consciously by its devotees. Avalokiteś-

vara is here represented as a god of mercy who will help anybody who finds himself in trouble spiritually as well as materially. In popular minds the god is no more masculine than feminine; if anything, more feminine, because of mercy being more reality associated with eternal femininity. That he can assume various forms (*vikurvaṇa*) in order to achieve his ends appeals very much to the religious imagination of the Eastern peoples. And this doctrine of transformation is one of the characteristic features of Mahayana Buddhism.

(3) *The Avataṁsaka-sūtra.* This is an encyclopedic sutra of which we find the *Gaṇḍavyūha* and the *Deśabhūmika* forming a part. It is another Mahayana sutra that has influenced the Chinese and the Japanese mind profoundly. The so-called Interpenetration which constitutes the central thought of the sutra is symbolically and effectively treated in the Chinese translations by Buddhabhadra (60 fas.), by Śikshānanda (80 fas.), and by Prajñā (40 fas.). The sutra as we have it now contains many sutras which may be considered independent though they no doubt belong to the same class of literature. The reading may be tedious from the modern point of view as the main theme is not so succinctly presented, and it takes some time before the reader can get into the mood of the sutra itself. After a quiet and patient pursuit of the text, however, he cannot help but be deeply impressed with its underlying spirit whose grandeur of outlook almost surpasses human comprehension. The huge rock-cut figure of Vairocana at Lung-men and the bronze figure in Nara are respectively the Chinese and the Japanese artistic response to the spiritual stimulation caused by the *Avataṁsaka*, or the *Gaṇḍavyūha* which is the same thing.

Another profound effect produced by this sutra on the Eastern mind is the conception of the Bodhisattva Samantabhadra with his "ten inexhaustible vows." He would not enter into Nirvana, that coveted object of all the Buddhists, because he would not have one single soul unsaved behind him. And by this "soul" was meant not only human soul but the soul of every being animate or inanimate. It was the vow of Samantabhadra to release animals, plants, and even such inanimate existences as mountains, waters, earths, etc., from the bondage of ignorance and karma. His universe, moreover, was far wider and more spiritualistic than our ordinary one

(4) *The Prajñā-pāramitā-sūtra.* This is regarded by most Mahayana scholars to have been one of the first Mahayana literature that was declared against the hair-splitting scholastic philosophy of early Buddhist doctors, gives us the doctrine of Emptiness or Void (*śūnyatā*), whereby every possible straw of attachment is taken away from us. To be left alone in the Void, even with this Void vanishing from around us, is the method of perfect emancipation proposed by the *Prajñā-pāramitā.* This was quite a direct straightforward proposition on the part of the Mahayanist. It appealed greatly to intellectual minds as well as the mystical. While the *Avataṁsaka* filled the universe with things of imagination even to its minutest particle, the *Prajñā-pāramitā* swept everything away from the universe which now becomes a vast Void indeed. And in six hundred fascicles of the sutra we are warned not to be afraid of, not to be taken aback by this vast Void. If we stagger at this gospel of absolute Emptiness, we are told by the Buddha that we cannot be good followers of the Mahayana.

(5) *The Vimalakīrti-sūtra.* This is a masterpiece, a drama with great literary merit, and because of this fact it is read more generally than other Buddhist sutras by the laity. The signification of this sutra lies in taking our soiled coat of attachment off our back which we have been wearing ever since we became aware of an external existence. Another significant feature of the sutra is that its chief figure of interest is not the Buddha but a wealthy layman called Vimalakīrti. It is this crafty old gentleman-philosopher who puts to shame all the Śrāvakas and Bodhisattvas coming to argue with him about the deepest truths of Buddhism, except Mañjuśrī, the head of the Bodhisattvas. The latter proved a good match for the eloquence of the lay-disciple of the Buddha. What we have to notice especially in this Mahayana text is that Buddhism does not require us to lead a

homeless life as a Bhikshu in order to attain enlightenment, that is, the householder's life is as good and pure as the mendicant's.

(6) In this respect the *Śrīmālā-sūtra* is also significant, for Śrīmālā the queen inspired by the wisdom and power of the Buddha delivers a great sermon on the Tathāgata-garbha. The Mahayana may be said to be the revolt of laymen and laywomen against the ascetic spirit of exclusion pervading among early advocates of Buddhism.

(7) *The Sukhāvatī-vyūha-sūtra.* The influence of this sutra on Oriental people is quite different from that of the other sutras, for it has awakened the faith-aspect of their religious consciousness, which is established on the general basis of Mahayana philosophy. Superficially, the faith of Amitābha looks very much like Christian faith in Christ, but the underlying thoughts are not at all the same. The Jōdo school could not take its rise from any other soil than Mahayana Buddhism. In Japan this school has achieved a unique development marking a spiritual epoch in the history of religious faith in the East.

(8) *The Parinirvāṇa-sūtra.* This once formed the foundation of the Nirvana school in the early history of Chinese Buddhism. Its main assertion is that the Buddha-nature is present in every one of us. Before the arrival of this sutra in China it was generally believed that there was a class of people known as Icchanti who had no Buddha-nature in them and therefore who were eternally barred from attaining enlightenment. This belief was entirely expelled, however, when a statement to the contrary was found in the sutra, saying that "There is something in all beings which is true, real, eternal, self-governing, and forever unchanging—this is called Ego, though quite different from what is generally known as such by the philosophers. This Ego is the Tathāgata-garbha, Buddha-nature, which exists in every one of us, and is characterised with such virtues as permanency, bliss, freedom, and purity."

(9) All these and other sutras of Mahayana Buddhism may seem to exhaust the many-sided aspects of this school,

but another is needed to tell us that mere understanding is not enough in the Buddhist life, that without self-realisation all intellection amounts to nothing. To tell us this is the office of the *Laṅkāvatāra-sūtra*, and Bodhidharma, father of Zen Buddhism, made use of the text quite effectively; for it was through him that a special school of Buddhism under the title of Zen or Ch'an has come to develop in China and in Japan. While Zen as we have it now is not the same in many respects as Bodhidharma first proclaimed it about fifteen centuries ago, the spirit itself flows quite unchanged in the East. And this is eloquently embodied in the *Laṅkāvatāra-sūtra*. It is not, however, necessary here for us to enter into details, for the point has been fully dwelt upon in my recent work, *Studies in the Laṅkāvatāra Sūtra*. Suffice it to touch lightly upon the characteristic features of the Sutra, which constitute its special message as distinguished from the other sutras already referred to.

There is no doubt that the *Laṅkā* is closely connected in time as well as in doctrine with *The Awakening of Faith in the Mahāyāna* generally ascribed to Aśvaghosha. While he may not have been the author of this most important treatise of Mahayana philosophy, there was surely a great Buddhist mind, who, inspired by the same spirit which pervades the *Laṅkā*, the *Avataṁsaka*, the *Parinirvāṇa*, etc., poured out his thoughts in *The Awakening*. Some scholars contend that *The Awakening* is a Chinese work, but this is not well grounded.

In a way *The Awakening* is an attempt to systematise the *Laṅkā*, for all the principal teachings of the latter are found there developed in due order. As far as the theoretical side is concerned, both teach the existence of th Garbha as ultimate reality. While this lies in ordinary people defiled by the evil passions and does not shine out in its native purity, we cannot deny its existence in them. When the external wrappage of impurities is peeled off we all become Buddhas and Tathagatas. In fact, the birth of a Tathagata is nowhere else than in this Garbha.

The Garbha is from the psychological point of view the

Ālayavijñāna, all-conserving mind, in which good and bad are mingled, and the work of the Yogin, that is, one who seeks the truth by means of self-discipline, is to separate the one from the other. Why is the Ālaya found contaminated by evil thoughts and desires? What is the evil? How does it come out in this world? How is the truth to be realised? These questions are answered by postulating a system of Vijñānas and by the doctrine of Discrimination (*vikalpa*), as has already been expounded above.

This is the point where the *Laṅkā* comes in contact with the Yogācāra school. The Yogācāra is essentially psychological standing in contrast in this respect to the Madhyamaka school which is epistemological. But the Ālayavijñāna of the Yogācāra is not the same as that of *Laṅkā* and the *Awakening of Faith*. The former conceives the Ālaya to be purity itself with nothing defiled in it whereas the *Laṅkā* and the *Awakening* make it the cause of purity and defilement. Further, the Yogācāra upholds the theory of Vijñaptimātra and not that of Cittamātra, which belongs to the *Laṅkā, Avataṁsaka,* and *Awakening of Faith*. The difference is this: According to the Vijñaptimātra, the world is nothing but ideas, there are no realities behind them; but the Cittamātra states that there is nothing but Citta, Mind, in the world and that the world is the objectification of Mind. The one is pure idealism and the other idealistic realism.

To realise the Cittamātra is the object of the *Laṅkā*, and this is done when Discrimination is discarded, that is, when a state of non-discrimination is attained in one's spiritual life. Discrimination is a logical term and belongs to the intellect. Thus we see that the end of the religious discipline is to go beyond intellectualism, for to discriminate, to divide, is the function of the intellect. Logic does not lead one to self-realisation. Hence Nāgārjuna's hair-splitting dialectics. His idea is to prove the ineffectiveness of logic in the domain of our spiritual life. This is where the *Laṅkā* joins hands with the Madhyamaka. The doctrine of the Void is indeed the foundation of Mahayana philosophy. But

INTRODUCTION xliii

this is not to be understood in the manner of analytical reasoning. The *Laṅkā* is quite explicit and not to be mistaken in this respect.

So far, the *Laṅkā* may seem to be only a philosophical treatise with nothing religious in it, but the fact is that the Sutra is deeply tinged with religious sentiments. For instance, the Bodhisattva would not enter into Nirvana because of his vows to save all sentient beings, and his vows are not limited in time and space, and for this reason they are called "inexhaustible". Not only are his vows inexhaustible but the "skilful means" he uses for the emancipation of all beings know no limits. He knows how to make the best use of his inexhaustible resources intellectual and practical for this single purpose. Here we may say that the Bodhisattva Samantabhadra of the *Avataṁsaka* or the *Gaṇḍavyūha* is reflected.

In the *Laṅkā* all the most fundamental conceptions of the Mahayana are thrown in without any attempt on the part of the compiler or compilers to give them a system. This is left to the thoughtful reader himself who will pick them up from the medley and string them into a garland of pearls out of his own religious experience.

The one significant Mahayana thought, however, which is not expressly touched upon in the Sutra is that of Pariṇāmana. *Pariṇāmana* means to turn one's merit over to somebody else so as to expedite the latter's attainment of Nirvana. If anybody does anything good, its merit is sure to come back to the doer himself—this is the doctrine of Karma; but according to the Mahayana the recipient need not always be the doer himself, he may be anybody, he may be the whole world; merit being of universal character can be transferred upon anything the doer wishes. This transferability is known as the doctrine of Pariṇāmana, the turning over of one's good work to somebody else. This idea comes from the philosophical teaching of Interpenetration as upheld in the *Avataṁsaka*.

IV

The Date of the Laṅkā

As is the case with other Buddhist texts it is quite impossible with our present knowledge of Indian history to decide the age of the *Laṅkā*. The one thing that is certain is that it was compiled before 443 A.D. when the first Chinese translation is reported to have been attempted. But this does not mean that the whole text as we have it now was then already in existence, for we know that the later translations done in 513 and 700-704 contain the Dhāraṇī and the Sagāthakam section which are missing in the 443 one (Sung). Further, the Meat-eating chapter also suffered certain modifications, especially in the 513 (Wei) one.

Even with the text that was in existence before 443 A.D. we do not know how it developed, for it was not surely written from the beginning as one complete piece of work as we write a book in these modern days. Some parts of it must be older than others, since there is no doubt that it has many layers of added passages.

To a certain extent, the contents may give a clue to the age of the text, but because of the difficulty of separating one part from another from the point of view of textual criticism, arguments from the contents as to the date are of very doubtful character. As long as we have practically no knowledge of historical circumstances in which the Buddhist texts were produced one after another in India or somewhere else, all the statements are more or less of the character of an ingenious surmise. All that we can say is this that the *Laṅkā* is not a discourse directly given by the founder of Buddhism, that it is a later composition than the Nikāyas or Āgamas which also developed some time after the Buddha, that when Mahayana thoughts began to crystallise in the Northern as well as in the Southern part of India probably about the Christian era or even earlier, the compiler or compilers began to collect passages as he or they came across in their study of the Mahayana, which finally resulted in the

Buddhist text now known under the title of *Laṅkāvatāra-sūtra.*

Some Remarks Concerning the Text

Certain irregularities of the chapter-endings are to be noticed in this connection. Generally these endings show that the chapters are composite parts of a sutra and belong to it; but in the case of the *Laṅkā* some endings are quite of an independent character, and their relation to the text is not at all definite. For instance:

Chapter I—"Chapter One Known as Rāvaṇa-invitation";

Chapter II—"Here Ends Chapter Two Known as the Collection of All the Dharmas in the 36,000 (śloka) Laṅkāvatāra";

Chapter III—"Here Ends Chapter Three on Impermanency in the Laṅkāvatāra, a Mahāyāna Sūtra";

Chapter IV—"Here Ends Chapter Four on Realisation";

Chapter V—"Here Ends Chapter Five on the Permamency and Impermanency of the Tathagata";

Chapter VI—"Here Ends Chapter Six on Momentariness";

Chapter VII—"Here Ends Chapter Seven on Egolessness";

Chapter VIII—"Here Ends Chapter Eight on Meat-eating from the Laṅkāvatāra which is the Essence of All the Buddha-Teachings";

Chapter IX—"Here Ends Chapter Nine Known as Dhāraṇī in the Laṅkāvatāra."

These irregularities, at least in one case, show that there was a larger *Laṅkā* containing 36,000 ślokas[1] as referred to in Fa-tsang's notices,[2] and in another case that the *Laṅkā* was also known, or contained, a chapter known as the "Essence of all the Buddha-teachings" which is indeed a sort of sub-

---

[1] Suggested by Mr Hokei Idzumi.
[2] See my *Studies in the Laṅkāvatāra Sūtra,* p. 42.

title given to the four-volume Chinese *Laṅkā* by Guṇabhadra (Sung), 443 A.D.

The Gāthā section called "Sagāthakam" presents peculiar difficulties. As the earliest Chinese translation by Guṇabhadra does not contain it, it is highly probable that it was not then included in the *Laṅkā* text. But the fact that both the Wei version and the Sanskrit edition contain not only the verses properly belonging to the Sagāthakam but those[1] already appearing in the prose section, hints at the existence of a larger or more complete text of the *Laṅkā* in which all these Sagāthakam verses were incorporated in the prose section, which, therefore, must have been naturally much fuller than the existing *Laṅkā*—perhaps something like the one containing 36,000 ślokas. There are many verses in the Sagāthakam which are too obscure to be intelligently interpreted without their corresponding prose passages. The verses are generally meant for memorising the principal doctrines, and they give sometimes no sense when they are separately considered, for some watch-words only are rhythmically arranged to facilitate the memory.

In the Sanskrit text, the Sagāthakam begins with this stanza:

> "Listen to the wonderful Mahayana doctrine,
> Declared in this Laṅkāvatāra Sūtra,
> Composed in verse-gems,
> And destroying a net of the philosophical views."

This may be understood to mean that this section is that part of the *Laṅkā* which is made up with the verses, that is to say, the verses taken from the entire text of the *Laṅkā*. The term *sagāthakam* also suggests this, for it means the "one with verses." But in this case the following questions may be asked:

If there were a larger *Laṅkā* containing all these verses in the Sagāthakam in the body of the text, or if there were a *Laṅkā* with the verses alone and as a separete text which was later on put together with the present one, are all these verses as a whole to be regarded as belonging to the same

---

[3] These are systematically excluded in the T'ang.

period? If so, what caused the disappearance of the prose passages which accompanied the verses now retained in the Sagāthakam only? Is there no possibility of some of the verses added later to the text independently? There is some evidence of such additions as we can see, for instance, in the conception of the Sambhogakāya (verse 384) and of the ninth Vijñāna (verse 13), which are surely of later development. The solution of these and some other possible questions is to be left to some future time when all the circumstances leading to the production of the Buddhist sutras Mahayana and Hinayana in various districts of India are ascertained.

The best way of reading the *Laṅkā*, as I said in my *Studies*, is to cut the whole text into as many pieces[1] as the sense allows and to regard each piece as completely expressing one chief thought in the philosophy of Mahayana Buddhism. In some cases the pieces so severed may seem to conflict with one another. In such cases a higher principle will be found somewhere else that unifies the two contradictory notions harmoniously. For after all there is but one highest truth in the *Laṅkā*, of which all others are so many aspects viewed at various angles of thought.

I thought I would treat the Sagāthakam in a similar manner, by dividing the whole portion into so many groups of verses, each of which is presumably concerned with one theme. But the verses being too concise and often merely mnemonic, one finds it too risky to cut them up into groups and to take the latter as containing so many definite sets of thoughts. As we notice in the cases of repetition occurring so frequently in the Sagāthakam the verses are not solidly transferred from the text, that is, they are not always found in the Sagāthakam in the same order as they are in the text proper, nor are they complete. Sometimes one single verse is taken out of the group where it belongs in the main text and inserted in an unexpected connection. In

---

[1] This cutting is indicated in the following translation by the Roman figures running consecutively through the entire text except the Rāvaṇa, the Dhāraṇī, and the Meat-eating chapter, where no such dividing is necessary.

these circumstances I thought it wise to leave the Sagāthakam as it stands and not to arrange the verses into groups until we know more exactly about the historical evolution of this portion of the *Laṅkā*.

In fact, the Sagāthakam is a curious mixture where subjects not at all referred to in the prose section are in juxtaposition with those that have to my view no proper bearing in the *Laṅkā*. Such subjects are those historical narratives concerning Vyāsa, Kātyāyana, Nāgahvaya, etc., and those relating to the monastery life. And then there are some passages in the Sagāthakam which may be regarded as later additions. For instance, when it refers to eight or nine several Vijñānas (verse 13), two forms of Ālaya (v. 59), the triple body (v. 434), thirty-six Buddhas (v. 380), etc., they are evidently later incorporations. The Sagāthakam requires more study from the point of text criticism, and also from the point of doctrinal, literary, and monachical history.

The Transmission History of the Laṅkā

In the book called 楞伽師資記, "Record of Master and Disciple in [the Transmission of] the Laṅkā," which is one of the Tung-huang findings, the transmission line of the *Laṅkā* is recorded. The author 淨覺, Ching-chüeh, living probably early in the eighth century apparently identified Zen Buddhism with the teaching of the *Laṅkā*, for his Fathers of the *Laṅkā* transmission are also those of Zen Buddhism. He considers Guṇabhadra, the translator of the Sung or four volume *Laṅkā*, the first Father of Zen in China, and not Bodhidharma as is generally done by Zen historians. In this the author may be in the right, for in his day there was yet no independent school which later came to be known as "Zen", and whatever represented this movement at the time was no more than the study of the *Laṅkā*. Moreover, Ching-chüeh belonged to the school of Hsüan-tsê (玄賾) and Shên-hsiu (神秀) who upheld the *Laṅkā* in opposition to their rival Hui-nêng's 慧能 *Vajracchedīkā*. This book is one of the most valuable documents for the historical students of early Zen Buddhism in China.¹ It contains so much information of definite character concerning its Fathers whose sayings and teachings have so far been shrouded in obscurity.

There is another equally valuable history of Zen Buddhism which was also discovered in the Tung-huang cave. It is entitled 歷代法寶記 "Record of the Succession of the Dharma-treasure." This was evidently written to contend the position of the 楞伽師資記, for it insists that the first Father of the Laṅkā as representing the Dharma-treasure was Bodhidharma and not Guṇabhadra who was mere translator and not the revealer of the inner meaning of the Sutra. Therefore, the history of Zen Buddhism in China, which is the "Dharma-treasure", should properly begin with Bodhidharma. The author evidently belongs to the school of Hui-nêng.

The discovery of these two important historical works on Zen, together with the *Sayings of Shên-hui*, 神會語錄, which was edited by 胡適, Professor Hu Hsi of Peking University, 1930, with his able critical notes, sheds an abundance of light on the early pages of Zen history in China. As a detailed discussion of the subject does not belong here, I reserve it for my *Essays in Zen Buddhism*, Series II.

The Present English Translation

As regards the English translation of the Sutra, I have decided after much hesitation to send it out to the public with all its many imperfections. It is a bold attempt on the part of the translator to try to render some of the deepest thoughts that have been nourished in the East into a language to which he was not born. But his idea is that if somebody did not make a first attempt, however poor and defective, the precious stones may remain buried unknown except to a few scholars, and this perhaps longer than necessary. And then

---

¹ The book has been quite recently edited by Kin Kyūkei, a librarian attached to Peking University and published in Peking. He was able to do this helped by Professor Hu Hsi, who is the owner of

things develop. As it is illustrated in the long history of the Chinese translations of the Buddhist texts, there must be several attempts before the work assumes something of finality. There are at present three Chinese translations and one Tibetan of the *Laṅkā,* and the first shows many traces of immaturity when compared with the third. We can easily understand the difficulties Chinese scholars encountered in trying to master the translations. The T'ang version could not perhaps be so perfect as it is unless it had two or three predecessors.

I have done all I could to make my translation as intelligible as possible to my readers. If I tried to be too literal, it would be quite unintelligible. The modes of expression are so different in the Sanskrit. There are still many obscure passages which I failed to interpret satisfactorily to myself. These obscurities are found more in the Sagāthakam, because the verses presuppose much knowledge of the matter treated therein, and this knowledge involves at present much more scholarship and intellectual perspicuity than the present translator can command. The Sagāthakam has never had any Chinese commentaries, and this fact adds more to the difficulties already in existence. Chinese and Japanese scholars have chosen, probably for brevity's sake, the four-volume text by Guṇabhadra for their study, and the Sagāthakam has thus inevitably been left out.

The Sanskrit text itself as we have it is still far from being perfect, and there is no doubt that Nanjo's edition requires many corrections in order to yield a more intelligible reading. Even with it, however, whatever shortcomings it may have, we are to be grateful to the editor who made the text more accessible to the public than ever before.

I have not always followed Nanjo in the reading of the text. I have used my own judgment in several cases when

the photographic copies of the original Manuscripts of 楞伽師資記 preserved in the British Museum and in the Bibliothèque Nationale. A collotype impression of the London MS which is not so complete as the Paris MS, though it is very much more legible than the latter, was published by Professor Keiki Yabuki of Japan, in his collection of the Tunhuang MSS, entitled 鳴沙餘韻, "Echoes of the Desert", 1930.

INTRODUCTION

I thought the sense became thereby clearer. In paragraphing too I have often disregarded Nanjo. As I said in my *Studies*, the *Laṅkā* is a highly chaotic text, and there are also some passages which have forced their way in wrong places where they do not belong.

The T'ang version in this respect gives on the whole the best rendering of the *Laṅkā*. While a first draft of the translation was prepared by Śikshānanda, the finishing touch was given by Fa-tsang, the great teacher of philosophy of the *Avataṁsaka*, with which the *Laṅkā* is in the closest relationship. When difficulties were encountered in the course of my English translation of the Sanskrit text, I have quite frequently followed the T'ang reading, though the fact has not regularly been noted.

A special index to the Sutra is being prepared and will be issued before long as a separate volume.

THE LANKĀVATĀRA SŪTRA

[CHAPTER ONE]

(1)[1] Om! Salutation to the Triple Treasure! Salutation to all the Buddhas and Bodhisattvas!

Here is carefully written down the *Laṅkāvatāra Sūtra* in which the Lord of the Dharma discourses on the egolessness of all things.

Thus have I heard. The Blessed One once stayed in the Castle of Laṅkā which is situated on the peak of Mount Malaya on the great ocean, and which is adorned with flowers made of jewels of various kinds.[2] He was with a large assembly of Bhikshus and with a great multitude of Bodhisattvas, who had come together from various Buddha-lands. The Bodhisattva-Mahāsattvas, headed by the Bodhisattva Mahāmati, were all perfect masters[3] of the various Samādhis, the [tenfold] self-mastery, the [ten] powers, and the [six] psychic faculties; they were anointed by the hands of all the Buddhas; they all well understood the significance of the objective world as the manifestation of their own Mind; (2) they knew how to maintain [various] forms, teachings, and disciplinary measures, according to the various mentalities and behaviours of beings; they were thoroughly versed in the five Dharmas, the [three] Svabhāvas, the [eight] Vijñānas, and the twofold Non-ātman.

At that time, the Blessed One who had been preaching in the palace of the King of Sea-serpents came out at the expiration of seven days and was greeted by an innumerable host of Nāgakanyās including Śakra and Brahma, and looking at Laṅkā on Mount Malaya smiled and said, "By the Tathagatas of the past, who were Arhats and Fully-

---

[1] These Gothic numerals in parentheses refer to pages of the Sanskrit edition.

[2] Much more fully described in Bodhiruci (Wei).

[3] Literally, "sporting" (*vikrīḍita*).

Enlightened Ones, this Truth was made the subject of their discourse, at that castle of Laṅkā on the mountain-peak of Malaya,—the Truth realisable by noble wisdom in one's inmost self, which is beyond the reasoning knowledge of the philosophers as well as the state of consciousness of the Śrāvakas and Pratyekabuddhas.[1] I, too, would now for the sake of Rāvaṇa, Overlord of the Yakshas, discourse on this Truth."

[Inspired] by the spiritual power of the Tathagata, Rāvaṇa, Lord of the Rākshasas, heard [his voice]. Indeed, the Blessed One, surrounded and accompanied by an innumerable host of Nāgakanyās including Śakra and Brahma, came out of the palace of the King of Sea-serpents; and looking at the waves of the ocean and also at the mental agitations going on in those assembled, [he thought of] the ocean of the Ālayavijñāna where the evolving Vijñānas [like the waves] are stirred by the wind of objectivity. While he was standing there [thus absorbed in contemplation, Rāvaṇa saw him and] uttered a joyous cry, saying: "I will go and request of the Blessed One to enter into Laṅkā; for this long night he would probably profit, do good, and gladden (3) the gods as well as human beings"

Thereupon, Rāvaṇa, Lord of the Rākshasas, with his attendants, riding in his floral celestial chariot, came up where the Blessed One was, and having arrived there he and his attendants came out of the chariot. Walking around the Blessed One three times from left to right, they played on a musical instrument. beating it with a stick of blue Indra (saphire), and hanging the lute at one side, which was inlaid with the choicest lapis lazuli and supported by [a ribbon of] priceless cloth, yellowish-white like Priyaṅgu, they sang with various notes such as Saharshya, Rishabha, Gāndhāra, Dhaivata, Nishāda, Madyama, and Kaiśika,[2] which were

---

[1] The Sanskrit text is here certainly at fault; there ought to be a negative particle somewhere in this passage, which is the case in the Chinese translations.

[2] Neither Bodhiruci nor Sikshānanda refers so specifically to these various notes.

melodiously modulated in Grāma, Mūrchana, etc.; the voice in accompaniment with the flute beautifully blended with the measure of the Gāthā.

1. "The truth-treasure whose principle is the self-nature of Mind, has no selfhood (*nairātmyam*), stands above all reasoning, and is free from impurities; it points to the knowledge attained in one's inmost self; Lord, show me here the way leading to the Truth.

2. "The Sugata is the body in whom are stored immaculate virtues; in him are manifested [bodies] transforming and transformed; he enjoys the Truth realised in his inmost self; may he visit Laṅkā. Now is the time, Muni!

3. (4) "This Laṅkā was inhabited by the Buddhas of the past, and [they were] accompanied by their sons who were owners of many forms. Lord, show me now the highest Truth, and the Yakshas who are endowed with many forms will listen."

Thereupon, Rāvaṇa, the Lord of Laṅkā, further adapting the Totaka rhythm sang this in the measure of the Gāthā.

4. After seven nights, the Blessed One leaving the ocean which is the abode of the Makara, the palace of the sea-king, now stands on the shore.

5. Just as the Buddha rises, Rāvaṇa, accompanied by the Apsaras and Yakshas numerous, by Śuka, Sāraṇa, and learned men,

6. Miraculously goes over to the place where the Lord is standing. Alighting from the floral vehicle, he greets the Tathagata reverentially, makes him offerings, tells him who he is, and stands by the Lord.

7. "I who have come here, am called Rāvaṇa, the ten-headed king of the Rākshasas, mayest thou graciously receive me with Laṅkā and all its residents.

8. "In this city, the inmost state of consciousness realised, indeed, by the Enlightened Ones of the past (5) was disclosed on this peak studded with precious stones.

9. "Let the Blessed One, too, surrounded by sons of the Victorious One, now disclose the Truth immaculate on

this peak embellished with precious stones; we, together with the residents of Laṅkā, desire to listen.

10. "The *Laṅkāvatāra Sūtra* which is praised by the Buddhas of the past [discloses] the inmost state of consciousness realised by them, which is not founded on any system of doctrine.

11. "I recollect the Buddhas of the past surrounded by sons of the Victorious One recite this Sutra; the Blessed One, too, will speak.

12. "In the time to come, there will be Buddhas and Buddha-Sons pitying the Yakshas; the Leaders will discourse on this magnificent doctrine on the peak adorned with precious stones.

13. "This magnificent city of Laṅkā is adorned with varieties of precious stones, [surrounded] by peaks, refreshing and beautiful and canopied by a net of jewels.

14. "Blessed One, here are the Yakshas who are free from faults of greed, reflecting on [the Truth] realised in one's inmost self and making offerings to the Buddhas of the past; they are believers in the teaching of the Mahāyāna and intent on disciplining one another.

15. "There are younger Yakshas, girls and boys, desiring to know the Mahāyāna. Come, Blessed One, who art our Teacher, come to Laṅkā on Mount Malaya.

16. (6) "The Rākshasas, with Kumbhakarṇa at their head, who are residing in the city, wish, as they are devoted to the Mahāyāna, to hear about this inmost realisation.

17. "They have made offerings assiduously to the Buddhas [in the past] and are to-day going to do the same. Come, for compassion's sake, to the Laṅkā, together with [thy] sons.

18. "Mahāmati, accept my mansion, the company of the Apsaras, necklaces of various sorts, and the delightful Aśoka garden.

19. "I give myself up to serve the Buddhas and their sons; there is nothing with me that I do not give up [for their sake]; Great Muni, have compassion on me!"

20. Hearing him speak thus, the Lord of the Triple

CHAPTER ONE 7

World said, "King of Yakshas, this mountain of precious stones was visited by the Leaders in the past.

21. "And, taking pity on you, they discoursed on the Truth revealed in their inmost [consciousness]. [The Buddhas of] the future time will proclaim [the same] on this jewel-adorned mountain.

22. "This [inmost Truth] is the abode of those Yogins who stand in the presence of the Truth. King of the Yakshas, you have the compassion of the Sugatas and myself."

23. The Blessed One accepting the request [of the King] remained silent and undisturbed; he now mounted the floral chariot offered by Rāvaṇa.

24. Thus Rāvaṇa and others, wise sons of the Victorious One, (7) honoured by the Apsaras singing and dancing, reached the city.

25. Arriving in the delightful city [the Buddha was] again the recipient of honours; he was honoured by the group of Yakshas including Rāvaṇa and by the Yaksha women.

26. A net of jewels was offered to the Buddha by the younger Yakshas, girls and boys, and necklaces beautifully ornamented with jewels were placed by Rāvaṇa about the neck of the Buddha and those of the sons of the Buddha.

27. The Buddhas together with the sons of the Buddha and the wise men, accepting the offerings, discoursed on the Truth which is the state of consciousness realised in the inmost self.

28. Honouring [him as] the best speaker, Rāvaṇa and the company of the Yakshas honoured Mahāmati and requested of him again and again:[1]

29. "Thou art the asker of the Buddha concerning the state of consciousness realised in their inmost selves, of which we here, Yakshas as well as the sons of the Buddha, are desirous of hearing. I, together with the Yakshas, the sons of the Buddha, and the wise men, request this of thee.

30. "Thou art the most eloquent of speakers, and the

[1] Verses 20–28, inclusive, are in prose in T'ang.

most strenuous of the Yogins; with faith I beg of thee. Ask [the Buddha] about the doctrine, O thou the proficient one!

31. "Free from the faults of the philosophers and Pratyekabuddhas and Śrāvakas is (8) the Truth of the inmost consciousness, immaculate and culminating in the stage of Buddhahood."

32.[1] Thereupon the Blessed One created jewel-adorned mountains and other objects magnificently embellished with jewels in an immense number.

33. On the summit of each mountain the Buddha himself was visible, and Rāvaṇa, the Yaksha, also was found standing there.

34. Thus the entire assembly was seen on each mountain-peak, and all the countries were there, and in each there was a Leader.

35. Here also was the King of the Rākshasas and the residents of Laṅkā, and the Laṅkā created by the Buddha rivaling [the real one].

36. Other things were there, too,—the Aśoka with its shining woods, and on each mountain-peak Mahāmati was making a request of the Buddha,

37. Who discoursed for the sake of the Yakshas on the Truth leading to the inmost realisation; on the mountain-peak he delivered a complete sutra with an exquisite voice varied in hundreds of thousands of ways.[2]

38. [After this] the teacher and the sons of the Buddha vanished away in the air, leaving Rāvaṇa the Yaksha himself standing [above] in his mansion.

39. Thought he, "How is this? What means this? and by whom was it heard? What was it that was seen? and by whom was it seen? Where is the city? and where is the Buddha?

40. "Where are those countries, those jewel-shining Buddhas, those Sugatas? (9) Is it a dream then? or a vision? or is it a castle conjured up by the Gandharvas?

---

[1] From this verse T'ang is in prose again.

[2] Thus according to Bodhiruci and Śikshānanda. The Sanskrit text has: "hundreds of thousands of perfect sutras."

CHAPTER ONE

41. "Or is it dust in the eye, or a fata morgana, or the dream-child of a barren woman, or the smoke of a fire-wheel, that which I saw here?"

42. Then [Rāvaṇa reflected], "This is the nature as it is (*dharmatā*) of all things, which belongs to the realm of Mind, and it is not comprehended by the ignorant as they are confused by every form of imagination.

43. "There is neither the seer nor the seen, neither the speaker nor the spoken; the form and usage of the Buddha and his Dharma—they are nothing but discrimination.

44. "Those who see things such as were seen before, do not see the Buddha; [even] when discrimination is not aroused, one does not see[1] the Buddha; the Buddha being fully-enlightened is seen where the world itself is not evolved.

The Lord of Laṅkā was then immediately awakened [from his reflection], feeling a revulsion (*parāvṛiti*) in his mind and realising that the world was nothing but his own mind: he was settled in the realm of non-discrimination, was urged by the stock of his past good deeds, acquired the cleverness of understanding all the texts, obtained the faculty of seeing things as they are, was no more dependent upon others, observed things excellently with his own wisdom (*buddhi*), gained the insight that was not of discursive reasoning, was no more dependent upon others,[2] became a great Yogin of the discipline, was able to manifest himself in all excellent forms, got thoroughly acquainted with all skilful means, had the knowledge of the characteristic aspects

---

[1] T'ang has: "He who sees in the way as was seen before, cannot see the Buddha; when no discrimination is aroused, this, indeed, is the seeing." According to Wei: "If he sees things and takes them for realities, he does not see the Buddha. Even when he is not abiding in a discriminating mind, he cannot see the Buddha. Not seeing anything doing [in the world]—this is said to be seeing the Buddha. If a man is able thus to see [things], he is the one who sees the Tathagata. When the wise observe all experiences in this manner, they are transformed assuming an exquisite body—this is the Enlightenment [attained by] the Buddha."

[2] This does not appear in T'ang, nor in Wei.

of every stage, by which he would surmount it skilfully, was delighted to look into[1] the self-nature of Citta, Manas, Manovijñāna, got a view whereby he could cut himself loose from the triple continuation, had the knowledge of disposing of every argument of (10) the philosophers on causation, thoroughly understood the Tathāgata-garbha, the stage of Buddhahood, the inmost self, found himself abiding in the Buddha-knowledge; [when suddenly] a voice was heard from the sky, saying, "It is to be known by oneself."

"Well done, well done, Lord of Laṅkā! Well done, indeed, Lord of Laṅkā, for once more! The Yogin is to discipline himself as thou doest. The Tathagatas and all things are to be viewed as they are viewed by thee; otherwise viewed, it is nihilism. All things are to be comprehended by transcending the Citta, Manas, and Vijñāna as is done by thee. Thou shouldst look inwardly and not become attached to the letter and a superficial view of things; thou shouldst not fall into the attainments, conceptions, experiences, views, and Samādhis of the Śrāvakas, Pratyekabuddhas, and philosophers; thou shouldst not have any liking for small talk and witticism; thou shouldst not cherish the notion of self-substance,[2] nor have any thought for the vainglory of rulership, nor dwell on such Dhyānas as belong to the six Dhyānas, etc.

"Lord of Laṅkā, this is the realisation of the great Yogins: to destroy the discourses advanced by others, to crush mischievous views in pieces, to keep themselves properly away from ego-centered notions, to cause a revulsion in the depths of the mind fittingly by means of an exquisite knowledge. Such are sons of the Buddha who walk in the way of the Mahāyāna. In order to enter upon the stage of self-realisation as attained by the Tathagatas, the discipline is to be pursued by thee.

"Lord of Laṅkā, conducting thyself in this manner, let thee be further purified in the way thou hast attained; (11) by disciplining thyself well in Samādhi and Samāpatti,

[1] T'ang: to go beyond.
[2] Wei and T'ang: Do not hold the views maintained in the Vedas.

follow not the state realised and enjoyed by the Śravakas, Pratyekabuddhas, and philosophers, which rises from the imagination of those who discipline themselves according to the practices of the puerile philosophers. They cling to the individual forms of the world created by their egotistical ideas; they maintain such notions as element, quality, and substance; they cling tenaciously to views originating from ignorance; they become confused by cherishing the idea of birth where prevails emptiness; they cling to discrimination [as real]; they fall into the way of thinking where obtains [the dualism of] qualifying and qualified.

"Lord of Laṅkā, this is what leads to various excellent attainments, this is what makes one grow aware of the inmost attainment, this is the Mahāyāna realisation. This will result in the acquirement of an excellent condition of existence.

"Lord of Laṅkā, by entering upon the Mahāyāna discipline the veils [of ignorance] are destroyed, and one turns away from the multitudinous waves of the Vijñāna and falls not into the refuge and practice of the philosophers.

"Lord of Laṅkā, the philosophers' practice starts from their own egotistic attachments. Their ugly practice arises from adhering to dualistic views concerning the self-nature of the Vijñāna.

"Well done, Lord of Laṅkā; reflect on the signification of this as you did when seeing the Tathagata before; for this, indeed, is seeing the Tathagata."

At that time it occurred to Rāvaṇa: "I wish to see the Blessed One again, who has all the disciplinary practices at his command, who has turned away from the practices of the philosophers, who is born of the state of realisation in the inmost consciousness, and who is beyond [the dualism of] the transformed and the transforming. He is the knowledge (12) realised by the Yogins, he is the realisation attained by those who enjoy the perfect bliss of the Samādhi which they gain by coming to an intuitive understanding through meditation. May I see thus [again] the Compassionate One by means of his miraculous powers in whom the fuel of passion and discrimination is destroyed, who is surrounded by sons of the Buddha, who has penetrated into the minds and thoughts of all beings, who moves about everywhere, who knows everything, who keeps himself away from work (*kriyā*) and form (*lakshaṇa*); seeing him may I attain what I have not yet attained, [retain] what I have already gained, may I conduct myself with non-discrimination, abide in the joy of Samādhi and Samāpatti, and attain the ground where the Tathagatas walk, and in these make progress."

At that moment, the Blessed One recognising that the Lord of Laṅkā is to attain the Anutpattikadharmakshānti showed his glorious compassion for the ten-headed one by making himself visible once more on the mountain-peak studded with many jewels and enveloped in a net-work of jewels. The ten-headed King of Laṅkā saw the splendour again as seen before on the mountain-peak, [he saw] the Tathagata, who was the Arhat and the Fully-Enlightened One, with the thirty-two marks of excellence beautifully adorning his person, and also saw himself on each mountain-peak, together with Mahāmati, in front of the Tathagata, the Fully-Enlightened One, putting forward his discourse on the realisation experienced by the Tathagata in his inmost self, and, surrounded by the Yakshas, conversing on the verbal teachings and stories [of the Buddha]. Those (13) [Buddha]-lands were seen with the Leaders.[1]

[1] There is surely a discrepancy here in the text. T'ang reads: "In all the Buddha-lands in the ten quarters were also seen such events going on, and there was no difference whatever." Wei is quite different and has the following: "Besides, he saw all the Buddha-lands and all the kings thinking of the transitoriness of the body. As they are covetously attached to their thrones, wives, children, and relatives, they find themselves bound by the five passions and have no time for emancipation. Seeing this, they abandon their dominions, palaces, wives, concubines, elephants, horses, and precious treasures, giving them all up to the Buddha and his Brotherhood. They now retreat into the mountain-woods, leaving their homes and wishing to study the doctrine. He [Rāvaṇa] then sees the Bodhisattvas in the mountain woods strenuously applying themseves to the mastery of the truth, even to the extent of throwing themselves to the hungry tiger, lion, and Rākshasas. He thus sees the Bodhisattvas reading and reciting the sutras under a tree in the woods and discoursing on them for others, seeking thereby the

CHAPTER ONE

Then the Blessed One beholding again this great assembly with his wisdom-eye, which is not the human eye, laughed loudly and most vigorously like the lion-king. Emitting rays of light from the tuft of hair between the eyebrows, from the ribs, from the loins, from the Śrivatsa[1] on the breast, and from every pore of the skin,—emitting rays of light which shone flaming like the fire taking place at the end of a kalpa, like a luminous rainbow, like the rising sun, blazing brilliantly, gloriously—which were observed from the sky by Śakra, Brahma, and the guardians of the world, the one who sat on the peak [of Laṅkā] vying with Mount Sumeru laughed the loudest laugh. At that time the assembly of the Bodhisattvas together with Śakra and Brahma, each thought within himself:

"For what reason, I wonder, from what cause does the Blessed One who is the master of all the world (*sarvadharma-vaśavartin*), after smiling first,[2] laugh the loudest laugh? Why does he emit rays of light from his own body? Why, emitting [rays of light], does he remain silent, with the realisation [of the Truth] in his inmost self, and absorbed deeply and showing no surprise in the bliss of Samādhi, and reviewing the [ten] quarters, looking around like the lion-king, and thinking only of the discipline, attainment, and performance of Rāvaṇa?"

At that time, Mahāmati the Bodhisattva-Mahāsattva who was previously requested by Rāvaṇa [to ask the Buddha concerning his self-realisation], feeling pity on him, (14) and knowing the minds and thoughts of the assembly of the

truth of the Buddha. He then sees the Bodhisattvas seated under the Bodhi-tree in the Bodhi-maṇḍala thinking of the suffering beings and meditating on the truth of the Buddha. He then sees the venerable Mahāmati the Bodhisattva before each Buddha preaching about the spiritual discipline of one's inner life, and also sees [the Bodhisattva] surrounded by all the Yakshas and families and talking about names, words, phrases, and paragraphs." This last sentence is evidently the translation of the Sanskrit *deśanāpāṭhakathām*, which is contrasted in the *Laṅkāvatāra* throughout with *pratyātmāryajñānagocara* (the spiritual realm realised by noble wisdom in one's inmost consciousness).

[1] Swastika.
[2] This is wanting in the Chinese translations.

Bodhisattvas, and observing that beings to be born in the future would be confused in their minds because of their delight in the verbal teaching (*deśanāpāṭha*), because of their clinging to the letter as [fully in accordance with] the spirit (*artha*), because of their clinging to the disciplinary powers of the Śrāvakas, Pratyekabuddhas, and philosophers, —which might lead them to think how it were that the Tathagatas, the Blessed Ones, even in their transcendental state of consciousness should burst out into loudest laughter —Mahāmati the Bodhisattva asked the Buddha in order to put a stop to their inquisitiveness the following question: "For what reason, for what cause did this laughter take place?"

Said the Blessed One: "Well done, well done, Mahāmati! Well done, indeed, for once more, Mahāmati! Viewing the world as it is in itself and wishing to enlighten the people in the world who are fallen into a wrong view of things in the past, present, and future, thou undertakest to ask me the question. Thus should it be with the wise men who want to ask questions for both themselves and others. Rāvaṇa, Lord of Laṅkā, O Mahāmati, asked a twofold question of the Tathagatas of the past who are Arhats and perfect Buddhas; and he wishes now to ask me too a twofold question in order to have its distinction, attainment, and scope ascertained—this is what is never tasted by those who practise the meditation of the Śrāvakas, Pratyekabuddhas, and philosophers; and the same will be asked by the question-loving ten-headed one of the Buddhas to come."

Knowing that, the Blessed One said to the Lord of Laṅkā, thus: "Ask, thou Lord of Laṅkā; the Tathagata has given thee permission [to ask], delay not, whatever questions thou desirest to have answered, I will answer each of them (15) with judgment to the satisfaction of your heart. Keeping thy seat of thought free from [false] discrimination, observe well what is to be subdued at each stage; ponder things with wisdom; [seeing into] the nature of the inner principle in thyself, abide in the bliss of Samādhi; embraced by the Buddhas in Samādhi, abide in the bliss of tranquillisation; going beyond the Samādhi and understanding attained by the Śrāvakas and Pratyekabuddhas, abide in [the attainment of the Bodhisattvas] in the stages of Acalā, Sādhumatī, and Dharmameghā; grasp well the egolessness of all things in its true significance; be anointed by the Buddhas in Samādhi at the great palace of lotus-jewels. [1]Surrounded by the Bodhisattvas who are sitting on lotuses of various sorts each supported by the gracious power of the Buddhas, thou shalt find thyself sitting on a lotus and each one of the Bodhisattvas looking at thee face to face. This is a realm beyond the imagination. Thou shouldst plan out an adequate plan and establish thyself at a stage of discipline by planning out such a plan as shall include [all kinds of] skilful means, so that thou comest to realise that realm which is beyond imagination; and thou shouldst attain the stage of Tathagatahood in which one is able to manifest oneself in various forms, and which is something never seen before by the Śrāvakas, Pratyekabuddhas, philosophers, Brahma, Indra, Upendra, and others."

At that moment the Lord of Laṅkā being permitted by the Blessed One, rose from his seat on the peak of the jewel-mountain which shone like the jewel-lotus immaculate and shining in splendour; he was surrounded by a large company of celestial maidens, and all kinds of garlands, flowers, perfumes, incense, unguents, umbrellas, banners, flags, necklaces, half-necklaces, diadems, tiaras, (16) and other ornaments whose splendour and excellence were never heard of or seen before, were created; music was played surpassing

---

[1] The following sentence is done by the aid of T'ang, as the Sanskrit does not seem to give any sense. Literally translated it reads: "There by the becoming lotuses, by those lotuses that are blessed variously by the benediction of his own person...." Wei has: "O King of Laṅkā, thou wilt before long see thy person, too, thus sitting on the lotus-throne and continuing to abide there in a most natural manner. There are innumerable families of lotus-kings and innumerable families of Bodhisattvas there, each one of whom is sitting on a lotus-throne, and surrounded by those thou wilt find thyself and looking face to face at one another, and each one of them will before long come to abide in a realm beyond the understanding."

anything that could be had by the gods, Nāgas, Yakshas, Rākshasas, Gandharvas, Kinnaras, Mahoragas, and men; musical instruments were created equal to anything that could be had in all the world of desire and also such superior musical instruments were created as were to be seen in the Buddha-lands; the Blessed One and the Bodhisattvas were enveloped in a net of jewels; a variety of dresses and high banners was made rising high in the air as high as seven tāla trees to great [the Buddha], showering great clouds of offerings, playing music which resounded [all around], and then descending from the air, [the Lord of Laṅkā] sat down on the peak of the jewel-mountain ornamented with magnificent jewel-lotus whose splendour was second only to the sun and lightning. Sitting he made courtesy smiling first to the Blessed One for his permission and proposed him a twofold question: "It was asked of the Tathagatas of the past, who were Arhats, Fully-Enlightened Ones, and it was solved by them. Blessed One, now I ask of thee; [the request] will certainly be complied with by thee as far as verbal instruction is concerned[1] as it was by the Buddhas [of the past]. Blessed One, duality was discoursed upon by the Transformed Tathagatas and Tathagatas of Transformation, but not by the Tathagatas of Silence.[2] The Tathagatas of Silence are absorbed in the blissful state of Samādhi, they do not discriminate concerning this state, nor do they discourse on it. Blessed One, thou assuredly wilt discourse on this subject of duality. Thou art thyself a master of all things, an Arhat, a Tathagata. The sons of the Buddha and myself are anxious to listen to it."

The Blessed One said, "Lord of Laṅkā, tell me what you mean by duality?"

The Lord of the Rākshasas, (17) who was renewed in his ornaments, full of splendour and beauty, with a diadem, bracelet, and necklace strung with vajra thread, said, "It is

---

[1] That is, as far as the teaching could be conveyed in words. *Deśanāpāṭha* stands in contrast with *siddhānta*, or *pratyātmagati* in the *Laṅkāvatāra*.

[2] In T'ang and Wei: "Original Tathagatas."

said that even dharmas are to be abandoned, and how much more adharmas. Blessed One, why does this dualism exist that we are called upon to abandon? What are adharmas? and what are dharmas? How can there be a duality of things to abandon—a duality that arises from falling into discrimination, from discriminating self-substance where there is none, from [the idea of] things created (*bhautika*) and uncreated, because the non-differentiating nature of the Ālayavijñāna is not recognised? Like the seeing of a hair-circle as really existing in the air, [the notion of dualism] belongs to the realm of intellection not exhaustively purgated. This being the case as it should be, how could there be any abandonment [of dharmas and adharmas]?"

Said the Blessed One, "Lord of Laṅkā, seest thou not that the differentiation of things, such as is perceived in jars and other breakable objects whose nature it is to perish in time, takes place in a realm of discrimination [cherished by] the ignorant? This being so, is it not to be so understood? It is due to discrimination [cherished by] the ignorant that there exists the differentiation of dharma and adharma. Noble wisdom (*āryajñāna*), however, is not to be realised by seeing [things this way]. Lord of Laṅkā, let it be so with the ignorant who follow the particularised aspect of existence that there are such objects as jars, etc., but it is not so with the wise. One flame of uniform nature rises up depending on houses, mansions, parks, and terraces, and burns them down; while a difference in the flames is seen according to the power of each burning material which varies in length, magnitude, etc. This being so, why (**18**) is it not to be so understood? The duality of dharma and adharma thus comes into existence. Not only is there seen a fire-flame spreading out in one continuity and yet showing a variety of flames, but from one seed, Lord of Laṅkā, are produced, also in one continuity, stems, shoots, knots, leaves, petals, flowers, fruit, branches, all individualised. As it is with every external object from which grows [a variety of] objects, so also with internal objects. From ignorance there develop the Skāndhas, Dhātus, Āyatanas, with all kinds of objects accompanying, which grow out in the triple world where we have, as we see, happiness, form, speech, and behaviour, each differentiating [infinitely]. The oneness of the Vijñāna is grasped variously according to the evolution of an objective world; thus there are seen things inferior, superior, and middling, things defiled and free from defilement, things good and bad. Not only, Lord of Laṅkā, is there such a difference of conditions in things generally, there is also seen a variety of realisations attained innerly by each Yogin as he treads the path of discipline which constitutes his practice. How much more difference in dharma and adharma do we not see in a world of particulars which is evolved by discrimination? Indeed, we do.

"Lord of Laṅkā, the differentiation of dharma and adharma comes from discrimination. Lord of Laṅkā, what are dharmas? That is, they are discriminated by the discriminations cherished by the philosophers, Śrāvakas, Pratyekabuddhas, and ignorant people. They think that the dharmas headed by quality and substance are produced by causes—[these are the notions] to be abandoned. Such are not to be regarded [as real] because they are appearances (*lakshaṇa*). It comes from one's clinging [to appearances] that the manifestations of his own Mind are regarded as reality (*dharmatā*). (19) Such things as jars, etc., are products of discrimination conceived by the ignorant, they exist not; their substances are not attainable. The viewing of things from this viewpoint is known as their abandonment.

"What, then, are adharmas? Lord of Laṅkā, [dharmas] are unattainable as to their selfhood, they are not appearances born of discrimination, they are above causality; there is in them no such [dualistic] happening as is seen as reality and non-reality. This is known as the abandoning of dharmas. What again is meant by the unattainability of dharmas? That is, it is like horns of a hare, or an ass, or a camel, or a horse, or a child conceived by a barren woman. They are dharmas the nature of which is unattainable; they are not to be thought [as real] because they are appearances. They

CHAPTER ONE

are only talked about in popular parlance if they have any sense at all; they are not to be adhered to as in the case of jars, etc. As these [unrealities] are to be abandoned as not comprehensible by the mind (*vijñāna*), so are things (*bhāva*) of discrimination also to be abandoned. This is called the abandoning of dharmas and adharmas. Lord of Laṅkā, your question as to the way of abandoning dharmas and adharmas is hereby answered.

"Lord of Laṅkā, thou sayest again that thou hast asked [this question] of the Tathagatas of the past who were Arhats and Fully-Enlightened Ones and that it was solved by them. Lord of Laṅkā, that which is spoken of as the past belongs to discrimination; as the past is thus a discriminated [idea], even so are the [ideas] of the future and the present. Because of reality (*dharmatā*) the Tathagatas do not discriminate, they go beyond discrimination and futile reasoning, they do not follow (20) the individuation-aspect of forms (*rūpa*) except when [reality] is disclosed for the edification of the unknowing and for the sake of their happiness.[1] It is by transcendental wisdom (*prajñā*) that

---

[1] This is one of the most important sections in this first introductory chapter, but singularly all the three texts, perhaps excepting T'ang, present some difficulties for clear understanding. Wei: "Lord of Laṅkā, what you speak of as past is a form of discrimination, and so are the future and the present, also of discrimination. Lord of Laṅkā, when I speak of the real nature of suchness as being real, it also belongs to discrimination; it is like discriminating forms as the ultimate limit. If one wishes to realise the bliss of real wisdom, let him discipline himself in the knowledge that transcends forms; therefore, do not discriminate the Tathagatas as having knowledge-body or wisdom-essence. Do not cherish any discrimination in [thy] mind. Do not cling in [thy] will to such notions as ego, personality, soul, etc. How not to discriminate? It is in the Manovijñāna that various conditions are cherished such as forms, figures, [etc.]; do not cherish such [discriminations]. Do not discriminate nor be discriminated. Further, Lord of Laṅkā, it is like various forms painted on the wall, all sentient beings are such. Lord of Laṅkā, all sentient beings are like grasses and trees, with them there are no acts, no deeds, Lord of Laṅkā, all dharmas and adharmas, of them nothing is heard, nothing talked...."
T'ang: "Lord of Laṅkā, what you speak of as past is no more than discrimination, so is the future; I too am like him. [Is this to be read, "the present, too, is like it"?] Lord of Laṅkā, the teaching of all the

the Tathagata performs deeds transcending forms (*animittacāra*); therefore, what constitutes the Tathagatas in essence as well as in body is wisdom (*jñāna*). They do not discriminate, nor are they discriminated. Wherefore do they not discriminate the Manas? Because discrimination is of the self, of soul, of personality. How do they not discriminate? The Manovijñāna is meant for the objective world where causality prevails as regards forms, appearances, conditions, and figures. Therefore, discrimination and non-discrimination must be transcended.

"Lord of Laṅkā, beings are appearances, they are like figures painted on the wall, they have no sensibility [or consciousness]. Lord of Laṅkā, all that is in the world is devoid of work and action because all things have no reality, and there is nothing heard, nothing hearing. Lord of Laṅkā, all that is in the world is like an image magically transformed. This is not comprehended by the philosophers and the ignorant. Lord of Laṅkā, he who thus sees things, is the one who sees truthfully. Those who see things otherwise walk in discrimination; as they depend on discrimination, they cling to dualism. It is like seeing one's own image reflected in a mirror, or one's own shadow in the water, or in the moonlight, or seeing one's shadow in the house, or hearing an echo in the valley. People grasping their own shadows of discrimination (21) uphold the discrimination of

Buddhas is outside discrimination; as it goes beyond all discriminations and futile reasonings, it is not a form of particularisation, it is realised only by wisdom. That [this absolute] teaching is at all discoursed about is for the sake of giving bliss to all sentient beings. The discoursing is done by the wisdom transcending forms. It is called the Tathagata; therefore, the Tathagata has his essence, his body in this wisdom. He thus does not discriminate, nor is he to be discriminated. Do not discriminate him after the notion of ego, personality, or being. Why this impossibility of discrimination? because the Manovijñāna is aroused on account of an objective world wherein it attaches itself to forms and figures. Therefore, [the Tathagata] is outside the discriminating [view] as well as the discriminated [idea]. Lord of Laṅkā, it is like beings painted in colours on a wall, they have no sensibility [or intelligence]. Sentient beings in the world are also like them; no acts, no rewards [are with them]. So are all the teachings, no hearing, no preaching."

dharma and adharma and, failing to carry out the abandonment of the dualism, they go on discriminating and never attain tranquillity, By tranquillity is meant oneness (*ekāgra*), and oneness gives birth to the highest Samādhi, which is gained by entering into the womb of Tathagatahood, which is the realm of noble wisdom realised in one's inmost self."

The First Chapter Called "Rāvaṇa Asking for Instruction."[1]

---

[1] It is noteworthy that the chapter endings are not the same throughout the entire text. Generally, reference is made to the Sutra itself at the end of a chapter, stating that the chapter bears such a title belonging to such a Sutra. But in the present case there is no mention at all of the *Laṅkāvatāra Sūtra* as if this Rāvaṇa section were something quite independent. While there is no doubt about its being a later addition, seeing what a complete piece of narrative it forms by itself, and again seeing that the rest of the text makes no further reference to Rāvaṇa, the trend of the discourse as presented by the Buddha shows that it is closely related to the Sutra, especially when it emphasises at the end the importance of self-realisation against the inanity or futility of the verbal teaching ordinarily given out by a master.

[CHAPTER TWO]

I[1]

(22) At that time Mahāmati the Bodhisattva-Mahāsattva who had visited all the Buddha-lands, together with all the Bodhisattvas, rose from his seat by the power of the Buddhas, drawing his upper garment over one shoulder, placing his right knee on the ground and with folded hands, turning in the direction of the Blessed One, respectfully saluted him, and praised him with the following verses:

1. As thou reviewest the world with thy transcendental knowledge and compassion, it is to thee like an ethereal flower, of which one cannot say whether it is born or destroyed, as [the category of] being and non-being is inapplicable to it.

2. As thou reviewest all things with thy transcendental knowledge and compassion, they are to thee like visions, they are beyond the reach of intellectual grasp, as [the category of] being and non-being is inapplicable to them.

3. As thou reviewest the world with thy transcendental knowledge and compassion, it is to thee always like a dream, of which one cannot say whether it is permanent or destructible, as [the category of] being and non-being is inapplicable to it.

4. In the Dharmakāya, whose self-nature is like a vision or a dream, what is there to praise? When no thought arises as to existence or as to not-having-self-nature, then there is praise.

5. Of a thing whose appearance is not visible because of its being beyond the senses and their objects (23), how can it be praised or blamed, O Muni?

6. With thy transcendental knowledge and compassion

---

[1] This division is made by the translator to facilitate the understanding of the text in which divers subjects are promiscuously treated.

CHAPTER TWO

which are above form, thou comprehendest the egolessness of things and persons, and art thyself always clean and free from the hindrances of passion and knowledge.

7. Thou dost not vanish in Nirvana, nor is Nirvana abiding in thee; for it transcends the duality of knowing and known and of being and non-being.

8. Those who see the Muni so serene and beyond birth [and death] will be cleansed of attachment, stainless both in this world and in the other.

II

At that time Mahāmati the Bodhisattva-Mahāsattva praising the Blessed One with such verses as these, made his own name known to the Blessed One.

9. I am Mahāmati, Blessed One, and am well versed in the Mahāyāna. I wish to ask one hundred and eight questions of thee who art most eloquent.

10. Hearing his words the Buddha, the best knower of the world, looking over the whole assembly, spoke to the son of the Sugata thus:

11. Ask me, sons of the Victorious, and Mahāmati, you ask and I will instruct you in self-realisation.

At that moment Mahāmati the Bodhisattva-Mahāsattva who was given by the Blessed One the opportunity to speak, prostrated himself at the feet of the Blessed One and asked:

(24) 12. How can one be cleansed of false intellection? Whence does it arise? How can one perceive errors? Whence do they arise?

13. Whence come lands, transformation, appearance, and philosophers? Wherefore is the state of imagelessness, the gradations, and whence are the sons of the Victorious?

14. Where is the way of emancipation? Who is in bondage? By what is he redeemed? What is the mental state of those who practise the Dhyānas? Whence is the triple vehicle?

15. What is that which is born of causation? What is effect? What is cause [or that which works]? Whence the doctrine of duality? Whence does it arise?

16. Wherefore is the tranquilising exercise of formlessness? And that of complete extinction? Wherefore the extinction of thoughts? And how is one awakened from it?

17. How does action rise? Whence is the behaviour of those who hold the body? Whence [this] visible [world]? Whence the conditions? Whence the entrance upon the stages?

18. Who is it that breaks through this triple existence? What is the abode? What is the body? Where does that which is abiding arise? Whence comes the son of the Buddha?

19. Who attains the psychic faculties, the self-masteries, the Samādhis? How is the mind tranquilised? Pray tell me, O Bull-like Victor?

20. What is the Ālaya? And whence the Manovijñāna? (25) How does the visible [world] rise? How does it cease from being visible?

21. Whence are families and no-families? What is meant by Mind-only? The setting up of marks? And whence [the doctrine of] egolessness?

22. Why is there no being? What kind of teaching is in accordance with popular thinking? How can one cease cherishing eternalism (*śāśvata-darshana*) and nihilism (*uccheda-darshana*)?

23. How is it that you do not differ from the philosophers as regards appearance? Tell me, whence is the rise of the Nyāya school? Its future?

24. What is meant by emptiness? What do you understand by momentary destruction? Whence is the Womb? And whence is the stability of the world?

25. Why is the world like a vision and a dream? How does it resemble the city of the Gandharvas? Why it is to be regarded as like a mirage, or like the moon reflected in water? Pray tell me.

26. What are the elements of enlightenment? Whence are the constituents of enlightenment? Wherefore is a revolution, and the disturbance of a kingdom? And how does the realistic view of existence (*bhavadṛishṭi*) take its rise?

CHAPTER TWO

27. What is meant by the world being above birth and death? or being like the flower in the air? How do you understand it? Why do you regard it as being beyond words?

28. How is it not subject to discrimination? How is it like the sky? Of how many sorts is suchness? How manifold is the Mind? How many Pāramitās are there?

29. Whence is the gradation of the stages? What is the state of imagelessness? (26) Wherefore is the twofold egolessness? How is one cleansed of [the hindrance of] knowledge?

30. Of how many kinds is knowledge (*jñāna*)? O Leader! How many moral precepts are there? and forms of being? Whence are the families born of gold and jewel and pearl?

31. Of whom is speech born? Whence is the differentiation of beings? Whence are the sciences, offices, arts? and by whom are they made manifest?

32. Of how many sorts are gāthās? What is prose? What is metre? Of how many sorts is reasoning and exegesis?

33. How many varieties of food and drink are there? Whence does sexual desire originate? Whence are there kings, sovereigns, and provincial rulers?

34. How does a king protect his dominion? Of how many groups are heavenly beings? Whence are the earth, stars, constellations, the moon, and the sun?

35. How many kinds of emancipation are there? of the Yogins? How many kinds of discipleship? And how about the masters?

36. How many kinds of Buddhahood are there? And how many of the Jātaka Tales? How numerous are the evil ones? How numerous are the heretics?

37. What is meant by [the doctrine] that there is nothing but thought-construction? Pray tell me, thou Most Eloquent One?

(27) 38. Whence are the clouds in the sky? the wind? What is meant by recollection? by wisdom (*medhā*)? Whence

are trees and vines? Pray tell me, Lord of the Triple World?

39. How do horses, elephants, and deer get caught? Wherefore are there fools and despicable people? Pray tell me, thou Charioteer of the Mind?

40. Wherefore are the six seasons mentioned? What is meant by the Icchantika [one who is without Buddha-nature]? Pray tell me whence is the birth of a man? of a woman? of a hermaphrodite?

41. How does one retrograde in the Yoga exercises? How does one make progress in them? How many exercises are there? and how are men kept abiding in them? Pray tell me.

42. Beings are born in the various paths of existence, what are their specific marks and forms? How is abundance of wealth acquired? Pray tell me, thou who art like the sky?

43. Whence is the Śākya family? And the one born of Ikshvāku? Whence is the Rishi Long-Penance? What is taught by him?

44. How is it that thou art thus apparent everywhere in every land, surrounded by such Bodhisattvas of such various names and forms?

45. Why is meat not to be eaten? Why is it forbidden? Whence was the carnivorous race born, who eats meat?

46. Why are the lands shaped like the moon, the sun, the Sumeru, the lotus, the swatika, and the lion? Pray tell me.

(28) 47. Wherefore are the lands shaped like a capsized and upturned net of Indra which is composed of all sorts of jewels? Pray tell me why?

48. Wherefore are [the lands] shaped in the form of a lute or a drum? Like various flowers and fruits? Like the sun and the moon which are so stainless? Pray tell me.

49. Whence are the Buddhas of Transformation? Whence are the Buddhas of Maturity [or Recompense]? Whence are the Buddhas who are endowed with transcendental knowledge of suchness? Pray tell me.

50. Why does not one attain enlightenment in the world of desire? Pray tell me. What is the meaning of your being enlightened in the Akanishṭha by shaking off all the passions?

51. After my passing who will be the upholder of the Discipline [or Doctrine, śāsana]? How long should the teacher abide? How long should the teaching continue?

52. How many sorts of established truths are there? And how many of philosophical views? Whence is morality? And what constitutes the being of a Bhikshu? Pray tell me.

53. What is meant by a state of revulsion [or turning-back]? Whence is a state of imagelessness, [which is realised] by the Pratyekabuddhas, Bodhisattvas, and Śrāvakas?

54. By whom are the psychic powers of this world attained? What are the super-worldly ones? By what means does the mind enter upon the seven stages? Pray tell me.

55. How many kinds of Brotherhood are there? And how does a dissension take place in a Brotherhood? Whence are medical treatises for beings? Pray tell me.

(29) 56. You say that you were among the Buddhas Kāśyapa, Krakuchanda, and Kanakamuni; tell me wherefore so, O Great Muni!

57. Whence is the doctrine that there is no ego-soul in beings? Whence is the doctrine of eternity, and of annihilation? Wherefore do you not everywhere announce the doctrine of Mind-only as the truth?

58. What is meant by the forest of men and women? And by the forest of Karītakī and Āmalī? Whence are the mountains Kailāsa, Cakravāḍa, and Vajrasaṃhananā?

59. Among these, whence are the mountains decorated with various sorts of jewels and filled with Ṛishis and Gandharvas? Pray tell me.

60. Hearing this [which constitutes] the wonderful doctrine of the Mahāyāna and also the most excellent heart of the Buddhas, the Great Hero, the Buddha, the One Most Excelled in the Knowledge of the World, [spoke thus]:

61. Well done! Well done! O Mahāprajñā-Mahāmati! Listen well, and I will tell you in order regarding your questions.

62. Birth, no-birth, Nirvana, emptiness, transmigration, having-no-self-nature, Buddhas, sons of the Pāramitās,

63. The Śrāvakas, Bodhisattvas, the philosophers, those who are capable of formless deeds, the Meru, oceans, mountains, islands, lands, the earth,

64. The stars, the sun, the moon, the philosophers, the Asura, (30) emancipations, the self-masteries, the psychic faculties, the Dhyānas, the Samādhis,

65. The extinctions (*nirodha*), the supernatural powers, the elements of enlightenment, and the paths, Dhyānas, the unmeasurables, the aggregates (*skandhas*), and the comings-and-goings.

66. Samāpattis, the extinctions, the stirrings of mind, explanations in words, the Citta, Manas, and Vijñānas, egolessness, the five Dharmas,

67. Self-nature, the discriminating, the discriminated, the visible [world], dualism—whence are they? Various forms of vehicles, families, those born of gold, jewels, and pearls?

68. The Icchantika, the original elements, the wandering-about, one Buddhahood, knowledge, the known, the marching, the attainment, and the existence and non-existence of beings?

69. How are horses, elephants, deer caught? Pray tell me how. What is a proposition, a teaching established by the conjunction of reason and illustration?

70. Whence is cause and effect? Various errors? and also reason? [Why the statement that there is] nothing but Mind, that there is no objective [literally, seen] world, that there is no ascending of the stages?

71. Whence is the state of imagelessness and revulsion which is a hundredfold?[1] You tell me. Likewise about medical treatises, arts, crafts, sciences, and teachings?

72. And also what are the measurements of the moun-

[1] Not found in T'ang.

tains, Sumeru, and the earth? What are the measurements of the ocean, moon, and sun? Tell me.

(31) 73. How many particles of dust are there in the body of a being? How many of the coarser ones, of the finer ones, and of the middle ones? How many particles of dust in every land? How many in every dhanva?

74. In measuring distance how much is a hasta, a dhanu, a krośa, a yojana, a half-yojana? How many of rabbit-hairs, of window-dust, louse-eggs, or ram-hairs, of barley?[1]

75. How many grains of barley in a prastha? How many grains of barley in a half-prastha? Likewise how many in a droṇa, in a khārya, a lakshā, a koṭi, a viṁvana?

76. How many atoms are there in a mustard-seed? How many mustard-seeds are there in a rakshikā? How many in a bean, in a dharaṇa, in a māshakā?

77. How many dharaṇās are there in a karsha? How many karshas in a pala? and how many palas are there in Mount Sumeru which is a huge accumulation [of masses]?

78. You should ask me thus, O son! Why do you ask me otherwise? How many atoms are there in the body of a Pratyekabuddha, of a Śrāvaka, of a Buddha, and of a Bodhisattva? (32) Why do you not ask me in this wise?

79. How many atoms are there at the top of a flame? How many atoms are in the wind? How many in each sense-organ? How many in a pore of the skin? in the eyebrows?

80. Whence are these men of immense wealth, kings, great sovereigns? How is the kingdom taken care of by them? And how about their emancipation?

81. Tell whence is prose and metre. Why is sexual desire universally cherished? Whence is the variety of foods and drinks? Whence the man-woman forest?

82. Wherefore are the mountains of Vajrasaṃhanana? Tell me whence, wherefore; are they like a vision, a dream, and a fata-morgana?

83. Whence is the arising of clouds? And whence do

[1] See the *Abhidharmakośa*, translated by Louis de la Vallée Poussin, Ch. III, p. 178.

the seasons rise? Whence is the nature of taste? Whence is woman, man, and hermaphrodite?

84. Whence are the adornments and the Bodhisattvas? Ask me, O my son! Whence are the divine mountains embellished by the Rishis and Gandharvas?

85. Whence is the way of emancipation? Who is in bondage? By whom is he delivered? What is the state of one who practises tranquillisation? What is transformation, and who are those philosophers?

86. What is meant by non-existence, existence, and no-effect? Whence arises the visible world? (33) How can one be cleansed of false intellection? Whence does false intellection arise?

87. Whence arises action? And whence its departure? Tell me. How does the extinction of thought take place? And what is meant by a Samādhi?

88. Who is the one that breaks through the triple world? What is the position? What is the body? Wherefore the doctrine that beings have no ego-soul? What is meant by a teaching in accordance with the world?[1]

89. Do you ask me about the marks? Do you ask me about egolessness? Do you ask me about the womb, about the Nyāya philosophers, O son of the Victor?

90. How about eternalism and nihilism? How is the mind tranquillised? Again [how about] speech, knowledge, morality, family, O son of the Victor?

91. What is meant by reasoning and illustrating, by master and disciple, by manifoldness of beings, food and drink, sky, intelligence, evil ones, and the statement that there is nothing but the thought-constructed?

92. What do you ask me concerning trees and vines, O son of the Victor? What about diversity of lands, and about Long-Penance the Ṛishi?

93. What is your family? Who is your master? You tell me, O son of the Victor. Who are the people who are despised? How is it that in the Yoga you do not attain

---

[1] *Saṁvṛityā deśanā* is contrasted to *paramārtha-satya*, highest truth.

enlightenment in the world of desire, but that in the Akanishṭha there is realisation?

94. What do you ask me about reasoning? (34) What about the psychic faculties belonging to this world, and about the nature of a Bhikshu?

95. Do you ask me about Buddhas of Transformation, Buddhas of Maturity [or Recompense]? About Buddhas of the Knowledge of Suchness? And whence is the Bodhisattva?

96. You ask me, O son of the Victor, about the lands that are devoid of light, resembling a lute, a drum, and a flower, and about the mind abiding in the seven stages?

97. You ask me such and many other questions, which are in accordance with the marks [of Truth?] and free from erroneous views.

III

98.[1] I will instruct you as regards realisation and its teaching; listen to me intently; I will give you an explanation of the statements, O son, listen to me, in regard to the one hundred and eight statements as recounted by the Buddhas.

At that moment Mahāmati the Bodhisattva-Mahāsattva said to the Blessed One: What is meant by the one hundred and eight statements?[2]

---

[1] This verse is probably to be separated from the foregoing ones as it forms a sort of introduction to what follows. The one hundred and eight questions (*praśna*) so called are not to be necessarily identified with the one hundred and eight statements (*pada*) which are uniformly negated in the paragraph that comes after. Some subjects are common to the Questions and the Negations, but others are not. I do not think there is any organic relationship between the two sections. What strikes one in both the Questions and the Negations is that trivial subjects are mixed up with important ones as equally constituting the content of self-realisation. The Sutra proper which is supposed to concern itself with them is also devoid of an intimate connection with them.

[2] Here is one of the most mysterious and unintelligible portions of the *Laṅkāvatāra Sūtra*. The Sanskrit word for "statement" is *pada*, which literally means, "foot-step," "a footing," "a position," "a subject," "an abode," "a matter of talk," "a portion of a line in a stanza," etc.

The Blessed One said: A statement concerning birth is no statement concerning birth; a statement concerning eternity is no statement concerning eternity. [The topics thus negated are as follows:[1]] the characteristic marks, abiding and changing, moment, self-nature, emptiness, annihilation, mind, the middle, permanence, causation, cause, the passions, desire, (35) means, contrivance, purity, inference [or conclusion], illustration, a disciple, a master, a family, the triple vehicle, imagelessness, vows, the triple circle, form, duality of being and non-being, bothness, the noble wisdom of self-realisation, the bliss of the present world, lands, atoms, water, a bow, reality, numbers and mathematics, the psychic powers, the sky, clouds, the arts and crafts and sciences, the wind, the earth, thinking, thought-constructions, self-nature, the aggregates, being, insight, Nirvana, that which is known, the philosophers, disorder, a vision, a dream, (36) a mirage, a reflection, a circle made in the dark by a fire-brand, the city of the Gandharvas, the heavens, food and drink, sexuality, philosophical views, the Pāramitās, morality, the moon and the sun and stars, truth, effect,

---

For the Sanskrit *pada* the Chinese translators have "句", "見", "位", "住", but as they stand these translations do not give any sense to the general context. 句 is perhaps the best in retaining the original sense, but it is to be understood in the sense of "a proposition," "a statement," and each sentence containing this word in the following negations means that each subject referred to is not properly conceived, because, for instance, the concept of birth is not in accordance with the true understanding of reality. Birth stands against death, they are relative notions, and do not apply to a world where things are perceived in their absolute aspect. Therefore, any statement that might be made concerning birth are not at all true; birth is no-birth, death is no-death, and so on. Even of such notions as truth, realisation, self-nature, mind, pāramitās, the same can be said; to make a statement about anything is to falsify it. Hence the series of negations as illustrated here. But the mysterious fact about them is the reference to so many trite subjects which are evidently in no direct connection with the teachings of the Mahāyāna. There must be something historical about these references of which the translator is at present quite ignorant. Another mystery here concerns the number of *padas*: why 108, and not more or less?

[1] To avoid repetitions, the subjects alone are mentioned which are systematically negated in the text.

annihilation and origination, medical treatment, the characteristic marks, the limbs, arts and sciences, Dhyāna, error, the seen [world], protection, dynasty, Rishi, kingdom, apprehension, treasure, explanation, the Icchantika, man, woman, and hermaphrodite, taste, action, the body, false intellection, motives, sense-organs, the Samskrita,[1] cause and effect, the Kanishṭha,[2] the seasons, a luxuriant growth of trees, vines and shrubs, (37) multiplicity, entering into the teaching, systems of morality, the Bhikshus, the powers added [by the Buddha], the lutes. These are the one hundred and eight statements recounted by the Buddhas of the past.

IV

At that moment, Mahāmati the Bodhisattva-Mahāsattva said again to the Blessed One: In how many ways, Blessed One, does the rise, abiding, and ceasing of the Vijñānas take place?

The Blessed One replied: There are two ways, Mahāmati, in which the rise, abiding, and ceasing of the Vijñānas take place, and this is not understood by the philosophers. That is to say, the ceasing takes place as regards continuation and form. In the rise of the Vijñānas, also, these two are recognisable: the rise as regards continuation and the rise as regards form. In the abiding, also, these two [are discernible]: the one taking place as regards continuation and the other as regards form.

[Further,] three modes are distinguishable in the Vijñānas: (1) the Vijñāna as evolving, (2) the Vijñāna as producing effects, and (3) the Vijñāna as remaining in its original nature.

[Further,] Mahāmati, in the Vijñānas, which are said to be eight, two functions generally are distinguishable: the perceiving and the object-discriminating. As a mirror reflects forms, Mahāmati, the perceiving Vijñāna perceives

---

[1] Anything that produces an effect.
[2] A class of deities.

[objects]. Mahāmati, between the two, the perceiving Vijñāna and the object-discriminating Vijñāna, there is no difference; they are mutually conditioning. Then, Mahāmati, the perciving Vijñāna functions because of transformation's taking place [in the mind] by reason of a mysterious habit-energy, while, Mahāmati, the object-discriminating Vijñāna (38) functions because of the mind's discriminating an objective world and because of the habit-energy accumulated by erroneous reasoning since beginningless time.

Again, Mahāmati, by the cessation of all the sense-Vijñānas is meant the cessation of the Ālayavijñāna's variously accumulating habit-energy which is generated when unrealities are discriminated. This, Mahāmati, is known as the cessation of the form-aspect of the Vijñānas.

Again, Mahāmati, the cessation of the continuation-aspect of the Vijñānas takes place in this wise: that is to say, Mahāmati, when both that which supports [the Vijñānas] and that which is comprehended [by the Vijñānas] cease to function. By that which supports [the Vijñānas] is meant the habit-energy [or memory] which has been accumulated by erroneous reasoning since beginningless time; and by that which is comprehended [by the Vijñānas] is meant the objective world perceived and discriminated by the Vijñānas, which is, however, no more than Mind itself.

Mahāmati, it is like a lump of clay and the particles of dust making up its substance, they are neither different nor not-different; again, it is like gold and various ornaments made of it. If, Mahāmati, the lump of clay is different from its particles of dust, no lump will ever come out of them. But as it comes out of them it is not different from the particles of dust. Again, if there is no difference between the two, the lump will be indistinguishable from its particles.

Even so, Mahāmati, if the evolving Vijñāna are different from the Ālayavijñāna, even in its original form, the Ālaya cannot be their cause. Again, if they are not different the cessation of the evolving Vijñānas will mean the cessation of the Ālayavijñāna, but there is no cessation of its original form. Therefore, Mahāmati, what ceases to function is not the Ālaya in its original self-form, but is the effect-producing form of the Vijñānas. When this original self-form ceases to exist, then there will indeed be the cessation of the Ālayavijñāna. (39) If, however, there is the cessation of the Ālayavijñāna, this doctrine will in no wise differ from the nihilistic doctrine of the philosophers.

This doctrine, Mahāmati, as it is held by the philosophers, is this: When the grasping of an objective world ceases the continuation of the Vijñānas is stopped; and when there is no more of this continuation in the Vijñānas, the continuation that has been going on since beginningless time is also destroyed. Mahāmati, the philosophers maintain that there is a first cause from which continuation takes place; they do not maintain that the eye-Vijñāna arises from the interaction of form and light; they assume another cause. What is this cause, Mahāmati? Their first cause is known as spirit (*pradhāna*), soul (*purusha*), lord (*iśvara*), time, or atom.

V

Again, Mahāmati, there are seven kinds of self-nature: collection (*samudaya*), being (*bhāva*), characteristic marks (*lakshana*), elements (*mahābhūta*), causality (*hetu*), conditionality (*pratyaya*), and perfection (*nishpatti*).[1]

VI

Again, Mahāmati, there are seven kinds of first principle [or highest reality, *paramārtha*]: the world of thought (*citta-gocara*), the world of knowledge (*jñāna-*), the world of super-knowledge (*prajñā-*), the world of dualistic views (*drishti-*), the world beyond dualistic views, the world beyond the Bodhisattva-stages, and a world where the Tathagata attains his self-realisation.[2]

[1] What is exactly meant by these concepts regarded as self-nature (*svabhāva*) is difficult to define as far as the *Laṅkāvatāra* is concerned.

[2] These seven principles or realities are not explained in the text. But we can state that they are so many different kinds of Paramārtha, as in the case of Svabhāva, so considered by different schools of philosophers or Buddhists.

(**40**) Mahāmati, this is the self-nature, the first principle, the essence, which constitutes the being of the Tathāgatas, Arhats, Fully-Enlightened Ones of the past, present, and future, whereby, perfecting things of this world and of a world beyond this, they, by means of a noble eye of transcendental wisdom, enter into various phases of existence, individual and general, and establish them. And what is thus established by them is not to be confused with the erroneous teachings generally held by the philosophers.

Mahāmati, what are these erroneous teachings accepted generally by the philosophers? [Their error lies in this] that they do not recognise an objective world to be of Mind itself which is erroneously discriminated; and, not understanding the nature of the Vijñānas which are also no more than manifestations of Mind, like simple-minded ones that they are, they cherish the dualism of being and non-being where there is but [one] self-nature and [one] first principle.

Again, Mahāmati, my teaching consists in the cessation of sufferings arising from the discrimination of the triple world; in the cessation of ignorance, desire, deed, and causality; and in the recognition that an objective world, like a vision, is the manifestation of Mind itself.

VII

Mahāmati, there are some Brahmans and Śramaṇas who assume something out of nothing, saying that there exists a substance which is bound up in causation and abides in time, and that the Skandhas, Dhātus, and Āyatanas have their genesis and continuation in causation and, after thus existing, pass away.

They are those, Mahāmati, who hold a destructive and nihilistic view concerning such subjects as continuation, activity, rising, breaking-up, existence, Nirvāṇa, the path, karma, fruition, and truth. (**41**) Why? Because they have not attained an intuitive understanding [of the Truth], because they have no fundamental insight of things. Mahāmati, it is like a jar broken in pieces which is unable to function as a jar; again, it is like a burnt seed which is

CHAPTER TWO 37

incapable of sprouting. Even so, Mahāmati, their Skandhas, Dhātus, and Āyatanas which they regard as subject to changes are really incapable of uninterrupted transformation because their views do not originate from the perception of an objective world as a manifestation of Mind itself which is erroneously discriminated.

If again, Mahāmati, something comes out of nothing and there is the rise of the Vijñānas by reason of a combination of the three effect-producing causes, we can say the same of a non-existing thing, that a tortoise would grow hair and sands produce oil. [As this is impossible] this proposition does not avail, it ends in affirming nothing. And, Mahāmati, it follows that deed, work, and cause [of which they speak] will be of no use, and so also with their reference to being and non-being. Mahāmati, when they argue that there is a combination of the three effect-producing causes, they do this by the principle of cause and effect [which is to say, by the principle that something comes out of something and not of nothing]; and thus there are [such things as] past, present, and future, and being and non-being. As long as they remain on their philosophic ground, their demonstration will be by means of their logic and text-books, for the memory of erroneous intellection will ever cling to them.[1] Thus, Mahāmati, simple-minded ones, poisoned by an erroneous view, declare the incorrect way of thinking taught by the ignorant to be the one presented by the All-Knowing One.

Again, Mahāmati, there are some Brahmans and

[1] The reasoning here may be a little difficult to follow. The general idea maintained by the *Laṅkāvatāra* is that as long as a world of relativity is asserted there is an ever-recurring chain of causation which cannot be denied in any circumstance. In this case we cannot talk of anything coming to an end or cessation. The fault with the philosophers is that they have no fundamental intuition into the essential nature of an objective world—a world of particulars—which is really the projection of mind by reason of memory or the habit-energy accumulated since beginningless time. When this thought is thoroughly grasped, the philosopher's point of view may also hold good as far as it goes. As they lack, however, the fundamental intuition, all the logical superstructure they build is essentially an error.

Śramaṇas who (42) recognising that the external world which is of Mind itself is seen as such owing to the discrimination and false intellection practised since beginningless time, know that the world has no self-nature and has never been born, it is like a cloud, a ring produced by a firebrand, the castle of the Gandharvas, a vision, a mirage, the moon as reflected in the ocean, and a dream; that Mind in itself has nothing to do with discrimination and causation, discourses of imagination, and terms of qualification (*lakshyalakshaṇa*); that body, property, and abode are objectifications of the Ālayavijñāna,[1] which is in itself above [the dualism of] subject and object; that the state of imagelessness which is in compliance with the awakening of Mind itself,[2] is not affected by such changes as arising, abiding, and destruction.

The Bodhisattvas-Mahāsattvas, Mahāmati, will before long attain to the understanding that Nirvana and Samsāra are one. Their conduct, Mahāmati, will be in accordance with the effortless exhibition of a great loving heart that ingeniously contrives means [of salvation], knowing that all beings have the nature of being like a vision or a reflection, and that [there is one thing which is] not bound by causation, being beyond the distinction of subject and object; [and further] seeing that there is nothing outside Mind, and in accordance with a position of unconditionality, they will by degrees pass through the various stages of Bodhisattvahood and will experience the various states of Samādhi, and will by virtue of their faith understand that the triple world is of Mind itself, and thus understanding will attain the Samādhi Māyopama. The Bodhisattvas entering into the state of imagelessness where they see into the truth of Mindonly, arriving at the abode of the Pāramitās, and keeping themselves away from the thought of genesis, deed, and discipline, they will attain the Samādhi Vajravimbopama which is in compliance with the Tathāgatakāya and with the transformations of suchness. After achieving a revulsion

---
[1] The translator here follows the T'ang reading.
[2] This clause does not appear in T'ang.

in the abode [of the Vijñānas], Mahāmati, they will gradually realise the Tathāgatakāya, which is endowed with the powers, the psychic faculties, self-control, love, compassion, and means; which can enter into all the Buddha-lands and into the sanctuaries of the philosophers; and which is beyond the realm of (43) Citta-mano-manovijñāna. Therefore, Mahāmati, these Bodhisattva-Mahāsattvas who wish, by following the Tathāgatakāya, to realise it, should exercise themselves, in compliance with the truth of Mind-only, to desist from discriminating and reasoning erroneously on such notions as Skandhas, Dhātus, Āyatanas, thought, causation, deed, discipline, and rising, abiding, and destruction.

VIII

Perceiving that the triple existence is by reason of the habit-energy of erroneous discrimination and false reasoning that has been going on since beginningless time, and also thinking of the state of Buddhahood which is imageless and unborn, [the Bodhisattva] will become thoroughly conversant with the noble truth of self-realisation, will become a perfect master of his own mind, will conduct himself without effort, will be like a gem reflecting a variety of colours, will be able to assume the body of transformation, will be able to enter into the subtle minds of all beings, and, because of his firm belief in the truth of Mind-only, will, by gradually ascending the stages, become established in Buddhahood. Therefore, Mahāmati, let the Bodhisattva-Mahāsattva be well disciplined in self-realisation.

IX

Then Mahāmati said: Teach me, Blessed One, concerning that most subtle doctrine which explains the Citta, Manas, Manovijñāna, the five Dharmas, the Svabhāvas, and the Lakshanas; which is put in practice by the Buddhas and Bodhisattvas; which is separated from the state of mind which recognises a world as something outside Mind itself; and which, breaking down all the so-called truths established by words and reasonings, constitutes the essence of the teachings of all the Buddhas. Pray teach this assembly headed by the Bodhisattvas gathering on Mount Malaya in the city of Laṅkā; teach them regarding the Dharmakāya which is praised by the Tathagatas and which is the realm of (44) the Ālayavijñāna which resembles the ocean with its waves.

Then the Blessed One again speaking to Mahāmati the Bodhisattva-Mahāsattva said this: The reasons whereby the eye-consciousness arises are four. What are they? They are: (1) The clinging to an external world, not knowing that it is of Mind itself; (2) The attaching to form and habit-energy accumulated since beginningless time by false reasoning and erroneous views; (3) The self-nature inherent in the Vijñāna; (4) The eagerness for multiple forms and appearances. By these four reasons, Mahāmati, the waves of the evolving Vijñānas are stirred on the Ālayavijñāna which resembles the waters of a flood. The same [can be said of the other sense-consciousnesses] as of the eye-consciousness. This consciousness arises at once or by degrees in every sense-organ including its atoms and pores of the skin; the sense-field is apprehended like a mirror reflecting objects, like the ocean swept over by a wind. Mahāmati, similarly the waves of the mind-ocean are stirred uninterruptedly by the wind of objectivity; cause, deed, and appearance condition one another inseparably; the functioning Vijñānas and the original Vijñāna are thus inextricably bound-up together; and because the self-nature of form, etc., is not comprehended, Mahāmati, the system of the five consciousnesses (*vijñānas*) comes to function. Along with this system of the five Vijñānas, there is what is known as Manovijñāna [i. e., the thinking function of consciousness], whereby the objective world is distinguished and individual appearances are distinctly determined, and in this the physical body has its genesis. But the Manovijñāna and other Vijñānas have no thought that they are mutually conditioned and that they grow out of their attachment to the discrimination which is applied to the projections of Mind itself. Thus the Vijñānas go on functioning mutually related in a most intimate manner and discriminating a world of representations.

(45) As the Vijñānas thus go on functioning [without being conscious of their own doings], so the Yogins while entering upon a state of tranquillisation (*samāpatti*) are not aware of the workings of the subtle habit-energy [or memory] within themselves; for they think that they would enter upon a state of tranquillisation by extinguishing the Vijñānas. But [in fact] they are in this state without extinguishing the Vijñānas which still subsist because the seeds of habit-energy have not been extinguished; and [what they imagine to be] an extinction is really the non-functioning of the external world to which they are no more attached. So it is, Mahāmati, with the subtle working of the Ālayavijñāna, which, except for the Tathagata and those Bodhisattvas who are established on the stages, is not easy to comprehend; [especially] by those who practise the discipline belonging to the Śrāvakas, Pratyekabuddhas, and philosophers, even with their powers of Samādhi and transcendental knowledge, it is difficult to distinguish. Only those who, understanding fully all the aspects of the different stages of Bodhisattvahood by the aid of their transcendental knowledge, acquiring a definite cognition as regards the meaning of the separate propositions, planting roots of goodness in the Buddha-lands that know no limits, and keeping themselves away from the discriminations and false reasonings that arise from recognising an external world which is of Mind itself, would retire into a secluded abode in the forest and devote themselves to the practice of the spiritual discipline, either high, or low, or middling, only those are capable of obtaining an insight into the flowing of Mind itself in a world of discrimination, of being baptised by the Buddhas living in the lands without limits, and of realising the self-control, powers, psychic faculties, and Samādhis. Surrounded by good friends and the Buddhas, Mahāmati, they are capable of knowing the Citta, Manas, Manovijñāna, which are the discriminating agents of an external world whose self-nature is of Mind itself; they are capable of crossing the ocean of birth and death which arises by reason of deed, desire, and ignorance. For this reason, Mahāmati, the Yogins ought to exercise

themselves in the discipline which has been given them by their good friends and the Buddhas.

(**46**) At that time the Blessed One recited the following verses:

99. Like waves that rise on the ocean stirred by the wind, dancing and without interruption,

100. The Ālaya-ocean in a similar manner is constantly stirred by the winds of objectivity, and is seen dancing about with the Vijñānas which are the waves of multiplicity.

101. Dark-blue, red, [and other colours], with salt, conch-shell, milk, honey, fragrance of fruits and flowers, and rays of sunlight;

102. They are neither different nor not-different: the relation is like that between the ocean and its waves. So are the seven Vijñānas joined with the Citta (mind).

103. As the waves in their variety are stirred on the ocean, so in the Ālaya is produced the variety of what is known as the Vijñānas.

104. The Citta, Manas, and Vijñānas are discriminated as regards their form; [but in substance] the eight are not to be separated one from another, for there is neither qualified nor qualifying.

105. As there is no distinction between the ocean and its waves, so in the Citta there is no evolution of the Vijñānas.

106. Karma is accumulated by the Citta, reflected upon by the Manas, and recognised by the Manovijñāna, and the visible world is discriminated by the five Vijñānas.

(**47**) 107. Varieties of colour such as dark-blue, etc., are presented to our Vijñāna. Tell me, Great Muni, how there are these varieties of colour like waves [on the ocean]?

108. There are no such varieties of colour in the waves; it is for the sake of the simple-minded that the Citta is said to be evolving as regards form.

109. There is no such evolving in the Citta itself, which is beyond comprehension. Where there is comprehension there is that which comprehends as in the case of waves [and ocean].

110. Body, property, and abode are presented as such

to our Vijñānas, and thus they are seen as evolving in the same way as are the waves.

111. The ocean is manifestly seen dancing in the state of waveness; how is it that the evolving of the Ālaya is not recognised by the intellect even as the ocean is?[1]

112. That the Ālaya is compared to the ocean is [only] for the sake of the discriminating intellect of the ignorant; the likeness of the waves in motion is [only] brought out by way of illustration.

113. When the sun rises it shines impartially on people high and low; so thou who art the light of the world shouldst announce the truth (*tattvam*) to the ignorant.

(48) 114. How is it that in establishing thyself in the Dharma thou announcest not the truth? If the truth is announced by me, the truth is not in the mind.[2]

115. As the waves appear instantly on the ocean, or [images] in a mirror or a dream, so the mind is reflected in its own sense-fields.[3]

116. Owing to a deficiency in conditions the evolution [of the Vijñānas] takes place by degrees.[4] The function of the Manovijñāna is to recognise and that of the Manas is to reflect upon,

117. While to the five Vijñānas the actual world presents itself. There is no gradation when one is in a state of collectedness (*samāhita*).[5] Like unto a master of painting or his pupils,

---

[1] This question according to Sung and T'ang is Mahāmati's.

[2] 113 and the first part of 114 are ascribed to Mahāmati in Sung and T'ang, but Wei gives both 113 and 114 to Mahāmati.

[3] This must have found its way here by mistake, for the ocean-waves simile in this text is generally used to illustrate the Ālaya's relation to the other Vijñānas, and not in connection with the immediacy of perception as in this case of the mirror-images simile.

[4] This ought to belong to the preceding verse. Not wishing, however, to disturb the original notation, the translator has followed the text. In that which follows, the reader is asked simply to look for the sense and to pay no attention to the division of verses.

[5] *Samāhita, samādhi, samāpatti, ekāgra* may be understood as synonymous, denoting a state of consciousness where the mind is most intensely concentrated on one thought. It is the receptive state of intuition, rather than the active state of thinking.

118.[1] Who arrange colours to produce a picture, I teach. The picture is not in the colours, nor in the canvas, nor in the plate;

119. In order to make it attractive to all beings, a picture is presented in colours. What one teaches, transgresses; for the truth (*tattva*) is beyond words.

120. Establishing myself in the Dharma, I preach the truth for the Yogins. The truth is the state of self-realisation and is beyond categories of discrimination.

121. I teach it to the sons of the Victorious; the teaching is not meant for the ignorant. What is seen as multitudinous is a vision which exists not.

122. The teaching itself is thus variously given, subject to transgression; (**49**) the teaching is no teaching whatever if it is not to the point in each case.

123. According to the nature of a disease the healer gives its medicine; even so the Buddhas teach beings in accordance with their mentalities.

124. This is indeed not a mental realm to be reached by the philosophers and the Śrāvakas; what is taught by the leaders is the realm of self-realisation.

X

Further, Mahāmati, if the Bodhisattva should wish to understand fully that an external world to be subsumed under categories of discrimination, such as the grasping (subject) and the grasped (object), is of Mind itself, let him be kept away from such hindrances as turmoil, social intercourse, and sleep; let him be kept away from the treatises and writings of the philosophers, from things belonging to the vehicles of Śrāvakahood and Pratyekabuddhahood; let the Bodhisattva-Mahāsattva be thoroughly acquainted with objects of discrimination which are to be seen as of Mind itself.

XI(a)

Further, Mahāmati, when the Bodhisattva-Mahāsattva

[1] Follow the sense and not necessarily the verse division as before.

establishes himself in the abode where he has gained a thorough understanding of Mind by means of his transcendental knowledge, he should later discipline himself in the cultivation of noble wisdom in its triple aspect. What are the three aspects of noble wisdom, Mahāmati, in which he has to discipline himself later? They are: (1) imagelessness; (2) the power added by all the Buddhas by reason of their original vows; and (3) the self-realisation attained by noble wisdom. Having mastered them, (50) the Yogin should abandon his knowledge of Mind gained by means of transcendental wisdom, which still resembles a lame donkey; and entering upon the eighth stage of Bodhisattvahood, he should further discipline himself in these three aspects of noble wisdom.

Then again, Mahāmati, the aspect of imagelessness comes forth when all things belonging to the Śrāvakas and Pratyekabuddhas and philosophers are thoroughly mastered. Again, Mahāmati, as to the power added, it comes from the original vows made by all the Buddhas. Again, Mahāmati, as to the self-realisation aspect of noble wisdom, it rises when a Bodhisattva, detaching himself from viewing all things in their phenomenality, realises the Samādhi-body whereby he surveys the world as like unto a vision, and further goes on to the attainment of the Buddha-stage. Mahāmati, this is the triplicity of the noble life. Furnished with this triplicity, noble ones will attain the state of self-realisation which is the outcome of noble wisdom. For this reason, Mahāmati, you should cultivate noble wisdom in its triple aspect.

XI(b)

At that moment, Mahāmati the Bodhisattva-Mahāsattva knowing what was going on in the minds of the Bodhisattvas who were gathered there, and empowered by the power added to him by all the Buddhas, asked the Blessed One concerning the doctrine known as examining into the reality of noble wisdom. Tell me, Blessed One, the doctrine of examining into the reality of noble wisdom, depending on which the one hundred and eight statements are to be distinguished—the doctrine depending on which the Tathagatas, Arhats, Fully-Enlightened Ones will analyse and disclose the nature and course of false imagination for the sake of (51) the Bodhisattva-Mahāsattvas who have fallen into the way of looking at things from their aspects of generality and individuality. Thus the Bodhisattvas will be instructed in the analysis and thorough examination of false imagination, and thereby they will have the passage purified which leads to the egolessness of things and persons, and get an illumination on the stages of Bodhisattvahood; and, further, going beyond the bliss of the tranquillisations[1] belonging to all the Śrāvakas, Pratyekabuddhas, and philosophers, will attain the Dharmakāya of the Tathagata, which belongs to the realm and course of Tathagatahood transcending thought and in which there is no rising of the five Dharmas. That is to say, they will attain the Tathagata-body which is the Dharma intimately bound up with the understanding born of transcendental knowledge, and which, entering into the realm of Māyā, reaches all the Buddha-lands, the heavenly mansions of Tushita, and the abode of the Akanishṭha.

XII

Said the Blessed One: Mahāmati, there are some philosophers who are addicted to negativism, according to whose philosophical view the non-existence of the hare's horns is ascertained by means of the discriminating intellect which affirms that the self-nature of things ceases to exist with the destruction of their causes; and they say that all things are non-existent just like the hare's horns.

Again, Mahāmati, there are others who, seeing distinctions existing in things as regards the elements, qualities, atoms, substances, formations, and positions, and, attached to the notion that the hare's horns are non-existent, assert that the bull has horns.

There are, Mahāmati, those who have fallen into the

[1] That is, *dhyāna*, *samādhi* and *samāpatti*, which practically belong to the same category.

dualistic way of thinking, being unable to comprehend the truth of Mind-only; they desire to discriminate a world which is of Mind itself. Mahāmati, body, property, and abode have their existence only when measured in discrimination. (52) The hare's horns neither are nor are not; no discrimination is to be made about them. So it is, Mahāmati, with all things, of which neither being nor non-being can be predicated; have no discrimination about them!

Again, Mahāmati, those who have gone beyond being and non-being, no more cherish the thought that the hare has no horns; for they never think that the hare has no horns because of mutual reference, nor do they think that the bull has horns because no ultimate substance is to be obtained however minutely the analysis of the horns may go on even to the subtlest particle known as atom: [that is,] the state in which noble wisdom is realised is beyond being and non-being.

At that time Mahāmati the Bodhisattva-Mahāsattva said this to the Blessed One: Is it not this way, Blessed One, that, seeing how discrimination takes place, we proceed to refer this to the non-rising of discrimination and infer that the horns exist not?

The Blessed One said: No, indeed, Mahāmati, the non-existence of the horns has no reference to the non-rising of discrimination. Why is it not so? Because there is discrimination owing to the idea of the horns. Indeed, depending upon the idea of the horns, Mahāmati, discrimination takes place. And because of this dependence of discrimination upon the idea of the horns, Mahāmati, and because of this relationship of dependence and apart from the *anyānanya*[1] relationship, one talks of the non-existence of the hare's horns, surely not because of the reference [to the horns of the bull]. If again, Mahāmati, discrimination is different (*anya*) from the hare's horns, (53) it will not take place by reason of the horns [and therefore the one is not different from the other]; but if it is not different (*anānya*), there is a discrimination taking place by reason of the horns [and

[1] Literally different and not-different.

therefore the one is different from the other]. However minutely the atoms are analysed, no horn[-substance] is obtainable; the notion of the horns itself is not available when thus reasoned. As neither of them [that is, the bull's nor the hare's] are existent, in reference to what should we talk of non-existence? Therefore, Mahāmati, the reasoning by reference as regards the non-existence of the hare's horns is of no avail. The non-existence of the hare's horns is asserted in reference to their existence [on the bull; but really a horn itself has no existence from the beginning]; have therefore no discrimination about it! Mahāmati, the dualism of being and non-being as held by the philosophers does not obtain as we see in the reasoning of horns.

Again, Mahāmati, there are other philosophers affected with erroneous views, who are attached to such notions as form, cause, and figure; not fully understanding the nature of space and seeing that space is disjoined from form, they proceed to discriminate about their separate existences. But, Mahāmati, space is form, and, Mahāmati, as space penetrates into form, form is space. To establish the relation of supporting and supported, Mahāmati, there obtains the separation of the two, space and form. Mahāmati, when the elements begin to evolve [a world] they are distinguishable one from another; they do not abide in space. and space is not non-existent in them.

It is the same with the hare's horns, Mahāmati, whose non-existence is asserted in reference to the bull's horns. But, Mahāmati, when the bull's horns are analysed to their minutest atoms, which in turn are further analysed, there is after all nothing to be known as atoms. The non-existence of what, is to be affirmed in reference to what? As to the other things, too, this reasoning from reference (54) does not hold true.

At that time, again, the Blessed One said this to Mahāmati the Bodhisattva-Mahāsattva; Mahāmati, you should discard the views and discriminations that are concerned with the horns of a hare and a bull, with space and form. And also, Mahāmati, let you and other Bodhisattvas reflect on the nature of discrimination which they have of the Mind itself, and let them go into all the Bodhisattva-lands where they should disclose the way of disciplining themselves in the manifestations of Mind itself.

XIII

Then at that time the Blessed One recited these verses:

125. The world [as we see it] exists not, pluralities of things rise from the Mind being seen [externally]; body, property, and abode are manifested to us as of the Ālaya-vijñāna.

126. The leaders talk about the Citta, Manas, [Mano-]vijñāna, the [triple] Svabhāva, the five Dharmas, the twofold egolessness, and purification.

127. Long and short, etc., exist mutually bound up; when existence is asserted, there is non-existence, and where non-existence is asserted, there is existence.

128. Analysed down to atoms, there is indeed no form to be discriminated as such; what can be established is the [truth of] Mind-only, which is not believed by those who cherish erroneous views.

129. This does not belong to the realm of the theoreticians nor to that of the Śrāvaka; (55) the Buddhas disclose the way of self-realisation.

XIV

At that time again, Mahāmati the Bodhisattva-Mahāsattva made a request of the Blessed One regarding the purification of the outflow which comes from recognising an objective world which is of Mind itself, saying, How, O Blessed One, is the outflow purified that takes place from recognising an external world which is of Mind itself? Is the purification instantaneous or gradual?

Replied the Blessed One: The outflow that takes place from recognising an external world which is of Mind itself is gradually purified and not instantaneously. Mahāmati, it is like the āmra fruit which ripens gradually and not instantaneously; in the same way, Mahāmati, the purification of beings[1] is gradual and not instantaneous. Mahāmati, it is like the potter making pots, which is done gradually and not instantaneously; in the same way, Mahāmati, the purification of beings by the Tathagata is gradual and not instantaneous. Mahāmati, it is like grass, shrubs, herbs, and trees, that grow up gradually from the earth and not instantaneously; in the same way, Mahāmati, the purification by the Tathagata of beings is gradual and not instantaneous; Mahāmati, it is like the mastery of comedy, dancing, singing, music, lute-playing, writing, and [other] arts, which is gained gradually and not instantaneously; in the same way, Mahāmati, the purification by the Tathagata of all beings is gradual and not instantaneous.

Mahāmati, it is like a mirror indiscriminately and instantaneously reflecting in it forms and images; (56) in the same way, Mahāmati, the purification by the Tathagata of all beings is instantaneous, who makes them free from discrimination and leads them to the state of imagelessness. Mahāmati, it is like the sun or the moon revealing all forms instantaneously by illuminating them with its light; in the same way, Mahāmati, the Tathagata, by making all beings discard the habit-energy which issues from the erroneous views they entertain in regard to an external world which is of the Mind, instantaneously reveals to all beings the realm of unthinkable knowledge which belongs to Buddhahood. It is like the Ālayavijñāna making instantaneously a world of body, property, and abode, which is what is seen of Mind itself; in the same way, Mahāmati, the Nishyanda-Buddha, instantaneously maturing the mentality of beings, places them in the palatial abode of the Akanishtha mansion where they will become practisers of various spiritual exercises. Mahāmati, it is like the Dharmatā-Buddha shining forth instantaneously with the rays that issue from the Nishyanda-Nirmāṇa [-Buddha]; in the same way, Mahāmati, the noble truth of self-realisation instantaneously shines out when the

---

[1] Abbreviated from "the outflowing that takes place in beings when they recognise an external world as real which is of Mind itself" (*svacittadṛiśyadhā- ī sattvānām*).

false [dualistic] views of existence and non-existence are discarded.

XV

And yet again, Mahāmati, what the Dharmatā-Nishyanda-Buddha [that is, the Buddha that flows out of the absolute Dharma] teaches is that all things are comprehensible under the aspects of individuality and generality, for they are bound up with causes and conditions of habit-energy which is accumulated by not recognising an external world as of Mind itself; that by reason of clinging to these false imaginations there is multitudinousness of unrealities, which resemble the various scenes and persons created magically and imagined as really in existence. Further again, Mahāmati, false imaginations arise from clinging to the notion of relativity. To illustrate: when the magician depending upon grass, (57) wood, shrubs, and creepers, exercises his art, all beings and forms take shape, magically-created persons are produced, which appear endowed with individuality and material body, and they are variously and fancifully discriminated. While they are thus manifesting themselves, Mahāmati, there is no substantiality in them. Likewise, Mahāmati, based on the notion of relativity the false imagination recognises a variety of appearances which are distinguished by a discriminating mind. And as their individual appearances are imagined and adhered to, there is habit-energy, and, Mahāmati, so long as the fancying goes on we have here all that is needed to constitute the self-nature of the false imagination. Mahāmati, this is the discourse of the Nishyanda Buddha.

Again, Mahāmati, it is the doing of the Dharmatā-Buddha to establish the exalted state of self-realisation which transcends the phenomena of the [empirical] mind.

Again, Mahāmati, what the Nirmita-Nirmāṇa-Buddha [or Buddha of transformation] establishes concerns such matters as charity, morality, meditation, tranquillisation, various forms of transcendental knowledge and of understanding, the Skandhas, Dhātus, and Āyatanas, emancipation, the Vijñānas, and the ways in which they function, the forms which they take, their distinctions and their performances. The Buddha discloses against the philosophical views that which surpasses forms.

Again Mahāmati, the Dharmatā-Buddha is unconditioned, free from conditions, has nothing to do with all doings, senses, and measurements, and does not belong to the world of the ignorant, Śrāvakas, Pratyekabuddhas, and philosophers, who are always clinging to the notion of an ego. For this reason, Mahāmati, you should discipline yourself in the excellent and exalted way leading to self-realisation; (58) you should keep yourself away from the views that recognise the reality of an external world apart from the Mind itself.

XVI

Further again, Mahāmati, in the life of the Śrāvaka-vehicle, there are two aspects to be distinguished, namely, the excellent and exalted state of self-realisation, and the attachment to the notion of self-nature arising from discrimination. What is the excellent, exalted state of self-realisation belonging to the Śrāvakas? This is a state of mental concentration which is attained when one realises states of emptiness, egolessness, suffering, and impermanence, and the truth that is free from passions and is ever serene; when one annihilates notions belonging to the externality of things, such as the Skandhas, Dhātus, Āyatanas, individuality and generality; and when one has an insight into reality as it is. Entering upon this state of mental concentration the Śrāvakas will attain the blissful abode of exalted self-realisation in which there is the emancipation belonging to a Dhyāna, the path and fruit of a Samādhi, and the deliverance of a Samāpatti, but in which there is as yet no discarding of habit-energy and no escape from the imperceivable transformation of death. This, Mahāmati, is the Śrāvaka's exalted state of self-realisation. Having attained this exalted and blissful condition of self-realisation as realised by the Śrāvakas, Mahāmati, the Bodhisattva-Mahāsattva may not enjoy by himself the bliss of cessation, the bliss of Samāpatti, but should think compassionately of other beings and keep ever fresh his original vows. Mahāmati, in whatever exalted and blissful state of self-realisation the Bodhisattva may find himself, he should never exert himself in the exalted and blissful state of self-realisation as attained by the Śrāvakas.

(59) Mahāmati, what is meant by the attachment to the notion of self-nature arising from discrimination? This attachment takes place when a man, seeing that the elements and the qualities such as blue, yellow, warmth, humidity, motility, and rigidity, have never been created by a creator, yet clings to the notions of individuality and generality in accordance with the measures laid down in books of logic. Mahāmati, the Bodhisattva, knowing what this is, must abandon it. Conforming himself to the egolessness of things and holding back the wrong views regarding the egolessness of a person, the Bodhisattva should keep himself on the continuously-ascending journey along the stages. This is the Śrāvaka's attachment to the notion of self-nature arising from the discrimination of existence.

XVII

At that time Mahāmati the Bodhisattva-Mahāsattva said this to the Blessed One: According to the Blessed One's teaching, the eternal-unthinkable is the exalted condition of self-realisation and also of highest reality. Now, do not the philosophers also talk about the creative agent being the eternal-unthinkable?

The Blessed One replied: No, Mahāmati, the eternal-unthinkable considered by the philosophers to be characteristic of their creator is untenable. Why? Because, Mahāmati, the eternal-unthinkable as held by the philosophers is not in conformity with the idea of a cause itself. When, Mahāmati, this eternal-unthinkable is not in conformity with the idea of a cause itself how can this be proved tenable? (60) Again, Mahāmati, if what is claimed to be the eternal-unthinkable is in conformity with the idea of a cause [which is eternal] in itself, it can be eternal; but since the idea of a creator is based upon that of a [further] cause, it cannot be the eternal-unthinkable.

But, Mahāmati, my highest reality is the eternal-unthinkable since it conforms to the idea of a cause and is beyond existence and non-existence. Because it is the exalted state of self-realisation it has its own character; because it is the cause of the highest reality it has its causation; because it has nothing to do with existence and non-existence it is no doer; because it is to be classed under the same head as space, Nirvana, and cessation it is eternal. Therefore, Mahāmati, it is not the same as the eternal-unthinkable of the philosophers; the eternal-unthinkable of the Tathagatas is thatness realised by noble wisdom within themselves. For this reason, Mahāmati, let the Bodhisattva-Mahāsattva discipline himself in order to attain by means of noble wisdom the truth of self-realisation which is the eternal-unthinkable.

Again, further, Mahāmati, the eternal-unthinkable of the philosophers is not characterised with eternality because it has a cause which is not eternal; what they regard as eternal is not eternal as it is not characterised with the power that can create itself. If again, Mahāmati, the philosophers prove the eternality of their eternal-unthinkable in contradistinction to the becoming and therefore the non-eternality of things created, Mahāmati, by the same reasoning (61) I can prove that their eternality has no reason to be known as such just because things created are non-eternal owing to their becoming.

If again, Mahāmati, the eternal-unthinkable of the philosophers is in conformity with the idea of a cause, what they regard as characteristic of a cause is a non-entity like the horns of a hare; and, Mahāmati, their eternal-unthinkable is no more than a verbal discrimination, in which, Mahāmati, the philosophers' fault consists. Why? Because, Mahāmati, mere verbal discriminations are, indeed, the hare's horns, on account of their having no characteristic of a self-cause. Mahāmati, moreover, my eternal-unthinkable is really eternal because it finds its cause in the exalted state of self-realisation, and because it has nothing to do with a creator, with being and non-being. Its eternality is not derived from the reasoning which is based upon the external notion of being and non-being, of eternity and non-eternity. If the eternal-unthinkable is eternal in consideration of the non-existence and eternality of external things, we can say of this kind of the eternal-unthinkable that the philosophers do not know what is meant by characteristically self-caused. As they are outside the state of self-realisation attainable by noble wisdom, Mahāmati, their discourse is not to the point.

XVIII

Further, Mahāmati, those who, afraid of sufferings arising from the discrimination of birth-and-death, seek for Nirvana, do not know that birth-and-death and Nirvana are not to be separated the one from the other; and, seeing that all things subject to discrimination have no reality, imagine that Nirvana consists in the future annihilation of the senses and their fields. (62) They are not aware, Mahāmati, of the fact that Nirvana is the Ālayavijñāna where a revulsion takes place by self-realisation. Therefore, Mahāmati, those who are stupid talk of the trinity of vehicles and not of the state of Mind-only where there are no images. Therefore, Mahāmati, those who do not understand the teachings of the Tathagatas of the past, present, and future, concerning the external world, which is of Mind itself, cling to the notion that there is a world outside what is seen of the Mind and, Mahāmati, go on rolling themselves along the wheel of birth-and-death.

XIX

Further, Mahāmati, according to the teaching of the Tathagatas of the past, present, and future, all things are unborn. Why? Because they have no reality, being manifestations of Mind itself, and, Mahāmati, as they are not born of being and non-being, they are unborn. Mahāmati, all things are like the horns of the hare, horse, donkey, or camel, but the ignorant and simple-minded who are given up to their false and erroneous imaginations, discriminate things where they are not; therefore, all things are unborn. That all things are in their self-nature unborn, Mahāmati, belongs to the realm of self-realisation attained by noble wisdom, and does not belong essentially to the realm of dualistic discrimination cherished by the ignorant and simple-minded. The self-nature and the characteristic marks of body, property, and abode evolve when the Ālayavijñāna is conceived by the ignorant as grasping and grasped; and then they fall into a dualistic view of existence where they recognise its rise, abiding, and disappearance, cherishing the idea that all things are born and subject to discrimination as to being and non-being. (63) Therefore, Mahāmati, you should discipline yourself therein [i.e in self-realisation].

XX

Again further, Mahāmati, there are five groups of people, each of whom attains its own [spiritual] insight. What are the five? They are: (1) the group of people whose insight belongs to the Śrāvaka-vehicle; (2) the group of people whose insight belongs to the Pratyekabuddha-vehicle; (3) the group of people whose insight belongs to the Tathagata-vehicle; (4) the group of indefinite character; and (5) the group of people to whom no insight is possible.

Mahāmati, how does one know the group of people whose insight belongs to the Śrāvaka vehicle? There are people the hair of whose body will stand on end when they know and realise the nature of the Skandhas, Dhātus, Āyatanas, and [what is meant by] generality and individuality; their intellect will leap with joy on knowing and practising what belongs to appearance and not on practising what they know of the uninterrupted chain of causation,—such ones, Mahāmati, are said to be of the group whose insight belongs to the Śrāvaka vehicle. Having had an insight into their own vehicle, they abide at the fifth or the sixth stage where they do away with the rising of the passions, but not with the habit-energy; they have not yet passed beyond the inconceivable transformation-death, and their lion-roar is, "My life is destroyed, my morality is established, etc."; they will

CHAPTER TWO 57

then discipline themselves in the egolessness of persons and finally gain the knowledge of Nirvana.

Again, Mahāmati, there are others who, believing in such things as ego, being, vital principle, nourisher, supreme spirit, or personal soul, will seek Nirvana in them. Again, Mahāmati, there are still others who, seeing that all things exist by depending upon causes, will recognise in this the way to Nirvana. (**64**) But, Mahāmati, as they have no insight into the egolessness of things, there is no emancipation for them. This, Mahāmati, is where those of the Śrāvaka-vehicle and the philosophers make the mistake in their insight by regarding non-deliverance as deliverance. Therefore, Mahāmati, you ought to discipline yourself in order to escape this wrong view.

Now, Mahāmati, they belong to the group of the Pratyekabuddha-vehicle who will shed tears and feel the hair of their body stand on end when the Pratyekabuddha's insight is shown to them. When the teaching to keep themselves away from social relations and entanglements, not to become attached to the external world and its manifold form, to perform miraculous powers by which they can divide their own body and appear double or perform the transformations, is disclosed to them, they are thereby entreated. Recognising that they are of the group whose insight belong to the Pratyekabuddha-vehicle, their discourses will be in conformity with the insight of the Pratyekabuddha-vehicle. This, Mahāmati, is the characteristic feature of the group of people whose insight belongs to the Pratyekabuddha-vehicle.

Now, Mahāmati, three aspects are distinguishable in the insight belonging to the group of the Tathagata-vehicle. They are: (1) an insight whereby one sees into the self-nature of things, which is no self-nature; (2) an exalted insight which is the attainment of self-realisation; and (3) an insight into the immensity of the external Buddha-lands. When, Mahāmati, these three aspects are disclosed one after another and also when the inconceivable realm of the Ālayavijñāna is disclosed, where body, property, and abode are seen to be the manifestation of Mind itself, a man will not be frightened, nor terrified, nor show any sign of fear; then such a one is to be known as of the group of people whose insight belongs to the Tathagata-vehicle. This is, (65) Mahāmati, the characteristic feature of the insight of those who belong to the Tathagata-vehicle.

Again, Mahāmati, when these three forms of insight are disclosed to a man, he may thereby be pursuaded to discipline himself in them. This, Mahāmati, is the stage of preparation for the establishment of his own group. In order that he may go up to the stage of imagelessness, there is this establishment. But the Śrāvaka who will purify his own habit-energy of passions by attaining an inner perception into the Ālaya and by seeing into the egolessness of things, will settle himself in the bliss of the Samādhi and finally will attain the body of Tathagatahood.[1]

XXI

Then the Blessed One recited these verses:

130. The fruit of the Stream-entered, and that of the Once-to-come; the fruit of the Not-to-come and Arhatship—all these are due to mental perturbation.

131. The triple vehicle, the one vehicle, and the no-vehicle, of these I talk, for the sake of the dull-witted, and [also] for the wise, solitude-loving ones.

132. The gate of highest reality has nothing to do with the two forms of thought-construction [subject and object]; Where the imageless stands, why should we establish the triple vehicles?

133. The Dhyānas, the immeasurables, and the no-form Samādhis, and the thought-cessation—all these are not at all found in Mind-only.

XXII

Again, Mahāmati, how is it that the Icchantika[2] never awaken the desire for emancipation? (66) Because they have

---

[1] What is stated about the group of indefinite character is not quite clear.
[2] Those who are destitute of the Buddha-nature.

abandoned all the stock of merit, and because they cherish certain vows for all beings since beginningless time. What is meant by abandoning all the stock of merit? It refers to [those Buddhists] who have abandoned the Bodhisattva collection [of the canonical texts], making the false accusation that they are not in conformity with the sutras, the codes of morality, and the emancipation. By this they have forsaken all the stock of merit and will not enter into Nirvana. Secondly again, Mahāmati, there are Bodhisattva-Mahāsattvas who, on account of their original vows made for all beings, saying, "So long as they do not attain Nirvana, I will not attain it myself," keep themselves away from Nirvana. This, Mahāmati, is the reason of their not entering into Nirvana, and because of this they go on the way of the Icchantika.

Again, Mahāmati said; Who, Blessed One, would never enter Nirvana?

The Blessed One replied: Knowing that all things are in Nirvana itself from the very beginning, the Bodhisattva-Icchantika would never enter Nirvana. But those Icchantikas who have forsaken all the stock of merit [finally] do. Those Icchantikas, Mahāmati, who have forsaken all the stock of merit might some day be influenced by the power of the Tathagatas and be induced at any moment to foster the stock of merit. Why? Because, Mahāmati, no beings are left aside by the Tathagatas. For this reason, Mahāmati, it is the Bodhisattva-Icchantika (67) who never enters into Nirvana.

XXIII

Further, Mahāmati, let the Bodhisattva-Mahāsattva be well acquainted with the three kinds of Svabhāva (self-nature). [What are the three? They are (1) false discrimination, (2) knowledge of relativity, and (3) perfect knowledge.] Now, Mahāmati, false discrimination rises from form (*nimitta*). How, Mahāmati, does it rise from form? In [the consideration of] the relativity aspect of Svabhāva, realities appear in various ways, as having forms, signs, and shapes; when, Mahāmati, these objects, forms, and signs are adhered to [as real], this adherence takes place in two ways. The Tathagatas, Arhats, and Fully-Enlightened Ones thus declare false discrimination to consist in attachment to names and attachment to objects. By the attachment to objects is meant, Mahāmati, to get attached to inner and external things [as realities]. By the attachment to names is meant to recognise in these inner and external things the characteristic marks of individuality and generality and to regard them as definitely belonging to the objects. These two modes of attachment, Mahāmati, constitute false discrimination. The knowledge of the relativity-aspect (*paratantra*) rises from the separation of subject (*āśraya*) and object (*ālambana*).

Now, Mahāmati, what is perfect knowledge? It is realised when one casts aside the discriminating notions of form, name, reality, and character; it is the inner realisation by noble wisdom. This (68) perfect knowledge, Mahāmati, is the essence of the Tathāgata-garbha.

Then the Blessed One recited this verse:

134. Form, Name, and Discrimination [correspond to] the two forms of Svabhāva, and Right Knowledge and Suchness [correspond to] the Perfect Knowledge aspect.

This, Mahāmati, is called the doctrine that examines into the nature of the five Dharmas and the two Svabhāvas (self-nature), and constitutes the state of self-realisation attained by noble wisdom, and in this you and other Bodhisattvas are to discipline yourselves.

XXIV

Further again, Mahāmati, let the Bodhisattva-Mahāsattva have a thorough understanding as to the nature of the twofold egolessness. Mahāmati, what is this twofold egolessness? [It is the egolessness of persons and the egolessness of things. What is meant by egolessness of persons? It means that] in the collection of the Skandhas, Dhātus, and Āyatanas there is no ego-substance, nor anything belonging to it; the Vijñāna is originated by ignorance, deed, and

CHAPTER TWO 61

desire, and keeps up its function by grasping objects by means of the sense-organs, such as the eye, etc., and by clinging to them as real; while a world of objects and bodies is manifested owing to the discrimination that takes place in the world which is of Mind itself, that is, in the Ālaya-vijñāna. By reason of the habit-energy stored up by false imagination since beginningless time, this world (*vishaya*) is subject to change and destruction from moment to moment; it is like a river, a seed, a lamp, wind, a cloud; [while the Vijñāna itself is] like a monkey who is always restless, like a fly who is ever in search of unclean things and defiled places, like a fire (**69**) which is never satisfied. Again, it is like a water-drawing wheel or a machine, it [i.e., the Vijñāna] goes on rolling the wheel of transmigration, carrying varieties of bodies and forms, resuscitating the dead like the demon Vetāla, causing the wooden figures to move about as a magician moves them. Mahāmati, a thorough understanding concerning these phenomena is called comprehending the egolessness of persons.

Now, Mahāmati, what is meant by the egolessness of things? It is to realise that the Skandhas, Dhātus, and Āyatanas are characterised with the nature of false discrimination. Mahāmati, since the Skandhas, Dhātus, and Āyatanas are destitute of an ego-substance, being no more than an aggregation of the Skandhas, and subject to the conditions of mutual origination which are causally bound up with the string of desire and deed; and since thus there is no creating agent in them, Mahāmati, the Skandhas are even destitute of the marks of individuality and generality; and the ignorant, owing to their erroneous discrimination, imagine here the multiplicity of phenomena; the wise, however, do not. Recognising, Mahāmati, that all things are devoid of the Citta, Manas, Manovijñāna, the five Dharmas, and the [three] Svabhāvas, the Bodhisattva-Mahāsattva will well understand what is meant by the egolessness of things.

Again, Mahāmati, when the Bodhisattva-Mahāsattva has a good understanding as regards the egolessness of things, before long he will attain the first stage [of Bodhisattvahood] when he gets a definite cognition of the imageless. When a definite acquisition is obtained regarding the aspect of the stages [of Bodhisattvahood], the Bodhisattva will experience joy, and, gradually and successively going up the scale, will reach the ninth stage where his insight is perfected, and [finally the tenth stage known as] Great Dharmameghā. Establishing himself here, (70) he will be seated in the great jewel palace known as "Great Lotus Throne" which is in the shape of a lotus and is adorned with various sorts of jewels and pearls; he will then acquire and complete a world of Māyā-nature; surrounded by Bodhisattvas of the same character and anointed like the son of the Cakravarti by the hands of the Buddhas coming from all the Buddhalands, he will go beyond the last stage of Bodhisattvahood, attain the noble truth of self-realisation, and become a Tathagata endowed with the perfect freedom of the Dharmakāya, because of his insight into the egolessness of things. This, Mahāmati, is what is meant by the egolessness of all things, and in this you and other Bodhisattva-Mahāsattvas should well exercise yourselves.

XXV

At that time, Mahāmati the Bodhisattva-Mahāsattva said this to the Blessed One: Pray teach me about making an assertion and refuting it so that I and other Bodhisattvas, getting rid of the erroneous views that may rise from assertion and refutation, may at once realise supreme enlightenment. Having been enlightened they would keep themselves away from the eternalistic assertions as well as from the nihilistic refutations, and leave your enlightenment eye unrefuted.

Then the Blessed One again, understanding the request of Mahāmati the Bodhisattva-Mahāsattva, recited this verse:

135. Assertions and refutations are not to be found in the Mind-only; the ignorant who understand not that the Mind is [seen in] the form of body, property, and abode, wander about with assertions and refutations.

CHAPTER TWO

(71) At that moment the Blessed One said this to elucidate the meaning of this verse: Mahāmati, there are four forms of assertion made concerning things not in existence. What are the four? (1) The assertion about individual marks that are non-existent; (2) the assertion about philosophical views which are non-existent [i.e., not true]; (3) the assertion about a cause which is non-existent; and (4) the assertion about objects that are non-existent. These, Mahāmati, are the four assertions.

Again, Mahāmati, what is meant by the refutation? It means not examining properly, because of ignorance, any assertions based on errors. This, Mahāmati, is what characterises assertion and refutation.

Further, Mahāmati, what are the characteristics of the assertion made about individual marks that have no existence? It concerns the marks of individuality and generality in the Skandhas, Dhātus and Āyatanas, which do not really exist; but taking them for realities and getting attached to them, a man may affirm that they are just so and not otherwise. This, Mahāmati, characterises the assertion of individual marks which are non-existent.[1] This assertion and discrimination, Mahāmati, concerning individual marks that are not existent, rises from one's attachment to the habit-energy which is amassed, since beginningless time, by varieties of erroneous views issuing from false imagination. This, Mahāmati, characterises the assertion of individual marks which are non-existent.

Again, Mahāmati, by the assertion of philosophical views which are non-existent [i.e., not true], is meant that in the Skandhas, Dhātus, and Āyatanas, [some philosophers] assume the existence of an ego, a being, a soul, a living being, a nourisher, or a spirit. This is said, Mahāmati, to be the assertion of some philosophical views which are non-existent [i.e., not true].

Again, Mahāmati, by the assertion of a cause that is non-existent is meant that [some philosophers] assume the causeless birth of a first (72) Vijñāna, which later comes to have

[1] This is repeated below and is evidently a clerical error.

a Māyā-like non-existence; that is to say, the originally unborn Vijñāna begins to function under the conditions of eye, form, light, and memory. The functioning goes on for a while and then ceases. This, Mahāmati, is the assertion of a cause that is non-existent.

Again, Mahāmati, the assertion about objects that are not-existent is an assertion arising from the attachment to such non-working existences as space, cessation, and Nirvana. These, Mahāmati, are neither existent nor non-existent; for all things are devoid of the alternatives of being and non-being and are to be known, Mahāmati, as the horns of a hare, a horse, or a camel, or like a hair-net. They are discriminated as realities by the ignorant who are addicted to assertions and refutations as their intelligence has not penetrated into the truth that there is nothing but what is seen of the Mind itself. It is otherwise with the wise. This, Mahāmati, is the characteristic point of the assertion about objects which are non-existent. For this reason, Mahāmati, one should avoid the views based on assertion and refutation.

XXVI

Further, Mahāmati, the Bodhisattvas who are thoroughly acquainted with the nature of the Citta, Manas, and Manovijñāna, of the five Dharmas, of the [three] Svabhāvas, and of the twofold Egolessness, will assume various personalities for the sake of benefitting others, just like the imagination that evolves from the seat of the relativity knowledge, and again, like the mysterious gem that reflects varieties of colours. Going over to all the Buddha-lands and assemblages, the Bodhisattvas will listen to the Buddhas, discourse on the nature of all things which are like a vision, a dream, an illusion, a reflection, and the lunar vision in water, and which have nothing to do with birth-and-death, eternality, and extinction; the Bodhisattvas, thus facing the Tathagatas, will listen to their discourses on the truth that does not belong to the Śrāvaka- and Pratyekabuddha-vehicle. They will then attain a hundred thousand Samādhis, (73) indeed, a hundred thousand niyutas of kotis of Samādhis, and by

CHAPTER TWO

means of these Samādhis they will go around from one country to another; they will do homage to the Buddhas, be born in all the celestial mansions, where they will discourse on the Triple Treasure, manifesting Buddha-bodies; and, surrounded by Śrāvakas and Bodhisattvas, they will, in order to free them from the alternatives of being and non-being, instruct them to understand thoroughly what is meant by an objective world which is nothing but Mind itself and in which there are no realities.

At that time the Blessed One recited this verse:

136. When those who are born of the Buddha see that the world is no more than Mind itself, they will obtain a body of transformation, which has nothing to do with effect-producing works, but which is endowed with the powers, psychic faculties, and self-control.

XXVII

At that time again Mahāmati the Bodhisattva-Mahāsattva made a request of the Blessed One. Tell me, Blessed One, how all things are empty, unborn, non-dual, and have no self-nature, so that I and other Bodhisattva-Mahāsattvas might be awakened in the teaching of emptiness, no-birth, non-duality, and the absence of self-nature, and, quitting the discrimination of being and non-being, quickly realise the highest enlightenment.

Then the Blesesd One said this to Mahāmati the Bodhisattva-Mahāsattva: Now, Mahāmati, listen well and reflect well upon what I tell you.

Replied Mahāmati the Bodhisattva-Mahāsattva, I will indeed, Blessed One. (74) The Blessed One said: Emptiness, emptiness, indeed! Mahāmati, it is a term whose self-nature is false imagination. Because of one's attachment to false imagination, Mahāmati, we have to talk of emptiness, no-birth, non-duality, and absence of self-nature. In short, then, Mahāmati, there are seven kinds of emptiness: (1) The emptiness of individual marks (*lakshaṇa*), (2) the emptiness of self-nature (*bhāvasvabbāva*), (3) the emptiness of no-work (*apracarita*), (4) the emptiness of work (*pracarita*), (5) the emptiness of all things in the sense that they are unpredicable (*nirabhilāpya*), (6) the emptiness in its highest sense of ultimate reality realisable only by noble wisdom, and (7) the emptiness of mutuality (*itaretara*) which is the seventh.

Mahāmati, what then is the emptiness of individual marks? It is that all things have no [such distinguishing] marks of individuality and generality. In consideration of mutuality and accumulation, [things are thought to be realities], but when they are further investigated and analysed, Mahāmati, they are non-existent, and not predicable with individuality and generality; and because thus no such ideas as self, other, or both, hold good, Mahāmati, the individual marks no longer obtain. So it is said that all things are empty as to their self-marks.

Again, Mahāmati, what is meant by the emptiness of self-nature? Mahāmati, it is that all things in their self-nature are unborn, hence the emptiness of self-nature, and it is therefore said that things are empty in their self-nature.

Again, Mahāmati, what is meant by the emptiness of no-work? It is that the Skandhas are Nirvana itself and there is no work doing in them from the beginning. Therefore, one speaks of the emptiness of no-work.

(75) Again, Mahāmati, what is meant by the emptiness of work? It is that the Skandhas are devoid of an ego and its belongings, and go on functioning when there is a mutual conjunction of cause and action. Thus one speaks of the emptiness of work.

Again, Mahāmati, what is meant by the emptiness of all things in the sense that they are unpredicable? It is that the nature of the false imagination is not expressible, hence the emptiness of all things in the sense of their unpredicability. Thus one speaks of the emptiness of unpredicability.

Again, Mahāmati, what is meant by the emptiness in its highest sense of ultimate reality realisable by noble wisdom? It is that in the attainment of an inner realisation by means of noble wisdom there is no trace of habit-energy generated by all the erroneous conceptions [of beginningless past].

CHAPTER TWO

Thus one speaks of the highest emptiness of ultimate reality realisable by noble wisdom.

Again, Mahāmati, what is meant by the emptiness of mutual [non-existence]? It is this: when a thing is missing here, one speaks of its being empty there. For instance, Mahāmati, in the lecture-hall of the Mṛigārama there are no elephants, no bulls, no sheep, but as to the Bhikshus I can say that the hall is not devoid of them; it is empty only as far as they [i.e. the animals] are concerned. Further, Mahāmati, it is not that the lecture-hall is devoid of its own characteristics, nor that the Bhikshu is devoid of this Bhikshuhood, nor that in some other places, too, elephants, bulls, and sheep are not to be found. Mahāmati, here one sees all things in their aspect of individuality and generality, but from the point of view of mutuality (*itaretara*) some things do not exist somewhere. Thus one speaks of the emptiness of mutual [non-existence].

These, Mahāmati, are the seven kinds of emptiness of which mutuality ranks the lowest of all and is to be put away by you.

(76) Again, Mahāmati, not that things are not born, but that they are not born of themselves, except when seen in the state of Samādhi—this is what is meant by "all things are unborn." To have no self-nature is, according to the deeper sense, to be unborn, Mahāmati. That all things are devoid of self-nature means that there is a constant and uninterrupted becoming, a momentary change from one state of existence to another; seeing this, Mahāmati, all things are destitute of self-nature. So one speaks of all things having no self-nature.

Again, Mahāmati, what is meant by non-duality? It means that light and shade, long and short, black and white, are relative terms, Mahāmati, and not independent of each other; as Nirvana and Samsara are, all things are not-two. There is no Nirvana except where is Samsara; there is no Samsara except where is Nirvana; for the condition of existence is not of mutually-exclusive character.[1] Therefore,

[1] Read after T'ang.

it is said that all things are non-dual as are Nirvana and Samsara. For this reason, Mahāmati, you should discipline yourself in [the realisation of] emptiness, no-birth, non-duality, and no-self-nature.

Then at that time the Blessed One recited this couplet of verses:

137. I always preach emptiness which is beyond eternalism and nihilism; Samsara is like a dream and a vision, and karma vanishes not.

138. Space, Nirvana, and the two forms of cessation— thus (77) the ignorant discriminate the things which are not effect-producing, but the wise stand above being and non-being.

At that time again, the Blessed One said this to Mahāmati the Bodhisattva-Mahāsattva; This [teaching of] emptiness, no-birth, non-duality, and no-self-nature is found in all the sutras of all the Buddhas, and this doctrine is recognised in every one of them. However, Mahāmati, the sutras are the teaching in conformity with the dispositions of all beings and deviate from the [real] sense, and not the truth-preserving statement. Mahāmati, it is like unto the mirage which entices the deer with its treacherous springs, the springs are not there but the deer are attached, imagining them to be real. So with the teachings disclosed in all the sutras, they are for all beings for the gratification of their own discriminating minds. They are not the truth-preserving statements meant for noble wisdom to grasp. For this reason, Mahāmati, be in conformity with the sense and be not engrossed in the word-teaching.

XXVIII

At that time, Mahāmati the Bodhisattva-Mahāsattva said this to the Blessed One: Now the Blessed One makes mention of the Tathāgata-garbha in the sutras, and verily it is described by you as by nature bright and pure, as primarily unspotted, endowed with the thirty-two marks of excellence, hidden in the body of every being like a gem of great value, which is enwrapped in a dirty garment, enveloped in the

CHAPTER TWO 69

garment of the Skandhas, Dhātus, and Āyatanas, and soiled with the dirt of greed, anger, folly, and false imagination, (78) while it is described by the Blessed One to be eternal, permanent, auspicious, and unchangeable. Is not this Tathāgata-garbha taught by the Blessed One the same as the ego-substance taught by the philosophers? The ego as taught in the systems of the philosophers is an eternal creator, unqualified, omnipresent, and imperishable.

The Blessed One replied: No, Mahāmati, my Tathāgata-garbha is not the same as the ego taught by the philosophers; for what the Tathagatas teach is the Tathāgata-garbha in the sense, Mahāmati, that it is emptiness, reality-limit, Nirvana, being unborn, unqualified, and devoid of will-effort; the reason why the Tathagatas who are Arhats and Fully-Enlightened Ones, teach the doctrine pointing to the Tathāgata-garbha is to make the ignorant cast aside their fear when they listen to the teaching of egolessness and to have them realise the state of non-discrimination and imagelessness. I also wish, Mahāmati, that the Bodhisattva-Mahāsattvas of the present and future would not attach themselves to the idea of an ego [imagining it to be a soul]. Mahāmati, it is like a potter who manufactures various vessels out of a mass of clay of one sort by his own manual skill and labour combined with a rod, water, and thread, Mahāmati, that the Tathagatas preach the egolessness of things which removes all the traces of discrimination by various skilful means issuing from their transcendental wisdom, that is, sometimes by the doctrine of the Tathāgata-garbha, sometimes by that of egolessness, and, like a potter, by means of various terms, expressions, and synonyms. For this reason, Mahāmati, the philosophers' doctrine of an ego-substance is not the same (79) as the teaching of the Tathāgata-garbha. Thus, Mahāmati, the doctrine of the Tathāgata-garbha is disclosed in order to awaken the philosophers from their clinging to the idea of the ego, so that those minds that have fallen into the views imagining the non-existent ego as real, and also into the notion that the triple emancipation is final, may rapidly be awakened to the state of supreme enlightenment.

Accordingly, Mahāmati, the Tathagatas who are Arhats and Fully-Enlightened Ones disclose the doctrine of the Tathāgata-garbha which is thus not to be known as identical with the philosopher's notion of an ego-substance. Therefore, Mahāmati, in order to abandon the misconception cherished by the philosophers, you must strive after the teaching of egolessness and the Tathāgata-garbha.

XXIX

At that moment then the Blessed One recited this verse:

139. The personal soul, continuity, the Skandhas, causation, atoms, the supreme spirit, the ruler, the creator,—[they are] discriminations in the Mind-only.[1]

XXX

At that time Mahāmati the Bodhisattva-Mahāsattva in consideration of future generations made this request again of the Blessed One: Pray tell me, Blessed One, about the perfecting of the discipline whereby the Bodhisattva-Mahāsattvas become great Yogins.

The Blessed One replied: There are four things, Mahāmati, by fulfilling which the Bodhisattvas become great Yogins. What are the four? They are: (1) To have a clear understanding as to what is seen of Mind itself,[2] (2) to discard the notions of birth, (80) abiding, and disappearance, (3) to look into [the truth] that no external world obtains, and (4) to seek for the attainment of inner realisation by noble wisdom. Provided with these four things the Bodhisattva-Mahāsattvas become great Yogins.

---

[1] This verse has strangely found its way here.

[2] This is rather a clumsy translation of *svacitta-dṛiśya*. *Dṛiśya* is "what is seen," that is, this visible world, or this external, objective world, which according to the *Laṅkāvatāra* is a manifestation of Mind itself. When this truth is realised, the objective world loses its reality as such, and we no more cling to it as if it were a final irreducible fact which stands oppressively against the mind. The Buddhist idea of interpreting existence idealistically is more religious than logical, for Buddhists want to elevate the value of spirit absolutely above matter so that the latter will be amenable to all the commands to be given by the former.

CHAPTER TWO

How, Mahāmati, does the Bodhisattva-Mahāsattva come to have a clear understanding as to what is seen of Mind itself? He comes to it by recognising that this triple world is nothing but Mind itself, devoid of an ego and its belongings, with no strivings, no comings-and-goings; that this triple world is manifested and imagined as real, under the influence of the habit-energy accumulated since beginningless time by false reasoning and imagination, and with the multiplicity of objects and actions in close relationship, and in conformity with the ideas of discrimination, such as body, property, and abode. Thus, Mahāmati, the Bodhisattva-Mahāsattva acquires a thoroughly clear understanding as to what is seen of Mind itself.

How again, Mahāmati, does the Bodhisattva-Mahāsattva discard notions of birth, abiding, and disappearance? By this it is meant that all things are to be regarded as forms born of a vision or a dream and have never been created since there are no such things as self, the other, or bothness. [The Bodhisattvas] will see that the external world exists only in conformity with Mind-only; and seeing that there is no stirring of the Vijñānas and that the triple world is a complicated network of causation and owes its rise to discrimination, (81) they find that all things, inner and external, are beyond predicability, that there is nothing to be seen as self-nature, and that [the world] is not to be viewed as born; and thereby they will conform themselves to the insight that things are of the nature of a vision, etc., and attain to the recognition that things are unborn. Establishing themselves on the eighth stage of Bodhisattvahood, they will experience a revulsion [in their consciousness] by transcending the Citta, Manas, and Manovijñāna, and the five Dharmas, and the [three] Svabhāvas, and the twofold Egolessness, and thereby attain the mind-made body (*manomayakāya*). Thus, Mahāmati, the Bodhisattva-Mahāsattva will discard the notion of birth, abiding, and disappearance.[1]

---

[1] The proper place of this last sentence is here as restored; it is found in the Sanskrit text near the end of page 81.

Said Mahāmati,[1] what is meant by the will-body, Blessed One? The Blessed One replied: It means that one [in this body] can speedily move unobstructed as he wills; hence the will-body, Mahāmati. For instance, Mahāmati, the will [or mind] travels unobstructed over mountains, walls, rivers, trees, etc., many a hundred thousand yojanas they may be away, when a man recollects the scenes which had previously come into his perception, while his own mind keeps on functioning in his body without the least interruption or hindrance. In the same fashion, Mahāmati, the will-body, in the attainment of the Samādhi called Māyā-like and adorned with such marks as the powers, the psychic faculties, and the self-control, will be born in the noble paths and assemblies, moving about as freely as he wishes, as he recalls his original vows and worlds in order to bring all beings to maturity.

Then, Mahāmati, what is meant by the Bodhisattva-Mahāsattva (82) having a good insight into the non-existence of external objects? It means, Mahāmati, that all things are like unto a mirage, a dream, a hair-net; and seeing that all things are here essentially because of our attachment to the habit-energy of discrimination which has been maturing since beginningless time on account of false imagination and erroneous speculation, the Bodhisattvas will seek after the attainment of self-realisation by their noble wisdom. Mahāmati, furnished with these four things, Bodhisattva-Mahāsattvas become great Yogins. Therefore, in these, Mahāmati, you should exercise yourself.

XXXI

At that time Mahāmati again made a request of the Blessed One: Pray tell me, Blessed One, about the causation of all things, whereby I and other Bodhisattva-Mahāsattvas can see into the nature of causation, and by getting rid of

---

[1] This whole paragraph is a digression, a sort of explanatory note. The will-body (*manomayakāya*) is again referred to later on, p. 115 et seq.

CHAPTER TWO 73

the discrimination [which issues in the philosophical views of] eternalism and nihilism, we may no more discriminate as to the gradual or simultaneous rising of all things.

Replied the Blessed One: Mahāmati, there are two factors of causation by which all things come into existence: external and inner. Mahāmati, the external factors are a lump of clay, a stick, a wheel, thread, water, a worker, and his labour, the combination of all of which produces a jar. As with the jar, Mahāmati, which is made of a lump of clay, or a piece of cloth made of thread, or a matting made of fragrant grass, or the sprout growing out of a seed, or fresh butter which is produced from sour milk by a man churning it with his own labour, (83) so it is, Mahāmati, with all things which, governed by external causes, appear one after another in continuous succession. As regards the inner factors of causation, Mahāmati, they are of such kind as ignorance, desire, and action, which make up our idea of causation. Born of these, Mahāmati, there is the manifestation of the Skandhas, Dhātus, and Āyatanas. They are not separable [realities][1] but discriminated [as such] by the ignorant.

Now, Mahāmati, there are six causes: (1) possibility-cause, (2) dependence-cause, (3) objectivity-cause, (4) agency-cause, (5) manifesting-cause, and (6) indifference-cause.[2] The possibility-cause means, Mahāmati, that when a cause to be becomes effective there is the rising of things inner and outer. The dependence-cause means, Mahāmati, that when conditions to be, become effective there is the rising of the Skandha-seeds, etc., inner and outer. Further, the objectivity-cause means, Mahāmati, that bound by the objective world [the Vijñāna] keeps up its continuous activity.

---

[1] Wei reads this without the negative particle, while T'ang omits the whole sentence together with the foregoing, *pratītyasamutpādasaṁjñānāṁ pratilabhante.* This latter is also omitted in this translation as the translator regards its insertion here as a clerical error, which perhaps was also the idea of the T'ang.

[2] The Chinese 觀待 (T'ang), 相待 (Wei), or simply 待 (Sung) points to *apeksha* rather than to *upeksha*. In this case, "mutual reference" is better.

Again, Mahāmati, the agency-cause means that like a sovereign king a cause invested with supreme authority asserts itself. Again, the manifesting-cause means that when the discriminating faculty rises, as the result it reveals individual marks as a lamp does forms, etc. Lastly, the indifference-cause means that when there is a dissolution (84) the power of combination discontinues, and there rises a state of non-discrimination.

These, Mahāmati, are the outcome of discrimination carried on by the ignorant and simple-minded, and there is no gradual nor simultaneous rising of existence. Why? Because, Mahāmati, if there is a simultaneous rising of existence, there would be no distinction between cause and effect, and there would be nothing to characterise a cause as such. If a gradual rising is admitted, there is no substance that holds together individual signs, which makes gradual rising impossible. While a child is not yet born, Mahāmati, the term father has no significance.[1] The logician argues that there is that which is born and that which gives birth by the mutual functioning of such causal factors as cause, subsistence, continuity, acceleration, and others; and they conclude that there is a gradual rising of existence. But, Mahāmati, this gradual rising does not obtain except by reason of their attachment to the notion of self-nature. When the [ideas of] body, property, and abode are cherished in what is nothing but the manifestation of Mind itself, the external world is perceived under the aspects of individuality and generality, which, however, are not realities; and therefore, Mahāmati, neither a gradual nor a simultaneous rising of things is possible. It is only when the Vijñāna evolves by reason of discrimination which discriminates the manifestation of Mind itself [that existence is said to come into view]. For this reason, Mahāmati, you must strive to get rid of notions of gradation and simultaneity in the combination of the causal activities. Thus it is said:

[1] In this and what follows the translator has adopted the reading of T'ang.

140. Nothing whatever is born or ceases to exist by reason of causation; when causation is discriminated there is birth and cessation.

(85) 141. It is not to keep off the idea of birth and disappearance which takes place in causation; it is to keep off the wrong imagination as to causation, which is cherished by the ignorant.

142. The being and non-being of things subject to causation has no reality; the triple world owes its existence to the Mind put into confusion by reason of habit-energy.

143. Not ever being in existence, what things are there that are born? [but] in causation nothing is lost; when effect-producing objects (*samskrita*) are regarded as like unto a barren woman's child or a flower in the sky, one perceives that grasping (subject) and grasped (object) are an error and desists [from committing the same error].

144. There is nothing that is to be born, nor is there anything that has been born; even causation is not; it is because of wordly usage that things are talked of as existing.

XXXII

At that moment again Mahāmati the Bodhisattva-Mahāsattva said this to the Blessed One: Pray tell me, Blessed One, about the teaching known as the essence of discrimination as regards words, whereby, Blessed One, I and other Bodhisattva-Mahāsattvas, comprehending and becoming well acquainted with the essence of discrimination as regards words, will be thoroughly informed of the signification of two things, expression and expressed, and, thereby immediately attaining supreme enlightenment, will explain the signification of these two things, expression and expressed, for the purification of all beings.

Replied the Blessed One: Then, Mahāmati, listen well and reflect well, (86) for I will tell you about it.

Well done! said Mahāmati the Bodhisattva-Mahasattva and listened to the Blessed One.

The Blessed One said this to him: There are, Mahāmati, four kinds of word-discrimination. They are: (1)

Words denoting individual marks, (2) dream-words, (3) words growing out of the attachment to erroneous speculations and discriminations, and (4) words growing out of the discrimination that knows no beginning.

Now, Mahāmati, the words denoting individual marks rise from discriminating forms and characteristic signs as real in themselves and becoming attached to them. The dream-words, Mahāmati, rise from the unreal surroundings which reveal themselves [before the mind] when it recollects its previous experience. The words growing out of the attachment to erroneous speculations and discriminations, Mahāmati, rise from recollecting deeds once previously committed. The words growing out of the discrimination that has been functioning since beginningless time, Mahāmati, rise from the habit-energy whose seeds have been growing out of the clinging to erroneous speculations and false imaginations since beginningless time. I say, Mahāmati, these are the four features of word-discrimination, which is the answer to your question.

XXXIII

At that time again, Mahāmati the Bodhisattva-Mahāsattva requested of the Blessed One to speak on this subject: Pray tell me again, Blessed One, about the conditions whereby the word-discrimination manifests itself. Where, whence, how, and by whom do words indicating discrimination take place among the people?

Said the Blessed One: Mahāmati, the word-discrimination goes on taking place by the coördination of the head, chest, nose, throat, palate, lips, tongue, and teeth.

Said Mahāmati; Again, Blessed One, (87) are words to be considered different (*anyā*) or not-different (*ananyā*) from discrimination?

Replied the Blessed One: Mahāmati, they are neither different nor not-different. Why? Because words rise, Mahāmati, with discrimination as their cause. If, Mahāmati, words are different from discrimination, they cannot have it for cause. Then if they are not different, words cannot express the sense, which they do. Therefore, words and discrimination are neither different nor not-different.

Then Mahāmati said: Again, Blessed One, are words themselves the highest reality? or is what is expressed in words the highest reality?

The Blessed One replied: Mahāmati, words are not the highest reality, nor is what is expressed in words the highest reality. Why? Because the highest reality is an exalted state of bliss, and as it cannot be entered into by mere statements regarding it, words are not the highest reality. Mahāmati, the highest reality is to be attained by the inner realisation of noble wisdom; it is not a state of word-discrimination; therefore, discrimination does not express the highest reality. And then, Mahāmati, words are subject to birth and destruction; they are unsteady, mutually conditioning, and are produced by the law of causation. And again, Mahāmati, what is mutually conditioning and produced by the law of causation cannot express the highest reality, because the indications [pointing to the distinction between] self and not-self are non-existent. Mahāmati, words are these indications and do not express [the highest reality].

(88) Further, Mahāmati, word-discrimination cannot express the highest reality, for external objects with their multitudinous individual marks are non-existent, and only appear before us as something revealed out of Mind itself. Therefore, Mahāmati, you must try to keep yourself away from the various forms of word-discrimination.

XXXIV

Thus it is said:

145. In all things there is no self-nature, words too are devoid of reality; as the ignorant understand not what is meant by emptiness, yes, by emptiness, they wander about.

146. In all things there is no self-nature, they are mere words of people; that which is discriminated has no reality; [even] Nirvana is like a dream; nothing is seen to be in transmigration, nor does anything ever enter into Nirvana.

147. As a king or a wealthy householder, giving his

children various clay-made animals, pleases them and makes them play [with the toys], but later gives them real ones;

148. So, I, making use of various forms and images of things, instruct my sons; but the limit of reality (*bhūtakoṭi*) can [only] be realised within oneself.

XXXV

At that time Mahāmati the Bodhisattva-Mahāsattva again (89) said this to the Blessed One: Pray tell me, Blessed One, about the attainment of self-realisation by noble wisdom, which does not belong to the path and the usage of the philosophers; which is devoid of [all such predicates as] being and non-being, oneness and otherness, bothness and not-bothness, existence and non-existence, eternity and non-eternity; which has nothing to do with the false imagination, nor with individuality and generality; which manifests itself as the truth of highest reality; which, going up continuously by degrees the stages of purification, enters upon the stage of Tathagatahood; which, because of the original vows unattended by any striving, will perform its works in infinite worlds like a gem reflecting a variety of colours; and which is manifested [when one perceives how] signs of individuation rise in all things as one realises the course and realm of what is seen of Mind itself, and thereby I and other Bodhisattva-Mahāsattvas are enabled to survey things from the point of view which is not hampered by marks of individuality and generality nor by anything of the false imagination, and may quickly attain supreme enlightenment and enable all beings to achieve the perfection of all their virtues.

Replied the Blessed One: Well done, well done, Mahāmati! and again, well done, indeed, Mahāmati! Because of your compassion for the world, for the benefit of many people, for the happiness of many people, for the welfare, benefit, happiness of many people, both of celestial beings and humankind, Mahāmati, you present yourself before me and make this request. Therefore, Mahāmati, listen well and truly, and reflect, for I will tell you.

Assuredly, said Mahāmati the Bodhisattva-Mahāsattva, and gave ear to the Blessed One.

(90) The Blessed One said this to him: Mahāmati, since the ignorant and the simple-minded, not knowing that the world is what is seen of Mind itself, cling to the multitudinousness of external objects, cling to the notions of being and non-being, oneness and otherness, bothness and not-bothness, existence and non-existence, eternity and non-eternity, as being characterised by self-nature which rises from discrimination based on habit-energy, they are addicted to false imaginings. Mahāmati, it is like a mirage in which the springs are seen as if they were real. They are imagined so by the animals who, thirsty from the heat of the season, would run after them. Not knowing that the springs are their own mental hallucinations, the animals do not realise that there are no such springs. In the same way, Mahāmati, the ignorant and simple-minded with their minds impressed by various erroneous speculations and discriminations since beginningless time; with their minds burning with the fire of greed, anger, and folly; delighted in a world of multitudinous forms; with their thoughts saturated with the ideas of birth, destruction, and subsistence; not understanding well what is meant by existent and non-existent, by inner and outer; the ignorant and simple-minded fall into the way of grasping at oneness and otherness, being and non-being. Mahāmati, it is like the city of the Gandharvas which the unwitted take for a real city, though it is not so in fact. This city appears in essence owing to their attachment to the memory of a city preserved in seed from beginningless time. This city is thus neither existent nor non-existent. In the same way, Mahāmati, clinging to the memory (*vāsanā*) of erroneous speculations and doctrines since beginningless time, they hold fast to ideas such as oneness and otherness, being and non-being, and their thoughts are not at all clear about what is seen of Mind-only. (91) Mahāmati, it is like a man, who, dreaming in his sleep of a country variously filled with women, men, elephants, horses, cars, pedestrians, villages, towns, hamlets, cows, buffalos, mansions, woods,

mountains, rivers, and lakes enters into its inner appartments and is awakened. While awakened thus, he recollects the city and its inner apartments. What do you think, Mahāmati? Is this person to be regarded as wise, who is recollecting the various unrealities he has seen in his dream?

Said Mahāmati: Indeed, he is not, Blessed One.

The Blessed One continued: In the same way the ignorant and simple-minded who are bitten by erroneous views and are inclined toward the philosophers, do not recognise that things seen of the Mind itself are like a dream, and are held fast by the notions of oneness and otherness, of being and non-being. Mahāmati, it is like the painter's canvas on which there is no depression nor elevation as imagined by the ignorant. In the same way, Mahāmati, there may be in the future some people brought up in the habit-energy, mentality, and imagination based on the philosophers' erroneous views; clinging to the ideas of oneness and otherness, of bothness and not-bothness, they may bring themselves and others to ruin; they may declare those people nihilists who hold the doctrine of no-birth apart from the alternatives of being and non-being. They [argue against] cause and effect, they are followers of the wicked views whereby they uproot meritorious causes of unstained purity. They are to be kept far away by those whose desires are for things excellent. They are those whose thoughts are entangled in the errors of self, other, and both, (**92**) in the errors of imagining being and non-being, assertion and refutation, and hell will be their final refuge. Mahāmati, it is like the dim-eyed ones who, seeing a hair-net, would exclaim to one another, saying: "It is wonderful! it is wonderful! Look, O honourable sirs!" And the said hair-net has never been brought into existence. It is in fact neither an entity nor a non-entity, because it is seen and not seen. In the same manner, Mahāmati, those whose minds are addicted to discrimination of the erroneous views as cherished by the philosophers, and who are also given up to the realistic ideas of being and non-being, oneness and otherness, bothness and not-bothness, will contradict the good Dharma, ending in the

CHAPTER TWO

destruction of themselves and others. Mahāmati, it is like a firebrand-wheel which is no real wheel but which is imagined to be of such character by the ignorant, but not by the wise. In the same manner, Mahāmati, those whose minds have fallen into the erroneous views of the philosophers will falsely imagine in the rise of all beings oneness and otherness, bothness and not-bothness.

Mahāmati, it is like those water-bubbles in a rainfall which have the appearance of crystal gems, and the ignorant taking them for real crystal gems run after them. Mahāmati, they are no more than water-bubbles, they are not gems, nor are they not-gems, because of their being so comprehended [by one party] and being not so comprehended [by another]. In the same manner, Mahāmati, those whose minds are impressed by the habit-energy of the philosophical views and discriminations will regard things born as non-existent and those destroyed by causation as existent.

[1]Further, Mahāmati, by setting up the three forms of measure and the [five] members of a syllogism, (93) [the philosophers] make the discrimination that there is a reality existing by itself, which is attained by the realisation of noble wisdom, and devoid of the two Svabhāvas. [This discrimination however is] not right. [The Buddhist doctrine is this:] Mahāmati, when a [psychological] revulsion takes place in the Yogins [by the transcendence of] the Citta, Manas, and Vijñāna, they cast off the [dualistic] discrimination of grasped and grasping in what is seen of Mind itself, and entering the Tathagata-stage attain the realisation of noble wisdom; and in this there is no thought of existence and non-existence. Again, Mahāmati, if there is the grasping of existence and non-existence in the realm attained by the Yogins, there will be in them the grasping of an ego, a nourisher, a supreme soul, or a person. Again, Mahāmati, the teaching pointing to self-nature, individuality and generality of things, is that of the Transformation Buddha and not that of the Dharmatā Buddha. Again, Mahāmati,

---

[1] This whole paragraph must be independently treated.

such teaching is meant for the ignorant, being in conformity with their mentality, their way of thinking and viewing things; any establishment that favours the way of self-nature, fails to reveal the truth of self-realisation to be attained by noble wisdom and the blissful abode of the Samādhi.

Mahāmati, it is like the trees reflected in water; they are reflections and yet are not-reflections, the trees are [real] figures, and yet no-figures. In the same manner, Mahāmati, those who are impressed by the habit-energy of the philosophical views carry on their discrimination regarding oneness and otherness, bothness and not-bothness, being and non-being, for their minds are not enlightened as regards what is seen of Mind-only.

Mahāmati, it is like a mirror reflecting all colours and images (94) as afforded by the conditions and without discrimination; and they are neither images nor not-images, because they are seen as images and also as not-images. And, Mahāmati, they are discriminated forms of what is seen of Mind itself, which are known to the ignorant as images. In the same manner, Mahāmati, oneness and otherness, bothness and not-bothness, are reflected images of Self-Mind while they appear as if real.

Mahāmati, it is like an echo giving the sound of a human voice, of a river, or of the wind; it is neither existent nor non-existent, because it is heard as a voice and yet as not a voice. In the same way, Mahāmati, the notions of being and non-being, oneness and otherness, bothness and not-bothness are the discriminations of Self-Mind and habit-energy.

Mahāmati, it is like a mirage which in conjunction with the sun appears with its flowing waves on the earth where there are no grass, shrubs, vines, and trees. They are neither existent nor non-existent, according to the desire for them or its absence. In the same way, Mahāmati, the discriminating Vijñāna of the ignorant which is impressed with the habit-energy of false imaginations and speculations since beginningless time, is stirred like a mirage even in the midst of reality revealed by means of noble wisdom, by the waves of birth, subsistence, and destruction, of oneness and otherness, bothness and not-bothness, being and non-being.

Mahāmati, it is like Piśāca who by means of his spell makes a corpse or a wooden image throb with life though it has no power of its own; but here the ignorant cling to the non-existent imagining them to have the power of movement. In the same way, Mahāmati, (95) the ignorant and simpleminded committing themselves to the erroneous philosophical views are thoroughly devoted to the ideas of oneness and otherness, but their assertion is not at all well grounded. For this reason, Mahāmati, in order to attain the noble reality attainable within yourself, you should cast off the discriminations leading to the notions of birth, abiding, and destruction, of oneness and otherness, bothness and not-bothness, being and non-being.

Therefore, it is said:

149. The Skandhas, of which the Vijñāna is the fifth, resemble the reflections of the trees in water; they are to be regarded as Māyā and a dream, they are so by thought-construction; make no discriminations!

150. This triple world resembles a hair-net, or water in a mirage which is agitated; it is like a dream, Māyā; and by thus regarding it one is emancipated.

151. Like a mirage in the spring-time, the mind is found bewildered; animals imagine water but there is no reality to it.

152. Thus the Vijñāna-seed is evolved and the world comes into view; the ignorant imagine it is born, just like the dim-eyed ones perceive things in the darkness.

153. Since beginningless time, the ignorant are found transmigrating through the paths, enwrapped in their attachment to existence; as a wedge is induced by another wedge, they are led to the abandonment [of their wrappage].

154. By regarding the world as always like a magically-moving corpse, or a machine, or like a dream, or a lightning, or a cloud; (96) the triple continuation is torn asunder and one is emancipated.

155. There is here nothing of thought-construction, it is like an image in the air; when they thus understand all there is nothing to know.

156. Here is nothing but thought-construction and name. You seek in vain for individual signs; the Skandhas are like a hair-net wherein discrimination goes on.

157. A world of multitudes[1] is a hair-net, a vision, a dream, and the city of the Gandharvas; it is [a wheel made by] a firebrand, a mirage; it is a non-entity, only an appearance to people.

158. Eternity and non-eternity; oneness, too, bothness and not-bothness as well: these are discriminated by the ignorant who are confused in mind and bound up by errors since beginningless time.

159. In a mirror, in water, in an eye, in a vessel, and on a gem, images are seen; but in them there are no images [i.e. realities] anywhere to take hold of.

160. Like a mirage in the air, so is a variety of things mere appearance; they are seen in diversity of forms, but are like a child in a barren woman's dream.

XXXVI

Further, Mahāmati, the religious teaching of the Tathagatas is free from the four statements. That is, it is devoid of oneness and otherness, of bothness and not-bothness, is free from being and non-being, assertion and refutation; the religious teaching of the Tathagatas is headed by the [four noble] truths, the [twelvefold] chain of origination, and [the eightfold noble] path leading to emancipation. **(97)** The religious teaching of the Tathagatas, Mahāmati, is not fastened to these ideas: Prakṛiti, Īśvara, causelessness, spontaneity, atoms, time and self-nature. Again, Mahāmati, [the Tathagatas, leading beings] successively forwards like the leader of a caravan, in order to purify them from the two hindrances of passion and knowledge, will establish them in the one hundred and eight statements of imagelessness and also in the characteristic distinctions of the vehicles, of the

[1] Read *cittram,* instead of *cittam.*

stages [of Bodhisattvahood], and of the constituents [of enlightenment].

XXXVII

Further, Mahāmati, there are four kinds of Dhyānas. What are the four? They are: (1) The Dhyāna practised by the ignorant, (2) the Dhyāna devoted to the examination of meaning, (3) the Dhyāna with Tathatā (suchness) for its object, and (4) the Dhyāna of the Tathāgatas.

What is meant by the Dhyāna practised by the ignorant? It is the one resorted to by the Yogins exercising themselves in the discipline of the Śrāvakas and Pratyekabuddhas, who perceiving that there is no ego-substance, that things are characterised with individuality and generality, that the body is a shadow and a skeleton which is transient, full of suffering and is impure, persistently cling to these notions which are regarded as just so and not otherwise, and who starting from them successively advance until they reach the cessation where there are no thoughts. This is called the Dhyāna practised by the ignorant.

Mahāmati, what then is the Dhyāna devoted to the examination of meaning? It is the one [practised by those who,] having gone beyond the egolessness of things, individuality and generality, the untenability of such ideas as self, other, and both, which are held by the philosophers, proceed to examine and follow up the meaning of the [various] aspects of the egolessness of things and the stages of Bodhisattvahood. This is the Dhyāna devoted to the examination of meaning.

What, Mahāmati, is the Dhyāna with Tathatā for its object? When [the Yogins recognise that] the discrimination of the two forms of egolessness is mere imagination, and that where he establishes himself in the reality of suchness (*yathābhūta*) there is no rising of discrimination, I call it the Dhyāna with Tathatā for its object.

(98) What, Mahāmati, is the Dhyāna of the Tathāgata? When [the Yogin], entering upon the stage of Tathāgatahood and abiding in the triple bliss which characterises self-

realisation attained by noble wisdom, devotes himself for the sake of all beings to the [accomplishment of] incomprehensible works, I call it the Dhyāna of the Tathagatas. Therefore, it is said:

161. There are the Dhyāna for the examination of meaning, the Dhyāna practised by the ignorant; the Dhyāna with Tathatā for its object, and the pure Dhyāna of the Tathagata.

162. The Yogin, while in his exercise, sees the form of the sun or the moon, or something looking like a lotus, or the underworld, or various forms like sky, fire, etc.

163. All these appearances lead him to the way of the philosophers; they throw him down into the state of Śrāvakahood, into the realm of the Pratyekabuddhas.

164. When all these are tossed aside and there is a state of imagelessness, then a condition in conformity with Tathatā presents itself; and the Buddhas will come together from all their countries and with their shining hands will stroke the head of this benefactor.

XXXVIII

At that time Mahāmati the Bodhisattva-Mahāsattva again said this to the Blessed One: Thou speakest of Nirvana, Blessed One. What is meant by this term Nirvana?

Replied the Blessed One: When the self-nature and the habit-energy of all the Vijñānas, including the Ālaya, Manas, and Manovijñāna, from which issues the habit-energy of wrong speculations—when all these go through a revulsion, I and all the Buddhas declare that there is Nirvana, and the way and the self-nature of this Nirvana is emptiness, which is the state of reality.

(99) Further, Mahāmati, Nirvana is the realm of self-realisation attained by noble wisdom, which is free from the discrimination of eternality and annihilation, existence and non-existence. How is it not eternality? Because it has cast off the discrimination of individuality and generality, it is not eternality. How about its not being annihilation? It is because all the wise men of the past, present, and future

have attained realisation. Therefore, it is not annihilation. Again, Mahāmati, the great Parinirvana is neither destruction nor death. Mahāmati, if the great Parinirvana is death, then it will be a birth and continuation. If it is destruction, then it will assume the character of an effect-producing deed. For this reason, Mahāmati, the great Parinirvana is neither destruction nor death. Neither has it anything to do with vanishing;[1] it is the goal of the Yogins. Again, Mahāmati the great Parinirvana is neither abandonment nor attainment, neither is it of one meaning nor of no-meaning; this is said to be Nirvana.

Further, Mahāmati, Nirvana conceived by the Śrāvakas and Pratyekabuddhas consists in recognising individuality and generality, in escaping social intercourse, in not having a perverted view of the world, and not raising discrimination. This is their notion of Nirvana.

XXXIX

Further, Mahāmati, there are two kinds of characteristic signs of self-nature. (100) What are these two kinds? They are the attachment to words as having self-nature, and the attachment to objects as having self-nature. The attachment to words as having self-nature, Mahāmati, takes place owing to one's clinging to the habit-energy of words and false imaginings since beginningless time. And the attachment to objects as having self-nature, Mahāmati, takes place from not knowing that the external world is no more than Self-Mind.

XL

Further, Mahāmati, there are two kinds of the sustaining power which issues from the Tathagatas who are Arhats and Fully-Enlightened Ones; and sustained by this power [the Bodhisattvas] would prostrate themselves at their feet and ask them questions. What is this twofold power that sustains the Bodhisattvas? The one is the power by which they are sustained to go through the Samādhis and Samā-

[1] *Maraṇam* repeated here in the text is a mistake.

pattis; while the other is the power whereby the Buddhas manifest themselves in person before the Bodhisattvas and baptise them with their own hands. Then, Mahāmati, sustained by the power of the Buddhas, the Bodhisattva-Mahāsattvas at their first stage will attain the Bodhisattva-Samādhi, known as the Light of Mahāyāna, which belongs to the Bodhisattva-Mahāsattvas. They will immediately see the Tathagatas, Arhats, Fully-Enlightened Ones appearing before them personally, who come from all the different abodes in the ten quarters of the world and who now facing the Bodhisattvas will impart to them their sustaining power displayed with the body, mouth, and words. Mahāmati, as is the case with Vajragarbha the Bodhisattva-Mahāsattva, and with other Bodhisattva-Mahāsattvas who are in possession of similar character and (101) virtue, so, Mahāmati, with the Bodhisattva-Mahāsattvas at the first stage, they will attain the Tathagatas' power sustaining them in their Samādhis and Samāpattis. By virtue of their stock of merit accumulated for a hundred thousand kalpas, they will, successively going up the stages and getting thoroughly acquainted with what they should do and should not do, finally reach the stage of Bodhisattvahood called Dharmameghā. Here the Bodhisattva-Mahāsattva finds himself seated on a throne in the Lotus Palace, and surrounded by the Bodhisattva-Mahāsattvas of a similar class; a tiara decorated and ornamented with all kinds of precious stones is on his head, and his body[1] shines brilliantly like the moon in the yellowish gold colour of the Campaka flower. The Buddhas now come from their worlds in the ten quarters, and with their lotus-like hands, sprinkle the forehead of the Bodhisattva-Mahāsattva who is seated on the throne in the Lotus Palace; the Buddhas thus give him a baptism personally by hand as when a great king invested with supreme authority [baptises his crown-prince]. This Bodhisattva and these Bodhisattvas are said to be sustained by the Buddhas' power, being thus baptised by [their] hands. Mahāmati, this is the twofold sustaining power imparted to the Bodhisattva-Mahāsattvas, who, sus-

[1] According to the Chinese translations.

tained by this twofold sustaining power, personally come into the presence of all the Buddhas. In no other way are the Tathagatas, Arhats, Fully-Enlightened Ones to be interviewed.

Further, Mahāmati, (102) whatever Samādhis, psychic faculties, and teachings are exhibited by the Bodhisattva-Mahāsattvas, they are sustained by the twofold sustaining power of all the Buddhas. If, Mahāmati, the Bodhisattva-Mahāsattvas show their eloquence without the Buddhas' sustaining power, the ignorant and simple-minded will also show their eloquence. [But the latter do not.] Why? Because of the sustaining power [on the one hand] and its absence [on the other]. Where the Tathagatas enter with their sustaining power there will be music not only in various musical instruments and vessels but also even in grass, shrubs, trees, and mountains, Mahāmati, yes, in towns indeed, palaces, houses, and royal abodes. How much more those endowed with sentiency! The mute, blind, and deaf will be cured of their deficiencies, Mahāmati, and will enjoy their emancipation. Such, Mahāmati, is the great extraordinary virtue of the sustaining power imparted by the Tathagatas.

Further, Mahāmati said: Why is it, Blessed One, that when the Bodhisattva-Mahāsattvas are established in the Samādhis and Samāpattis, and when they are baptised at the most exalted stage, the Tathagatas, Arhats, Fully-Enlightened Ones, bestow their sustaining power on them?

Replied the Blessed One: It is in order to make them avoid the evil ones, karma, and passions, to keep them away from the Dhyāna and stage of the Śrāvakahood, to have them realise the stage of Tathagatahood, and to make them grow in the truth and experience already attained. For this reason, Mahāmati, the Tathagatas, Arhats, Fully-Enlightened Ones sustain with their power the Bodhisattva-Mahāsattvas. If they were not thus sustained, Mahāmati, (103) they would fall into the way of thinking and feeling as cherished by the wrong philosophers, Śrāvakas, or evil ones, and would not attain the highest enlightenment. For this reason, the Bodhisattva-Mahāsattvas are upheld by the

Tathagatas, Arhats, Fully-Enlightened Ones. Thus it is said:

165. The sustaining power is purified by the Buddhas' vows; in the baptism, Samādhis, etc., from the first to the tenth [stage], [the Bodhisattvas are in the embrace of the Buddhas].

XLI

At that time again Mahāmati the Bodhisattva said thus to the Blessed One: The chain of origination as told by the Blessed One depends on a cause producing an effect, and that it is not a theory established on the principle of a self-originating substance. The philosophers also proclaim a causal origination when they say that all things rise conditioned by a supreme spirit, Iśvara, a personal soul, time, or atom. How is it that the rise of all things is explained by the Blessed One in another terminology bearing on causation but in its meaning not different? Blessed One, the philosophers explain birth from being and non-being, while, according to the Blessed One, all things coming into existence from nothingness pass away by causation,[1] that is to say, the Blessed One has Ignorance from which there rises Mental Conformation until we reach Old Age and Death. This teaching as explained by the Blessed One is the doctrine of no-causation and not that of causation. According to the Blessed One,[2] "that being so, this is"—if this is simultaneous conditionality and not successive mutuality, it is not right. There, Blessed One, the philosophers, (104) teaching excels, and not thine. Why? The cause assumed by the philosophers is not dependent upon the chain of origination and produces effects. But, Blessed One, thy cause has reference to its effect and the effect to its cause, and thus there is an interconnection of causal links, and from this mutuality follows the fault of non-finality. When people talk about, "That being so, this is," there is a state of causelessness.

---

[1] This is according to the Chinese translations; in the Sanskrit text there is apparently an omission.

[2] The T'ang reading seems to give the best sense.

CHAPTER TWO

Replied the Blessed One: Not so, Mahāmati, mine is not a causeless theory of causation which results in an [endless] interconnection of causes and conditions. I speak of "That being so, this is" because of my seeing into the nature of the external world which is nothing but Self-Mind and because of its unreality of grasped (object) and grasping (subject). However, Mahāmati, when people clinging to the notion of grasped and grasping fail to understand the world as something seen of Mind itself; and, Mahāmati, by them the fault is committed as they recognise the external world as real with its beings and non-beings, but not by my theory of causation.

XLII

Further, Mahāmati said: Blessed One, is it not because of the reality of words that all things are? If not for words, Blessed One, there would be no rising of things. Hence, Blessed One, the existence of all things is by reason of the reality of words.

Said the Blessed One: Even when there are no [corresponding] objects there are words, Mahāmati; for instance, the hare's horns, the tortoise's hair, a barren woman's child, etc. (105)—they are not at all visible in the world but the words are; Mahāmati, they are neither entities nor non-entities but expressed in words. If, Mahāmati, you say that because of the reality of words the objects are, this talk lacks in sense. Words are not known in all the Buddha-lands; words, Mahāmati, are an artificial creation. In some Buddha-lands ideas are indicated by looking steadily, in others by gestures, in still others by a frown, by the movement of the eyes, by laughing, by yawning, or by the clearing of the throat, or by recollection, or by trembling. Mahāmati, for instance, in the worlds of the Steady-Looking and in those of Exquisite Odours, and in the Buddha-land of Samantabhadra the Tathagata, Arhat, Fully-Enlightened One, the Bodhisattva-Mahāsattvas by steadily looking without a wink attain the recognition of all things as unborn and also various most excellent Samādhis. For this reason, Mahāmati, the validity of all things has nothing to do with the reality of words. It is observed, Mahāmati, even in this world that in the kingdom of such special beings as ants, bees, etc., they carry on their work without words. Thus it is said:

166. As space, the hare's horns, and a barren woman's child are non-entities except as expressed in words, so is this existence imagined.

167. When causes and conditions are in combination the ignorant imagine the birth /[of this world]; **(106)** as they fail to understand this reason, they wander about in the triple world which is their dwelling.

XLIII

At that time Mahāmati the Bodhisattva-Mahāsattva again said this to the Blessed One: Blessed One, where dost thou pronounce sound to be eternal?

The Blessed One replied: According to error, Mahāmati; since even to the wise there is this error, only that they are free from perversion. Mahāmati, it is like the unwitted in the world who conceive a perverted idea regarding a mirage, a firebrand wheel, a hair-net, the city of the Gandharvas, Māyā, a dream, a reflected image, and an Aksha-purusha, but with the knowing it is not so, though it does not mean that those illusions do not appear to them. When, Mahāmati, there is this error, diversities of forms are seen, though to this error the idea of impermanence is inapplicable. Why? Because it cannot be characterised with the ideas of being and non-being. Again, Mahāmati, how are the ideas of being and non-being inapplicable to this error? Because all the ignorant take in varieties of situations, like the waves of the ocean and the waters of the Ganges which are not seen by the Pretas, but seen [by others]. For this reason, Mahāmati, the error-existence [or this world of illusion] is not, but as this water is manifest to other people it is not a non-existence either. Thus to the wise, the error is neither a perversion nor a non-perversion. And for this reason, Mahāmati, the error in itself is characterised

CHAPTER TWO 93

with permanency, having the nature of non-distinction [as far as its own appearance is concerned]. Mahāmati, being discriminated as regards its diversified individual signs, (107) the error is perceived as differentiated. Thus the error, [as far as its own nature is concerned], is characterised with permanency. Again, Mahāmati, how is the error to be considered reality? Mahāmati, for this reason that as regards this error the wise cherish neither a perverted knowledge nor an unperverted knowledge. It is [such as it is and] not otherwise. In case, Mahāmati, the wise should cherish any thought whatever in this error, it goes contrary to the reality attainable by noble wisdom. If there is anything at all here it is the prattling of the ignorant, it is not the talk of the wise.

Again, when the error is discriminated according to a perverted and an unperverted view, it gives rise to two classes of family, one of which is the family of the wise, and the other the family of the ignorant and simple-minded. Now, Mahāmati, the family of the wise is divisible into three kinds, that is, the Śrāvakas, the Pratyekabuddhas, and the Buddhas. Mahāmati, how does the Śrāvakayāna family rise from the discrimination whereby the ignorant conceive the error? Mahāmati, there is the rise of the Śrāvakayāna family where the attachment to the notions of individuality and generality is kept up. This is the way, Mahāmati, this error gives rise to the Śrāvakayāna family. Mahāmati, how does the Pratyekabuddhayāna family rise as the error is discriminated? Mahāmati, when in this error the attachment to the notions of individuality and generality (108) leads one to a retirement from social life, there rises the Pratyebuddhayāna family. Mahāmati, how is there the rise of the Buddhayāna family when this error is discriminated by the intelligent? Mahāmati, when the world is understood to be nothing but Mind itself, the existence and non-existence of external objects ceases to be discriminated, and there is the rise of the Buddhayāna family. Mahāmati, this is the family, that is, what is meant by the family.

Again, Mahāmati, when the error is discriminated by

the ignorant, there is the manifestation of varieties of objects which calls forth the assertion [on their part] that this is so and not otherwise; whence rises the family of the transmigration vehicle. For this reason, Mahāmati, the error is discriminated by the ignorant as characterised by multitudinousness, and this error is neither a reality nor an unreality. Thus, Mahāmati, this error being discriminated by the wise turns into Tathatā (suchness) with them, by virtue of a revulsion which takes place in them concerning the Citta, Manas, Manovijñāna, false reasoning, habit-energy, the [three] Svabhāvas, and the [five] Dharmas. Thus, Mahāmati, there is this statement that Tathatā is Mind emancipated. Mahāmati, the meaning of this statement is here thus clearly expressed by me, that is, by the discarding of discrimination is meant the abandonment of all discriminations. So much for this statement.

Mahāmati said, Blessed One, is the error an entity or not?

The Blessed One replied: It is like Māyā, Mahāmati, the error has no character in it making for attachment; if, Mahāmati, the error had any character in it making for attachment, (109) no liberation would be possible from the attachment to existence, the chain of origination would be understood in the sense of creation as held by the philosophers.

Mahāmati said: Blessed One, if the error is like Māyā, it will thereby be the cause of another error.

The Blessed One said: No, Mahāmati, Māyā cannot be the cause of the error, because of its incapability of producing evils and faults; and thus, Mahāmati, Māyā does not give rise to evil thoughts and faults. Again, Mahāmati, Māyā has no discrimination of itself; it rises when invoked by the magical charm of a certain person. It has in itself no habit-energy of evil thoughts and faults that, issuing from self-discrimination, affect it. [Therefore,] there are no faults in it. This is only due to the confused view fondly cherished by the ignorant regarding Mind, and the wise have nothing to do with it. So it is said:

CHAPTER TWO 95

168. The wise do not see [the(?)] error, nor is there any truth in its midst; if truth is in its midst, [the(?)] error would be truth.

169. If there is the rising of individual forms (*nimitta*) apart from all error, this will indeed be error, the defiled is like darkness.[1]

XLIV

Further, Mahāmati, Māyā is not an unreality, because it has the appearance of reality; and all things have the nature of Māyā.

Said Mahāmati: Is it, Blessed One, that all things are like Māyā because Māyā is something imagined and clung to as having multitudinousness of individual forms? (110) Or is it due to the incorrect imagining of individual forms? If all things have the likeness of Māyā because Māyā is something imagined and clung to as having multitudinousness of individual forms, then see, Blessed One, things are not like Māyā. Why? Because forms are seen in the multitudinousness of individual signs not without due causes. If they ever appear without due causes, assuming the multitudinousness of individual signs and shapes, [then] they would be like Māyā. For this reason, Blessed One, that things are like Māyā is not because they [i.e. all things and Māyā] are both alike in being imagined and clung to as having multitudinousness of individual signs.

Said the Blessed One: It is not, Mahāmati, that all things are Māyā because they are both alike in being imagined and clung to as having multitudinousness of individual signs, but that all things are like Māyā because they are unreal and like a lightning-flash which is seen as quickly disappearing. Mahāmati, a lightning appears and disappears in quick succession as is manifest to the ignorant; in the same way, Mahāmati, all things assume individuality and generality according to the discrimination [of the Mind] itself. When the state of imagelessness[2] is recognised,

[1] What is exactly meant by these two verses, especially the latter, is difficult to find in this connection.
[2] According to T'ang.

objects which are imagined and clung to as in possession of individual signs cease to assert themselves. Thus it is said:

170. Māyā is not without reality, because it has something resembling it; the reality of all things is talked of [in a similar manner]; they are unreal like a lightning-flash [appearing and disappearing] quickly, and therefore they are regarded as resembling Māyā.

XLV

Further, Mahāmati said: Now according to the Blessed One, all things are unborn (111) and resemble Māyā; but, Blessed One, is there not the fault of contradiction between the previous statement and the later one? It is asserted by thee that that all things are unborn is due to their having the nature of Māyā.[1]

The Blessed One replied: Mahāmati, when all things are asserted to be unborn because of their having the nature of Māyā, there is no fault of contradiction between my previous statement and my later one. Why? Because birth is no-birth, when it is recognised that the world that presents itself before us is no more than Mind itself; and as to all external objects of which we state that they are or are not, they are to be seen as non-existent and unborn; and thus, Mahāmati, there is here no fault of contradiction between my previous statement and my later one. But, Mahāmati, in order to cast aside the philosophers' thesis on birth by causation, it is asserted that all things are like Māyā and unborn. Mahāmati, the philosophers who are the gathering of the deluded, foster the notion of deriving the birth of all things from that of being and non-being, and fail to regard it as caused by the attachment to the multidinousness which rises from the discrimination [of the Mind] itself. Mahāmati, no fear rises in me [by making this statement].[2] In this light, Mahāmati, the term "unborn" is to be understood.

[1] This last sentence is missing in T'ang, whereas Wei has: "It is said by the Tathagata that all things are unlike māyā."

[2] T'ang, says: I say that all things are non-existent because of their being unborn. Wei: I say that all things are unborn when ex-

Again, Mahāmati, the teaching that all things exist is given in order to admit transmigration, to check nihilism which says "Nothing is," and to make my disciples accept the doctrine that asserts the reality of karma in various forms and birth in the various worlds, for by admitting the terminology of existence we admit transmigration. Mahāmati, the teaching that all things are characterised with the self-nature of Māyā is meant to make the ignorant and simple-minded cast aside the idea of self-nature in anything; (112) as they cherish the thoughts characterised with error, as they do not clearly grasp the meaning of the world which is no more than the Mind itself, they imagine and cling to causation, work, birth, and individual signs; in order to check this I teach that all things are characterised in their self-nature with the nature of Māyā and a dream. Attached to erroneous thoughts they contradict both themselves and others by not seeing all things as they really and truly are. Mahāmati, to see all things as they really and truly are means to realise that there is nothing to be seen but Mind itself. So it is said:

171. In the theory of no-birth, causation is not accepted [as is maintained by the ignorant]; where existence is accepted transmigration prevails; seeing that [all things] are like Māyā, etc., one does not discriminate individual signs.

XLVI

Further, Mahāmati, we will explain the characteristics of name-body, the sentence-body, and the syllable-body; for when name-body, sentence-body, and syllable-body are well understood, the Bodhisattva-Mahāsattvas conformable to the signification of a sentence and a syllable will quickly realise supreme enlightenment and thereby awaken all beings to it. Mahāmati, by name-body is meant the object depending on which a name obtains, the body is this object; in another sense the body means substance (*śarīra*). Mahāmati, this is the body of a name. By the body of a sentence is meant

istent, unborn when non-existent. Sung: I do not [say] that the existent and the non-existent are born.

what it signifies, the real object, determining its sense definitely. In another sense, it completes its reference. Mahāmati, this is my teaching as regards the sentence-body. By the syllable-body (113) is meant that by which names and sentences are indicated; it is a symbol, a sign; in another sense, it is something indicated.

Again, Mahāmati, the sentence(*pada*)-body means the completion of the meaning expressed in the sentence. Again, Mahāmati, a name (or a letter, *nāma*) means each separate letter distinguished as to its self-nature from *a* to *ha*. Again, Mahāmati, a syllable (*vyañjana*) is short, long, or lengthy. Again, Mahāmati, regarding the sentence(*pada*)-body the idea of it is obtained from the foot-prints left on the road by elephants, horses, people, deer, cattle, cows, buffalos, goats, rams, etc. Again, Mahāmati, names(*nāma*) and syllables (*vyañjana*) belong to the four Skandhas which being formless are indicated by names; thus are names made. By means of the differently characterised names there are syllables (*vyañjana*); thus are syllables made. This, Mahāmati, is the meaning of the body of a name(*nāma*), a sentence (*pada*), and a syllable(*vyañjana*). You should endeavour to have a thorough understanding of these terms. It is thus said:

172. Because of the distinction between *nāma, pada,* and *vyañjana,* the ignorant, the dull-witted, stick to them like the elephant in deep mud.

XLVII

(114) Further, Mahāmati, in the time to come, those wrong-headed ones who are inclined to false speculations owing to their deficiency of knowledge concerning truth and cause may be asked by the wise, regarding that which is liberated from the dualistic conceptions of things such as oneness and otherness, bothness and not-bothness; and thus asked, they may answer, saying, "It is no question; it is not at all properly put—that is to say, the question: Are form, etc. and transiency to be considered one or different?"

In the same way, Nirvana and the Skandhas, indices

and indicated, qualities and qualified, realities and the elements, seen and seeing, dust and atoms, knowledge and the Yogins—[are these to be considered one or different?] Such questions concerning the various aspects of existence lead successively from one thing to another without end, and those who are asked about these unexplainable questions would declare that they were put aside by the Blessed One as impossible to answer. However, these deluded people are unable to realise [the meaning of] what they heard [from the Buddha] because of their deficiency of knowledge. The Tathagatas, Arhats, Fully-Enlightened Ones do not explain these things to all beings because of their wish to keep the latter from the fear-inspiring phrases.

Mahāmati, these inexplicables (*vyāhṛitāni*) are not taken up for consideration by the Tathagatas in order to keep the philosophers away from their wrong views and theories. Mahāmati, the philosophers may declare thus: what life is that is the body, or life is one thing, body is another. In these they make inexplicable statements. Mahāmati, entirely bewildered by the idea of a creator, the philosophers make an inexplicable statement, but that is not found in my teaching. In my teaching, Mahāmati, discrimination does not take place because I teach to stand above grasped and grasping. (115) How could there be any setting aside here? But, Mahāmati, to those who are addicted to grasped and grasping, as they do not have a thorough understanding of the world which is no more than what is seen of the Mind itself, there is something to be set aside [as inexplicable]. Mahāmati, the Tathagatas, Arhats, Fully-Enlightened Ones teach the Dharma to all beings by means of the four forms of questioning and answering. As to the propositions that are set aside [as inexplicable], Mahāmati, they are made use of by me on some other occasions for those whose senses are not yet fully matured; but for those of matured senses there is nothing to set aside.

XLVIII

Further, Mahāmati, all things being devoid of doing and

doer are unborn; as there is no doer, all things are therefore said to be unborn. Mahāmati, all things are without self-nature. Why? Because, Mahāmati, when they are examined by self-knowledge, there are no such signs obtainable which characterise them with individuality and generality; therefore, all things are said to have no self-nature. Again, Mahāmati, in all things there is no taking birth, no going-out. Why? Because, Mahāmati, the signs of individuality and generality are seen as existing and yet they are non-existent; they are seen as going out, and yet they do not go out. For this reason, Mahāmati, all things are neither taking birth, nor are they going out. Again, Mahāmati, all things are never annihilated. Why? For this reason that the individual signs that make up the self-nature of things are non-existent, and all things are beyond reach. Therefore, all things are said never to be annihilated. Again, Mahāmati, all things are not eternal. Why? (116) Because the rising of individual signs is characterised with non-eternality. Therefore, all things are said not to be eternal. Again, Mahāmati, all things are eternal. Why? Because the rising of individual signs is no-rising and is non-existent; and all things are eternal because of their non-eternality. Therefore, Mahāmati, all things are said to be eternal.

Thus it is said:

173. [1]The four kinds of explanation are: direct statement, questioning, discernment, and setting aside; whereby the philosophers are kept away.

174. The Sāṅkha and the Vaiśeshika philosophers teach birth from a being or from a non-being; all that are proclaimed by them are the inexplicables.

175. When the self-nature [of all things] is examined by knowledge, it is beyond reach; therefore, they are without self-nature and unattainable.

XLIX

At that time Mahāmati the Bodhisattva-Mahāsattva again said this to the Blessed One: Pray tell me, Blessed

[1] These three verses ought to follow § 47.

One, regarding the Stream-entered and their special attainment which characterises the state of the Stream-entered, whereby I and other Bodhisattva-Mahāsattvas thoroughly becoming acquainted with the Stream-entered and their special attainment characterising the state of the Stream-entered, will proceed to know the means and conduct which characterises the state of the Once-returning, Never-returning, and Arhatship; and they will then explain the Dharma to all beings in this manner. Having understood the twofold form of egolessness and (**117**) having cleansed themselves of the twofold hindrance, they will by degrees go through the stages of Bodhisattvahood each of which has its own characteristics, and attaining Tathagatahood whose spiritual realm is beyond conceivability, they will be like a multicoloured gem and will accomplish what is good for the lives of all beings, providing them with every teaching, condition, deportment, body, and enjoyment.

Replied the Blessed One: Listen well Mahāmati, and take well to heart; I will tell you.

Mahāmati the Bodhisattva-Mahāsattva answering him said: Very well, Blessed One.

The Blessed One then said this: Mahāmati, in the fruit attained by the Śrāvakas, three kinds are distinguishable. What are the three? They are graded, Mahāmati, low, middle, and the highest. The low ones will be reborn seven times when their existence will come to an end; the middling will attain Nirvana in three or five births; the highest will attain Nirvana in this birth. Mahāmati, for these three classes [of the Stream-entered] there are three kinds of knots: weak, middling, and strong. What are these three knots, Mahāmati? They are: (1) the view of an individual personality, (2) doubt, and (3) the holding-on to moral practices. Mahāmati, when all these three knots are in succession promoted to the higher stage there will be the attainment of Arhatship.

Mahāmati, there are two kinds of the view of an individual personality; that is, (1) the inborn one and (2) the one due to the false imagination; it is like [the relation between] the relativity view and the false imagination [of the three] Svabhāvas. (118) For instance, Mahāmati, depending on the relativity view of things there arise varieties of attachments to the false imagination. But this [existence] is neither a being, nor a non-being, nor a being-and-non-being; it is not a reality because of the false imagination, and, being discriminated by the ignorant, assumes varieties of individual signs to which they are strongly attached just as the deer does to a mirage. Mahāmati, this is the view of an individual personality falsely imagined by the Stream-entered, which has been accumulated for a long time by their ignorance and attachment. This is destroyed when the egolessness of a person is attained by which the clinging ceases.

Mahāmati, the inborn view of an individual personality as held by the Stream-entered [is destroyed in this way]. When this body which belongs equally to each of us is considered, it is perceived that it consists of form and the other four Skandhas, that form takes its rise from the elements and their belongings, that the elements are mutually conditioning, and that hence there is no aggregate known as form. When thus the Stream-entered realise that the idea of being and non-being is a partial view [of truth], the view of individual personality is destroyed. When the view of individual personality is thus destroyed, covetousness will never assert itself. This, Mahāmati, is what characterises the view of individual personality.

Again, Mahāmati, as regards the nature of doubt, when the Dharma is attained, and realised, and thoroughly understood as to its characteristics, and when the twofold view of individual personality is destroyed as previously described, no doubt is cherished in the teaching [of the Buddhas]. And there is no thought [in the minds of the Stream-entered] to follow the lead of any other teacher because of [the difference between] purity and non-purity. This, Mahāmati, is what is meant by doubt [discarded] (119) by the Stream-entered.

Again, Mahāmati, how is it that the Stream-entered do

not hold themselves to the morality? They do not because they clearly see into the nature of suffering wherever they may be reborn. [What is meant by] the holding? Mahāmati, that the ignorant and simple-minded observe the rules of morality, piety, and penance, is because they desire thereby to attain worldly enjoyments and happinesses; they cherish the hope of being born in agreeable conditions. And [the Stream-entered] do not hold [to the rules of morality], for their thoughts are turning only towards the exalted state of self-realisation, and the reason why they devote themselves to the details of morality is that they wish to master such truths as are in conformity with non-discrimination and undefiled outflows. This, Mahāmati, is the way in which the Stream-entered Ones hold to morality and piety. Mahāmati, by thus breaking up the three knots the Stream-entered will discard covetousness, anger, and folly.

Mahāmati said: Many kinds of covetousness are taught by the Blessed One; which one of them is to be cast aside?

The Blessed One replied: The world where love grows, i.e., the desire for sexual embrace, showing itself in beating, slapping, suggesting, kissing, embracing, smelling, looking-sidewise, or gazing may give one momentary pleasures but is productive of future grief. [With the Stream-entered] there is no greed for such. Why? Because they are abiding in the bliss of the Samādhi which they have attained. Hence this casting aside, but not of the desire for Nirvana.

(120) Again, Mahāmati, what is the fruit of the Once-returning? There is once in them the discrimination of forms, signs, and appearances; but as they learn not to view individual objects under the aspect of qualified and qualifying, and as they know well what marks the attainment of the Dhyāna, they once come back into the world, and putting an end to suffering, realise Nirvana. Hence the appellation "Once-returning."

Again, Mahāmati, what is meant by Never-returning? It means that while there is yet the viewing of individual objects as characterised by being and non-being in the past, present, and future, the discrimination does not return with its errors and faults, the dormant passions do not assert themselves, and the knots are completely cut off never to return. Hence the appellation "Never-returning."

Again, Mahāmati, the Arhat is the one who has attained the Dhyānas, Samādhis, emancipations, powers, psychic faculties, and with whom there are no more passions, sufferings, and discriminations. Hence the appellation "Arhat."

Mahāmati said: Now, the Blessed One declares that there are three kinds of Arhats: to which one of the three is this term "Arhat" to be applied? To one who makes straightway for the path of cessation? Or to one who neglects all his accumulated stock of merit for the sake of his vow to enlighten others? Or to one who is a form of the Transformation [Buddha]?

Replied the Blessed One: Mahāmati, [the term "Arhat"] applies to the Śrāvaka who makes straightway for the path of cessation, and to no others. Mahāmati, as for the others, they are those who have finished practising the deeds of a Bodhisattva; they are forms of the Transformation Buddha. With skilful means born of their fundamental and original vows (121), they manifest themselves among the multitudes in order to adorn the assemblages of the Buddhas. Mahāmati, here in these paths and abodes of existence they give out varieties of teachings which are based on discrimination; that is to say, as they are above such things as the attainment of the fruit, the Dhyānas, the Dhyāna-practisers, or subjects for meditation, and as they know that this world is no more than what is seen of the Mind itself, they discourse on the fruit attained [for the sake of all beings]. Further, Mahāmati, if the Stream-entered should think. "These are the fetters, but I am disengaged from them," they commit a double fault: they still hold to the vices of the ego, and they have not freed themselves from the fetters.

Further, Mahāmati, in order to go beyond the Dhyānas, the immeasurables, and the formless world, the signs of this visible world which is Mind itself should be discarded. The Samāpatti leading to the extinction of thought and sensation does not enable one to transcend the world of particulars, for there is nothing but Mind. So it is said:

176. The Dhyānas, the immeasurables, the formless, the Samādhis, and the complete extinction of thought (*nirodha*)—these do not exist where the Mind alone is.

177. The fruit of the Stream-entered, and that of the Once-returning, and that of the Never-returning, and Arhatship—these are the bewildered states of mind.

178. The Dhyāna-practiser, the Dhyāna, the subject for it, the destruction, the seeing of the truth,—these are no more than discriminations; when this is recognised there is emancipation.

L

(122) Further, Mahāmati, there are two kinds of intellect: the intellect as an examining function, and the intellect which functions in connection with the attachment to ideas of discrimination. As for the intellect that examines, Mahāmati, it is that act of intellect which examines into the self-nature of things, finding it to be devoid of the four propositions, and unattainable. This is known as the intellect that examines. What is meant by [being devoid of] the four propositions? It means to be devoid of oneness and otherness, bothness and not-bothness, being and non-being, eternity and non-eternity. These are called the four propositions. Mahāmati, train yourself to examine carefully all things as regards these four propositions. What, Mahāmati, is the intellect which functions in connection with the attachment to ideas of discrimination? It is the intellect with which the Mind is discriminated and the ideas arising therefrom are adhered to [as real]; and this adherence gives rise to the conceptions of warmth, fluidity, motility, and solidity as characterising the gross elements; while the tenacious holding to proposition, reason, definition, and illustration, leads to the assertion of a non-entity [as entity]. This is called the intellect that functions in connection with the attachment to ideas of discrimination.

This, Mahāmati, is what characterises the two kinds of

intellect, in accordance with which the Bodhisattvas, thoroughly mastering the signs of egolessness of persons and things, (123) and, by means of knowledge of imagelessness, becoming conversant with the stage of examination and practice, will attain the first stage [of Bodhisattvahood] and acquire one hundred Dhyānas. Attaining the excellent Samādhis, they will see one hundred Buddhas and Bodhisattvas, they will enter into one hundred kalpas that were prior to the present and also into those that will follow the present, they will illuminate one hundred Buddha-lands, and, illuminating one hundred Buddha-lands, they will understand the signs belonging to the higher stages; and by virtue of the most exalted vows they will manifest wonderful powers, they will be baptised by [the Buddhas] when they reach the stage of Dharmameghā (law-cloud); and realising the inmost realm of the Tathagatas, they will be provided with things which are closely connected with the ten inexhaustible vows; and, in order to bring all beings into maturity, they will shine out in various forms with the rays of transformation; they will be quite absorbed in the bliss of self-realisation.

LI

Further, Mahāmati, the Bodhisattva-Mahāsattvas are to be well acquainted with the primary and the secondary elements. How do the Bodhisattvas know the primary and the secondary elements? Mahāmati, the Bodhisattva-Mahāsattvas are to know this that the truth is that the primary elements have never come into existence, and that, Mahāmati, these elements are unborn. Thus understood, there is nothing in the world but what is discriminated [by our imagination]. When it is recognised that the visible world is no more than Mind itself, external objects cease to be realities, and there is nothing but what is discriminated by the mind and perceived [as external]. That is to say, let it be understood that the triple world has nothing to do with the primary and the secondary elements, (124) that it is removed from the four propositions and philosophical

CHAPTER TWO 107

systems, that it has nothing to do with a personal ego and what belongs to it; and that it establishes itself in the abode of real reality, where it is seen in its own form, i.e. in its unborn state.

Mahāmati, what is meant by the elements derived from the primary elements? The element discriminated as vascidity produces the realm of water, inner and outer; the element discriminated as energy produces the realm of fire, inner and outer; the element discriminated as motility produces the realm of air, inner and outer; the element discriminated as divisibility of form gives birth to the realm of earth together with space, inner and outer. Because of the attachment to the incorrect truths there is the aggregation of the five Skandhas giving rise to the elements primary and secondary.

Again, Mahāmati, the Vijñāna has its cause in our attachment to and the desire for the multitudinousness of statements and objective fields; and it continues to evolve in another path of existence. Mahāmati, the secondary elements such as earth, etc., [are said] to have their cause in the primary elements which, however, are non-existent. Because, Mahāmati, of things endowed with being, characteristics, marks, perceivableness, abode, and work, one can say that they are born of the combination of various effect-producing [elements]; but not of things which are devoid of characteristic marks. For this reason, Mahāmati, the elements primary and secondary are the discriminations of the philosophers and not mine.

LII

Further, Mahāmati, I will explain what characterises the self-nature of the Skandhas. Mahāmati, what are the five Skandhas? They are form, (125) sensation, thought, conformation, and consciousness. Mahāmati, four of these have no material forms—sensation, thought, conformation, and consciousness. Form, Mahāmati, belongs to what is made of the four primary elements, and these elements differ from one another in their individual signs. But the four

Skandhas that are without form cannot be reckoned as four, they are like space. For instance, Mahāmati, space cannot be numbered, and it is due to our discrimination that it is designated as such; in the same way, Mahāmati, the Skandhas that are beyond calculability as they have no number-marks, are not to be predicated as existing and non-existing, and are beyond the four propositions; but to the ignorant they are described as subject to numeration, but not so to the wise.

Again, Mahāmati, by the wise the five Skandhas are regarded as thought-constructions, devoid of [dualisties such as] otherness and not-otherness; for they are like varieties of forms and objects in a vision, like images and persons in a dream. As they have no better substance for their support, and as they obstruct the passage of noble wisdom, there is what is known as the Skandha-discrimination. This, Mahāmati, is what characterises the self-nature of the Skandhas. This discrimination must be discarded by you, and having discarded this, you should declare the truth of solitude. Keeping back the views held by the philosophers, the truth of solitude is to be announced in all the Buddha-assemblies, Mahāmati, and thereby the teaching of the egolessness of things is purified and you will enter upon the stage of Far-going (dūraṁgamā). Entering upon the stage of Dūraṁgamā you will become the master of many Samādhis, and, attaining the will-body (126) you will realise the Samādhi known as Māyopama (Māyā-like). Thoroughly conversant with the powers, psychic faculties, and self-control, you will be the supporter of all beings like the earth. Mahāmati, as the great earth is the supporter of all beings, so is the Bodhisattva-Mahāsattva the supporter of all beings.

LIII

Further, Mahāmati, there are four kinds of Nirvana. What are the four? They are: (1) the Nirvana which is attained when the self-nature of all things is seen as non-entity; (2) the Nirvana which is attained when varieties of individual marks characterising all things are seen as non-entities; (3) the Nirvana which is attained when there is the recognition of the non-existence of a being endowed with its own specific attributes; and (4) the Nirvana which is attained when there takes place the severance of the bondage conditioning the continuation of individuality and generality of the Skandhas. Mahāmati, these four views of Nirvana belong to the philosophers and are not my teaching. According to my teaching, Mahāmati, the getting rid of the discriminating Manovijñāna—this is said to be Nirvana.

Mahāmati said: Does not the Blessed One establish eight Vijñānas?

The Blessed One replied: I do, Mahāmati.

Mahāmati said: If eight Vijñānas are established, why do you refer to the getting-rid of the Manovijñāna and not of the seven [other] Vijñānas [as well]?

The Blessed One said: With the Manovijñāna as cause and supporter, Mahāmati, there rise the seven Vijñanas. Again, Mahāmati, the Manovijñāna is kept functioning, as it discerns a world of objects and becomes attached to it, and by means of manifold habit-energy [or memory] (127) it nourishes the Ālayavijñāna. The Manas is evolved along with the notion of an ego and its belongings, to which it clings and on which it reflects. It has no body of its own, nor its own marks; the Ālayavijñāna is its cause and support. Because the world which is the Mind itself is imagined real and attached to as such, the whole psychic system evolves mutually conditioning. Like the waves of the ocean. Mahāmati, the world which is the mind-manifested, is stirred up by the wind of objectivity, it evolves and dissolves. Thus, Mahāmati, when the Manovijñāna is got rid of, the seven Vijñānas are also got rid of. So it is said:

179. I enter not into Nirvana by means of being, of work, of individual signs; I enter into Nirvana when the Vijñāna which is caused by discrimination ceases.

180. With it [i.e. the Manovijñāna] for its cause and support, the Manas secures its use; the Vijñāna causes the Citta to function, and is supported [by it].

181. Like a great flood where no waves are stirred

because of its being dried up, the Vijñāna[-system] in its various forms ceases to work when there is the annihilation [of the Manovijñāna].

LIV

Further, Mahāmati, I will tell you about the various features of the false imagination (*parikalpita*); and when you and the Bodhisattva-Mahāsattvas are well acquainted with each of them in its specific form, you will get away from discrimination; and seeing well and knowing the way of inner realisation by noble wisdom and also the ways of speculation by the philosophers, (128) you will cast off discriminations such as grasped and grasping, and will not be induced to discriminate in respect to the multiple aspects of relativity-knowledge (*paratantra*), as well as the forms of the false imagination. What are the various features of the false imagination, Mahāmati? They are the discriminations as regards (1) words (*abhilāpa*), (2) meaning, (3) individual marks, (4) property, (5) self-nature, (6) cause, (7) philosophical views, (8) reasoning, (9) birth, (10) no-birth, (11) dependence, and (12) bondage and emancipation. These, Mahāmati, are the various features of the false imagination.

Now, Mahāmati, what is the discrimination of words? That is the becoming attached to various sweet voices and singing—this is the discrimination as regards words.

What is the discrimination of meaning? It is the discrimination by which one imagines that words rise depending on whatever subjects they express, and which subjects one regards as self-existent and belonging to the realisation of noble wisdom.

What is the discrimination of individual marks? It is to imagine in whatever is denoted by words the multitudinousness of individual marks which are like a mirage, and, clinging tenaciously to them, to discriminate all things according to these categories: warmth, fluidity, motility, and solidity.

What is the discrimination of property? It is to desire

a state of wealth such as gold, silver, and various precious stones.

What is the discrimination of self-nature? It is to make discrimination according to the imaginary views of the philosophers in reference to the self-nature of all things (**129**) which they stoutly maintain, saying, "This is just it, and there is no other."

What is the discrimination of cause? That is, to distinguish the notion of causation in reference to being and non-being and to imagine that there are cause-signs—this is the discrimination of cause.

What is the discrimination of philosophical views? That means getting attached to the philosophers' wrong views and discriminations concerning such notions as being and non-being, oneness and otherness, bothness and not-bothness.

What is the discrimination **of reasoning?** It means the teaching **whose** reasoning is **based** on the grasping of the notion of an ego-substance **and** what belongs to it.

What is the discrimination of birth? It means getting attached to the notion that things come into existence and go out of it according to causation.

What is the discrimination of no-birth? It is to discriminate that all things are from the beginning unborn, that the causeless substances which were not, come into existence by reason of causation.

What is the discrimination of dependence? It means the mutual dependence of gold and the filament [which is made of gold].

What is the discrimination of bondage and emancipation? It is like imagining that there is something bound because of something binding as in the case of a man who by the help of a cord ties a knot or loosens it.

These, Mahāmati, are the various features of the false imagination, to which all the ignorant and simple-minded ones cling, imagining that things are or are not. Those attached to the notion of relativity are attached to the notion of multitudinousness of things rising from the false imagination. It is like seeing varieties of objects depending on Māyā, but these varieties thus revealing themselves are discriminated by the ignorant as something other than Māyā itself according to their way of thinking. (130) Now, Mahāmati, Māyā and varieties of objects are neither different nor one. If they were different, varieties of objects would not have Māyā for their cause. If Māyā were one with varieties of objects, there would be no distinction between the two, but as there is the distinction these two—Māyā and varieties of objects—are neither one nor different. For this reason you and the Bodhisattva-Mahāsattvas should never give yourselves up to the notion of being and non-being.

LV

So it is said:

182. The Citta is bound up with the objective world; the intellect's function is to speculate; and in the excellent state of imagelessness there is the evolving of transcendental wisdom (*prajñā*).

183. According to the false imagination, [self-substance] is, but from the point of view of relativity (*paratantra*) it is not; owing to perversion, what is discriminated is grasped [as real]; in the relativity there is no discrimination.

184. Multitudinousness of differentiations is imagined [as real by the ignorant], but being like Māyā they obtain not; varieties of individual forms are discriminated as such, but they [really] do not obtain.

185. [To imagine] individual forms is wrong, it puts one in bondage; they are born of Mind due to the false imagination of the ignorant; based on the relativity they are discriminated.

186. The existence thus subjected to discrimination is no other than its relativity aspect; (131) the false imagination is of various forms; based on the relativity, discrimination is carried on.

187. Conventional truth (*saṁvṛiti*) and ultimate truth (*paramārtha*)—if there be a third, non-entity is its cause;

CHAPTER TWO 113

the false imagination belongs to the conventional; when it is cut asunder, there is the realm of the wise.

188. As to the Yogins there is one reality which reveals itself as multiplicity and yet there is no multiplicity in it; so is the nature of the false imagination.

189. As by the dim-eyed a variety of objects is seen and imagined while the dimness itself is neither a form (*rūpa*) nor a no-form (*arupa*), so is the relativity [discriminated] by the unknowing ones.

190. As is pure gold, water free from dirt, the sky without a cloud, so is [the Mind] pure when detached[1] from the false imagination.

191. Falsely-imagined existence is not, but from the relativity point of view it is, assertion and refutation are destroyed when one is freed from the imagination.

192. If the relativity-aspect of existence is, while the imagination is not, this means that there is a being apart from being and that a being is born of a non-being.

193. Depending on the false imagination there obtains the relativity-aspect of existence; from the conjunction of form and name there rises false imagination.

194. False imagination can never be perfect knowledge (*nishpanna*), it is not productive of anything else [but itself]; (132) then one knows what is meant by ultimate truth whose self-nature is purity.

195. There are ten kinds[2] of false imagination and six kinds of relativity; in the knowledge of Tathatā innerly attained there is no differentiation.

196. Truth consists in [knowing] the five Dharmas and also the three Svabhāvas; when the Yogin thus comprehends [the truth], he does not transgress Tathatā.

197. According to the form of relativity, there are those names that belong to false imagination; and the various aspects of false imagination arise from relativity.

---

[1] Throughout the text, *vikalpa* is translated "discrimination" or "imagination," but here the term is evidently used as negating the function of *kalpita* which stands in these verses for *parikalpita*.

[2] All the Chinese texts have "twelve" instead of "ten."

198. When well pondered with intelligence (*buddhi*) there is neither relativity nor false imagination; where perfect knowledge is, there is nothing [dualistically] existent; for how with intelligence can discrimination take place?

199. Where perfect knowledge is, the existent cannot be qualified with being and non-being; in what cannot be qualified with being and non-being, how can there be these two Svabhāvas?

200. Because of false imagination, the two Svabhāvas are established; where there is false imagination multitudinousness of things is recognised, which being purified the [spiritual] condition of the wise obtains.

201. Where there is false imagination there is multitudinousness of objects, which are discriminated under the aspect of relativity; if otherwise discriminated, one becomes attached to the teachings of the philosophers.

202. What is imagined being subjected to further imagination, there are various views from which rises the doctrine of causal origination; (**133**) when the dualistic discrimination is got rid of, there indeed is perfect knowledge.[1]

LVI

Further, Mahāmati said: Pray tell me, Blessed One, about the one vehicle that characterises the inner realisation of noble wisdom, whereby, Blessed One, I and other Bodhisattva-Mahāsattvas, becoming conversant with the one vehicle which marks the inner attainment of noble wisdom, may be established without depending on anybody else in the teaching of the Buddha.

Said the Blessed One: Then, Mahāmati, listen well and reflect within yourself as I tell you.

---

[1] This whole section treats of the threefold Svabhāva, chiefly explaining where Parikalpita (false imagination) is differentiated from Paratantra (relativity view). While the explanation sometimes appears quite complicated, the main point is clear enough. The Kalpita is a net of wrong interpretations woven about the Paratantra, which is the dualistic view of existence, and which is valid as far as it goes. But to reach the Nishpanna (perfect knowledge) it is necessary to transcend all forms of dualism, for the Paratantra is by no means ultimate truth.

CHAPTER TWO

Mahāmati the Bodhisattva-Mahāsattva said, Yes, I will, Blessed One; and gave ear to the Blessed One.

Thereupon the Blessed One said: In accordance with the authoritative teachings in which there are no discriminations, Mahāmati, let the Bodhisattva-Mahāsattva retire by himself to a quiet secluded place, where he may reflect within himself, not relying on anybody else, but by means of his own inner intelligence, in order to discard erroneous views and discriminations, make successive advances and exert himself to finally enter upon the stage of Tathagatahood. This, Mahāmati, is the characteristic feature of the inner realisation to be gained by means of noble wisdom.

What characterises the way of the one vehicle? I call it the one vehicle because thereby one recognises and realises the path leading to the one vehicle. How is this path of the one vehicle to be recognised and realised? The recognition of the one vehicle is obtained when there is no rising of discrimination by doing away with the notion of grasped and grasping and by abiding in the reality of suchness (*yathābhūta*). Mahāmati, this recognition of the one vehicle, (134) except by the Tathagata himself, has never been obtained before by anybody else—the philosophers, Śrāvakas, Pratyekabuddhas, Brahmans, etc. For this reason, Mahāmati, this is known as the one vehicle.

Mahāmati said: For what reason is it that the Blessed One speaks of the triple vehicle and not of the one vehicle?

The Blessed One replied: Because there is no teaching whereby the Śrāvakas and Pratyekabuddhas can realise Nirvana by themselves, I do not speak of the one vehicle. Thus, Mahāmati, the Śrāvakas and Pratyekabuddhas are disciplined, segregated, and trained in meditation according to the discourse of the Tathagata, whereby they are led to emancipation, and not by themselves.

Further, Mahāmati, as they have not yet destroyed the habit-energy (memory) of karma and the hindrance of knowledge, all the Śrāvakas and Pratyekabuddhas are unable to realise the egolessness of things and have not attained the inconceivable transformation-death, I preach to the Śrāvakas [and Pratyekabuddhas] the triple vehicle and not the one vehicle.[1] When, Mahāmati, destroying all the evil habit-energy, they realise the egolessness of things, they who are now free from the evil habit-energy will not be intoxicated by the Samādhis and will be awakened into the realm of no-evil-outflows. Now being taken into a super-world which is the realm of no-evil-outflows, they will gather up all the material for the attainment of the Dharmakāya which is of severeign power and beyond conception. So it is said:

203. The Deva vehicle, the Brahma vehicle, the Śrāvaka vehicle, (135) the Pratyekabuddha vehicle, and the Tathagata vehicle, of these I speak.

204. So long as there is a mind making conscious efforts, there can be no culmination as regards the various vehicles; when a revulsion takes place in the mind, there is neither a vehicle nor one who rides in it.

205. There is really no establishment of various vehicles, and so I speak of the one vehicle;[2] but in order to carry the ignorant I talk of a variety of vehicles.

206. There are three emancipations, and in all things there is no ego-substance; knowledge and passions are of the same nature, when [one is] emancipated they are discarded.

207. Like a piece of wood floating on the waves of the ocean, the Śrāvaka obsessed with individual marks is driven along [the stream of existence].

208. Though disengaged from the actively-functioning passions, they [the Śrāvakas] are still bound up with the habit-energy of the passions; intoxicated with the liquor of the Samādhi, they still have their abode in the realm of outflows.

209. In this there is no course of finality, nor retrogression either; [losing himself] in the attainment of the Samādhi-body, he is not at all awakened even to the end of kalpas.

210. Like unto the drunkard who, being awakened from his intoxication, regains his intelligence, [the Śrāvakas]

---

[1] Transfer *naikayānam* (line 9) to line 10 after *yānatrayam*.
[2] According to the Chinese translations.

will have the realisation of the Buddha's truth, which is his own body.

Here Ends the Second Chapter, [Known as] the "Collection of All the Dharmas," Taken from the *Laṅkāvatāra* of 36,000 [Ślokas].

[CHAPTER THREE]

LVII

(136) At that time again the Blessed One said this to Mahāmati the Bodhisattva-Mahāsattva: I will tell you, Mahāmati, about the various forms of the will-body; listen well and reflect well within yourself. I will tell you.

Mahāmati the Bodhisattva-Mahāsattva said; I will, Blessed One, and gave ear to the Blessed One.

The Blessed One then said this: There are three kinds of will-body, Mahāmati. What are the three? They are: (1) the will-body obtained in the enjoyment of the Samādhi; (2) the will-body obtained by recognising the self-nature of the Dharma; and (3) the will-body which is assumed [by a Bodhisattva according to] the class of beings [to be saved] and which perfects and achieves [without a thought of its own achievement]. By realising the higher stages successively after the first is attained, the Yogin will experience them [all].

Now, Mahāmati, what is the will-body attained in the enjoyment of the Samādhi? It is this: when [the Yogin] in the third, fourth, fifth stages removes the various discriminations going on in his mind and is at rest,[1] the waves of consciousness are no more stirred in the Mind-ocean and the Vijñāna functions are quieted, the bliss of which is

---

[1] It will be interesting for the Chinese readers of the *Laṅkāvatāra* to notice that the compound, *svacitta-vividha-viveka-vihāra*, is here read in three different ways by the three Chinese translators, showing how variously a Sanskrit compound allows itself to be interpreted. This is one of numerous such examples to be met with throughout the text.

Sung: 種種自心寂靜安住. The mind itself, variously [discriminating], grows quiet and finds its rest.

Wei: 自心寂靜行種種行. The mind itself is quiet and practises various deeds.

T'ang: 離種種心寂然不動. Discarding various [mentations], the mind is quiet and immovable.

enjoyed by him; and when he thus recognises the nonexistence of the external world, which is no more than his own mind, he is said to have the will-body.[1]

(137) What is the will-body obtained by recognising the self-nature of the Dharma? When [the Yogin] of the eighth stage has a thoroughgoing penetration into the nature of things which is like Māyā and not image-producing, he experiences a revulsion at the seat of consciousness and obtains the Samādhi known as Māyā-like and other Samādhis. By entering upon the Samādhis he gains a body which exhibits various powers of self-mastery and supernatural activity, which moves according to his wish as quickly as a flower opens up, which resembles Māyā, a dream, and a reflected image, and which is not a product of the elements but has something analogous to what is produced of the elements, which is furnished with all the differences appertaining to the world of forms and yet is able to follow up all the assemblages in the Buddha-lands. This is the body which has a thoroughgoing knowledge of the self-nature of the Dharma and for this reason is called will-body.

Now what is the will-body which is born in accordance with the class and which perfects and achieves? When [the Yogin] is thoroughly conversant with all the characteristics of self-realisation and its bliss which pervades the teachings of the Buddha, he is said to have the body which is willmade, born with [the class], perfecting and achieving. Mahāmati, you should exert yourself in order to have a thoroughly penetrating knowledge of these three marks of the will-body. So it is said:

1. My Mahāyāna is neither a vehicle, nor a sound, nor words; it is neither the truth, nor emancipation, nor the realm of imagelessness.

2. Yet the Mahāyāna is a vehicle on which the Samādhis are carried leading to various creative activities; the several forms of the will-body are adorned with the flowers of the sovereign will.

---

[1] Page 136, line 14, delete *abhāva* and *manaso*.

LVIII

(138) At that time again Mahāmati the Bodhisattva-Mahāsattva said this to the Blessed One: The five immediacies are preached by the Blessed One; and what are these five, Blessed One, which being committed by a son or a daughter of a good family cause them to fall into the Avici hell?

The Blessed One replied: Then, Mahāmati, listen well and reflect, for I will tell you.

Mahāmati the Bodhisattva-Mahāsattva said; Certainly, Blessed One, and gave ear to the Blessed One.

The Blessed One said thus to him: What are the five immediacies? They are: (1) the murdering of the mother, (2) of the father, (3) of the Arhat, (4) the breaking-up of the Brotherhood, and (5) causing the body of the Tathagata to bleed from malice.

Now what is meant by the mother of all beings? It is desire which is procreative, going together with joy and anger and upholding all with motherliness. Ignorance representing fatherhood brings about one's rebirth in the six villages of the sense-world. When there takes place a complete destruction of both roots, fatherhood and motherhood, it is said that mother and father are murdered. When there is a complete extermination of the subordinate group of passions such as anger, etc., which are like an enemy, a venomous rat, the murdering of the Arhat is said to take place. What is meant by the breaking-up of the Brotherhood? When there is a complete fundamental breaking-up of the combination of the Skandhas whose characteristic mark is a state of mutual dependence among dissimilarities, it is said that the Brotherhood is split up. (139) Mahāmati, when the body of the eight Vijñānas, which erroneously recognises individuality and generality as being outside the Mind—which is seen [by the ignorant] in the form of an external world—is completely extirpated by means of faulty discriminations, that is, by means of the triple emancipation and the non-outflows, and when thus the faulty mentality of the Vijñāna-Buddha is made to bleed, it is known as an immediacy-deed. These,

Mahāmati, are the five inner immediacies, and when they are experienced by a son or a daughter of a good family, there is an immediacy-deed of realisation as regards the Dharma.

Further, Mahāmati, there are five external immediacies which I will point out to you, in order that you and other Bodhisattvas in the future may thereby be saved from ignorance. What are these five? They are those immediacies which are described in the canonical texts, and those who commit these crimes can never experience any one of these manifestations, except those Transformation [-Buddhas] who are sustained by the power [of the Tathagatas] and have already attained a realisation. The Śrāvakas of transformation, Mahāmati, who are sustained by the sustaining power either of the Bodhisattvas or Tathagatas, may see somebody else practising deeds of wickedness, and they will repeatedly make great efforts to turn him away from his wickness and faulty views, and to make him realise the non-reality of wickedness and faulty views by laying down his burden. This is the way I demonstrate facts of the transformation, the sustaining power, and the realisation. Mahāmati, there is, however, no realisation for those who are sheer offenders of the immediacies, (140) except when they come to the recognition of the truth that an external world is nothing but[1] the Mind itself, seeing that body, property, and abiding place are discriminations, and that the notion of an ego and its belongings are to be kept away; or, when they are released from the fault of self-discrimination by encountering a good friend at some time or other, or at any time, and being born in some other path of existence. So it is said:

3. Desire is said to be the mother and ignorance the father; the Vijñāna which recognises an objective world is [compared to] the Buddha.

4. The secondary group of passions is the Arhat, the amassing of the five Skandhas the Brotherhood; as these are to be destroyed immediately they are known as immediacy-deeds.

[1] Page 140, line 1: *bhavana* is to be deleted.

LIX

Again Mahāmati said: Pray tell me, Blessed One, what makes the Buddhas and the Blessed Ones such as they are: that is, [what is] the Buddha-nature of the Buddhas?[1]

Said the Blessed One: when the egolessness of things as well as of persons is understood, when the knowledge of the twofold hindrance is thoroughly taken hold of, when the twofold death (*cyuti*) is accomplished, and when the twofold group of passions is destroyed, there, Mahāmati, is the Buddda-nature of the Buddhas and the Blessed Ones. When these teachings are experienced by the Śrāvakas and Pratyekabuddhas, this is their Buddha-nature. So it is said:

5. The twofold egolessness, the twofold group of passions, the twofold hindrance, and the inconceivable transformation-death,—when these are attained, there is the Tathagata.

LX

(141) At that time again, Mahāmati the Bodhisattva-Mahāsattva said this to the Blessed One: According to what deeper sense[2] did you make this announcement before the congregation, that "I am all the Buddhas of the past," and that "I have gone through many a birth in varieties of forms, being thus at times the king Māndhātṛi, Elephant, Parrot, Indra, Vyāsa, Sunetra, and other beings in my one hundred thousand births?"

Said the Blessed One: There are, according to the deeper sense, four kinds of sameness distinguished, Mahāmati, and the Tathagatas, Arhats, Fully-Enlightened Ones make this assertion: I was thus at that time the Buddha Krakucchanda, Kanakamuni, and Kāśyapa. What are the four kinds of sameness which are distinguished according to the deeper sense? They are: (1) sameness of letters, (2) sameness of words, (3) sameness of teachings, and (4) sameness of the body. According to this fourfold sameness in

---

[1] *Bhagavān buddhānām*, page 140, line 10, may better be dropped.

[2] *Samdhāya*. There is no reference to this in Wei and Sung. The term has a special sense here and elsewhere in the *Laṅkāvatāra*.

CHAPTER THREE 123

the deeper sense, the Tathagatas, Arhats, Fully-Enlightened Ones make the announcement before the congragation.

Now, Mahāmati, what is the sameness of letters? It is that my name is [spelt] B-u-d-d-h-a, and these letters are also used for other Buddhas and Blessed Ones; Mahāmati, these letters in their nature are not to be distinguished one from another; therefore, Mahāmati, there is the sameness of letters.

Now, Mahāmati, what is the sameness of words with regard to the Tathagatas, Arhats, and (142) Fully-Enlightened Ones? It is that sixty-four sounds of the Brahman language are distinguished by me, and these identical sixty-four sounds of the Brahman language are also uttered by the Tathagatas, Arhats, and Fully-Enlightened Ones, and their Kalaviṅka-like notes are the same with all of us, as we are indistinguishable in this respect.

Now, Mahāmati, what is the sameness of the body? It is that I and other Tathagatas, Arhats, Fully-Enlightened Ones are the same as regards our Dharmakāya and the [thirty-two] signs and the [eighty] minor excellencies of bodily perfection—no distinction existing among us, except that the Tathagatas manifest varieties of forms according to the different dispositions of beings, who are to be disciplined by varieties of means.

Now, Mahāmati, what is the sameness of the teaching? It is that I as well as they [other Tathagatas] are all conversant with the teachings belonging to the thirty-seven branches of enlightenment. According to the deeper sense which is concerned with this fourfold sameness, the Tathagatas, Arhats, Fully-Enlightened Ones make their announcement before the congregation. So it is said:

6. "I am Kāśyapa, Krakucchanda, and Kanakamuni"; this I preach who come out of the sameness for the sake of the sons of the Buddha.

LXI

Again Mahāmati said: It is said by the Blessed One that from the night of the Enlightenment till the night of the Parinirvana, the Tathagata (143) in the meantime has not uttered even a word, nor will he ever utter; for not-speaking is the Buddha's speaking. According to what deeper sense is it that not-speaking is the Buddha's speaking?

The Blessed One replied: By reason of two things of the deeper sense, Mahāmati, this statement is made. What are the two things: They are the truth of self-realisation and an eternally-abiding reality. According to these two things of the deeper sense the statement is made by me. Of what deeper sense is the truth of self-realisation? What has been realised by the Tathagatas, that is my own realisation, in which there is neither decreasing nor increasing; for the realm of self-realisation is free from words and discriminations, having nothing to do with dualistic terminology.

What is meant by an eternally-abiding reality? The ancient road of reality, Mahāmati, has been here all the time, like gold, silver, or pearl preserved in the mine, Mahāmati; the Dharmadhātu abides forever, whether the Tathagata appears in the world or not; as the Tathagata eternally abides so does the reason (*dharmatā*) of all things; reality foreover abides, reality keeps its order, like the roads in an ancient city. For instance, Mahāmati, a man who is walking in a forest and discovering an ancient city with its orderly streets may enter into the city, and having entered into it, he may have a rest, conduct himself like a citizen, and enjoy all the pleasures accruing therefrom. (144) What do you think, Mahāmati? Did this man make the road along which he enters into the city, and also the various things in the city?

Mahāmati said: No, Blessed One.

The Blessed One said: Just so, Mahāmati, what has been realised by myself and other Tathagatas is this reality, the eternally-abiding reality (*sthititā*), the self-regulating reality (*niyāmatā*), the suchness of things (*tathatā*), the realness of things (*bhūtatā*), the truth itself (*satyatā*). For this reason, Mahāmati, it is stated by me that from the night of the Tathagata's Enlightenment till the night of his entrance into Nirvana, he has not in the meantime uttered, nor ever will utter, one word. So it is said:

7. From the night of Enlightenment till that of Nirvana, I have not in the meantime made any proclamation whaever.[1]

8. It is on account of the deeper meaning that the eternally-abiding reality of self-realisation is talked of by me; and between myself and [all the other] Buddhas, in this respect, there is no distinction whatever.

LXII

At that time, Mahāmati made this request of the Blessed One: Pray tell me, Blessed One, about the being and non-being of all things; and when myself and other Bodhisattva-Mahāsattvas are freed of the notions of being and non-being, may we quickly attain supreme enlightenment.

(145) The Blessed One replied: Then, Mahāmati, listen well and reflect well within yourself; I will tell you.

Mahāmati the Bodhisattva-Mahāsattva said, Certainly, Blessed One, and gave ear to the Blessed One.

Then the Blessed One said: People of this world are dependent on two things, Mahāmati, that is, they are dependent on the idea of being and on that of non-being, and they fall into the views whereby they take pleasure either in nihilism or in realism. They imagine emancipation where there is no emancipation.

Now, Mahāmati, who are the people dependent on the notion of being? It means this that they regard the world as rising from causation which is really existent, and that the actually existing and becoming world does not take its rise from causation which is non-existent. This will not be the case if the world is something non-existing. They thus talk of the really-existing world as arising from the reality of causation. This is the realistic view of causation as held by some people.

Now, Mahāmati, what is meant by being dependent upon the idea of non-being? It means, Mahāmati, admitting greed, anger, and folly, and yet discriminating as regards the non-reality of what makes up greed, anger, and folly; and, Mahā-

[1] The Zen masters frequently refer to this important declaration.

mati, there is one who does not admit the reality of things because of their being devoid of individual marks; and there is another who, seeing that the Buddhas, Śrāvakas, and Pratyekabuddhas are free from greed, anger, and folly, because of all things being devoid of individual marks, [think that greed, anger, and folly] do not exist.

Now, Mahāmati, who of these is the one doomed to ruin?

Said Mahāmati; Blessed One, it is he who, admitting greed, anger, and folly, yet refuses to admit them.

(146) The Blessed One said: Well said indeed, Mahāmati! Again thou hast indeed spoken well, Mahāmati! Not only is he himself doomed to ruin because of his notion of greed, anger, and folly as existent and yet as not-existent, but he ruins even the character of the Buddha, the Śrāvaka, and the Pratyekabuddha. Why? Because the passions are not to be taken hold of innerly and outwardly, because they are neither different nor not-different. Mahāmati, greed, anger, and folly too are not to be taken hold of innerly as well as outwardly; they have no substance of their own and they are not to be admitted; Mahāmati, as there is no reality in the nature of greed, anger, and folly, [he who fails to understand this] is the one who ruins the character of the Buddha, Śrāvaka, and Pratyekabuddha. The Buddha, Śrāvaka, and Pratyekabuddha are by nature emancipated as there is in them no cause for being bound and binding; Mahāmati, [on the other hand,] where there is a state of being bound there are the binding and the cause of bondage. [And yet there is] one who talks thus, [that is, denies causation]; such is doomed to ruin. Mahāmati, this characterises nihilism and realism.

This is stated by me in accordance with the deeper sense. It is better to cherish the notion of an ego-substance as much as Mount Sumeru than to have the notion of emptiness derived from the self-conceited view of being and non-being. One who is conceited in the view of being and non-being is indeed doomed to ruin. Those who are delighted in cherishing notions of individuality and generality fail to understand that an external world is nothing but Mind itself and has no reality; and as they do not understand this they regard things external as transient, for they suffer every moment changes which follow one after another, now splitting, now dividing, while the Skandhas, Dhātus, and Āyatanas succeeding one another and combining with one another, now come forward and (147) now pass away. They who thus disregarding words of the scriptures are given up to wrong discriminations are also doomed to ruin. So it is said:

9. As far as the duality of being and non-being extends, there is the realm of intellection; when this realm vanishes, intellection completely ceases.

10. When the external world is not grasped [as real] there is neither causation nor reality; there is the essence of suchness (*thatatā*), which is the [spiritual] realm of the wise.

11. Those who believe in the birth of something that has never been in existence and, coming to exist, finally vanishes away,—which leads them to assert that things come to exist, things pass away, according to causation,—such people have no foothold in my teaching.

12. It is not by the philosophers, not by the Buddhas, not by myself, not by anybody else, but by causation that being obtains; how can one talk of non-being?

13. When being obtains by causation, who can bring about non-being? By reason of the wrong views based on the doctrine of birth, being and non-being are discriminated.

14. When it is realised that there is nothing born, nothing passing away, there is no way to admit its being and not-being; the world is to be regarded as quiescent.

LXIII

At that time again Mahāmati the Bodhisattva-Mahāsattva requested of the Blessed One, saying: Pray point out to me, Blessed One; pray point out to me, Sugata; pray point out to me, Tathagata, Arhat, Fully-Enlightened One! Pray tell me, Most Excellent One! (148) What is the characteristic of the realisation by which I and other Bodhisattva-Mahāsattvas, becoming thoroughly conversant with its meaning, may quickly attain the highest enlightenment, and, relying upon themselves, will not be led away by any speculations or philosophies?

Said the Blessed One: Then listen well, Mahāmati, and well reflect within yourself; I will tell you.

Mahāmati the Bodhisattva-Mahāsattva said; Certainly, I will; and gave ear to the Blessed One.

Thereupon the Blessed One said this: There are two ways of characterising the realisation attained by all the Śrāvakas, the Pratyekabuddhas, and the Bodhisattvas: the realisation itself and the teaching [about it]. Now, Mahāmati, by the realisation itself is meant that it is the realm of inner attainment; its characteristic features are that it has nothing to do with words, discriminations, and letters; that it leads one up to the realm of non-outflows; that it is the state of an inner experience; that it is entirely devoid of philosophical speculations and [the doings of] evil beings; and that, destroying philosophical speculations and [the doings of] evil beings, it shines out in its own inner light of attainment. These, Mahāmati, are the characteristics of the realisation.

Now, Mahāmati, what is meant by the teaching [concerning it]? It is variously given in the nine divisions of the doctrinal works; it keeps one away from the dualistic notions of being and non-being, of oneness and otherness; first making use of skilful means and expedients, it induces all beings to have a perception [of this teaching] so that whoever is inclined towards it, may be instructed in it. This, Mahāmati, is the characteristic of the teaching. Let, therefore, Mahāmati, you and other Bodhisattva-Mahāsattvas (149) exert yourselves in this.

15. Realisation and teaching, self-attainment and doctrinal instruction—those who have an insight into the difference will not be led away by philosophical authorities.

16. There is no truth in any object that is imagined by the ignorant; deliverance is where there is no objective world; why is this not sought by the speculators?

17. The world of the Saṁskritas is observed as the continuation of birth-and-death, whereby dualisms are nour-

ished, and because of this perversion [the truth] is not perceived.

18. There is just one truth, which is Nirvana—it has nothing to do with the Manas (intellection); the world seen as subject to discrimination resembles a plantain tree, a dream,[1] a vision.

19. No greed there is, no anger, nor folly either, and again, no personal ego; from desire start the Skandhas, which resemble a dream.

LXIV

At that time again Mahāmati the Bodhisattva-Mahāsattva requested of the Blessed One, saying: Pray tell me, Blessed One, pray tell me, Sugata, regarding what characterises wrong discrimination (*abhūtaparikalpa*). Blessed One, tell me as to the how, what, why, and who of wrong discrimination, which, when rising and going on, constitutes what is known as wrong discrimination; that is to say, to what kind of thought is the term wrong discrimination applicable? or what kind of discrimination is to be called wrong?

(150) The Blessed One said: Well said, well said, Mahāmati; and again, well said, indeed, Mahāmati! You who have been admitted [into the order of Bodhisattvas], Mahāmati, think of this matter which is worth asking about, for the welfare of many people, for the happiness of many people, because of your compassion for the world, for the benefit of the multitudes, for the welfare and happiness of celestial beings and humankind. Therefore, Mahāmati, listen well and reflect well within yourself as I tell you.

Certainly, Blessed One; said Mahāmati the Bodhisattva-Mahāsattva, and gave ear to the Blessed One.

Then the Blessed One said thus to him: When the multitudinousness of objects is wrongly imagined [as real] and attached to, discrimination goes on evolving; and, Mahāmati, as people are attached tenaciously to the notion of grasping, as they have not ascertained in their minds as to the nature of the objective world which is no more than the

---

[1] The text has *skandha*; but *svapna* seems to be better.

Mind itself, as they have fallen into the dualistic view of being and non-being, and, Mahāmati, as they are nourished by the habit-energy of the views and discriminations of the philosophers, they perceive the multitudinousness of external objects [as real] and become attached to them; and for this reason a system of mentation—mind and what belongs to it—is discriminated and is spoken of [as real], and with the assertion of an ego-soul and its belongings, the system goes on functioning.

Said Mahāmati: As you say, Blessed One, when the multitudinousness of external objects is wrongly imagined [as real] and attached to by people, discrimination goes evolving on; and they fall into the dualistic view of being and non-being,[1] they nourish the views and discriminations of the philosophers which are based on the notion of grasped and grasping; (151) and as they perceive the multitudinousness of external objects [as real] and become attached to them, a system of mentation—mind and what belongs to it—is discriminated and is spoken of [as real] and goes on functioning owing to the fact that the external world is not recognised as nothing but the Mind itself, and that the multitudinousness of things is tenaciously clung to as subject to [the notion of] being and non-being. This being the case, Blessed One, the multitudinousness of external objects which is characterised with the dualism of being and non-being, is to be said neither existent nor non-existent, and does not render itself to the formation of the philosophical views. [Inasmuch as the external world owes its existence to discrimination, it in itself must be said to be devoid of all forms of dualism.] Blessed One, in the same way the highest reality is declared to be devoid of [all forms of logical analysis such as] the means of proof, sense-perception, syllogistic arguments, illustration, reasoning, etc. How is it, Blessed One, that while, on the one hand, the discrimination of multiplicity is said to go on operating on the strength of the attachment which attaches itself to the multiplicity of external unrealities, the attachment, on the other hand, to

[1] This is omitted in T'ang.

CHAPTER THREE 131

the highest reality does not give rise to discrimination which goes on functioning in its own way? Is it not, Blessed One, unfair reasoning on your part to say, "It gives rise [to discrimination]" in one place, and to say in another place, "It does not"? [1]According to the Blessed One, depending on and attaching to the dualism of being and non-being, there evolve views characteristic of wrong discrimination as when the magician produces varieties of people that are not at all real and complete objects. Thus signs of existence and non-existence are falsely imagined and go on so imagined; [but in fact existence itself is] devoid of discrimination. If so, how does one come to cherish the dualism as held by a man of the world?

Said the Blessed One: Mahāmati, discrimination, indeed, does not evolve, nor is it put away. Why? Because there is no evolving of discrimination as regards being and non-being; because the perception of objective realities is not real; because all that is seen is to be recognised as nothing but the Mind itself. (152) Mahāmati, discrimination does not evolve, nor is it put away. But, Mahāmati, for the sake of the ignorant who are addicted to discriminating the multiplicity of things which are of their own Mind, it is said by me that discrimination whose first function is to produce effects takes its rise owing to the attachment to the aspect of multiplicity as charactersitic of objects. How otherwise, Mahāmati, can the ignorant and simple-minded have an insight into the Mind itself which they discriminate, and see themselves freed from the notion of an ego and what belongs to it, and also freed from the wrong conception of cause and effect? And, again, how can they recognise that there is nothing but Mind itself and cause a revulsion at the inmost seat of consciousness (*cittāśraya*)? How can they have a clear perception of all the stages and attain the inner realisation of the Tathāgatas, which transcends the five Dharmas,

---

[1] The whole passage below does not appear in Sung. The text seems to be confused and it is difficult to make out what it really means. The present translation is merely tentative. It mainly follows the T'ang interpretation; Wei gives no sense as far as one can see.

the three Svabhāvas, and the idea of reality as well as discrimination? For this reason, Mahāmati, I state that discrimination takes its rise from our attachment to the multiplicity of objects which are not real, and that emancipation comes from our thoroughly understanding the meaning of reality as it is and also the meaning of multiplicity of things which evolve from discrimination. So it is said:

20. Those who, regarding the world as evolving from causes and conditions, are attached to these notions as well as to the fourfold proposition, fail to understand my teaching.

21. The world cannot be predicated anywhere as being, or as non-being, or as being-and-non-being, as is discriminated by the ignorant who regard it as subject to causes and conditions.

22. When the world is seen [to be unpredicable with such notions as] being, non-being, or being-and-non-being, (153) a change takes place in the mind, and egolessness is attained.

23. All things are unborn because they are born of causation; anything that is born of causation is an effect, and from an effect nothing is produced.

24. From an effect no effect is produced; [if you assert this,] you commit the fault of a double effect; and this double effect being untenable, no existence comes from an effect.

25. When the Saṁskṛita [i.e. anything produced] is regarded as free from [the dualism of] depended and depending, there decidedly is Mind-only, and hence my teaching of Mind-only.

26. The [Mind as] norm is the abode of self-nature which has nothing to do with a world of causation; of this norm which is perfect existence and the highest Brahma,[1] I speak.

27. An ego-soul is a truth belonging to thought-construction, in which there is no real reality; the self-nature of the Skandhas is also a thought-construction, as there is no reality in it.

---

[1] The Chinese all have "the Pure" for this. Does it mean "the Absolute" cleansed of all dualistic impurities?

28. The sameness is of four kinds: individual forms, cause, the coming into being,[1] and the sameness of non-ego is the fourth: these are subjects of discipline for the Yogins.

29. [There is a state which is] removed from all philosophical views, free from imagined and imagining, of no attainment, and of no birth—this I call Mind-norm.

30. Of neither existence nor non-existence do I speak, but of Mind-only which has nothing to do with existence and non-existence, and which is thus[2] free from intellection.

(154) 31. Suchness (*tathatā*), emptiness, realm of truth (*dharmadhātu*), the various forms of the will-body—these I call Mind-only.

32. Multiplicity of objects evolves from the conjunction of habit-energy and discrimination; it is born of Mind, but is regarded by people as existing outwardly: this I call Mind-only.

33. The external world is not, and multiplicity of objects is what is seen of Mind; body, property, and abode—these I call Mind-only.

LXV

At that time Mahāmati the Bodhisattva-Mahāsattva said this to the Blessed One: This is said by the Blessed One that the Bodhisattva-Mahāsattva and others should not grasp meaning [or reality, *artha*], according to words. But, Blessed One, why should not the Bodhisattva-Mahāsattva grasp meaning from words? What are words? What is meaning?

Said the Blessed One: Then, Mahāmati, listen well and reflect within yourself well; I will tell you.

Thereupon said Mahāmati the Bodhisattva-Mahāsattva, Certainly, Blessed One; and gave ear to the Blessed One.

The Blessed One then said this to him: Now, Mahāmati, how is speech produced? Depending on discrimination and habit-energy [or memory] as the cause, there is the conjunction and the distinction of sounds and letters, which,

---

[1] *Bhāvaja*, coming into existence.
[2] *Tathā*, not *tathatā*, according to the Chinese versions.

issuing from the teeth, jaws, palate, tongue, lips, and the cavity of the mouth, make mutual conversations possible. This is speech. Now, Mahāmati, what is meaning? (155) The Bodhisattva-Mahāsattva is said to have grasped meaning well, when, all alone in a lonely place, he walks the path leading to Nirvana, by means of his transcendental wisdom (*prajñā*) which grows from learning, thinking, and meditation, and causing a revulsion first at the source of habit-energy by his self-knowledge (*svabuddhi*), abides on the stages of self-realisation where he leads a life full of excellent deeds.

Further, Mahāmati, the Bodhisattva-Mahāsattva who is conversant with words and meaning observes that words are neither different nor not-different from meaning and that meaning stands in the same relation to words. If, Mahāmati, meaning is different from words, it will not be made manifest by means of words; but meaning is entered into by words as things [are revealed] by a lamp. It is, Mahāmati, like a man carrying a lamp to look after his property. [By means of this light] he can say: This is my property and so is kept in this place. Just so, Mahāmati, by means of the lamp of words and speech originating from discrimination, the Bodhisattva-Mahāsattvas can enter into the exalted state of self-realisation which is free from speech-discrimination.

Further, Mahāmati, if a man becomes attached to the [literal] meaning of words and holds fast to their agreement in regard to the original state of Nirvana which is unborn and undying, the triple vehicle, the one vehicle, the five [Dharmas], mentation, the [three] Svabhāvas, etc., he will come to cherish views either affirmative or negative. As varieties of objects are seen in Māyā and are discriminated [as real], statements are erroneously made, discriminations erroneously go on. (156) It is by the ignorant that discriminations thus go on; it is otherwise with the wise.[1]

So it is said:

[1] The reading is more or less after T'ang. *Abhiniveśaṁ pratītya* (p. 155, line 15) is dropped, and *tad yathā mahāmate anyathā hi māyā-vaicitryaṁ draṣṭavyam anyathā* (p. 155, line 17—p. 156, line 1) does not

34. [1]Those who following words, discriminate and assert various notions, are bound for hell because of their assertions.

35. The ego-soul is not with the Skandhas, nor are the Skandhas in the ego-soul. They are not as they are discriminated, nor are they otherwise.

36. The reality of objects is seen being discriminated by the ignorant; if it were so as they are seen, all would be seeing the truth.

37. As all things are unreal, there is neither defilement nor purity; things are not as they are seen, nor are they otherwise.

LXVI

Further, Mahāmati, I will tell you about the features of Jñāna (absolute knowledge) and Vijñāna (relative knowledge)[2]; and when you and other Bodhisattva-Mahāsattvas are well conversant with these distinctive features of Jñāna and Vijñāna, you will quickly realise supreme enlightenment. There are three kinds of Jñāna—worldly, super-worldly, and transcendental. Now, worldly knowledge belongs to the philosophers and to the ignorant and simple-minded who are attached to the dualistic views of being and non-being. Super-worldly knowledge belongs to all the Śrāvakas and Pratyekabuddhas who are attached to the notions of individuality and generality. Transcendental knowledge which is free from the dualism of being and non-being, belongs to the Bodhisattvas and takes its rise when they thoroughly examine things of imagelessness, see into the state of no-birth and no-annihilation, and realise egolessness at the stage of Tathagatahood.[3]

appear in T'ang, and as it is partly a repetition of what precedes, not to speak of its making the whole passage obscure, it is omitted in this translation.

[1] According to the Chinese versions.
[2] The use of *vijñāna* in this sense is unusual in the *Laṅkā*; while *jñāna, āryajñāna, prajñā,* and *buddhi* are frequently used as synonyms.
[3] The passage between "Now, worldly knowledge" and "Tathagatahood" which is restored here according to T'ang and Sung, is found in the Sanskrit text inserted after the next paragraph, p. 157, ll. 8–13.

(157) Vijñāna is subject to birth and destruction, and Jñāna is not subject to birth and destruction. Further, Mahāmati, Vijñāna falls into [the dualism of] form and no-form, being and non-being, and is characterised with multiplicity; but Jñāna is marked with the transcendence of [the dualism of] form and no-form. Further, Mahāmati, Vijñāna is characterised with accumulation and Jñāna with non-accumulation. Jñāna is of three kinds: that which assertains individuality and generality, that which assertains birth and decay, and that which assertains no-birth and no-decay.

Further, Mahāmati, Jñāna is devoid of attachment; Vijñāna attaches itself to the multitudinousness of objects. Again, Vijñāna is produced from the concordance of the triple combination;[1] Jñāna, in its self-nature, has nothing to do with combination or concordance. Again, Mahāmati,[2] Jñāna is characterised with unattainability; it is the inner state of self-realisation by noble wisdom, (158) and as it neither enters nor goes out, it is like the moon in water. So it is said:

38. Karma is accumulated by Citta, and discriminated by Jñāna; and one acquires by Prajñā the state of imagelessness and the powers.

39. Citta is bound up with an objective world, Jñāna evolves with reflection; and Prajñā evolves in the exalted state of imagelessness and in the excellent conditions.

40. Citta, Manas, and Vijñāna are devoid of thoughts and discriminations;[3] it is the Śrāvakas and not the Bodhisattvas that try to reach reality by means of discrimination.

41. The Tathagata's Jñāna is pure, [resting] in quietude in the most excellent patience [or recognition of truth];

---

[1] Read *trisaṁgatyutpādayogalakṣaṇam* (lines 15–16), and *asaṁgatiyogasva°* (line 16), according to Sung and T'ang.

[2] T'ang and Sung have inserted here: Vijñāna is characterised with attainability.

[3] Is this in accord with the general drift of thought maintained in the text? T'ang and Sung have: Citta, Manas, and Vijñāna, when devoid of thought and discrimination, attain the state of non-discrimination; this belongs to the Bodhisattvas and not to the Śrāvakas.

CHAPTER THREE 137

it is productive of excellent sense and is devoid of purposiveness (*samudācāra-varijitam*).

42. Prajñā, with me, is of three kinds; whereby the wise grow powerful, individual signs are discriminated, and all things are manifested.[1]

43. My Prajñā has nothing to do with the two vehicles, it excludes the world of beings; that of the Śrāvakas evolves from their attachment to the world of beings; the Tathagata's Prajñā is spotless[2] because of its being in accord with Mind-only.

LXVII

Further, Mahāmati, there are nine kinds of transformation as held by the philosophers endorsing the doctrine of transformation. They are: (1) the transformation of form; **(159)** (2) the transformation of characteristics; (3) the transformation of cause; (4) the transformation of concordance; (5) the transformation of view; (6) the transformation of origin; (7) the transformation of nature; (8) the transformation of manifest conditions; and (9) the transformation of manifest work. These, Mahāmati, are the nine views of transformation expounded by all the philosophers in accordance with their secret teaching, and they are all founded upon the dualism of being and non-being.

Now, Mahāmati, by the transformation of form is meant the alteration of form in appearance as gold takes various shapes when made into all kinds of ornament. For example: gold is seen made into a bracelet, a necklace, a fylfot, or what not; though the gold itself remains the same, varieties of articles [made of it] are all different in form, that is, in their transformations. In the same way, Mahāmati, there is a general transformation of things which is discriminated by other philosophers as coming from a causal agency. They are not right, nor are they otherwise. All differentiation in transformation is to be regarded as due to discrimination, such as the thickening of milk into curds and the ripening

---

[1] After T'ang.
[2] Read *amalā*, not *matā*.

of fruit into a liquor. Mahāmati, like this thickening and ripening each transformation is a transformation rising from discrimination, which is discriminated by the philosophers; really there is nothing transformed, for the external objects of which being and non-being are discriminated, are what is seen of Mind itself and have no reality of their own. In the same way, Mahāmati, what is regarded by the ignorant and simple-minded as the evolving of objects is no more than the discrimination of their own mind, and, (160) Mahāmati, there is really nothing evolving, nothing disappearing, as it is like seeing things that evolve in a vision and a dream. Mahāmati, it is like perceiving the rise and disappearance of things in a dream; it is like the birth and death of a barren woman's child. So it is said:

44. The transformation of the form in time, and the embracing [of the soul] in the elements and sense-organs, which is in its middle-way existence (*antarābhava*)—they who [thus] imagine [the birth of a child] are not wise men.

45. The Buddhas do not discriminate the world as subject to the chain of origination; but they regard the causation which rules this world as something like the city of the Gandharvas.

LXVIII

At that time, Mahāmati the Bodhisattva-Mahāsattva asked the Blessed One to explain concerning the deep-seated attachment to the existence of all things and the way of emancipation, saying: Pray tell me, Blessed One, pray tell me Tathagata, Arhat, Fully-Enlightened One, concerning the characteristics of our deep attachment to existence and of our detachment from it. When I and other Bodhisattva-Mahāsattvas understand well the distinction between attachment and detachment, we shall know what is the skilful means concerning them, and shall no more become attached to words according to which we grasp meaning. When we understand well what is meant by attachment to the existence of all things and the detachment from them, we shall destroy our discrimination of words and letters; and, by means of our wisdom (*buddhi*), enter into all the Buddha-lands and assemblies; be well stamped with the stamp of the powers, the self-control, the psychic faculties, and the Dhāraṇīs; and, well furnished with the wisdom (*buddhi*) in the ten inexhaustible vows and shining with varieties of rays pertaining to the Transformation Body, (**161**) behave ourselves with effortlessness like the moon, the sun, the jewel, and the elements; and hold such views at every stage as are free from all the signs of self-discrimination; and, seeing that all things are like a dream, like Māyā, etc., [shall be able to] enter the stage and abode of Buddhahood, and deliver discourses on the Dharma in the world of all beings and in accordance with their needs, and free them from the dualistic notion of being and non-being in the contemplation of all things which are like a dream and Māyā, and free them also from the false discrimination of birth and destruction; and, finally, [shall be able to] establish ourselves where there is a revulsion at the deepest recesses [of our consciousness], which is more than words [can express].

Said the Blessed One: Well said, well said, Mahāmati! Listen well to me then, Mahāmati, and reflect well within yourself; I will tell you.

Mahāmati the Bodhisattva-Mahāsattva said, Certainly, I will, Blessed One; and gave ear to the Blessed One.

The Blessed One said to him thus: Mahāmati, immeasurable is our deep-seated attachment to the existence of all things the significance of which we try to understand after words. For instance, there are the deep-seated attachments to signs of individuality, to causation, to the notion of being and non-being, to the discrimination of birth and no-birth, to the discrimination of cessation and no-cessation, to the discrimination of vehicle and no-vehicle, of Saṁskṛita and Asaṁskṛita, of the characteristics of the stages and no-stages, and the attachment to discrimination itself, and to that arising from enlightenment, the attachment to the discrimination of being and non-being on which the philosophers are so dependent, and the attachment to the triple vehicle and the one vehicle, which are discriminated.

These and others, Mahāmati, are the deep-seated attachments cherished by the ignorant and simple-minded (162) to their discriminations. Tenaciously attaching themselves to these the ignorant and simple-minded go on ever discriminating like the silk-worms who, with their own thread of discrimination and attachment, enwrap not only themselves but others and are charmed with the thread; and thus they are ever tenaciously attached to the notions of existence and non-existence. [But really] Mahāmati, there are no signs here of deep-seated attachment or detachment. All things are to be seen as abiding in solitude where there is no evolving of discrimination. Mahāmati, the Bodhisattva-Mahāsattva should have his abode where he can see all things from the viewpoint of solitude.

Further, Mahāmati, when the existence and non-existence of the external world are understood to be due to the seeing of the Mind itself in these signs, [the Bodhisattva] can enter upon the state of imagelessness where Mind-only is, and [there] see into the solitude which characterises the discrimination of all things as being and non-being and the deep-seated attachments resulting therefrom. This being so, there are in all things no signs of a deep-rooted attachment or of detachment. Here, Mahāmati, is nobody in bondage, nobody in emancipation, except those who by reason of their perverted wisdom[1] recognise bondage and emancipation. Why? Because in all things neither being nor non-being is to be taken hold of.

Further, Mahāmati, there are three attachments deep-seated in the minds of the ignorant and simple-minded. They are greed, anger, and folly; and thus there is desire which is procreative and is accompanied by joy and greed; closely attached to this there takes place a succession of births in the [five] paths. Thus there are the five paths of existence for all beings who are found closley attached [to greed, anger, and folly]. When one is cut off from this attachment, (163) no signs will be seen indicative of attachment or of non-attachment.

[1] Read *buddhyā*, instead of *budhyā*.

CHAPTER THREE

Further, Mahāmati, depending upon and attaching to the triple combination which works in unison, there is the continuation of the Vijñānas incessantly functioning; and because of the attachment there is a continued and deep-felt assertion of existence. When the triple combination which causes the functioning of the Vijñānas no more takes place, there is the triple emancipation, and when this is kept in view, there is no rising of any combination. So it is said:

46. The imagining of things not existent—this is characteristic of attachment [deeply seated in all beings]; when the truth of this is thoroughly understood, the net of attachment is cleared away.

47. The ignorant take hold of the knowledge of existence according to words and are bound up like the silk-worm with their own discriminations; hence their ignorance of attachment [deeply seated in their minds].

LXIX

Further, Mahāmati said: According to the Blessed One, in all things that are variously discriminated by discrimination there is no self-nature, as it is nothing but [the creation of] false imagination (*parikalpita*); if, Blessed One, it is but [the creation of] false imagination and there is nothing in the world which is to be conceived as indicative of self-nature, does it not, Blessed One, come to this, according to your statement, that there is neither defilement nor purification, because all things are of the nature of false imagination?

Said the Blessed One: Mahāmati, it is just as you say. The self-nature of things is the discrimination of the ignorant and simple-minded, and it is not as it is discriminated by them. (164) Mahāmati, it is the creation of false imagination; nothing indicative of self-nature is to be ascertained. But, Mahāmati, there is the self-nature of things such as is ascertained by the wise, by their wise knowledge, by their wise insight, by their wise transcendental vision.

Said Mahāmati: Blessed One, if there is the self-nature of things such as is ascertained by the wise, by their wise knowledge, by their wise insight, by their wise transcendental vision which is neither human nor celestial vision, and if there is no such self-nature as is discriminated by the ignorant and simple-minded, how, Blessed One, can the ignorant and the simple-minded abandon their discriminations, as they have no way to recognise the presence of an exalted reality (*āryabhāvavastu*)? For they are neither perverted nor unperverted, Blessed One, [that is, they are what they are]. Why? Because they are unable to have an insight into the self-nature of exalted reality, because they see the course of things in the aspect of being and non-being. And Blessed One, the reality[1] cannot be such as is discriminated even by the wise, because the aspect of reality as it is in itself cannot be an object [of discrimination by anybody]; because, Blessed One, what appears to the wise as the self-nature of reality is no more than the creation of their imagination, which is predicable with the notion of causation and no-causation; that is, they also cherish in their own way the idea of a being with self-nature. [And they would say] that this is a realm that belongs to somebody else and is not that [of the ignorant]. This is committing the fault of non-finality, for thus what constitutes the self-nature of reality becomes impossible to know. Blessed One, what is derived from the imagination cannot be the self-nature of reality. How is it (165) that while things are said to exist owing to the imagination[2] [or discrimination], they are said again not to be such as are imagined?

Blessed One, [it is true that] according to the way the imagination is carried on, the self-nature of reality conceived may vary; for when the cause is not alike, the notion of reality that thus comes to be cherished may not be alike. But according to you, Blessed One, while the imagination is kept on going with the wise as well as with the ignorant, the latter alone fail to see reality as it is; and yet you tell us that the reason why it is said that things are not really such

---

[1] *Vastu* and *bhāva* are both used here in the sense of reality.
[2] Throughout this text, *parikalpa, vikalpa, pratikalpa,* and *prativikalpa* are used interchangeably

as are imagined by the imagination is to make all beings discard their imagination. Now, Blessed One, is it that in order to have all beings free from the notion of being [which is realism] and of non-being [which is nihilism], you in turn make them cherish a realistic view of existence[1] by telling them to uphold the idea of the self-nature of reality, whereby they are led to cling to the realm of noble wisdom? Why do you deny the truth of solitude by teaching the doctrine of reality whose self-nature is [according to you] noble wisdom?[2]

Said the Blessed One: Mahāmati, it is not true that I deny truth of solitude, nor that I fall into a realistic view by upholding the noble doctrine of self-existing reality. But in order to save all beings from becoming frightened, who are addicted from beginningless past to the notion of self-nature, it is told them that there is truth of solitude, after making them realise by means of noble wisdom that reality in its self-nature is made the subject of attachment [by the ignorant]. Mahāmati, the doctrine of self-nature is not taught by me. But, Mahāmati, those who have realised by themselves truth of solitude as it really is and are abiding in it, will see that [this existence of] error has no form; and thereby knowing that what is seen is nothing but the Mind itself, (166) they are kept away from [dualistically] viewing an external world[3] under the aspect of being and non-being; they are stamped well with the stamp of suchness which is gained by the triple emancipation; they will have an intuition into the self-nature of all things by the wisdom which is acquired within themselves, and thus get away from such ideas of reality as to lead themselves to realism and nihilism.

[1] Not *abhiniveśānnāstitvadrishṭih* (lines 8–9) as it stands in the text, but *abhiniveśādastitva°* according to T'ang and Sung.

[2] This whole passage ascribed to Mahāmati is one of the most difficult passages in the *Laṅkāvatāra*, partly due to discrepancies. The translator is not at all satisfied with the result. In the Appendix the whole section 69 is given in the original Sanskrit together with all the four versions, Chinese and Tibetan.

[3] *Viviktadharma......yathātathya* (lines 2–3) being a curious repetition of the preceding lines is dropped in the translation.

LXX

Further, Mahāmati, the thesis: "All things are unborn" is not to be maintained by the Bodhisattva-Mahāsattva as valid. Why? Of this thesis it is to be stated that anything of which something is asserted partakes thereby of the nature of being, and that the reason for this thesis is characterised with the quality of birth; while it is being asserted by the Bodhisattva-Mahāsattva that all things are unborn, the very assertion destroys his thesis. The thesis that all things are unborn acts against the one who holds it because it is born of the principle of mutuality. Even when this thesis of no-birth is to be maintained within the extent of existence itself, the notion of no-birth cannot hold itself in it, and the statement, the thesis, that all things are unborn is destroyed since it is dependent on the members of the syllogism. As regards the thesis maintaining the no-birth[1] of being and non-being, Mahāmati, this thesis, to be valid, must be within the limits of existence itself; but there is no aspect of existence which can be regarded either as being or as non-being. If, Mahāmati, the no-birth of all things is to be asserted by this thesis of no-birth, (167) the very attempt defeats the thesis itself.[2] Therefore, this thesis is not to be upheld. Because many faults come out in connection with the members of the syllogism, and because in these syllogistic members there is a mutual mixing-up of reasons, this thesis is not to be upheld.

As with [the thesis that] all things are unborn, so with [the thesis that] all things are empty and have no self-nature—neither is to be maintained by the Bodhisattva-Mahāsattva. But, Mahāmati, this is to be pointed out by the Bodhisattva-Mahāsattva, that things in their self-nature are like Māyā, like a dream; for they are in one way perceived [as existing] and in another way are not perceived

---

[1] Literally, "is not born."

[2] *Pratijñāyām......pratijñā bhavati* (lines 1-4) is omitted in the translation following T'ang and Sung, as it does not add to the clearing up of the meaning.

CHAPTER THREE 145

[as such], and all things are thus seen in [two] ways, in accordance either with knowledge or ignorance. Let it be pointed out that all things are like Māyā and a dream, except when the feeling of fear is aroused in the minds of the ignorant. Mahāmati, the ignorant and the simple-minded are addicted to the views of being and non-being, and are liable to tremble [at our teaching]; Mahāmati, let them not be frightened away from the Mahāyāna. So it is said:

48. There is no self-nature, no thought-construction, no reality, no Ālaya-vijñāna; these, indeed, are so many discriminations cherished by the ignorant who like a corpse are bad logicians.

(168) 49. All things are unborn—[this thesis] is established by all the philosophers; [but] nothing whatever is ever born, [no establishment is needed,] things are all linked by causation.

50. All things are unborn—no such discrimination is made by transcendental knowledge; when a certain conclusion is made depending on a cause, there is no sound judgment in it.

51. As a hair-net is what is wrongly perceived by those who are dim-eyed, so existence discriminated [as real] is due to the wrong discrimination of the ignorant.

52. The triple world is no more than thought-construction (*prajñapti*), there is no reality in its self-nature; by means of this thought-constructed reality, logicians go on discriminating.

53. Individual form, reality, thought-construction,—these are [only] a mental disturbance; transcending all this, my sons will walk where there is no discrimination.

54. As in a mirage in the air, the thought of water is cherished where there is no water, so things are seen by the ignorant otherwise than by the wise.

55. The insight of the wise, who move about in the realm of imagelessness, is pure, is born of the triple emancipation, is released from birth and destruction.

56. Where all things are wiped away, even a state of imagelessness ceases to exist for the Yogins; in the sameness

of existence and non-existence, the fruit [of wisdom] is born to the wise.

(169) 57. How does existence cease to exist? How does the sameness take place? When the mind fails to understand [the truth], there is disturbance inside, outside, and in the middle; with the cessation [of the disturbance] the mind sees the sameness.

LXXI

Further, Mahāmati said: It is told by the Blessed One, again, that [true] knowledge is gained independent of any object supporting it, and whatever statements one makes about it are no more than thought-construction, and that as this thought-construction is not to be seized as real, the seizing act of the seizer itself ceases, and when there is thus no seizing, knowledge which is known as discrimination no more evolves. Now, Blessed One, [how is transcendental knowledge unobtainable?] Is it unobtainable because of our not recognising the generality and individuality of things, their pluralities, their unities? Or is it unobtainable because [such ideas as] individuality, generality, multiplicity, and self-nature overpower one another? Or is it unobtainable because of the obstructions presented by a wall, a mountain, an earth-work, a rampart, or by earth, wind, water, or fire? Or because of remoteness or nearness? Or does the knowledge fail to obtain its object of cognition because of [the imperfection of] the sense-organs due to youth, age, or blindness? If, Blessed One, knowledge was not obtainable because of our not recognising individuality, generality, unity and plurality, then, Blessed One, such cannot be [transcendental] knowledge; it is to be called ignorance (ajñāna), for in spite of the fact that objects to be known are before us we do not know them. Again, if knowledge is unobtainable because [such ideas as] individuality, generality, multiplicity, and self-nature overpower one another, such is ignorance (ajñāna). (170) Blessed One, it is not [transcendental] knowledge. Where there is something to be known, Blessed One, knowledge evolves; where there is nothing, none evolves;

knowledge is possible [only] where there is a correspondence with that which is known. Again, if knowledge is unobtainable because of the obstruction presented by a wall, mountain, earthwork, rampart, or by earth, water, wind, or fire, or due to farness or nearness, or on account of the imperfection of the sense-organs as in the case of an infant, the aged, and the blind, such as is unattainable is not [transcendental] knowledge; it is ignorance, for the object to be known is there but the knowing faculty is lacking.

Said the Blessed One: Mahāmati, such [knowledge as is unobtainable] is not ignorance, such is [transcendental] knowledge; Mahāmati, it is not ignorance. It is not because of the deeper sense that I say this, but when [we know that] there is knowledge gained independent of any supporting object, whatever statements we make about it are no more than thought-constructions. That [transcendental] knowledge is unobtainable is due to the recognition that there is nothing in the world but what is seen of the Mind, and that these external objects to which being and non-being are predicated are non-existent. As this [knowledge] is unobtainable, there is no evolving of knowing and known, and as thus the triple emancipation is realised, there is unattainable knowledge [which is transcendental]. But logicians being under the habit-energy of the wrong reasoning which has been carried on since beginningless time as to existence and non-existence are unable to know all this, and, while not knowing it, they are concerned with [such notions as] external objects, substances, forms, indications, existence and non-existence; and yet they declare that the cessation of discrimination is [the state of] the Mind-only. As they are tenaciously clinging to the thought of an ego-soul and all that belongs to it, they are really unable to understand what is meant by the doctrine of Mind-only, (**171**) and go on discriminating knowing and known. And because of their discriminating knowing and known, they think of things as existent and non-existent, and declaring that [transcendental knowledge] is unobtainable, abide in nihilism. So it is said:

58. If [transcendental] knowledge fails to see an objective world which lies before it, such is ignorance and not knowledge; this teaching belongs to the logicians.

59. If [transcendental] knowledge fails to see, though various obstructions far and near, its own unique object that does not present itself [as an object], such is to be called wrong knowledge.

60. If [transcendental] knowledge fails to know, on account of defective senses such as infancy, old age, and blindness, its own object which is present, such is to be called wrong knowledge.

LXXII

Further, Mahāmati, the ignorant and simple-minded keep on dancing and leaping fascinated with their wrong reasonings, falsehoods, and self-discriminations, and are unable to understand the truth of self-realisation and its discourse in words; clinging to the external world which is seen of the Mind itself, they cling to the study of the discourses which are a means and do not know properly how to assertain the truth of self-realisation which is the truth unspoiled by the fourfold proposition.

Said Mahāmati: Blessed One, it is just as you say. Pray tell me, Blessed One, about the characteristic features of the truth of self-realisation and about the discourses on it, whereby I and other Bodhisattva-Mahāsattvas in future time, understanding what they are, may keep ourselves away from the wrong logicians such as the philosophers and those who belong to the vehicles of the Śrāvaka and the Pratyekabuddha.

(172) Said the Blessed One: Then, Mahāmati, listen well and reflect well within yourself; I will tell you.

Certainly, Blessed One; said Mahāmati the Bodhisattva-Mahāsattva and gave ear to the Blessed One.

The Blessed One said this to him: Mahāmati, there are two forms of teaching the truth attained by the Tathagatas, Arhats, Fully-Enlightened Ones of the past, present, and future. They are: the teaching by discourses, and the teaching by the establishment of self-realisation. What is meant by the studying of the discourses is this, Mahāmati: there are various materials and canonical texts and discourses by which sentient beings are taught according to their dispositions and inclinations. What then is the truth of self-realisation by which the Yogins turn away from discriminating what is seen of the Mind itself? There is an exalted state of inner attainment which does not fall into the dualism of oneness and otherness, of bothness and not-bothness; which goes beyond the Citta, Manas, and Manovijñāna; which has nothing to do with logic, reasoning, theorising, and illustrating; which has never been tasted by any bad logicians, by the philosophers, Śrāvakas, and Pratyekabuddhas, who have fallen into the dualistic views of being and non-being—this I call self-realisation. This, Mahamati, is what characterises the truth of self-realisation and discoursing on it, and in this you and the other Bodhisattva-Mahāsattvas are to discipline themselves. So it is said:

61. I have two forms of teaching the truth: self-realisation and discoursing. I discourse with the ignorant and [disclose] self-realisation to the Yogins.

LXXIII

(173) At that time again, Mahāmati the Bodhisattva-Mahāsattva said this to the Blessed One: It was told at one time by the Blessed One, the Tathagata, the Arhat, the Fully-Enlightened One, that the Lokāyatika who is [skilled in] various forms of incantation and in the art of eloquence is not to be honoured, adored, and reverently attended upon; for what one gains from such devotions is worldly enjoyments and not the Dharma [or Truth]. For what reason is this said, Blessed One, that by devoting ourselves to the Lokāyatika who is skilled in varieties of incantations and in the art of eloquence, worldly enjoyments are gained but not the Dharma [or Truth]?

Said the Blessed One: The Lokāyatika who is skilled in varieties of incantations and in the art of eloquence, Mahāmati, puts the minds of the ignorant in utter confusion by means of various reasonings, by [clever manipulation of] words and phrases, and what he teaches being the mere prattle of a child as far as one can make out is not at all in accordance with truth nor in unison with sense. For this reason, Mahāmati, the Lokāyatika is said to be skilled in varieties of incantations and in the art of eloquence. He attracts the ignorant by making clever use of various words, [but] he never leads them to the way of truth and right teaching. As he himself does not understand what all things mean, he puts the minds of the ignorant into utter confusion by his dualistic views, thus ruining himself. Not being released of the transition from one path to another, not understanding that there is nothing but what is seen of the Mind itself, and attaching himself to the idea of self-nature in external things, the Lokāyatika knows no deliverance from discrimination. For this reason, Mahāmati, the Lokāyatika who is clever in various incantations (174) and in the art of eloquence, being thus never emancipated from such calamities[1] as birth, age, disease, sorrow, lamentation, pain, and despair, leads the ignorant into bewilderment by means of various words, phrases, reasons, examples, and conclusions.

Mahāmati, Indra was a brilliant [Lokāyatika] whose knowledge made him master of many treatises and who was himself the author of a work on sound. He had a disciple who assuming the body of a serpent went up to heaven and got into the society of the god Indra. Making up a thesis he challenged the god: Either your one-thousand-spoked chariot be smashed to pieces, or every one of my own serpent-hoods be cut off. In the argument the Lokāyatika disciple who had assumed the form of a serpent defeated [the god-opponent], whereupon the one-thousand-spoked chariot was smashed to pieces. The disciple then came down again to this world. In such a way, Mahāmati, [the Lokāyatika] has a system composed of various reasonings and exemplifications, and, knowing well even the minds of the animal world, puts the gods and fighting demons in utter confusion by means of various words and phrases; he then makes them

[1] Read *apāyāsa* instead of *upāyāsa*.

tenaciously adhere to the notion of coming and going (*āyavyaya*); how much more human beings! For this reason, Mahāmati, the Lokāyatika is to be shunned, for he carries with him the cause leading to the birth of pain. No homage, no reverence, no service is to be shown him. Mahāmati, the attainment of the Lokāyatika does not go beyond the realm of the body and knowledge belonging to it, though he may explain his materialism by using varieties of words and phrases (**175**) amounting to a hundred thousand. But in after times, after five hundred years, divisions will take place [among his followers] leading them to wrong reasonings and demonstrations; divisions will abound because of this, not being able to hold disciples. Thus, Mahāmati, materialism splitting into many parties and adhering to varieties of reasonings is explained by the philosophers, each of whom clings to his way of reasoning as he knows no truth existing by itself. While this is not at all the case with [all] the philosophers who have their own treatises and doctrines, materialism is asserted under various disguises which are explained by a hundred thousand different methods; there is in them [also] no truth existing by itself, and they do not recognise that theirs is materialism because of their stupidity.[1]

Said Mahāmati: If all the philosophers teach materialism by means of various words, phrases, examples, and conclusions, which are not the truth as it is, but are their own selfish assertions tenaciously maintained, does not the Blessed One too teach materialism by means of various words and phrases, to the assemblages of the gods, demons, and human beings, who come from various countries—I say, materialism which is not the truth of self-realisation but is something like the discourses of all the philosophers?

The Blessed One said: I do not teach materialism, nor coming-and-going (*āyavyaya*). But I teach, Mahāmati, that which is not coming-and-going. Now, Mahāmati, coming means production and mass, it is born of accumulation. Going, Mahāmati, means destruction. That which is not

[1] Read *mohāt* instead of *mohohāt*.

coming-and-going is designated unborn. (176) Mahāmati, I do not teach anything approaching the discrimination of the philosophers. For what reason? Because there are no external objects, there is nothing to get attached to; when one abides in Mind-only, beyond which there is no external world, dualism ceases; as there is no realm of form based on discrimination, one comes to recognise that there is nothing but what is seen of the Mind itself; and for these reasons the discrimination of what is seen of the Mind itself does not take place. Owing to the cessation of discrimination, one enters into the triple emancipation where is the state of no-form, emptiness, and effortlessness. Hence it is called deliverence.

I remember, Mahāmati, when I was staying in a certain place, a Brahman Lokāyatika approached where I was and having approached suddenly asked me, saying: Gautama, is all created?

I said this to him: Brahman, if all is created, this is the first school of materialism.

Guatama, is all uncreated?

Brahman, if all is uncreated, this is the second school of materialism. Thus [to state that] all is non-eternal, or that all is eternal, or that all is born, or that all is unborn, this, Brahman, is the sixth school of materialism.

Again, Mahāmati, the Brahman Lokāyatika said this to me: Gautama, is all one? Is all different? Is all characterised with bothness? Is all characterised with not-bothness? Is all to be regarded as subject to causation since all is seen as born of varieties of causes?

This, Brahman, is the tenth school of materialism.

Again, Gautama, is all explainable? Is all unexplainable? Is there an ego-soul? Is there no ego-soul? Is this world real? (177) Is this world not-real? Is there another world? Is there no other world? Is another world existent or non-existent?[1] Is there emancipation? Is there no emancipation? Is all momentary? Is all not momentary? Are

---

[1] The Chinese translations omit this question.

space, Apratisamkhya-nirodha,[1] and Nirvana, O Gautama, are they created or uncreated? Is there the middle existence? Is there no middle existence?

I then said this to him, Mahāmati: If so, Brahman, this is materialism. It is not mine. O Brahman, it is your worldly philosophy. I explain, Brahman, that the triple world has its cause in the habit-energy of discrimination going on since beginningless time on account of error and wrong reasoning: for discrimination takes place. Brahman, because it is not recognised that there is no external world but the Mind itself, and not because an external world is seen as the object of cognition. According to the philosophers, there is a triple concordance of an ego-soul, sense-organs, and an objective world, but such is not mine. Brahman, I do not belong to the school of causation, nor to the school of no-causation, except that I teach the chain of origination as far as the thought-constructed world of grasped and grasping exists depending on discrimination. This is not understood by you and others who cherish the notion of an ego-soul and its continuity. Mahāmati, space, Nirvana, and causation exist in enumeration; as realities they are unobtainable. Hence the question whether they are created or not requires no answering.

Again, Mahāmati, the Brahman Lokāyatika said this: Is the triple world to be regarded as caused by ignorance, desire, and action? or is it causeless?

Brahman, this twofold question again belongs to materialism.

Gautama, are all things to be conceived (178) under the aspect of individuality and generality?

This, too, Brahman, belongs to materialism. So long as there is a mental perturbation which makes one cling to an objective world of discrimination, there is materialism.

Further, Mahāmati, this Brahman materialist said this to me: Gautama, is there any philosophy that is not of the world? All the truth that is taught by all the philosophers

[1] "Annihilation taking place without premeditation"—one of the three non-effect-producing objects (*asamskṛita*).

by means of varieties of words and phrases, by means of reasons, examples, and conclusions, by general consent, Gautama, belongs to me.

Brahman, there is something that does not belong to you, though it is not beyond the truth of general consent, nor independent of varieties of words and phrases, and further, it is not out of accord with reason.

[The Brahman asked,] Is there any philosophy that is not of the world and yet belongs to the general opinion of the world?

Brahman, there is that which does not belong to materialism and which is not reached by your wisdom nor by that of the philosophers who cling to false discriminations and wrong reasonings as they fail to see the unreality of external objects. By this is meant the cessation of discrimination. When it is recognised that there is nothing beyond what is seen of the Mind itself, the discrimination of being and non-being ceases; as thus there is no external world as the object of perception, discrimination abides in its own abode.[1] This is not of materialism; it belongs to me, it does not belong to you. By abiding in its own abode is meant that it ceases to evolve; as discrimination is no more born, it is said to have ceased to evolve. This, Brahman, is not of materialism. In short, Brahman, if there is any coming-and-going of the Vijñānas, (**179**) a vanishing-and-appearing, a solicitation, an attachment, an intense affection, a philosophical view, a theory, an abode, a touch, the clinging to various signs, assemblage, continuity,[2] desire (*trishṇā*), and

---

[1] A better reading of the Nanjo text may be to follow the T'ang and the Wei, according to which *vikalpaḥ* (1.16) is negated and *svasthāne 'vatishṭhate* forms a separate sentence, thus: "Discrimination ceases, and one abides in the self-abode." That by this self-abode is meant the self-abode of reality is gathered from such phrases as *yathābhūtārthasthāna-darśanam* (p. 200, 1.6), *yathābhūtāvasthānadarśanam* (p. 112, 1.6), *yathābhūtasvalakshaṇāvasthānāvasthitam* (p. 124, 1.1), *vikalpasyāpravṛitteh svastho, loko nishkriyaḥ* (p. 199, 1.3), etc. The self-abode of reality is where reality is seen as it is in itself, or as the suchness of existence, or as something solitary (*viviktadharma*), i.e. absolute.

[2] *Saṃtatiḥ* instead of *sattvānām*, according to T'ang and Sung.

attachment to a cause, this, Brahman, is materialism of yours but not mine.

Mahāmati, I was thus questioned by the Brahman materialist, who came to me, and when he was thus sent off he silently departed.

At that time there came to the Blessed One the King of the Nāgas, called Krishṇapakshaka, who assumed the body of a Brahman and said thus: Gautama, is there not another world?

Now, young man, whence do you come?

Gautama, I am come from White Isle.

Brahman, that is another world.

The young man thus refuted and put to silence made himself invisible without asking me anything about my own teaching, which stands in opposition to his;[1] he thought within himself: This son of the Śākyas stands outside of my own system; he is a pitiable fellow, he belongs to the school which holds the cessation of signs and causes, he talks of the cessation of discrimination which will take place when there is the cognition of an external world as something seen of one's own discrimination. And, Mahāmati, you too ask me how, for one who serves the Lokāyatika skilled in various incantations and in the art of eloquence, there are worldly enjoyments and not the attainment of the Dharma.

Said Mahāmati; What is meant, Blessed One, by the words, "the objects of worldly enjoyment" and "the Dharma"?

(180) Said the Blessed One: Well said, well said, Mahāmati! You have thought deeply about this twofold meaning, having in view present and future generations. Then, Mahāmati, listen well and reflect well within yourself; I will tell you.

Certainly, Blessed One; said Mahāmati the Bodhisattva-Mahāsattva and gave ear to the Blessed One.

The Blessed One said this to him: What is meant by a worldly object of enjoyment, Mahāmati? It means that

---

[1] There is no allusion in the Chinese versions to this dialogue between Krishnapakshaka and the Buddha.

which can be touched, attracted by, wiped off, handled, and tasted; it is that which makes one get attached to an external world, enter into a dualism on account of a wrong view, and appear again in the Skandhas, where, owing to the procreative force of desire, there arise all kinds of disaster such as birth, age, disease, death, sorrow, lamentation, pain, despair, etc. This is called the object of worldly enjoyment by myself and other Buddhas. This, Mahāmati, is the attainment of worldly enjoyments and not that of the Truth. It is materialism which one learns by serving the Lokāyatika.

Mahāmati, what is meant by the attainment of the Dharma (Truth)? When the truth of Self-mind and the twofold egolessness are understood, and further, when the nature of the egolessness of things and persons is seen into, discrimination ceases to assert itself; when the various stages of Bodhisattvahood are thoroughly perceived one after another, the Citta, Manas, and Manovijñāna are turned away; and when one enters upon the path of baptism by the wisdom of all the Buddhas, and takes hold of the [ten] inexhaustible vows,[1] one becomes (181) sovereign master of all things by virtue of a life of effortlessness. Hence it is called the Dharma, as one is thereby released from all philosophical views, unsound reasonings, discriminations, and dualistic notions. As a rule, Mahāmati, the philosophical views lead the ignorant, though not the wise, to a dualism, that is, to nihilism and eternalism. Eternalism rises from embracing a doctrine of no-causation, while nihilism rises from believing in the annihilation of causal conditions and in the non-existence of a cause. I teach, however, the Dharma so called which is [subject to] the conditions of rising, abiding, and destruction. This, Mahāmati, is the conclusion with regard to worldly enjoyment and the Dharma. So it is said:

62. Beings are subdued by the reception (saṁgraha),[2] and are brought into subjection by the moral precepts (śīla); they are removed from philosophical views by transcendental

---

[1] Read anishṭhāpada, instead of anadishṭhāpada.
[2] There are four ways of receiving others, catvāri saṁgrahavastūni: charity, kindly spirit, benevolent deeds, and impartiality.

knowledge (*prajñā*) and are nourished by the emancipations.[1]

63. All that is taught by the philosophers to no purpose is materialism; where the realistic view of cause and effect is cherished, there is no self-realisation.

64. I teach to my group of disciples one self-realisation which has nothing to do with cause and effect, being free from materialism.

65. There is nothing but that which is seen of the Mind itself, the duality too is of the Mind; while existence[2] is [observed as divided into] the grasped and the grasping, it has nothing to do with eternalism or nihilism.

(182) 66. As long as mentation goes on, there is materialism; when there is no rising of discrimination, the world is seen as of Mind itself.

67. "Coming" (*āyam*) means the originating of the objective world as effect, and "going" (*vyayam*) is the not-seeing[3] of the effect; when one thoroughly understands the "coming-and-going," discrimination ceases.

68. Eternity and non-eternity, the made and not-made, this world and that world—all these and other [ideas] belong to materialism.

LXXIV

At that time again, Mahāmati the Bodhisattva-Mahāsattva said this to the Blessed One: Nirvana, Nirvana is talked of by the Blessed One; what does this term designate? What is the Nirvana that is discriminated by all the philosophers?

Said the Blessed One: Then, Mahāmati, listen well and reflect well within yourself; I will tell you.

Certainly, Blessed One; said Mahāmati the Bodhisattva-Mahāsattva and gave ear to the Blessed One.

The Blessed One said this to him: As to such Nirvanas as are discriminated by the philosophers, there are really

---

[1] Missing in Sung.
[2] *Abhāvena*(?) in Sung.
[3] According to the Chinese translations.

none in existence. Some philosophers conceive Nirvana to be found where a system of mentation no more operates owing to the cessation of the Skandhas, Dhātus, and Āyatanas, or to the indifference to the objective world, or to the recognition that all things are impermanent; (183) or where there is no recollection of the past and present, just as when a lamp is extinguished, or when a seed is burnt, or when a fire goes out, because then there is the cessation of all the substrate, which is explained by the philosophers as the non-rising of discrimination. But, Mahāmati, Nirvana does not consist in mere annihilation.

Again, some explain deliverance by going to another quarter and abode, as when a wind stops blowing, when the discrimination of objects ceases. Again, some philosophers explain deliverance by the getting-rid of the [dualistic] view of knower and known. Some conceive deliverance to be the cessation of discrimination where one sees permanence and impermanence.

Again, some explain the discrimination of various forms as the bearer of pain, and yet not understanding that there is nothing but what is seen of the Mind itself, are alarmed by the notion of form, and seek their happiness in formlessness.[1] In this they cherish the notion of Nirvana.

Again some conceive this to be Nirvana: that in consideration of generality and individuality recognisable in all things inner and outer, they are never destroyed, maintaining their being throughout the past, present, and future. Again some conceive that Nirvana is an ego-soul, a being, a vital force, a nourisher, a supreme spirit, and the indestructability of all things.

Again, Mahāmati, some philosophers owing to their foolishness declare this to be Nirvana: that there is a primary substance, there is a supreme soul, and they are seen differently by each, and that they produce all things from the transformations of the qualities.

Some conceive Nirvana to consist in the extinction of

---

[1] According to the Chinese translations, *nimitto* (line 10) is to be cancelled.

merit and demerit; some in the destruction of the passions by means of knowledge; (**184**) some in regarding Iśvara as the free creator of the world. Some think that the world is born of interaction and that there is no [special] cause other than this cause, and clinging to it they have no awakening because of stupidity, and they conceive Nirvana to consist in this non-awakening.

Again, Mahāmati, some philosophers conceive Nirvana to be the attaining of the true path. Some cherish the thought of Nirvana as where there is the union of qualities and their owner, from which there is oneness and otherness, bothness and not-bothness. Some imagine that Nirvana is where they see the self-nature of things existing all by its own nature, such as the variegated feathers of the peacock, variously formed precious stones, or the pointedness of a thorn.

Some, Mahāmati, conceive Nirvana in the recognition of the twenty-five Tattvas (truths); some in the king's observance of the teaching of the six virtues. Some, seeing that time is a creator and that the rise of the world depends on time, conceive that Nirvana consists in recognising this fact. Again, Mahāmati, some conceive being to be Nirvana, some non-being, while some conceive that all things and Nirvana are not to be distinguished one from the other.

All these views of Nirvana severally advanced by the philosophers with their reasonings are not in accord with logic, nor are they acceptable to the wise. Mahāmati, they all conceive Nirvana dualistically and in a causal connection. By these discriminations, Mahāmati, all philosophers imagine Nirvana, but there is nothing rising, nothing disappearing here, [and there is no room for discrimination.] Mahāmati, each philosopher relying on his own text-book from which he draws his understanding and intelligence, examines [the subject] and sins against [the truth], because [the truth] is not such as is imagined by him; [his reasoning] ends in setting the mind to wandering about and becoming confused, as Nirvana is not to be found anywhere.

Again, Mahāmati, there are others who, roaring with

their all-knowledge as a lion roars, explain Nirvana in the following wise: that is, Nirvana is where it is recognised that there is nothing but what is seen of the Mind itself; where there is no attachment to external objects, existent or nonexistent; where, getting rid of the four propositions, there is an insight into the abode of reality as it is; where, recognising the nature of the Self-mind, (185) one does not cherish the dualism of discrimination; where grasped and grasping are no more obtainable; where all logical measures are not seized upon as it is realised that they never assert themselves; where the idea of truth is not adhered to but treated with indifference because of its causing a bewilderment; where, by the attainment of the exalted Dharma which lies within the inmost recesses of one's being, the two forms of egolessness are recognised, the two forms of passions subsided, and the two kinds of hindrance cleared away; where the stages of Bodhisattvahood are passed one after another until the stage of Tathagatahood is attained, in which all the Samādhis beginning with the Māyopama (Māyā-like) are realised, and the Citta, Manas, and Manovijñāna are put away:[1] [here indeed they say Nirvana is to be found].

69. Nirvana is severally conceived by the philosophers; (186) but theirs is no more than imagination, it is not the way of emancipation.

70. Released of bound and binding and free from all expediencies, the philosophers imagine they are emancipated, but emancipation is not to be found there.

71. Divided into many a school are the systems of the philosophers; there is thus no emancipation in them, because of their imagination stupidly carried on.

72. Wrongly imbued with the ideas of cause and effect, all the philosophers are beguiled, and their is thus no emancipation for them who are of the dualistic school of being and non-being.

73. The ignorant are delighted with discoursing and

---

[1] This whole paragraph which ought to be where it is in the present translation, is put after the paragraph preceding the last one in the Sanskrit text and also in Sung. Delete *kalpayanti* (p. 185, 1. 6).

false reasoning [but] they are unable to raise any great intelligence towards truth (*tattva*), discoursing is a source of suffering in the triple world, while truth is the extinguisher of suffering.

74. Like an image seen in a mirror, which is not real, the Mind is seen by the ignorant in a dualistic form in the mirror of habit-energy.

75. When it is not thoroughly understood that there is nothing but what is seen of the Mind itself, dualistic discriminations take place; when it is thoroughly understood that there is nothing but what is seen of the Mind itself, discrimination ceases.

76. Mind is no other than multiplicity, [and yet it is] devoid of qualified and qualifying; forms are visible but not in the way as seen discriminated by the ignorant.

77. The triple world is no other than discrimination, there are no external objects; discrimination sees multiplicity, this is not understood by the ignorant.

(187) 78. [The truth] is told [differently] discriminated in the different sutras because of names and notions; [yet] apart from words no meaning is attainable.

LXXV

At that time Mahāmati the Bodhisattva-Mahāsattva said this to him: Tell me, Blessed One, Tathagata, Arhat, Fully-Enlightened One, concerning the self-nature of Buddhahood, whereby I and other Bodhisattva-Mahāsattvas, understanding well what constitutes the self-nature[1] of the Tathagata, may have both ourselves and others awakened [in the truth].

The Blessed One said: Then, Mahāmati, ask me as you desire, according to which I will answer.

Mahāmati replied: Blessed One, is the Tathagata, the Arhat, the Fully-Enlightened One to be considered unmade or made, an effect or a cause, predicated or predicating, an expression or that which is expressed, knowledge or that which is knowable? Is the Blessed One different from all these expressions, or not?

[1] *Tathāgata-svabhāvakuśalā*, instead of *svakuśalā*.

The Blessed One said: If the Tathagata, Arhat, Fully-Enlightened One is to be described by those expressions, he is neither made nor unmade, neither an effect nor a cause. Why? Because the error of dualism would here be committed. If, Mahāmati, the Tathagata is something made, he is impermanent; if he is impermanent, anything made would be a Tathagata, which is not desired by myself and other Tathagatas. If he is something unmade, his self-essence being attainment, all the preparations brought forward [for the realisation of Tathagatahood] will be useless, (188) like a hare's horns, or a barren woman's child, because of their never having been made. That which is neither an effect nor a cause, Mahāmati, is neither a being nor a non-being; and that which is neither a being nor a non-being is outside the four propositions. The four propositions, Mahāmati, belong to worldly usage. That which is outside the four propositions is no more than a word, like a barren woman's child. Mahāmati, a barren woman's child is a mere word and is beyond the four propositions. As it is beyond them, the wise know it to be not subject to measurement. So is the meaning of all the terms concerning the Tathagata to be understood by the wise.

It is told by me that all things are egoless; by this is meant, Mahāmati, that they are devoid of selfhood; hence this egolessness. What I mean is that all things have each its own individuality which does not belong to another, as in the case of a cow and a horse. For example, Mahāmati, the being of a cow is not of horse-nature, nor is the being of a horse of cow-nature. This [exemplifies] the case of neither being nor non-being. Each of them is not without its own individuality, each is such as it is by its own nature. In the same way, Mahāmati, things are not each without its own individuality, they are such as they are, and thus the ignorant and simple-minded fail to understand the signification of egolessness by reason of their discrimination; indeed, they are not free from discrimination. The same is to be known exactly about all things being empty, unborn, and without self-nature.

In the same way the Tathagata and the Skandhas are neither not-different nor different. If he is not different from the Skandhas, he is impermanent as (**189**) the Skandhas are something made. If they are different, they are two separate entities; the case is like a cow's horns. As they look alike, they are not different; as the one is short and the other long, they are different. [This can be said] of all things. Mahāmati, the right horn of a cow is thus different from her left horn; so is the left from the right; the one is longer or shorter than the other. The same can be said of varieties of colours. Thus the Tathagata and the Skandhas are neither different nor not-different the one from the other.

In the same way, the Tathagata is neither different nor not-different from emancipation, he can be described in terms of emancipation. If the Tathagata is different from emancipation, he partakes of the nature of a material object; if he does he is impermanent. If he is not different, there will be no distinction in the attainments of the Yogins, and, Mahāmati, a distinction is seen in the Yogins; therefore, [the Tathagata] is neither different nor not-different [from emancipation].

In the same way, knowledge is neither different nor not-different from that which is known. That, Mahāmati, which is neither eternal nor not-eternal, neither effect nor cause, neither effect-producing nor not-effect-producing, neither knowledge nor that which is knowable, neither predicated nor predicating, neither the Skandhas nor different from the Skandhas, neither that which is expressed nor expression, nor bound-up with oneness and otherness, with bothness and not-bothness,—this is something removed from all measurement; that which is removed from all measurement is not expressible in words;[1] that which is not expressible[1] is something unborn; that which is unborn is not subject to destruction; that which is not subject to destruction (**190**) is like space, and, Mahāmati, space is neither an effect nor a cause. That which is neither an effect nor a cause is something unconditioned. That which is unconditioned

[1] After Sung.

goes beyond all idle reasonings. That which goes beyond all idle reasonings, that is the Tathagata. Mahāmati, this is the essence of perfect enlightenment, this is the self-nature of Buddhahood which is removed from all senses and measurements. So it is said:

79. That which is released from senses and measurements is neither an effect nor a cause; it has nothing to do with knowledge and that which is to be known; it is free from predicated and predicating.

80. There is something which is nowhere to be seen by anybody as the Skandhas, causation, enlightenment; of that which is nowhere to be seen by anybody, what description can we make?

81. It is not something made nor unmade, it is neither an effect nor a cause, it is neither the Skandhas nor not-Skandhas, nor is it other than the combination.

82. There is something that is not to be seen by the discrimination of its being, nor is it to be known as non-existent; such is the self-essence of all things.

83. Accompanied by being, there is non-being; accompanied by non-being there is being; as thus non-being is not to be known [by itself], being is not to be discriminated.

84. Those who cling to mere words, not knowing what is meant by an ego-soul and egolessness, are immersed in dualism; they are corrupted and lead the ignorant to corruption.

(**191**) 85. When they see my religion liberated from all detriments, they behold properly, they do not defile the world-leaders.

LXXVI

At that time again, Mahāmati the Bodhisattva-Mahāsattva said this to the Blessed One: Tell me, Blessed One; tell me, Sugata. Mention is made in the canonical books of the Blessed One's being subject neither to birth nor to destruction, and it is declared by you that this being subject neither to birth nor to destruction is an epithet of the Tathagata. Now, Blessed One, by this being subject neither to birth nor to destruction, is a non-entity meant? And is it another name for the Tathagata, as is declared by the Blessed One? It is taught by the Blessed One that all things are subject neither to birth nor to destruction because they are not to be seen in the dualistic aspect of being and non-being. If all things are unborn, Blessed One, no one can take hold of anything because nothing has ever been born; and if that is another name of something, what can this something be, Blessed One?

The Blessed One said: Then, Mahāmati, listen well and reflect well within yourself; I will tell you.

Certainly, Blessed One, said Mahāmati the Bodhisattva-Mahāsattva and gave ear to the Blessed One.

The Blessed One said this to him: Mahāmati, the Tathagata is not a non-entity; nor is he to be conceived as all things are, as neither born nor disappearing; nor is he to look around for causation [in order to appear before others]; nor is he without signification; I refer to him as unborn. (192) Nevertheless, Mahāmati, there is another name for the Tathagata when his Dharmakāya assumes a will-body. This is what goes beyond the comprehension of the philosophers, Śrāvakas, Pratyekubuddhas, and those Bodhisattvas still abiding in the seventh stage. The unborn, Mahāmati, is synonymous with the Tathagata.

For instance, Mahāmati, Indra is [sometimes known as] Śakra, [sometimes? as] Purandara; hand is *hasta, kara, pani*; the body is *tanu, deha, śarīra*; the earth is *pṛthivī, bhūmi, vasumdhara*; the sky is *kha, ākāśa, gagana*; all these objects each in its way are designated with many names, synonymously used and discriminated; but on account of these different names different objects are not to be imagined, nor are they without their self-nature. The same, Mahāmati, can be said of myself, for I come within the range of hearing of ignorant people, in this world of patience, under many names, amounting to a hundred thousand times three asaṁkhyeyas, and they address me by these names not knowing that they are all other names of the Tathagata. Of these, Mahāmati, some recognise me as the Tathagata, some as the

Self-existent One, some as Leader, as Vinayaka (Remover), as Pariṇāyaka (Guide), as Buddha, as Rishi (Ascetic), as Bull-king, as Brahma, as Vishṇu, as Īsvara, as Original Source (*pradhāna*), as Kapila, as Bhūtānta (End of Reality), as Arishṭa, as Nemina, as Soma (moon), as the Sun, as Rāma, as Vyāsa, as Śuka, as Indra, as Balin, as Varuṇa, as is known to some; while others recognise me as One who is never born and never passes away, as Emptiness, as Suchness, as Truth, as Reality, as Limit of Reality, (**193**) as the Dharmadhātu, as Nirvana, as the Eternal, as Sameness, as Non-duality, as the Undying, as the Formless, as Causation, as the Doctrine of Buddha-cause, as Emancipation, as the Truth of the Path, as the All-Knower, as the Victor, as the Will-made Mind. Mahāmati, thus in full possession of one hundred thousand times three asaṁkhyeyas of appellations, neither more nor less, in this world and in other worlds, I am known to the peoples, like the moon in water which is neither in it nor out of it. But this is not understood by the ignorant who have fallen into the dualistic conception of continuity.[1] Though they honour, praise, esteem, and revere me, they do not understand well the meaning of words and definitions; they do not distinguish ideas, they do not have their own truth, and, clinging to the words of the canonical books, they imagine that not being subject to birth and destruction means a non-entity, and fail to see that it is one of the many names of the Tathagata as in the case of Indra, Śakra, Purandara. They have no confidence in the texts where the self-standing truth is revealed, since in their study of all things they follow mere words as expressed in the texts trying thereby to gain into the meaning.

Thus, Mahāmati, these deluded ones would declare that as words are so is meaning, that meaning is not otherwise than words. For what reason? Because meaning has no body of its own and cannot be different from words. That the unintelligent declare words to be identical with meaning, is due to their ignorance as to the self-nature of words. They do not know, Mahāmati, that words (**194**) are subject

[1] This is missing in T'ang and Sung.

CHAPTER THREE 167

to birth and death whereas meaning is not. Mahāmati, words are dependent on letters, but meaning is not. As meaning is freed from existence and non-existence, it is not born, it has no substratum. And, Mahāmati, the Tathagatas do not teach the doctrine that is dependent upon letters. As to letters, their being or non-being is not attainable; it is otherwise with the thought that is never dependent on letters. Again, Mahāmati, anyone that discourses on a truth that is dependent on letters is a mere prattler because truth is beyond letters. For this reason, Mahāmati, it is declared in the canonical text by myself and other Buddhas and Bodhisattvas that not a letter is uttered or answered by the Tathagatas. For what reason? Because truths are not dependent on letters. It is not that they never declare what is in conformity with meaning; when they declare anything, it is according to the discrimination [of all beings]. If, Mahāmati, the truth is not declared[1] [in words] the scriptures containing all truths will disappear, and when the scriptures disappear there will be no Buddhas, Śrāvakas, Pratyekabuddhas, and Bodhisattvas; and when there is no one [to teach], what is to be taught and to whom? For this reason, then, Mahāmati, the Bodhisattva-Mahāsattva is not to become attached to the words of the canonical texts. Mahāmati, owing to the functioning of the minds of sentient beings, the canonical texts sometimes deviate from their straightforward course; religious discourses are given by myself and other Tathagatas, Arhats, Fully-Enlightened Ones in response to varieties of faiths on the part of beings, in order to remove them from [the bondage of] the Citta, Manas and Manovijñāna, and not for the attainment and establishment of self-realisation which issues from noble wisdom. When there is the recognition of the fact that all things are characterised with imagelessness and that there is nothing in the world but what is seen of the Mind itself, there is the discarding of the dualistic discrimination.

Therefore, Mahāmati, let the Bodhisattva-Mahāsattva

---

[1] According to the Chinese versions. *Upādāyānupādāyāt* in this connection is not quite intelligible.

be in conformity with the meaning (195) and not with the letter. Mahāmati, a son or a daughter of a good family who conforms himself or herself to the letter will ruin his or her understanding of ultimate reality[1] and will cause others to fail to recognise [the truth]. Continuing to cherish wrong views, one's own assertion is confounded by the philosophers who do not understand well what characterises all the stages of the Dharma, and who have no adequate knowledge as to the interpretation of words. If they well understand what characterises all the stages of the Dharma and are adequately equipped with the interpretation of words and expressions, and have a good understanding of the meaning and reason of all things, they will properly enjoy by themselves the bliss of formlessness while others are properly established in the Mahāyāna. Being properly embraced in the Mahāyāna they will, Mahāmati, be in the embrace of the Buddhas, Śrāvakas, Pratyekabuddhas, and Bodhisattvas. Being embraced by the Buddhas, Bodhisattvas, Pratyekabuddhas, and Śrāvakas, they will [in turn] embrace all beings. Embracing all beings they will embrace the good Dharma. The good Dharma being embraced, the Buddha-seeds will not be destroyed. When the Buddha-seeds are not destroyed, the excellent abodes will be attained. When thus these excellent abodes are attained, Mahāmati, the Bodhisattva-Mahāsattvas will see to it that [all beings], being established in the Mahāyāna, are born there [in the excellent abodes], and fortifying themselves with the tenfold supernatural power and assuming various forms, (196) they will discourse on the Dharma in conformity to its true nature (*tathātva*), and with a thorough knowledge of various wishes and characteristics of beings. Now the true nature of things (*tathātva*) is characterised by non-differentiation and trueness, it is neither coming nor departing, it puts a stop to all idle reasonings, and it is called the truth (*tattvam*).

Therefore, Mahamati, let son or daughter of a good family take good heed not to get attached to words as being in perfect conformity with meaning, because the truth is not

[1] Read *paramārtha* after Sung and Wei.

of the letter. Be not like the one who looks at the finger-tip. For instance, Mahāmati, when a man with his finger-tip points at something to sombody, the finger-tip may be taken wrongly for the thing pointed at; in like manner, Mahāmati, the people belonging to the class of the ignorant and simple-minded, like those of a childish group, are unable even unto their death to abandon the idea that in the finger-tip of words there is the meaning itself, and will not grasp ultimate reality because of their intent clinging to words which are no more than the finger-tip to them. To give another illustration, Mahāmati: boiled rice is the proper food for infants, to whom [suppose] somebody gave uncooked food to eat. In this case, this one is to be considered to be out of his sense because of his not knowing how to prepare food properly. So it is with that which is neither born nor destroyed, Mahāmati; it will not manifest itself to anybody unless he is well disciplined in it. Therefore, you should most assuredly discipline yourself in this and not be like one who grasping his own finger-tip sees the meaning there. For this reason, Mahāmati, (197) you should energetically discipline yourself to get at the meaning itself.

Mahāmati, the meaning is alone with itself (*vivikta*) and is the cause of Nirvana. Words are bound up with discrimination and are the carrier of transmigration. Meaning, Mahāmati, is attained from much learning, and this much learning, Mahāmati, means to be conversant with meaning and not with words. To be conversant with meaning means [to ascertain] the view which is not at all associated with any philosophical school and which will keep not only yourself but others from falling into [the false views]. Being so, Mahāmati, this is said to be learned much in meaning. Therefore, let seekers for meaning reverently approach those [who are much learned in it], but those who are attached to words as being in accord with meaning, they are to be left to themselves and to be shunned by truth-seekers.

LXXVII

Further, Mahāmati to whom the Buddha's spiritual powers were added, said: There is nothing specially distinguishable in the Buddha's teaching of no-birth and no-annihilation. Why? Because all the philosophers also declare, Blessed One, their causes to be unborn and not to be annihilated; and you, too, Blessed One, declare space, Apratisaṁkhyanirodha (annihilation), and Nirvana to be unborn and not to be annihilated. The philosophers declare, Blessed One, that the world rises from causal agencies and causation, while the Blessed One too declares that the world takes its rise from ignorance, desire, deed, discrimination, which work in accordance with the law of causation. Both thus refer to causation, the difference being in names only.

So with the rise of external objects, both you and they assume external causation. Thus, there is no distinction between your teaching, Blessed One, and that of the philosophers. [With them] there are nine substances which are regarded as unborn and not to be annihilated: atoms, supreme soul (*pradhāna*), Iśvara, creator (*prajāpati*), etc., (198) while, Blessed One, you assert that all things are neither born nor annihilated as their being and non-being is unattainable. Now as the elements are indestructible, their self-nature is neither born nor annihilated; while following various courses of transformation, what constitutes their essential nature is not abandoned. Though your notion of the elements may differ in form, Blessed One, it is what has been imagined by all the philosophers as well as by yourself. For this reason this teaching of yours has nothing distinctive. If there is anything distinctive by which the teaching of the Tathagata excels that of the philosophers, pray tell me. Blessed One, if there is nothing distinctive in your own teaching, we can say that there is something of Buddhahood in the teaching of all the philosophers, because in them there is a cause pointing to no-birth and no-annihilation. It was declared by the Blessed One that many Tathagatas are not born simultaneously in the same district in

CHAPTER THREE 171

one world. But if the rule of cause and effect with regard to being and non-being holds true, and your own teaching leaves nothing contradicting behind, there must be many Tathagatas [rising at the same time and in the same locality].

The Blessed One said: Mahāmati, my [teaching of] no-birth and no-annihilation is not like that of philosophers who also speak of no-birth and no-annihilation; nor is it like their doctrine of birth and impermanency. Why? Because, Mahāmati, that to which the philosophers ascribe the characteristics of no-birth and no-change is the self-nature of all things. But mine is not that which falls into the dualism of being and non-being. Mine, Mahāmati, goes beyond the dualism of being and non-being; has nothing to do with birth, abiding, and destruction; is neither existent nor non-existent. How is it not non-existent? Because (**199**) multitudinousness of objects is to be seen as like Māyā and a dream; I say that it is not non-existent. How is it not existent? Because there are no characteristic signs to be perceived as belonging to the self-nature of things; they are seen [in one sense as individual objects] and not seen [as such in another sense]; again they are [something in one sense] graspable [and in another sense] ungraspable. For this reason, things are existent and non-existent.

But when it is understood that there is nothing in the world but what is seen of the Mind itself, discrimination no more rises, and one is thus established in his own abode which is the realm of no-work. The ignorant work and discriminate but not the wise. Mahāmati, [the doings of the ignorant] are unrealities discriminated, realities confounded; they are like the city of the Gandharvas, like magically-created figures. To illustrate, Mahāmati, here is a city of the Gandharvas where children see magically-created people, merchants, and many others, going in or coming out, and imagine that they are really people going in and coming out. It is owing to this discrimination characterised by perturbation that such takes place. It is the same, Mahāmati, with the ignorant that they have a confused perception of birth and no-birth. There is really nothing made or unmade, like the rising of magically-created people; for magically-created people are neither born nor annihilated, because here is no question whatever as to their existence or non-existence. In like manner, all things have nothing to do with birth and destruction, except that the ignorant cherishing false ideas imagine the birth and annihilation of objects. It is, however, not so with the wise. By false ideas it is meant that objects are not judged as they are in themselves. They are nothing else. When [reality] is discriminated other than it is, there is the clinging to the idea that all things have their self-nature (200) and what is alone by itself is not seen, and when what is alone by itself is not seen there is no disappearance of discrimination. For this reason, Mahāmati, an insight into formlessness excels, and not an insight into form; as form causes another birth, it excels not. By formlessness, Mahāmati, is meant the disappearance of discrimination.

No-birth and no-annihilation,[1] this I call Nirvana. By Nirvana, Mahāmati, is meant the looking into the abode of reality as it really is in itself; and when, along with the turning-back of the entire system of mentation (*citta-caitta-kalāpa*), there is the attainment of self-realisation by means of noble wisdom, which belongs to the Tathagatas, I call it Nirvana.[2]

LXXVIII

So it is said:

86. In order to remove [the notion of] birth and to accomplish [that of] no-birth, I teach the doctrine of no-cause; but this is not understood by the ignorant.

87. This all is unborn, but that does not mean that there are no objects; they are seen to be like the city of the Gandharvas, a dream, and Māyā; objects are here, but causeless.

---

[1] Added after the Chinese translations; but Wei has *animitta* instead of *anirodha*.

[2] This digression on Nirvana somehow found its way here.

88. Tell me how things are unborn, without self-nature[1] and empty. When things are seen by [transcendental] knowledge, they are not subject to combination and are unobtainable; therefore, I declare that they are empty, unborn, and without self-nature.

89. Considered one by one combination is there, the world appears to exist, but nothing is really existing; it is not as it is conceived by the philosophers; when combination is dissolved, nothing is left to be seen.

90. As is a dream, a hair-net, Māyā, the city of the Gandharvas, and a mirage, (201) which rise into view causelessly, so is the multitudinousness of the world.

91. By keeping down the theory of no-causation,[2] no-birth is demonstrated; when the theory of no-birth is declared, my law-eye[3] is never destroyed; when the theory of no-cause is pointed out, the philosophers are horrified.

92. [Mahāmati asked].[4] How, by whom, where, and wherefore does the theory of no-cause make its appearance? [The Blessed One answered.][4] When things (saṁskṛita) are perceived as neither subject to causation nor above it, then the view maintained by the philosophers of birth and destruction is done away with.

93. [Mahāmati asked;] Is non-being no-birth? or does it look for causation? or is it a being's name without a [corresponding] reality? Pray tell me.

94. [The Blessed One answered,] Non-being is not no-birth, nor does it look for causation, nor is it a being's name, nor is it a name without a [corresponding] object.

95. Here is a reality which does not belong to the Śrāvakas, Pratyekabuddhas, nor to the philosophers; neither does it belong to the Bodhisattvas who have entered upon the seventh stage; this is what characterises no-birth.

96. The doing away with the notion of cause and con-

---

[1] According to Sung and T'ang.
[2] According to T'ang and Sung, "theory of causation."
[3] *Netrī*, according to T'ang; Sung has "law-stream" and Wei "my law."
[4] According to Sung.

dition, the giving up of a causal agency, the establishment of the Mind-only—this I state to be no-birth.

97. The getting-rid of [the idea that] things are caused, the removal of [the dualism of] imagined and imagining, (202) the being liberated from the alternatives of being and non-being—this I state to be no-birth.

98. The mind liberated from its objective world, the getting-rid of the twofold Svabhāva [*parikalpita* and *paratantra*], a turning-up at the seat of mentation—this I state to be no-birth.

99. No external existence, no non-existence, not even the grasping of mind; [things are like] a dream, a hair-net, Māyā, [the city of] Gandharvas, a mirage;[1] the abandonment of all the philosophical views,—this is what characterises no-birth.

100. Thus too all these words will be understood, that is, emptiness, having no self-nature, etc.; [the world] is empty, not, indeed, because of its being empty, but because of its being empty in the sense of being unborn.

101. A system [of mentality] may have its rise and fall owing to causation; when there is a dissolution of the system, there is neither birth nor annihilation.

102. When a dissolution somewhere takes place among the members of the system, such existence ceases as is discriminated by the philosophers by means of [such categories as] oneness and separateness.

103. Nothing is born; being is not, non-being is not, nowhere is being-and-non-being; except that where there is a system, there is the rising of things and their dissolution.

104. It is only in accordance with general convention that a chain[2] of mutual dependence is talked of; (203) birth has no sense when the chain of dependence is severed.

105. As there is nothing generating, there is no-birth, free from the faults of the philosophers; I talk of this conventionally according [to the theory of] concatenation, and this is not intelligible to the ignorant.

---

[1] This line may better be dropped as an interpolation.
[2] *Saṁkata.*

CHAPTER THREE 175

106. If there is anything born somewhere apart from concatenation, here is one who is to be recognised as an advocate of no-causation as he destroys concatenation.

107. If concatenation works [from outside] like a lamp revealing all kinds of things, this means the presence of something outside concatenation itself.

108. All things are devoid of self-nature, have never been born, and in their original nature are like the sky; things separated from concatenation belong to the discrimination of the ignorant.

109. There is another kind of no-birth which is the self-essence of things realised by the wise; its birth is no-birth, and in this no-birth there is a recognition.[1]

110. When this entire world is regarded as concatenation, as nothing else but concatenation, then the mind gains tranquillity.

111. Ignorance, desire, karma, etc.—these are the inner concatenation; a ladle, clay, a vessel, a wheel, etc., or seeds, the elements, etc.—these are external concatenations.

112. If there is any other existence born of concatenation, this goes against the law of concatenation; those [who hold this view] are not established in the principles of correct reasoning.

(204) 113. If there is an object coming to exist and yet is non-existent, by what law of causation is there the recognition of it? Things here are of mutual origination, and for this reason causation is declared.

114. Heat, fluidity, motility, solidity—such notions are discriminated by the ignorant; there is a system of relations, no individual objects exist; hence the denial of self-nature [as constituting the realness of objects].

115. The physician varies his treatment according to diseases though there is no difference in the principle [of healing]; the difference comes from varieties of diseases.

116. In like manner, [in order to save] generations of

---

[1] This is what constitutes *anutpattikadharmakshānti*, the "recognition of all things as unborn," which is considered the supreme spiritual attainment of Bodhisattvas.

beings from their disease of passions with which they are ill, I teach people with my doctrines, knowing the power of their senses.

117. My doctrine does not vary, but the passions and powers are differentiated; there is just one vehicle; auspicious is the eightfold path.

LXXIX

At that time again, Mahāmati the Bodhisattva-Mahāsattva said this to the Blessed One: Impermanence, impermanence—this is the discrimination of the philosophers, Blessed One, and you, too, declare in the canonical texts that all composite things are impermanent, to be subject to birth and destruction is the nature of things; but, Blessed One, is this right or wrong? And how many kinds of impermanency [are there], Blessed One?

Said the Blessed One: Mahāmati, there are eight[1] kinds of impermanency as discriminated by the philosophers, but not by me. What are the eight kinds? (1) Some say (205) that there is origination and then cessation—this is impermanency: that is to say, Mahāmati, in the beginning there is something born which ceases to exist—this is impermanency. (2) Some explain impermanency as the changing of shape. (3) Some say, form[2] itself is impermanent. (4) Some regard impermanency to consist in the changing of form (*rūpa*), saying that in a continuous, uninterrupted existence of all things there takes place a change in their natural flavour; for instance, milk going through a transformation turns into sour milk, and that such an invisible decomposition happens to all things; this is called impermanency. (5) Some imagine that there is an objective existence (*bhāva*) which is called impermanency. (6) Some imagine that existence and non-existence—this is impermanency. (7) Some say that not being born is impermanency;

---

[1] Both T'ang and Sung have seven, not eight. The present text also enumerates only seven; the missing one is supplied in a footnote from Wei.

[2] Or matter, *rūpa*.

because of all things being impermanent, and because of impermanency being inherent in them.¹

Now, Mahāmati, by impermanency that exists in existence and non-existence, is meant that things made of the elements² are by nature subject to destruction and have nothing in them one can take hold of, while the elements themselves are never set in motion.

By impermanency that is no-birth is meant that there is neither³ permanency nor impermanency; that in all things there is no [dualistic] evolution of being and non-being, and that nothing is seen to exist, even when they are examined into the last atom. This not seeing of anything is another name for no-birth, and not for birth. This, Mahāmati, is the nature of impermanency that is no-birth, and as this is not understood, all the philosophers cherish the view of impermanency that is based on birth.

Further, Mahāmati, by the conception of impermanency as objective existence is meant that there is a discrimination in [the philosopher's] own mind as to that which is not permanent and that which is not impermanent. What is the sense of this? (206) It means that there is a thing called impermanency which in itself is not subject to destruction, but by whose working there is the disappearance of all things; and if not for impermanency there will be no disappearance of all things. It is like a stick or a stone, or like a hammer breaking other things to pieces while itself remains unbroken. [This is the philosopher's meaning but] as we actually see things about us, there is no such mutual differentiation which compels us to say that here is impermanency the cause, and there is the disappearance of all things as the effect; there is no such differentiation of cause

---

¹ This is the eighth in Wei, and for the seventh Wei has this: "Again there are other philosophers according to whom impermanency consists in not being [existent] at first but coming later to exist. That is to say, when things born of the elements cease to exist, nothing is seen, nothing is born, as they are seperated from the substances that subsist—this is called impermanency."

² *Bhūta* before *bhautika* (line 10) may better be dropped.

³ The negative particle *na* is inserted here according to Sung.

and effect, and we cannot say: Here is impermanency as cause and there is the effect. When there is thus no differentiation of cause and effect, all things are permanent since no cause exists to render them otherwise. Mahāmati, as to the disappearance of all things, there is a cause, but it is not in the understanding of the ignorant and simple-minded. When the cause is of a dissimilar nature, the [same] effect is not produced. In case it does, the impermanency of all things is an example of dissimilar effect, and there is no distinction between cause and effect. But the distinction between cause and effect is observed in them. If there is an [objective] existence to be known as impermanence, it will be characterised with the nature of an effect-producing cause, and there will be one entity contained in all things. When the notion is cherished of a cause-producing effect, this means that impermanence the cause is impermanent because it partakes of the nature of the effect which is impermanent. All things then are not to be regarded as impermanent but as permanent.

If impermanency [as the cause] resides within all things, it will come under the three divisions of time. It passes away together with things past; its future is not yet here as things of the future are still unborn; in the present it breaks up together with things of the present.

(207) Form [or matter] results from the combination and variation of the elements; as the primary elements and the secondary elements are neither different nor not-different, they are by nature not subject to destruction, because according to the philosophers the elements are indestructible. [But, Mahāmati,] it is an established fact that the entire triple world with its elements primary and secondary is born, abides, and disappears. How do the philosophers conceive a separate existence of impermanency which is independent of the elements primary and secondary, while the elements themselves are neither set in motion nor destroyed because they cling to the notion of self-nature [as eternally unchangeable]?

The conception of impermanency as existing in the first

CHAPTER THREE

origination which ceases to continue [is not tenable for three reasons]; the elements cannot produce one another, because each has its self-nature different from the others. Each individual one cannot produce itself because there is no differentiation in it. The [mutually] separated origination of the elements is impossible because there is no correspondence between the two. Hence the conclusion that the conception of origination-impermanency is untenable.

By the conception of impermanency in consideration of changes taking place in external form is meant that the elements primary and secondary are not subject to dissolution. What is known as dissolution, Mahāmati, even when closely examined until atoms are reached, is not the destruction of the elements primary and secondary but of their external forms whereby the elements assume different appearances as short or long; but, in fact, nothing is destroyed in the elemental atoms. What is seen as ceased to exist is the external formation of the elements. This view is cherished by the Sāmkhya school.

By the impermanency of external shapes is meant the impermanency of form (*rūpa*); (**208**) what is impermanent is thus the external shape and not the elements. If the elements themselves are impermanent all our everyday experiences come to naught. This is cherishing the view of the Lokāyatika, according to which all things are reducible to mere words because their self-nature is never seen as born.

By the impermanency of changes is meant the changing of forms (*rūpa*) and not the changing of the elements themselves as is seen in various ornamental articles of gold which assume various forms. While there is no disappearance in the nature of gold, the ornamental articles variously change in form.

These and other views of impermanency as changes are discriminated variously by the philosophers as is here described. Fire may burn all the elements but their self-nature can never be burned; when each goes asunder by itself, there is the destruction of what constitutes the elements primary and secondary.

However, Mahāmati, I am neither for permanency nor for impermanency. Why? For these reasons: external objects are not admitted; the triple world is taught as not being anything else but the Mind itself; multiplicities of external existences are not accepted; there is no rising of the elements, nor their disappearance, nor their continuation, nor their differentiation; there are no such things as the elements primary and secondary; because of discrimination there evolve the dualistic indications of perceived and perceiving; when it is recognised that because of discrimination there is a duality, the discussion concerning the existence and non-existence of the external world ceases because Mind-only is understood. Discrimination (209) rises from discriminating a world of effect-producing works; no discrimination takes place when this world is not recognised.[1] Then a man ceases to cherish the discrimination of existence and non-existence which rises out of his own mind, he sees that things, either of this world or of a higher world, or of the highest, are not to be described as permanent or impermanent, because he does not understand the truth that there is nothing in the world but what is seen of the Mind itself. As [the meaning of] discrimination is not understood by all the philosophers who have fallen into wrong ideas of dualism and who are people of no [spiritual] attainment, impermanency comes up to them as a subject for discussion. Mahāmati,[2] the triple aspect of all things as distinguished as of this world, of a higher world, and of the highest, is the outcome of word-discrimination, but this is not understood by the ignorant and simple-minded. So it is said:

118. By the deluded philosophers the notion of impermanency is discriminated as origination-cessation, as transformation of external forms, as an [independent] existence, as form.

119. There is no destruction of things; the elements abide for ever as regards their self-essence; immersed in

[1] Read after the Chinese.
[2] *Sarvatīrthakara* (line 6) is dropped, according to the Chinese.

varieties of views the philosophers discriminate impermanency.

120. To these philosophers there is no destruction, no birth; the elements are permanent as regards their self-essence; who ever discriminates impermanency? [This is the position of the philosophers.]

121. [According to the Buddha,] there is nothing in the world but the Mind itself, and all that is of duality has its rise from the Mind and is seen as perceived and perceiving; an ego-soul and what belongs to it—they exist not.

122. The abode and realm of Brahma, etc.—I declare all to be of Mind-only, (210) outside Mind-only, Brahma, etc., are not attainable.

Here Ends the Third Chapter, "On Impermanency," in the *Laṅkāvatāra-Mahāyāna-Sūtra*.

[CHAPTER FOUR]

LXXX

(211) At that time again Mahāmati the Bodhisattva-Mahāsattva said this to the Blessed One: Pray tell me, Blessed One, about the state of perfect tranquillisation (*nirodha*) and its further development as attained by all the Bodhisattvas, Śrāvakas, and Pratyekabuddhas; for when this further development is thoroughly understood by myself and other Bodhisattva-Mahāsattvas all may be saved from being confounded by the happiness which comes from the attainment of perfect tranquillisation and also from falling into the confused state of mind of the Śrāvakas, Pratyekabuddhas, and philosophers.

Said the Blessed One: Then listen well and reflect well within yourself; I will tell you.

Certainly, Blessed One, said Mahāmati the Bodhisattva-Mahāsattva and gave ear to the Blessed One.

The Blessed One said this to him: Those Bodhisattva-Mahāsattvas who have reached the sixth stage as well as all the Śrāvakas and Pratyekabuddhas attain perfect tranquillisation. At the seventh stage, the Bodhisattva-Mahāsattvas, giving up the view of self-nature as subsisting in all things, attain perfect tranquillisation in every minute of their mental lives, which is not however the case with the Śrāvakas and Pratyekabuddhas; for with them there is something effect-producing, and in their attainment of perfect tranquillisation there is a trace [of dualism], of grasped and grasping. Therefore, they do not attain perfect tranquillisation in every minute of their mental lives which is possible at the seventh stage. They cannot attain to [the clear conviction of] an undifferentiated state of all things (212) and the cessation of [all] multiplicities. Their attainment is due to understanding the aspect of all things in which their self-nature is discriminated as good and as not-good. Therefore, until the seventh stage there is not a well-established attainment of tranquillisation in every minute of their mental lives.

Mahāmati, at the eighth stage the Bodhisattva-Mahāsattvas, Śrāvakas, and Pratyekabuddhas cease cherishing discriminative ideas that arise from the Citta, Manas, and Manovijñāna. From the first stage up to the sixth, they perceive that the triple world is no more than the Citta, Manas, and Manovijñāna, that as it is born of a discriminating mind there is no ego-soul and what belongs to it, and that there is no falling into the multitudinousness of external objects except through [the discrimination of] the Mind itself. The ignorant turning their self-knowledge (*svajñāna*) towards the dualism of grasped and grasping fail to understand, for there is the working of habit-energy which has been accumulating since beginningless time owing to false reasoning and discrimination.

Mahāmati, at the eighth stage there is Nirvana for the Śrāvakas and Pratyekabuddhas and Bodhisattvas; but the Bodhisattvas are kept away by the power of all the Buddhas[1] from [being intoxicated by] the bliss of the Samādhi, and thereby they will not enter into Nirvana. When the stage of Tathagatahood is not fulfilled there would be the cessation of all doings, and if [the Bodhisattvas] were not supported [by the Buddhas] the Tathagata-family would become extinct. Therefore, the Buddhas, the Blessed Ones, point out the virtues of Buddhahood which are beyond conception. (213) Therefore, [the Bodhisattvas] do not enter into Nirvana, but the Śrāvakas and Pratyekabuddhas, engrossed in the bliss of the Samādhis, therein cherish the thought of Nirvana.

At the seventh stage, Mahāmati, the Bodhisattva properly examines into the nature of the Citta, Manas, and Manovijñāna; he examines into [such subjects as] ego-soul and what belongs to it, grasped and grasping, the egolessness of persons and things, rising and disappearing, individuality

[1] Read according to T'ang.

and generality; he skilfully ascertains the fourfold logical analysis; he enjoys the bliss of self-mastery; he enters successively upon the stages; he knows the differences obtaining in the various elements of enlightenment. The grading of the stages is arranged by me lest the Bodhisattva-Mahāsattva, not knowing what is meant by individuality and generality and failing to understand the continuous development of the successive stages, should fall into the philosophers' wrong way of viewing things. But, Mahāmati, there is really nothing rising, nothing disappearing, all is nothing except what is seen of the Mind itself; that is, the continuous development of the successive stages and all the multiple doings of the triple world [—they are all of Mind itself]. This is not understood by the ignorant. I and all the Buddhas[1] establish the doctrine of the stages which develop successively as do all the doings of the triple world.

Further, Mahāmati, the Śrāvakas and Pratyekabuddhas at the eighth stage of Bodhisattvahood are so intoxicated with the happiness that comes from the attainment of perfect tranquillisation, and, failing to understand fully that there is nothing in the world but what is seen of the Mind itself, they are thus unable to overcome the hindrances and habit-energy growing out of their notions of generality and individuality; and adhering to the egolessness of persons and things and (214) cherishing views arising therefrom, they have the discriminating idea and knowledge of Nirvana, which is not that of the truth of absolute solitude. Mahāmati, when the Bodhisattvas face and perceive the happiness of the Samādhi of perfect tranquillisation, they are moved with the feeling of love and sympathy owing to their original vows, and they become aware of the part they are to perform as regards the [ten] inexhaustible vows. Thus, they do not enter Nirvana. But the fact is that they are already in Nirvana because in them there is no rising of discrimination. With them the discrimination of grasped and grasping no more takes place; as they [now] recognise that there is nothing in the world but what is seen of the Mind

[1] The Chinese reading is here adopted.

itself, they have done away with the thought of discrimination concerning all things. They have abandoned adhering to and discriminating about such notions as the Citta, Manas, and Manovijñāna, and external objects, and self-nature; however, they have not given up the things promoting the cause of Buddhism; because of their attainment of the inner insight which belongs to the stage of Tathagatahood; whatever they do all issues from their transcendental knowledge.

It is like a man crossing a stream in a dream. For instance, Mahāmati, suppose that while sleeping a man dreams that he is in the midst of a great river which he earnestly endeavours with all his might to cross by himself; but before he succeeds in crossing the stream, he is awakened from the dream, and being awakened he thinks: "Is this real or unreal?" He thinks again: "No, it is neither real nor unreal. By reason of the habit-energy of discrimination which has been accumulated by experience ever since beginningless time, as multiplicities of forms and conditions are seen, heard, thought, and recognised, there is the perception and discrimination of all things as existent and non-existent; and for this reason my Manovijñāna experiences even in a dream all that has been seen by myself."

In the same way, Mahāmati, the Bodhisattva-Mahāsattvas of the eighth stage of Bodhisattvahood, (215) after passing through the first up to the seventh stage, observe that there is no more rising in them of discrimination since all things are seen as like Māyā, etc., when they have an intuitive understanding of the [true] nature of all things, and [further] observing that, therefore, there is the cessation of all things as to grasped and grasping which rise from one's ardent desire for things, and also observing how the mind and what belongs to it carry on their discrimination, the Bodhisattva-Mahāsattvas never relax their efforts to practise the teachings of the Buddhas. Mahāmati, they will exercise themselves to make those who have not yet attained the truth attain it. For the Bodhisattvas, Nirvana does not mean extinction; as they have abandoned thoughts of discrimination evolving from the Citta, Manas, and Manovijñāna, there is for them the attainment of the recognition that all things are unborn. And, Mahāmati, in ultimate reality there is neither gradation nor continuous succession; [only] the truth of absolute solitude (*viviktadharma*) is taught here in which the discrimination of all the images is quieted. So it is said:

1. The abodes and the stages of Buddhahood are established in[1] the Mind-only which is imageless—this was told, is told, and will be told by the Buddhas.

2. The [first] seven stages are [still] of the mind, but here the eighth is imageless; the two stages, [the ninth and the tenth,] have [still] something to rest themselves on; the [highest] stage that is left belongs to me.

3. Self-realisation and absolute purity—this stage is my own; it is the highest station of Maheśvara, the Akanishtha [heaven] shining brilliantly.

4. Its rays of light move forward like a mass of fire; they who are bright-coloured, charming, and auspicious transform the triple world.

5. Some worlds are being transformed, while others have already been transformed;[2] there I preach the various vehicles which belong to my own stage.

(216) 6. But [from the absolute point of view] the tenth is the first, and the first is the eighth; and the ninth is the seventh, and the seventh is the eighth.

7. And the second is the third, and the fourth is the fifth, and the third is the sixth; what gradation is there where imagelessness prevails?

The Fourth Chapter, "On Intuitive Understanding."

---

[1] The Sagāthakam, V. 105, has *cittamātram nirābhāsam*...... instead of *cittamātre nirābhāse*......, as it stands here.

[2] According to T'ang.

[CHAPTER FIVE]

LXXXI

(217) At that time again, Mahāmati the Bodhisattva-Mahāsattva said this to the Blessed One: Is the Blessed One, the Tathagata, the Arhat, the Fully-Enlightened One, permanent or impermanent?

Said the Blessed One: Mahāmati, the Tathagata is neither permanent nor impermanent. Why? Because either way there is a fault connected with it. Mahāmati, what fault is connected with either assertion?[1] If the Tathagata is permanent, he will be connected with the creating agencies. For, Mahāmati, according to all the philosophers the creating agencies are something uncreated and permanent. But the Tathagata is not permanent [in the same sense] as the uncreated are permanent. If he is impermanent, he will be connected with things created. Because the Skandhas which are predicable as qualified and qualifying are non-existent, and because the Skandhas are subject to annihilation, destructibility is their nature. Mahāmati, all that is created is impermanent as is a jug, a garment, straw, a piece of wood, a brick, etc., which are all connected with impermanency. Thus all the preparations for the knowledge of the All-Knowing One will become useless as they are things created. On account of no distinction being made, the Tathagata, indeed, would be something created. For this reason, the Tathagata is neither permanent nor impermanent.

Again, Mahāmati, the Tathagata is not permanent for the reason that [if he were] he would be like space, and the preparations one makes for Tathagatahood would be useless. That is to say, Mahāmati, space is neither permanent nor impermanent as it excludes [the idea of] permanence and impermanence, (218) and it is improper to speak of it

[1] Following T'ang.

as characterised with the faults of oneness and otherness, of bothness and not-bothness, of permanence and impermanence. Further, Mahāmati, it is like the horns of a hare, or a horse, or an ass, or a camel, or a frog, or a snake, or a fly, or a fish; [with the Tathagata] as with them here is the permanency of no-birth. Because of this fault of the permanency of no-birth, the Tathagata cannot be permanent.

However, Mahāmati, there is another sense in which the Tathagata can be said to be permanent. How? Because the knowledge arising from the attainment of enlightenment [=an intuitive understanding] is of a permanent nature, the Tathagata is permanent. Mahāmati, this knowledge, as it is attained intuitively by the Tathagatas, Arhats, Fully-Enlightened Ones, is, indeed, permanent. Whether the Tathagatas are born or not, this Dharmatā, which is the regulative and sustaining principle to be discoverable in the enlightenment of all the Śrāvakas, Pratyekabuddhas, and philosophers, abides, and this sustaining principle of existence is not like the emptiness of space, which, however, is not understood by the ignorant and simple-minded. Mahāmati, this knowledge of enlightenment belonging to the Tathagatas comes forth from transcendental knowledge (*prajñājñāna*); Mahāmati, the Tathagatas, Arhats, Fully-Enlightened Ones do not come forth from the habit-energy of ignorance which is concerned with the Citta, Manas, and Manovijñāna, and the Skandhas, Dhātus, and Āyatanas. The triple world originates from the discriminating of unrealities, but the Tathagatas do not originate from the discriminating of unrealities. Where duality obtains, Mahāmati, there is permanency and impermanency because of its not being one. Mahāmati, [the truth of] absolute solitude is, indeed, non-dualistic[1] because all things are characterised with non-duality and no-birth. For this reason, Mahāmati, the Tathagatas, Arhats, Fully-Enlightened Ones are neither permanent nor impermanent. Mahāmati, as long as there is word-discrimination, (**219**) there follows the faulty notion of permanency and impermanency. The destruction of the

[1] Read *advayam*, not *dvayam*.

notion of permanency and impermanency as held by the ignorant, Mahāmati, comes from the getting rid of the knowledge that is based on discrimination, and not from the getting rid of the knowledge that is based on the insight of solitude. So it is said:

1. By keeping away permanency and impermanency, [and yet] by keeping permanency and impermanency in sight, those who always see the Buddhas will not expose themselves to the power of the philosophical doctrines.

2. When permanency and impermanency are adhered to all the accumulation [one makes for the attainment of reality] will be of no avail; by destroying the knowledge that is based on discrimination, [the idea of] permanency and impermanency is kept back.

3. As soon as an assertion is made, all is in confusion; when it is understood that there is nothing in the world but what is seen of the Mind itself, disputes never arise.

Here Ends the Fifth Chapter, "On the Deduction of the Permanency and Impermanency of Tathagatahood."

[CHAPTER SIX]

LXXXII

(220) At that time again, Mahāmati the Bodhisattva-Mahāsattva made a request of the Blessed One, saying: Blessed One, tell me; Sugata, tell me about the rising and disappearing of the Skandhas, Dhātus, and Āyatanas. In case there is no ego-soul, what is it that comes to exist and to disappear? The ignorant who are attached to the notion of rising and disappearing, fail to understand the extinction of pain, and thus they know not what Nirvana is.

Said the Blessed One: Then, Mahāmati, listen well and reflect well within yourself; I will tell you.

Mahāmati the Bodhisattva-Mahāsattva said: Certainly, Blessed One; and gave ear to the Blessed One.

The Blessed One said this to him: Mahāmati, the Tathāgata-garbha holds within it the cause for both good and evil, and by it all the forms of existence are produced. Like an actor it takes on a variety of forms, and [in itself] is devoid of an ego-soul and what belongs to it. As this is not understood, there is the functioning together of the triple combination from which effects take place. But the philosophers not knowing this are tenaciously attached to the idea of a cause [or a creating agency]. Because of the influence of habit-energy that has been accumulating variously by false reasoning since beginningless time, what here goes under the name of Ālayavijñāna is accompanied by the seven Vijñānas which give birth to a state known as the abode of ignorance. It is like a great ocean in which the waves roll on permanently but the [deeps remain unmoved; that is, the Alaya-] body itself subsists uninterruptedly, quite free from fault of impermanence, unconcerned with the doctrine of ego-substance, and (221) thoroughly pure in its essential nature.

CHAPTER SIX 191

As to the other seven Vijñānas beginning with the Manas and Manovijñāna, they have their rise and complete ending from moment to moment; they are born with false discrimination as cause, and with forms and appearances and objectivity as conditions which are intimately linked together; adhering to names and forms, they do not realise that objective individual forms are no[1] more than what is seen of the Mind itself; they do not give exact information regarding pleasure and pain; they are not the cause of emancipation; by setting up names and forms which originate from greed, greed is begotten in turn, thus mutually conditioned and conditioning. When the sense-organs which seize [upon the objective world] are destroyed and annihilated, the other things immediately cease to function, and there is no recognition of pleasure and pain which are the self-discrimination of knowledge; thus there is the attainment of perfect tranquillisation in which thoughts and sensations are quieted, or there is the realisation of the four Dhyānas, in which truths of emancipation are well understood; whereupon the Yogins are led to cherish herein the notion of [true] emancipation, because of the not-rising [of the Vijñānas].

[But] when a revulsion [or turning-back] has not taken place in the Ālayavijñāna known under the name of Tathāgata-garbha, there is no cessation of the seven evolving Vijñānas. Why? Because the evolution of the Vijñānas is depending on this cause; but this does not belong to the realm of the Śrāvakas, Pratyekabuddhas, and those who are disciplining themselves in the exercises of the philosophers. As they [only] know the egolessness of the self-soul, as they [only] accept the individuality and generality of the Skandhas, Dhātus, and Āyatanas, there is the evolving of the Tathāgata-garbha. When an insight into the five Dharmas, the three Svabhāvas, and the egolessness of all things is obtained, the Tathāgata-garbha becomes quiescent. By causing a revulsion in the continuous development of the graded stages, [the Bodhisattva] may not be led astray in the path [of enlightenment] by those philosophers who

[1] According to T'ang and Sung.

hold different views. Thus establishing himself at the Bodhisattva stage of Acalā (immovable), (222) he obtains the paths leading to the happiness of the ten Samādhis. Supported by the Buddhas in Samādhi, observing the truths of the Buddha which go beyond thought and his own original vows, not entering into the happiness of the Samādhi which is the limit of reality, but by means of the self-realisation which is not generally gained by the paths of discipline belonging to the Śrāvakas, Pratyekabuddhas, and philosophers, he obtains the ten paths of discipline which belong to the noble family [of the Tathagatas], and [also obtains] the knowledge-body created by the will which is removed from the [premeditated] workings of Samādhi. For this reason, Mahāmati, let those Bodhisattva-Mahāsattvas who are seeking after the exalted truth effect the purification of the Tathāgata-garbha which is known as Ālayavijñāna.

Mahāmati, if you say that there is no Tathāgata-garbha known as Ālayavijñāna, there will be neither the rising nor the disappearing [of an external world of multiplicities] in the absence of the Tathāgata-garbha known as Ālayavijñāna. But, Mahāmati, there is the rising and disappearing of the ignorant as well as the holy ones. [Therefore], the Yogins, while walking in the noble path of self-realisation and abiding in the enjoyment of things as they are, do not abandon working hard and are never frustrated [in their undertakings]. Mahāmati, this realm of the Tathāgata-garbha is primarily undefiled and is beyond all the speculative theories of the Śrāvakas, Pratyekabuddhas, and philosophers; but it appears to them devoid of purity, as it is soiled by these external defilements. This is not the case with the Tathagatas, Mahāmati; with the Tathagatas it is an intuitive experience as if it were an Āmalaka fruit held in the palm of the hand.

This, Mahāmati, was told by me in the canonical text relating to Queen Śrīmālā, (223) and in another where the Bodhisattvas, endowed with subtle, fine, pure knowledge, are supported [by my spiritual powers[—that the Tathāgata-garbha known as Ālayavijñāna evolves together with the seven Vijñānas. This is meant for the Śrāvakas who are not free from attachment, to make them see into the egolessness of things; and for Queen Śrīmālā to whom the Buddha's spiritual power was added, the [pure] realm of Tathagatahood was expounded. This does not belong to the realm of speculation as it is carried on by the Śrāvakas, Pratyekabuddhas, and other philosophers, except, Mahāmati, that this realm of Tathagatahood which is the realm of the Tathāgata-garbha-Ālayavijñāna is meant for those Bodhisattva-Mahāsattvas who like you are endowed with subtle, fine, penetrating thought-power and whose understanding is in accordance with the meaning; and it is not for others, such as philosophers, Śrāvakas, and Pratyekabuddhas, who are attached to the letters of the canonical texts. For this reason, Mahāmati, let you and other Bodhisattva-Mahāsattvas discipline yourselves in the realm of Tathagatahood, in the understanding of this Tathāgata-garbha-Ālayavijñāna, so that you may not rest contented with mere learning. So it is said:

1. The Garbha of the Tathagatas is indeed united with the seven Vijñānas; when this is adhered to, there arises duality, but when rightly understood, duality ceases.

2. The mind, which is the product of intellection since beginningless time, is seen like a mere image; when things are viewed as they are in themselves, there is neither objectivity nor its appearance.

3. As the ignorant grasp the finger-tip and not the moon, (224) so those who cling to the letter, know not my truth.

4. The Citta dances like a dancer; the Manas resembles a jester; the [Mano-] vijñāna together with the five [Vijñānas] creates an objective world which is like a stage.[1]

LXXXIII

At that time, Mahāmati the Bodhisattva-Mahāsattva made a request of the Blessed One, saying: Pray tell me, Blessed One; pray tell me, Sugata, concerning the distin-

[1] Sung and T'ang seem to be incorrect in their reading of this verse.

guishing aspects of the five Dharmas, the [three] Svabhāvas, the [eight] Vijñānas, and the twofold egolessness. By [recognising] the distinguishing aspects of the twofold egolessness, I and other Bodhisattva-Mahāsattvas will be able to establish those truths while effecting a continuous development through the various stages of Bodhisattvahood. It is said that by these truths we can enter into all the Buddha-truths, and that by entering into all the Buddha-truths we can enter even into the ground of the Tathagata's inner realisation.

Said the Blessed One: Then, Mahāmati, listen well and reflect well within yourself; I will tell you.

Certainly, Blessed One, said Mahāmati the Bodhisattva-Mahāsattva and gave ear to the Blessed One.

The Blessed One said this to him: Mahāmati, I will tell you about the distinguishing aspects of the five Dharmas, the [three] Svabhāvas, the [eight] Vijñānas, and the twofold egolessness. The five Dharmas are: name, form, discrimination, right knowledge, and suchness. [When these are thoroughly comprehended] by the Yogins, they enter into the course of the Tathagata's inner realisation, where they are kept away from such views as eternalism and nihilism, realism and negativism, and (225) where they come face to face with the abode of happiness belonging to the present existence as well as to the Samāpatti (tranquillisation). But, Mahāmati, as the ignorant do not understand that the five Dharmas, the [three] Svabhāvas, the [eight] Vijñānas, and the twofold egolessness, together with the external objects which are regarded as existent and non-existent—[all these are no more than] what is seen of the Mind itself—they are given to discrimination, but it is otherwise with the wise.

Said Mahāmati: How is it that the ignorant are given up to discrimination and the wise are not?

Said the Blessed One: Mahāmati, the ignorant cling to names, ideas, and signs; their minds move along [these channels]. As thus they move along, they feed on multiplicities of objects, and fall into the notion of an ego-soul and what belongs to it, and cling to salutary appearances. As thus they cling, there is a reversion to ignorance, and they become tainted, karma born of greed, anger, and folly is accumulated. As karma is accumulated again and again, their minds become swathed in the cocoon of discrimination as the silk-worm; and, transmigrating in the ocean of birth-and-death (*gati*), they are unable, like the water-drawing wheel, to move forward. And because of folly, they do not understand that all things are like Māyā, a mirage, the moon in water, and have no self-substance to be imagined as an ego-soul and its belongings; that things rise from their false discrimination; that they are devoid of qualified and qualifying; and have nothing to do with the course of birth, abiding, and destruction; that they are born of the discrimination of what is only seen of the Mind itself; and assert[1] that they are born of Iśvara, time, atoms, or a supreme spirit, for they follow names and appearances. Mahāmati, the ignorant move along with appearances.

Further, Mahāmati, by "appearance" is meant that which reveals itself to the visual sense (226) and is perceived as form, and in like manner that which, appearing to the sense of hearing, smelling, tasting, the body, and the Manovijñāna, is perceived as sound, odour, taste, tactility, and idea,—all this I call "appearance."

Further, Mahāmati, by "discrimination" is meant that by which names are declared, and there is thus the indicating of [various] appearances. Saying that this is such and no other, for instance, saying that this is an elephant, a horse, a wheel, a pedestrian, a woman, or a man, each idea thus discriminated is so determined.

Further, Mahāmati, by "right knowledge" is meant this: when names and appearances are seen as unobtainable owing to their mutual conditioning, there is no more rising of the Vijñānas, for nothing comes to annihilation, nothing abides everlastingly; and when there is thus no falling back into the stage of the philosophers, Śrāvakas, and Pratyekabuddhas, it is said that there is right knowledge. Further,

[1] According to T'ang and Wei.

Mahāmati, by reason of this right knowledge, the Bodhisattva-Mahāsattva does not regard name as reality and appearance as non-reality.

When erroneous views based on the dualistic notion of assertion and negation are gotten rid of, and when the Vijñānas cease to rise as regards the objective world of names and appearances, this I call "suchness." Mahāmati, a Bodhisattva-Mahāsattva who is established on suchness attains the state of imagelessness and thereby attains the Bodhisattva-stage of Joy (*pramuditā*).

When [the Bodhisattva] attains the stage of Joy, he is kept away from all the evil courses belonging to the philosophers and enters upon the path of supra-worldly truths. When [all] the conditions [of truth] are brought to consummation, he discerns that the course of all things starts with the notion of Māyā, etc.; and after the attainment of the noble truth of self-realisation, he earnestly desires to put a stop to speculative theorisation; (227) and going up in succession through the stages of Bodhisattvahood he finally reaches the stage of Dharma-Cloud (*dharmameghā*). After being at the stage of Dharma-Cloud, he reaches as far as the stage of Tathagatahood where the flowers of the Samādhis, powers, self-control, and psychic faculties are in bloom. After reaching here, in order to bring all beings to maturity, he shines like the moon in water, with varieties of rays of transformation. Perfectly fulfilling[1] the [ten] inexhaustible vows, he preaches the Dharma to all beings according to their various understandings. As the Bodhisattva-Mahāsattvas, Mahāmati, have entered into suchness, they attain the body which is free from the will and thought-constructions.[2]

Again, Mahāmati said: Are the three Svabhāvas to be regarded as included in the five Dharmas, or as having their own characteristics complete in themselves?

The Blessed One said: The three Svabhāvas, the eight Vijñānas, and the twofold egolessness—they are all included

[1] According to Sung and T'ang.
[2] T'ang and Wei have *citta-mano-manovijñānarahitam*.

CHAPTER SIX   197

[in the five Dharmas]. Of these, name and appearance are known as the Parikalpita [false imagination]. Then, Mahāmati, discrimination which rises depending upon them, is the notion of an ego-soul and what belongs to it,—the notion and the discrimination are of simultaneous occurrence, like the rising of the sun and its rays. Mahāmati, the discrimination thus supporting the notion of self-nature which subsists in the multiplicities of objects, is called the Paratantra [dependence on another]. Right knowledge and suchness, Mahāmati, are indestructible, and thus they are known as Parinishpanna [perfect knowledge].

Further, Mahāmati, by adhering to what is seen of the Mind itself there is an eightfold discrimination. This comes from imagining unreal individual appearances [as real]. (228) When the twofold clinging to an ego-soul and what belongs to it is stopped, there is the birth of the twofold egolessness. Mahāmati, in these five Dharmas are included all the Buddha-truths and also the differentiation and succession of the [Bodhisattva-] stages, and the entrance of the Śrāvakas, Pratyekabuddhas, Bodhisattvas, and Tathagatas into the state of self-realisation by means of their noble wisdom.

LXXXIV

Further, Mahāmati, of the five Dharmas—name, appearance, discrimination, right knowledge, and suchness—appearance is that which is seen as having such characteristics as form, shape, distinctive features, images, colours, etc.—this is "appearance." Out of this appearance ideas are formed such as a jar, etc., by which one can say, this is such and such, and no other; this is "name." When names are thus pronounced, appearances are determined[1] and there is "discrimination," saying this is mind and this is what belongs to it. That these names and appearances are after all unobtainable because when intellection is put away the aspect of mutuality [in which all things are determined]

[1] *Samadharmeti vā* that follows here is probably to be dropped on the strength of the Chinese versions.

ceases to be perceived and imagined—this is called the "suchness" of things. And this suchness may be characterised as truth, reality, exact knowledge, limit, source, self-substance, the unattainable. This has been realised by myself and the Tathagatas, truthfully pointed out, recognised, made public, and widely shown. When, in agreement with this, [the truth] is rightly understood as neither negative nor affirmative, discrimination ceases to rise, and there is a state conformable to self-realisation by means of noble wisdom, which is not the course of controversy pertaining to the philosphers, Śrāvakas, and Pratyekabuddhas; this is "right knowledge."

(229) These are, Mahāmati, the five Dharmas, and in them are included the three Svabhāvas, the eight Vijñānas, the twofold egolessness, and all the Buddha-truths. In this, Mahāmati, reflect well with your own wisdom and let others do [the same] and do not allow yourself to be led by another. So it is said:

5. The five Dharmas, the Svabhāvas, the eight Vijñānas, and the twofold egolessness—they are all embraced in the Mahāyāna.

6. Name, appearance, and discrimination [correspond to] the first two Svabhāvas, while right knowledge and suchness are the Parinishpanna.

LXXXV

At that time again, Mahāmati the Bodhisattva-Mahāsattva said this to the Blessed One: It is told by the Blessed One in the canonical text the Tathagatas of the past, present, and future are like the sands of the river Gaṅgā. Blessed One, is this to be accepted literally? or is there another distinct meaning? Pray tell me, Blessed One.

The Blessed One said: Mahāmati, do not take it in its literal sense; for, Mahāmati, the Buddhas of the three divisions of time are not measurable by the measurement of the sands of the Gaṅgā. Why? Because an analogy which is superior to anything of the world and surpasses it cannot be called an analogy, since there is in it something resembling and something not resembling. (230) The Tathagatas, Arhats,

CHAPTER SIX   199

Fully-Enlightened Ones do not give out such an analogy that has in it something resembling and something not resembling and that is superior to the world and surpasses it. But this comparison is only given out, Mahāmati, by myself and the Tathagatas, in which the Tathagatas, Arhats, Fully-Enlightened Ones are said to be like the sands of the river Gangā; the idea is to terrify those ignorant and simple-minded ones who, tenaciously clinging to the idea of permanency and impermanency, and giving themselves up to the ways of thinking and the erroneous views of the philosophers, follow up the wheel of transmigration. To those who, anxious to escape the intricacies of the wheel of existence, seek after the excellent state, thinking how this could be realised, it is told them that the appearance of the Tathagatas is not like the blooming of the Udumbara flower, because they will thereby see that the attainment of Buddhahood is not a difficult undertaking and will put forward their energy. But it is told in the canonical text that the Tathagatas appear as rarely as the Udumbara flower, and this is in consideration of those people who are to be led by me. Mahāmati, however, no one has ever seen the Udumbara flower blooming, nor will anyone; while, Mahāmati, the Tathagatas are at present in the world, they were seen and are to be seen. To say that the Tathagatas appear as rarely as the Udumbara flower has [really] no reference to the establishment of the truth itself. When, Mahāmati, the establishment of the truth itself is pointed out, it surpasses beyond measure anything in the world that can be offered as an analogy to it, because [the ignorant] are incapable of believing. And thus there is an unbelief on the part of the ignorant and simple-minded. (231) There is indeed no room for analogies to enter in the realm of self-realisation which is effected by means of noble wisdom. The truth transcends all the notions that are characteristic of the Citta, Manas, and Manovijñāna. The truth is the Tathagatas, and, therefore, in them there is nothing describable by analogy.

But, Mahāmati, [sometimes] a comparison is made use

of; that is to say, the Tathagatas are said to be like the sands of the river Gaṅgā, because they are the same and impartial [to all things], because they are free from imagination and discrimination. For example, Mahāmati, the sands of the river Gaṅgā are tossed about by the fishes, tortoises, porpoises, crocodiles, buffalos, lions, elephants, etc., but they are free from imagination and discrimination; for they do not resent, saying. "We are down-trodden," or "We are not." They are non-discriminative, pure in themselves, separated from defilement. In the same way, Mahāmati, the self-realisation of noble wisdom which has been attained by the Tathagatas, Arhats, Fully-Enlightened Ones, is like the river Gaṅgā, and their powers, psychic faculties, and self-control are like the sands; and however much they are tossed about by the fishes of the philosophers, by the ignorant who belong to other schools, they are not troubled by imaginations and discriminations. Because of their original vows, the Tathagatas [whose hearts are] filled with all the happiness of the Samāpatti are not troubled by imaginations and discriminations with regard to beings. Therefore, the Tathagatas, like the sands of the river Gaṅgā, are free from partiality because of their being devoid of likes and dislikes.

To illustrate, Mahāmati: as the sands of the river Gaṅgā partake of the character of the earth, the conflagration that will break out at the end of the Kalpa may burn the earth but does not destroy its self-nature. Mahāmati, the earth is not consumed because of its being inseparably connected with the element of fire, (232) and it is only the ignorant and simple-minded that on account of their falling into false ideas imagine the earth being consumed by fire. But as it supplies the material cause to the element fire, it is never consumed. In the same way, Mahāmati, the Dharmakāya of the Tathagatas, like the sands of the river Gaṅgā, is never destroyed.

To illustrate, Mahāmati: the sands of the river Gaṅgā are immeasurable. In the same way, Mahāmati, the rays of light of the Tathagatas are beyond measure, which are emitted by them in all the Buddha-assemblies in order to bring beings to maturity and arouse them [to the knowledge of the truth].

To illustrate, Mahāmati: the sands of the river Gaṅgā do not assume another nature than itself remaining forever the same. In the same way, Mahāmati, the Tathagatas, Arhats, Fully-Enlightened Ones are neither evolving nor disappearing in transmigration because in them the cause of making them come into existence is destroyed.

To illustrate, Mahāmati: the sands of the river Gaṅgā are unconcerned whether they are carried away or whether more is added into them. In the same way, Mahāmati, the knowledge of the Tathagatas which is exercised for the maturing of beings is neither exhausted nor augmented, because the Dharma is without a physical body. Mahāmati, that which has a physical body is subject to annihilation, but not that which has no physical body; and the Dharma is not a physical body.

To illustrate, Mahāmati: the sands of the river Gaṅgā, however much they are compressed for the sake of the ghee and oil, are destitute of them. In the same way, (233) Mahāmati, the Tathagatas never abandon their deep concerns[1] and original vows and happiness as regards the Dharmadhātu, however hard they are oppressed with pain for the sake of beings, as long as all beings have not yet been led into Nirvana by the Tathagatas, who are endowed with a great compassionate heart.

To illustrate, Mahāmati: the sands of the river Gaṅgā are drawn along with the flow of the stream, but not where there is no water. In the same way, Mahāmati, the Tathagata's teaching in regard to all the Buddha-truths takes place along the flow of the Nirvana-stream; and for this reason the Tathagatas are said to be like the sands of the river Gaṅgā.

Mahāmati, in *tathāgata* ("thus come") there is no sense of "going away"; Mahāmati, "going away" means destruction. Mahāmati, the primary limit of transmigration is unknown. Not being known, how can I talk of the sense

[1] After T'ang.

of "gong away"? The sense of "going away," Mahāmati, is annihilation, and this is not known by the ignorant and simple-minded.

Mahāmati said: If, Blessed One, the primary limit of transmigration of all beings is unknowable, how is the emancipation of beings knowable?

The Blessed One said: Mahāmati, when it is understood that the objective world is nothing but what is seen of the Mind itself, the habit-energy of false speculations and erroneous discriminations which have been going on since beginningless time is removed, and there is a revulsion [or turning-back] at the basis of discrimination—this is emancipation, Mahāmati, and not annihilation. Therefore, Mahāmati, there cannot be any talk about endlessness. To be endless in limit, Mahāmati, is another name for discrimination. Apart from discriminations (234) there are no other beings. When all things external or internal are examined with intelligence, Mahāmati, knowing and known are found to be quiescent. But when it is not recognised that all things rise from the discrimination of the Mind itself, discrimination asserts itself. When this is understood discrimination ceases. So it is said:

7. Those who regard the removers of obstruction [i. e., Buddhas] as neither destroyed nor departed for ever, like the sands of the Gangā, see the Tathagata.

8. Like the sands of the Gangā they are devoid of all error: they flow along the stream and are permanent, and so is the essence [or nature] of Buddhahood.

LXXXVI

At that time again, Mahāmati the Bodhisattva-Mahāsattva said this to the Blessed One; Tell me, Blessed One; tell me, Sugata, Tathagata, Arhat, Fully-Enlightened One, regarding the momentary destruction of all things and their distinctive signs. Blessed One, what is meant by all things being momentary?

The Blessed One replied: Then, Mahāmati, listen well and reflect well within yourself; I will tell you.

CHAPTER SIX

Certainly, Blessed One; said Mahāmati the Bodhisattva-Mahāsattva and gave ear to the Blessed One.

The Blessed One said this to him: Mahāmati, all things, all things we speak of, and they are good or bad, effect-producing or not effect-producing, of this world (235) or of super-world, faulty or faultless, of evil flowings or the non-flowings, receptive or non-receptive. In short, Mahāmati, the five appropriating[1] Skandhas have their rise from the habit-energy of the Citta, Manas, and Manovijñāna, they are imagined good or bad. Mahāmati, the happiness of the Samādhi and the attainments [resulting therefrom], which belong to the wise by reason of their abiding in the happiness of the existing world, are called the non-outflowing goods.

Again, Mahāmati, by good and bad are meant the eight Vijñānas. What are the eight? They are the Tathāgata-garbha known as the Ālayavijñāna, Manas, Manovijñāna, and the system of the five Vijñānas as described by the philosophers. Now, Mahāmati, the system of the five Vijñānas is together with the Manovijñāna, and there is an undivided succession and differentiation of good and bad, and the entire body moves on continuously and closely bound together; moving on, it comes to an end; but as it fails to understand that there is nothing in the world but what is seen of Mind-only, there is the rising of another Vijñāna [-system] following the cessation of the first; and the Manovijñāna in union with the system of the five Vijñānas, perceiving the difference of forms and figures, is set in motion, not remaining still even for a moment—this I call momentariness. Mahāmati, momentary is the Ālayavijñāna known as the Tathāgata-garbha, which is together with the Manas and with the habit-energy of the evolving Vijñānas— this is momentary. But [the Ālayavijñāna which is together] with the habit-energy of the non-outflows (*anāsrava*) (236) is not momentary. This is not understood by the

---

[1] All the Skandhas are self-appropriating, or self-grasping, as long as there is attachment to the notion of an ego-soul. When that is got rid of, the Skandhas are *anāsrava*, i.e. not tainted with evil outflows.

ignorant and simple-minded who are addicted to the doctrine of momentariness. Not understanding the momentariness and non-momentariness of all things, they cherish nihilism whereby they even try to destroy the unmade (*asaṁskṛita*). Mahāmati, the system itself of the five Vijñānas is not subject to transmigration, nor does it suffer pleasure and pain, nor is it conducive to Nirvana. But, Mahāmati, the Tathāgata-garbha is together with the cause that suffers pleasure and pain; it is this that is set in motion and ceases to work; it is stupefied by the fourfold habit-energy. But the ignorant do not understand it, as their thoughts are infused with the habit-energy of discrimination which cherishes the view of momentariness.

Further, Mahāmati, gold, vajra, and the relics of the Buddha, owing to their specific character, are never destroyed but remain the same until the end of time. If, Mahāmati, the nature of enlightenment is momentary, the wise would lose their wiseness (*āryatva*), but they have never lost it. Mahāmati, gold and vajra remain the same until the end of time; remaining the same they are neither diminished nor increased. How is it that the ignorant, failing to recognise the hidden meaning of all things internal and external, discriminate in the sense of momentariness?

LXXXVII

Further, Mahāmati said: It is again said by the Blessed One that by fulfilling the six Pāramitās Buddhahood is realised. What are the six (237) Pāramitās? And how are they fulfilled?

The Blessed One replied: Mahāmati, there are three kinds of Pāramitās. What are the three? They are the worldly, the super-worldly, and the highest super-wordly. Of these, Mahāmati, the worldly Pāramitās [are practised thus]: Adhering tenaciously to the notion of an ego-soul and what belongs to it and holding fast to dualism, those who are desirous for this world of form, etc., will practise the Pāramitā of charity in order to obtain the various realms of existence. In the same way, Mahāmati, the

CHAPTER SIX

ignorant will practise the Pāramitās of morality, patience, energy, Dhyāna, and Prajñā. Attaining the psychic powers they will be born in Brahma's heaven.

As to the super-worldly Pāramitās, they are practised by the Śrāvakas and Pratyekabuddhas whose thoughts are possessed by the notion of Nirvana; the Pāramitās of charity, etc. are thus performed by them, who, like the ignorant, are desirous of enjoying Nirvana for themselves.

Again, Mahāmati, as to the highest super-worldly Pāramitās, [they are practised] by the Bodhisattva-Mahāsattvas who are the practisers of the highest form of spiritual discipline; that is, perceiving that there is nothing in the world but what is only seen of the Mind itself, on account of discrimination, and understanding that duality is of the Mind itself, they see that discrimination ceases to function; and, that seizing and holding is non-existent; and, free from all thoughts of attachment to individual objects which are of the Mind itself, and in order to benefit and give happiness to all sentient beings, [the Bodhisattvas] practise the Pāramitā of charity. While dealing with an objective world there is no rising in them of discrimination; they just practise morality and this is the Pāramitā [of morality]. To practise patience with no thought of discrimination rising in them (238) and yet with full knowledge of grasped and grasping —this is the Pāramitā of patience. To exert oneself with energy from the first part of the night to its end and in conformity with the disciplinary measures and not to give rise to discrimination—this is the Pāramitā of energy. Not to cherish discrimination, not to fall into the philosopher's notion of Nirvana—this is the Pāramitā of Dhyāna. As to the Pāramitā of Prajñā: when the discrimination of the Mind itself ceases, when things are thoroughly examined by means of intelligence, there is no falling into dualism, and a revulsion takes place at the basis, while previous karma is not destroyed; when [transcendental knowledge] is exercised for the accomplishment of self-realisation, then there is the Pāramitā of Prajñā. These, Mahāmati, are the Pāramitās and their meanings.

LXXXVIII[1]

So it is said:

9. The created (*saṁskṛita*) are empty, impermanent, momentary—so the ignorant discriminate; the meaning of momentariness is discriminated by means of the analogies of a river, a lamp, and seeds.

10. All things are non-existent, they are not-momentary, quiescent, not subject to destruction, and unborn—this, I say, is the meaning of momentariness.

11. Birth and death succeed without interruption—this I do not point out for the ignorant. Owing to the uninterrupted succession of existence, discrimination moves on in the [six] paths.

12. Ignorance is the cause and there is the general rising of minds, when form is not yet born, where is the abode of the middle existence?

13. If another mind is set in motion in an uninterrupted succesion of deaths, (**239**) where does it find its dependence as form is not established in time?

14. If mind is set in motion, somewhere, somehow, the cause is an unreal one; it is not complete; how can one know of its momentary disappearances?

15. The attainment of the Yogins, gold, the Buddha-relics, and the heavenly palace of Abhāsvara are indestructible by any worldly agencies.

16. Ever abiding are the truths attained by the Buddhas and their perfect knowledge; the nature of Buddhahood as realised [by them]—how can there be momentariness in them?

17. The city of the Gandharvas, Māyā-like forms—how can they be otherwise than momentary? Realities are characterised with unreality, and how can they be causal agencies?

Here Ends the Sixth Chapter "On Momentariness."

---

[1] The proper place for this section is after the section on "Momentary" and before the "Pāramitā," or what is the same thing the latter is wrongly inserted where it is found in in the text.

[CHAPTER SEVEN]
LXXXIX

(240) At that time again, Mahāmati the Bodhisattva-Mahāsattva said this to the Blessed One: [How was it that] the Arhats were given assurance by the Blessed One of their attainment of supreme enlightenment? [How can] all beings attain Tathagatahood without realising the truths of Parinirvana? [What does it mean that] from the night when the Tathagata was awakened to supreme enlightenment until the night when he entered into Parinirvana, between these times the Tathagata has not uttered, has not pronounced, a word. [What is the meaning of this] that being always in Samādhi the Tathagatas neither deliberate nor contemplate? [How do] Buddhas of transformation, being in the state of transformation, execute the works of the Tathagatas? How is the succession of momentary decomposition explained which takes place in the Vijñānas?

[Further, what do these statements mean] that Vajrapāṇi is constantly with [the Tathagata] as his personal guard; that the primary limit is unknown and yet cessation is knowable; that there are evil ones, their activities, and left-over karma? Blessed One, [facts of] karma-hindrance are said to be shown [by the Tathagata in the incident of] Cañcā the daughter of a Brahmin, of Sundarī the daughter of a mendicant, an empty bowl, etc.; how can the Blessed One with these unexhausted evils attain all-knowledge?

The Blessed One replied: Then, Mahāmati, listen well and reflect well within yourself; I will tell you.

Certainly, Blessed One; (241) said Mahāmati the Bodhisattva-Mahāsattva and gave ear to the Blessed One.

The Blessed One said this to him: The realm of Nirvana where no substratum is left behind is according to the hidden meaning and for the sake of the practisers who are thereby inspired to exert themselves in the work of the Bodhisattvas. Mahāmatī, there are Bodhisattvas practising the work of the Bodhisattva here and in other Buddha-lands, who, however, are desirous of attaining the Nirvana of the Śrāvakayāna. In order to turn their inclination away from the Śrāvakayāna and to make them exert themselves in the course of the Mahāyāna, the Śrāvakas in transformation are given assurance [as to their future Buddhahood] by the Body of Transformation; but this is not done by the Dharmatā-Buddha. This giving assurance to the Śrāvakas, Mahāmati, is declared according to the hidden meaning. Mahāmati, that the abandonment of passion-hindrance by the Śrāvakas and Pratyekabuddhas is not different [from that by the Tathagatas] is due to the sameness of the taste of emancipation, but this does not apply to the abandonment of knowledge-hindrance. Knowledge-hindrance, Mahāmati, is purified when the egolessness of things is distinctly perceived; but passion-hindrance is destroyed when first the egolessness of persons is perceived and acted upon, for [then] the Manovijñāna ceases to function. Further, dharma-hindrance is given up because of the disappearance of the habit-energy [accumulated in] the Ālayavijñāna, it is now thoroughly purified.

There is an eternally-abiding reality [which is to be understood] according to the hidden meaning, because it is something that has neither antecedents nor consequents. The Tathagata points out the Dharma without deliberation, without contemplation, and by means of such words that are original and independent. Because of his right thinking and because of his unfailing memory, he neither deliberates nor contemplates, he is no more at the stage of the fourfold habit-energy, (242) he is free from the twofold death, he has relinquished the twofold hindrance of passion and knowledge.

Mahāmati, the seven Vijñānas, that is, Manas, Manovijñāna,, eye-vijñāna, etc., are characterised with momentariness because they originate from habit-energy, they are destitute of the good non-flowing factors, and are not transmigratory. What transmigrates, Mahāmati, is the Tathāgata-garbha which is the cause of Nirvana as well as that of pleasure and pain. This is not understood by the ignorant whose minds are torn asunder by the notion of emptiness.

Mahāmati, the Tathagatas who are accompanied by Vajrapāṇi are the Tathagatas transformed in transformation and are not the original Tathagatas, Arhats, Fully-Enlightened Ones. The original Tathagatas, Mahāmati, are indeed beyond all sense and measurement, beyond the reach of all ignorant ones, Śrāvakas, Pratyekabuddhas, and philosophers. [These Tathagatas] are abiding in the joy of existence as it is, as they have reached the truth of intuitive knowledge by means of Jñānakshānti. Thus Vajrapāṇi is not attached to them. All the Buddhas of Transformation do not owe their existence to karma; in them there is no Tathagatahood, but apart from them there is no Tathagatahood either. Like the potter who is dependent on various combinations, [the Buddha of Transformation] does his work for sentient beings; he teaches the doctrine meeting conditions, but not the doctrine that will establish the truth as it is, which belongs to the noble realm of self-realisation.

Further, Mahāmati, on account of the cessation of the six Vijñānas the ignorant and simple-minded look for nihilism, and on account of their not understanding the Ālayavijñāna they have eternalism. The primary limit of the discrimination of their own minds (**243**) is unknown, Mahāmati. Emancipation is obtained when this discrimination of Mind itself ceases. With the abandonment of the fourfold habit-energy the abandonment of all faults takes place.

So it is said :[1]

1. The three vehicles are no-vehicle; there is no Nirvana with the Buddhas; it is pointed out that the assurance of Buddhahood is given to all that are freed from faults.

2. Ultimate intuitive knowledge, Nirvana that leaves no remnant,—this is told according to the hidden meaning in order to give encouragement to the timid.

The following gāthās do not seem to have any specific relation to the prose section.

3. Knowledge is produced by the Buddhas, and the path is pointed out by them: they move in it and not in anything else, therefore there is no Nirvana with them.

4. Existence, desire, form (*rūpa*), theorising—this is the fourfold habit-energy; this is where the Manovijñāna takes its rise and the Ālaya and Manas abide.

5. Nihilism and the idea of impermanency rise because of the Manovijñāna, the eye-vijñāna, etc.; eternalism rises from [the thought that] there is no beginning in Nirvāna, intelligence, and theorisation.

Here Ends the Seventh Chapter, "On Transformation."

[CHAPTER EIGHT][1]

(244) At that time Mahāmati the Bodhisattva-Mahāsattvt asked the Blessed One in verse and again made a request, saying: Pray tell me, Blessed One, Tathagata, Arhat, Fully-Enlightened One regarding the merit and vice of meat-eating; thereby I and other Bodhisattva-Mahāsattvas of the present and future may teach the Dharma to make those beings abandon their greed for meat, who, under the influence of the habit-energy belonging to the carnivorous existence, strongly crave meat-food. These meat-eaters thus abandoning their desire for [its] taste will seek the Dharma for their food and enjoyment, and, regarding all beings with love as if they were an only child, will cherish great compassion towards them. Cherishing [great compassion], they will discipline themselves at the stages of Bodhisattvahood and will quickly be awakened in supreme enlightenment; or staying a while at the stage of Śrāvakahood and Pratyekabuddhahood, they will finally reach the highest stage of Tathagatahood.

Blessed One, even those philosophers who hold erroneous doctrines and are addicted to the views of the Lokāyata such as the dualism of being and non-being, nihilism, and eternalism, will prohibit meat-eating and will themselves refrain from eating it. How much more, O World Leader, he who promotes one taste for mercy and is the Fully-Enlightened One; (245) why not prohibit in his teachings

---

[1] This chapter on meat-eating is another later addition to the text, which was probably done earlier than the Rāvaṇa chapter. It already appears in the Sung, but of the three Chinese versions it appears here in its shortest form, the proportion being S=1, T=2, W=3. It is quite likely that meat-eating was practised more or less among the earlier Buddhists, which was made a subject of severe criticism by their opponents. The Buddhists at the time of the Laṅkāvatāra did not like it, hence this addition in which an apologetic tone is noticeable.

the eating of flesh not only by himself but by others? Indeed, let the Blessed One who at heart is filled with pity for the entire world, who regards all beings as his only child, and who possesses great compassion in compliance with his sympathetic feelings, teach us as to the merit and vice of meat-eating, so that I and other Bodhisattva-Mahāsattvas may teach the Dharma.

Said the Blessed One: Then, Mahāmati, listen well and reflect well within yourself; I will tell you.

Certainly, Blessed One; said Mahāmati the Bodhisattva-Mahāsattva and gave ear to the Blessed One.

The Blessed One said this to him: For innumerable reasons, Mahāmati, the Boddhisattva, whose nature is compassion, is not to eat any meat; I will explain them: Mahāmati, in this long course of transmigration here, there is not one living being that, having assumed the form of a living being, has not been your mother, or father, or brother, or sister, or son, or daughter, or the one or the other, in various degrees of kinship; and when acquiring another form of life may live as a beast, as a domestic animal, as a bird, or as a womb-born, or as something standing in some relationship to you; [this being so] how can the Bodhisattva-Mahāsattva who desires to approach all living beings as if they were himself and to practise the Buddha-truths, eat the flesh of any living being that is of the same nature as himself? Even, Mahāmati, the Rakshasa, listening to the Tathagata's discourse on the highest essence of the Dharma, attained the notion of protecting [Buddhism], and, feeling pity, (**246**) refrains from eating flesh; how much more those who love the Dharma! Thus, Mahāmati, wherever there is the evolution of living beings, let people cherish the thought of kinship with them, and, thinking that all beings are [to be loved as if they were] an only child, let them refrain from eating meat. So with Bodhisattvas whose nature is compassion, [the eating of] meat is to be avoided by him. Even in exceptional cases, it is not [compassionate] of a Bodhisattva of good standing to eat meat. The flesh of a dog, an ass, a buffalo, a horse,

CHAPTER EIGHT

a bull, or man, or any other [being], Mahāmati, that is not generally eaten by people, is sold on the roadside as mutton for the sake of money; and therefore, Mahāmati, the Bodhisattva should not eat meat.

For the sake of love of purity, Mahāmati, the Bodhisattva should refrain from eating flesh which is born of semen, blood, etc. For fear of causing terror to living beings, Mahāmati, let the Bodhisattva who is disciplining himself to attain compassion, refrain from eating flesh. To illustrate, Mahāmati: When a dog sees, even from a distance, a hunter, a pariah, a fisherman, etc., whose desires are for meat-eating, he is terrified with fear, thinking, "They are death-dealers, they will even kill me." In the same way, Mahāmati, even those minute animals that are living in the air, on earth, and in water, seeing meat-eaters at a distance, will perceive in them, by their keen sense of smell, (247) the odour of the Rakshasa and will run away from such people as quickly as possible; for they are to them the threat of death. For this reason, Mahāmati, let the Bodhisattva, who is disciplining himself, to abide in great compassion, because of its terrifying living beings, refrain from eating meat. Mahāmati, meat which is liked by unwise people is full of bad smell and its eating gives one a bad reputation which turns wise people away; let the Bodhisattva refrain from eating meat. The food of the wise, Mahāmati, is what is eaten by the Rishis; it does not consist of meat and blood. Therefore, Mahāmati, let the Bodhisattva refrain from eating meat.

In order to guard the minds of all people, Mahāmati, let the Bodhisattva whose nature is holy and who is desirous of avoiding censure on the teaching of the Buddha, refrain from eating meat. For instance, Mahāmati, there are some in the world who speak ill of the teaching of the Buddha; [they would say,] "Why are those who are living the life of a Śramaṇa or a Brahmin reject such food as was enjoyed by the ancient Rishis, and like the carnivorous animals, living in the air, on earth, or in the water? Why do they go wandering about in the world thoroughly terrifying living beings, disregarding the life of a Śramaṇa and destroying the vow of a Brahmin? There is no Dharma, no discipline in them." There are many such adverse-minded people who thus speak ill of the teaching of the Buddha. For this reason, Mahāmati, in order to guard the minds of all people, (248) let the Bodhisattva whose nature is full of pity and who is desirous of avoiding censure on the teaching of the Buddha, refrain from eating meat.

Mahāmati, there is generally an offensive odour to a corpse, which goes against nature; therefore, let the Bodhisattva refrain from eating meat. Mahāmati, when flesh is burned, whether it be that of a dead man or of some other living creature, there is no distinction in the odour. When flesh of either kind is burned, the odour emitted is equally noxious. Therefore, Mahāmati, let the Bodhisattva, who is ever desirous of purity in his discipline, wholly refrain from eating meat.

Mahāmati, when sons or daughters of good family, wishing to exercise themselves in various disciplines such as the attainment of a compassionate heart, the holding a magical formula, or the perfecting of magical knowledge, or starting on a pilgrimage to the Mahāyāna, retire into a cemetery, or to a wilderness, or a forest, where demons gather or frequently approach; or when they attempt to sit on a couch or a seat for the exercise; they are hindered [because of their meat-eating] from gaining magical powers or from obtaining emancipation. Mahāmati, seeing that thus there are obstacles to the accomplishing of all the practices, let the Bodhisattva, who is desirous of benefiting himself as well as others, wholly refrain from eating meat.

As even the sight of objective forms gives rise to the desire for tasting their delicious flavour, let the Bodhisattva, whose nature is pity and who regards all beings as his only child, wholly refrain from eating meat. (249) Recognising that his mouth smells most obnoxiously, even while living this life, let the Bodhisattva whose nature is pity, wholly refrain from eating meat.

[The meat-eater] sleeps uneasily and when awakened

is distressed. He dreams of dreadful events, which makes his hair rise on end. He is left alone in an empty hut; he leads a solitary life; and his spirit is seized by demons. Frequently he is struck with terror, he trembles without knowing why, there is no regularity in his eating, he is never satisfied. In his eating[1] he never knows what is meant by proper taste, digestion, and nourishment. His visceras are filled with worms and other impure creatures and harbour the cause of leprosy. He ceases to entertain any thoughts of aversion towards all diseases. When I teach to regard food as if it were eating the flesh of one's own child, or taking a drug, how can I permit my disciples, Mahāmati, to eat food consisting of flesh and blood, which is gratifying to the unwise but is abhorred by the wise, which brings many evils and keeps away many merits; and which was not offered to the Rishis and is altogether unsuitable?

Now, Mahāmati, the food I have permitted [my disciples to take] is gratifying to all wise people but is avoided by the unwise; it is productive of many merits, it keeps away many evils; and it has been prescribed by the ancient Rishis. (250) It comprises rice, barley, wheat, kidney beans, beans, lentils, etc., clarified butter, oil, honey, molasses, treacle, sugar cane, coarse sugar, etc.; food prepared with these is proper food. Mahāmati, there may be some irrational people in the future who will discriminate and establish new rules of moral discipline, and who, under the influence of the habit-energy belonging to the carnivorous races, will greedily desire the taste [of meat]: it is not for these people that the above food is prescribed. Mahāmati, this is the food I urge for the Bodhisattva-Mahāsattvas who have made offerings to the previous Buddhas, who have planted roots of goodness, who are possessed of faith, devoid of discrimination, who are all men and women belonging to the Śākya family, who are sons and daughters of good family, who have no attachment to body, life, and property, who do not covet delicacies, are not at all greedy, who being

---

[1] Delete *pitakhāditā* (line 7).

compassionate desire to embrace all living beings as their own person, and who regard all beings with affection as if they were an only child.

Long ago in the past, Mahāmati, there lived a king whose name was Siṁhasaudāsa. His excessive fondness for meat, his greed to be served with it, (251) stimulated his taste for it to the highest degree so that he [even] ate human flesh. In consequence of this he was alienated from the society of his friends, counsellors, kinsmen, relatives, not to speak of his townsmen and countrymen. In consequence he had to renounce his throne and dominion and to suffer great calamities because of his passion for meat.

Mahāmati, even Indra who obtained sovereignty over the gods had once to assume the form of a hawk owing to his habit-energy of eating meat for food in a previous existence; he then chased Viśvakarma appearing in the guise of a pigeon, who had thus to place himself on the scale. King Śivi feeling pity for the innocent [pigeon had to sacrifice himself to the hawk and thus] to suffer great pain. Even a god who became Indra the Powerful, after going through many a birth, Mahāmati, is liable to bring misfortune both upon himself and others; how much more those who are not Indra!

Mahāmati, there was another king[1] who was carried away by his horse into a forest. After wandering about in it, he committed evil deeds with a lioness out of fear for his life, and children were born to her. Because of their descending from the union with a lioness, (252) the royal children were called the Spotted-Feet, etc. On account of their evil habit-energy in the past when their food had been flesh, they ate meat even [after becoming] king, and, Mahāmati, in this life they lived in a village called Kuṭīraka ("seven huts"), and because they were excessively attached and devoted to meat-eating they gave birth to Ḍākas and Ḍākinīs who were terrible eaters of human flesh. In the life of transmigration, Mahāmati, such ones will fall into the wombs of such excessive flesh-devouring creatures as the

---

[1] The text has all this in the plural.

CHAPTER EIGHT 217

lion, tiger, panther, wolf, hyena, wild-cat, jackal, owl, etc.; they will fall into the wombs of still more greedily flesh-devouring and still more terrible Rākshasas. Falling into such, it will be with difficulty that they can ever obtain a human womb; how much more [difficult] attaining Nirvana!

Such as these, Mahāmati, are the evils of meat-eating; how much more numerous [evil] qualities that are born of the perverted minds of those devoted to [meat-eating][1]. And, Mahāmati, the ignorant and simple-minded are not aware of all this and other evils and merits [in connection with meat-eating]. I tell you, Mahāmati, that seeing these evils and merits the Bodhisattva whose nature is pity should eat no meat.

If, Mahāmati, meat is not eaten by anybody for any reason, there will be no destroyer of life. Mahāmati, in the majority of cases (253) the slaughtering of innocent living beings is done for pride and very rarely for other causes. Though nothing special may be said of eating the flesh of living creatures such as animals and birds, alas, Mahāmati, that one addicted to the love of [meat-] taste should eat human flesh! Mahāmati, in most cases nets and other devices are prepared in various places by people who have lost their sense on account of their appetite for meat-taste, and thereby many innocent victims are destroyed for the sake of the price [they bring in]—such as birds, Kaurabhraka, Kaivarta, etc., that are moving about in the air, on land, and in water. There are even some, Mahāmati, who are like Rākshasas hard-hearted and used to practising cruelties,[2] who, being so devoid of compassion, would now and then look at living beings as meant for food and destruction— no compassion is awakened in them.

It is not true, Mahāmati, that meat is proper food and permissible for the Śrāvaka when [the victim] was not killed by himself, when he did not order others to kill it, when it was not specially meant for him. Again, Mahāmati,

---

[1] Both T'ang and Wei have here a sentence to the following effect: "Those who do not eat meat acquire a large sum of merit."
[2] According to T'ang.

there may be some unwitted people in the future time, who, beginning to lead the homeless life according to my teaching, are acknowledged as sons of the Śākya, and carry the Kāshāya robe about them as a badge, but who are in thought evilly affected by erroneous reasonings. They may talk about various discriminations which they make in their moral discipline, being addicted to the view of a personal soul. Being under the influence of the thirst for [meat-] taste, they will string together in various ways (254) some sophistic arguments to defend meat-eating. They think they are giving me an unprecedented calumny when they discriminate and talk about facts that are capable of various interpretations. Imagining that this fact allows this interpretation, [they conclude that] the Blessed One permits meat as proper food, and that it is mentioned among permitted foods and that probably the Tathagata himself partook of it. But, Mahāmati, nowhere in the sutras is meat permitted as something enjoyable, nor it is referred to as proper among the foods prescribed [for the Buddha's followers].

If however, Mahāmati, I had the mind to permit [meat-eating], or if I said it was proper for the Śrāvakas [to eat meat], I would not have forbidden, I would not forbid, all meat-eating for these Yogins, the sons and daughters of good family, who, wishing to cherish the idea that all beings are to them like an only child, are possessed of compassion, practise contemplation, mortification, and are on their way to the Mahāyāna. And, Mahāmati, the interdiction not to eat any kind of meat is here given to all sons and daughters of good family, whether they are cemetery-ascetics of forest-ascetics, or Yogins who are practising the exercises, if they wish the Dharma and are on the way to the mastery of any vehicle, and being possessed of compassion, conceive the idea of regarding all beings as an only child, in order to accomplish the end of their discipline.

(255) In the canonical texts here and there the process of discipline is developed in orderly sequence like a ladder going up step by step, and one joined to another in a regular and methodical manner; after explaining each point

CHAPTER EIGHT 219

meat obtained in these specific circumstances is not interdicted.[1] Further, a tenfold prohibition is given as regards the flesh of animals found dead by themselves. But in the present sutra all [meat-eating] in any form, in any manner, and in any place, is unconditionally and once for all, prohibited for all. Thus, Mahāmati, meat-eating I have not permitted to anyone, I do not permit, I will not permit. Meat-eating, I tell you, Mahāmati, is not proper for homeless monks. There may be some, Mahāmati, who would say that meat was eaten by the Tathagata thinking this would caluminate him. Such unwitted people as these, Mahāmati, will follow the evil course of their own karma-hindrance, and will fall into such regions where long nights are passed without profit and without happiness. Mahāmati, the noble Śrāvakas do not eat the food taken properly by [ordinary] men, how much less the food of flesh and blood, which is altogether improper. Mahāmati, the food for my Śrāvakas, Pratyekabuddhas, and Bodhisattvas is the Dharma and not flesh[2]-food; how much more the Tathagata! The Tathagata is the Dharmakāya, Mahāmati; he abides in the Dharma as food; his is not a body feeding on flesh; he does not abide in any flesh-food. He has ejected the habit-energy of thirst and desire which sustain all existence; he keeps away the habit-energy of all evil passions; he is thoroughly emancipated in mind and knowledge; he is the All-knower; (256) he is All-seer; he regards all beings impartially as an only child; he is a great compassionate heart. Mahāmati, having the thought of an only child for all beings, how can I, such as I am, permit the Śrāvakas to eat the flesh of their own child? How much less my eating it! That I have permitted the Śrāvakas as well as myself to partake of [meat-eating], Mahāmati, has no foundation whatever.

So it is said:

1. Liquor, meat, and onions are to be avoided, Mahāmati, by the Bodhisattva-Mahāsattvas and those who are Victor-heroes.

---

[1] The text as it stands requires fuller explanation.
[2] *Amiśra* (mixed) in T'ang.

2. Meat is not aggreeable to the wise: it has a nauseating odour, it causes a bad reputation, it is food for the carnivorous; I say[1] this, Mahāmati, it is not to be eaten.

3. To those who eat [meat] there are detrimental effects, to those who do not, merits; Mahāmati, you should know that meat-eaters bring detrimental effects upon themselves.

4. Let the Yogin refrain from eating flesh as it is born of himself, as [the eating] involves transgression, as [flesh] is produced of semen and blood, and as [the killing of animals] causes terror to living beings.

5. Let the Yogin always refrain from meat, onions, various kinds of liquor, allium, and garlic.

6. Do not anoint the body with sesamum oil; do not sleep on a bed, perforated with spikes; (257) for the living beings who find their shelter in the cavities and in places where there are no cavities may be terribly frightened.[2]

7. From eating [meat] arrogance is born, from arrogance erroneous imaginations issue, and from imagination is born greed; and for this reason refrain from eating [meat].

8. From imagination, greed is born, and by greed the mind it stupefied; there is attachment to stupefaction, and there is no emancipation from birth [and death].

9. For profit sentient beings are destroyed, for flesh money is paid out, they are both evil-doers and [the deed] matures in the hells called Raurava (screaming), etc.

10. One who eats flesh, trespassing against the words of the Muni, is evil-minded; he is pointed out in the teachings of the Śākya as the destroyer of the welfare of the two worlds.

11. Those evil-doers go to the most horrifying hell; meat-eaters are matured in the terrific hells such as Raurava, etc.

12. There is no meat to be regarded as pure in three ways: not premeditated, not asked for, and not impelled; therefore, refrain from eating meat.

---

[1] *Brūmi*, instead of *brūhi* as in the text.
[2] Unintelligible as far as the translator can see.

13. Let not the Yogin eat meat, it is forbidden by myself as well as by the Buddhas; those sentient beings who feed on one another will be reborn among the carnivorous animals.

14. [The meat-eater] is ill-smelling, contemptuous, and born deprived of intelligence; (**258**) he will be born again and again among the families of the Caṇḍāla, the Pukkasa, and the Domba.

15. From the womb of Dākinī he will be born in the meat-eaters' family, and then into the womb of a Rākshasī and a cat; he belongs to the lowest class of men.

16. Meat-eating is rejected by me in such sutras as the *Hastikakshya,* the *Mahāmegha,* the *Nirvāna,* the *Aṅglimālika,* and the *Laṅkāvatāra.*

17. [Meat-eating] is condemned by the Buddhas, Bodhisattvas, and Śrāvakas; if one devours [meat] out of shamelessness he will always be devoid of sense.

18. One who avoids meat, etc., will be born, because of this fact, in the family of the Brahmins or of the Yogins, endowed with knowledge and wealth.

19. Let one avoid all meat-eating [whatever they may say about] witnessing, hearing, and suspecting; these theorisers born in a carnivorous family understand this not.

20. As greed is the hindrance to emancipation, so are meat-eating, liquor, etc., hindrances.

21. There may be in time to come people who make foolish remarks about meat-eating, saying, "Meat is proper to eat, unobjectionable, and permitted by the Buddha."

22. Meat-eating is a medicine; again, it is like a child's flesh; (**259**) follow the proper measure and be averse [to meat, and thus] let the Yogin go about begging.

23. [Meat-eating] is forbidden by me everywhere and all the time for those who are abiding in compassion; [he who eats meat] will be born in the same place as the lion, tiger, wolf, etc.

24. Therefore, do not eat meat which will cause terror among people, because it hinders the truth of emancipation; [not to eat meat—] this is the **mark** of the wise.

Here Ends the Eighth Chapter, "On Meat-eating," from the *Laṅkāvatāra*, the Essence of the Teaching of All the Buddhas.[1]

---

[1] For the phrase "The essence of the teaching of the Buddhas (*sarvabuddhapravacanahṛidaya*)," see pp. 39–40.

[CHAPTER NINE][1]

(260) At that time the Blessed One addressed Mahāmati the Bodhisattva-Mahāsattva: Mahāmati, you should hold forth these magical phrases of the *Laṅkāvatāra*, which were recited, are recited, and will be recited by the Buddhas of the past, present, and future. I will recite them here for the benefit of the proclaimers of the Dharma, who will retain them in memory. They are:

Tuṭṭe, tuṭṭe—vuṭṭe, vuṭṭe—paṭṭe, paṭṭe—kaṭṭe, kaṭṭe—amale, amale—vimale, vimale—nime, nime—hime, hime—vame, vame—kale, kale, kale, kale—aṭṭe, maṭṭe—vaṭṭe, tuṭṭe—jñeṭṭe, spuṭṭe—kaṭṭe, kaṭṭe—laṭṭe, paṭṭe—dime dime—cale, cale—pace, pace—badhe, bandhe—añce, mañce—dutāre, dutāre—patāre, patāre—arkke, arkke—sarkke, sarkke—cakre, cakre—dime, dime—hime, hime—ṭu ṭu ṭu ṭu (4)—ḍu ḍu ḍu ḍu (4)— ru ru ru ru (4)—phu phu phu phu (4)—svāhā.

(261) These, Mahāmati, are the magical phrases of the *Laṅkāvatāra Mahāyāna Sūtra*: If sons and daughters of good family should hold forth, retain, proclaim, realise these magical phrases, no one should ever be able to effect his

---

[1] Another later addition probably when Dhāraṇī was extensively taken into the body of Buddhist literature just before its disappearance from the land of its birth. Dhāraṇī is a study by itself. In India where all kinds of what may be termed abnormalities in religious symbology are profusely thriving, Dhāraṇī has also attained a high degree of development as in the case of Mudrā (holding the fingers), Āsana (sitting), and Kalpa (mystic rite). When a religious symbolism takes a start in a certain direction, it pursues its own course regardless of its original meaning, and the symbolism itself begins to gain a new signification which has never been thought of before in connection with the original idea. The mystery of an articulate sound which infinitely fascinated the imagination of the primitive man has come to create a string of meaningless sounds in the form of a Dhāraṇī. Its recitation is now considered by its followers to produce mysterious effects in various ways in life.

descent upon them. Whether it be a god, or a goddess, or a Nāga, or a Nāgī, or a Yaksha, or a Yakshī, or an Asura, or an Asurī, or a Garuḍa, or a Garuḍī, or a Kinnara, or a Kannarī, or a Mahoraga, or a Mahoragī, or a Gandharva, or a Gandharvī, or a Bhūta, or a Bhutī, or a Kumbhāṇḍa, or a Kumbhāṇḍī, or a Piśāra, or a Piśācī, or an Austāraka, or an Austārakī, or a Apasmāra, or an Apasmārī, or a Rākshasa, or a Rākshasī, or a Ḍāka, or a Ḍākinī, or an Aujohāra, or an Aujohārī, or a Kaṭapūtana, or a Kaṭapūtanī, or an Amanushya, or an Amanushyī,—no one of these will be able to effect his or her descent [upon the holder of these magical phrases]. If any misfortune should befall, let him recite the magical phrases for one hundred and eight times, and [the evil ones] will, wailing and crying, turn away and go in another direction.

I will tell you, Mahāmati, other magical phrases. They are:

Padme, padmadeve—hine, hini, hine—cu, cule, culu, cule (262)—phale, phula, phule—yule, ghule, yula, yule—ghule, ghula, ghule—pale, pala, pale—muñce, muñce, muñce—cchinde, bhinde, bhañje, marde, pramarde, dinakare—svāhā.

If, Mahāmati, any son or daughter of good family should hold forth, retain, proclaim, and realise these magical phrases, on him or her no [evil beings] should be able to make their descent. Whether it be a god, or a goddess, or a Nāga, or a Nāgī, or a Yaksha, or a Yakshī, or an Asura, or an Asurī, a Garuḍa, or a Garuḍī, or a Kinnara, or a Kinnarī, or a Mahoraga, or a Mahoragī, or a Gandharva, or a Gandharvī, or a Bhūta, or a Bhūtī, or a Kumbhāṇḍa, or a Kumbhāṇḍī, or a Piśāca, or a Piśācī, or an Austāraka, or an Austārakī, or an Apasmāra, or an Apasmārī, or a Rākshasa, or a Rākshasī, or a Ḍāka, or a Ḍākinī, or an Aujohara, or an Aujoharī, or a Kaṭapūtana, or a Kaṭapūtanī, or an Amanushya, or an Amanushyī—no one of these will be able to effect his or her descent upon [the holder of these magical phrases]. By him who will recite these magic phrases, the [whole] *Laṅkāvatāra Sūtra* will be recited. (263) These magic

CHAPTER NINE

phrases are given by the Blessed One to guard against the interference of the Rākshasas.

Here Ends the Ninth Chapter Called "Dhāraṇī" in the *Laṅkāvatāra*.

[SAGĀTHAKAM][1]

(264) Listen to the wonderful Mahāyāna doctrine,
Declared in this *Laṅkāvatāra Sūtra*,
Composed into verse-gems,
And destroying a net of the philosophical views.

At that time Mahāmati the Bodhisattva-Mahāsattva said this to the Blessed One:[2]
1. (Chapter II, verse 1.)
2. (Chapter II, verse 3.)
3. (Chapter II, verse 2.)
4, 5. (Chapter II, verses 6, 7.)
(265) 6. (Chapter II, verse 8.)[3]
7, 8. (Chapter II, verses 151, 152.)
9. (Chapter II, verse 178.)
10. These individual objects are not solid [realities];

---

[1] This section entitled, "Sagāthakam," consists entirely of verses. It is probable that it was added later into the text. The subjects treated are many and varied, including those that have never appeared in the text. The verses are in a most confused condition, and it is frequently quite difficult to disentangle them and give them a semblance of order. The reader may use his own judgment in the matter.

[2] This remark refers only to the first six verses. The Chinese translations have here the following: "At that time the Blessed One wishing to declare again the deep signification of the Sutra uttered the following verses." The verses enumerated in the Sanskrit text are 884, out of which about 208 are repetitions of those which have already appeared in the main text. These repetitions are systematically excluded in T'ang, while Wei, with a few exceptions, repeats them all. In this English translation I have followed the method of T'ang. When we know more about the historical circumstances of the compilation of the various sutras we may be able to see how these repetitions came to be inserted here and also may learn something regarding the relation which this "Sagāthakam" section stands to the preceding part of the Sutra.

[3] These verses are not repeated in the same order as they are in the prose section of the text. There are some omissions, too. These irregularities take place throughout the "Sagāthakam," showing that the verses were originally an independent body.

they rise because of imagination; as the imagination itself is empty, what is imagined is empty.

11. (Chapter II, verse 149.)

12. (Chapter II, verse 154.)

13. By wrong discrimination the Vijñāna[-system] rises; severally as eightfold, as ninefold,[1] like waves on the great ocean.

14. The root is constantly nourished by habit-energy, firmly attached to the seat; (**266**) the mind moves along with an objective world as iron is drawn by the loadstone.

15. The original source on which all sentient beings are dependent is beyond theorisation; all doings cease and emancipation obtains, knowing and known are transcended.

16. In the Samādhi known as Māyā-like, one goes beyond the ten stages of Bodhisattvaship; one who is removed from thought and knowledge perceives the Mind-king.

17. When a "turning-back" takes place in the mind, one abides permanently in the palace of lotus-form, which is born of the realm of Māyā.

18. Abiding in it one attains a life of imagelessness, and, like a many-coloured jewel, performs religious deeds for all beings.

19. Except for discrimination, there is neither Saṁskṛita (or things made) nor Asaṁskṛita (or things not made); the ignorant hold on to them as a barren woman does to the child of her dream; what fools they are!

20. Let it be known that without self-nature, unborn, and empty are a personal soul, the Skandha-continuity, causation, the Dhātus, and [the notion of] existence and non-existence.

21. To me teaching is an expedient, but I do not teach external signs; the ignorant because of their attachment to existence seize on signified and signifying.

22. A knower of all things is not an all-knower, and all is not within all; the ignorant discriminate and [think] "I

---

[1] This requires attention. The Sutra itself maintains a system of eight Vijñānas, and not a ninefold one, which is a later development.

am the enlightened one in the world"; but I am not enlightened nor do I enlighten others.

(267) 23. (Chapter II, verse 156.)

24. (Chapter II, verse 143 and the first half of 144.)

25. (Chapter II, verse 179.)[1]

26. (Chapter II, verse 181.)

27. These things are empty, without self-nature, and unborn, like Māyā, like a dream, and their being and non-being is unobtainable.

28. One self-nature (*svabhāva*) I teach, which is removed from speculation and thought-construction, which belongs to the exquisite [spiritual] realm of the wise, removed from the two Svabhāvas [i.e., the Parikalpita and the Paratantra].

(268) 29. Though multitudinousness of things has no [real] existence as such, they appear to the intoxicated as like fire-fies because of their constitutional disturbance; likewise is the world essentially [appearance].

30. As Māyā is manifested depending on grass, wood, and brick, though Māyā itself is non-existent, so are all things essentially [mere appearances].

31. There is neither seizing nor seized, neither bound nor binding; all is like Māyā, like a mirage, like a dream, like an affected eye.

32. When the truth-seeker sees [the truth] devoid of discrimination and free from impurities, then he is accomplished in his contemplation; he sees me, there is no doubt.

33. In this there is nothing of thought-construction; it is like a mirage in the air; those who thus see all things, see nothing whatever.[2]

34. In causation which governs being and non-being things do not originate; in the triple world the mind is perturbed, therefore multiplicities appear.

35. The world is the same as a dream, and so are the multiplicities of things in it; [the wise] see property, touch,

---

[1] Omit the line in parentheses.

[2] This verse and the following one do not appear in T'ang, and they are also missing in the prose section.

death, a world-teacher, and work as of the same nature.[1]

36. This mind is the source of the triple world; when the mind goes astray there appears this world and that; (269) recognising the world as such, as it is non-existent, [a wise man] does not discriminate a world.

37. The ignorant because of their stupidity see [an objective world] as taking its rise and disappearing, but he who has transcendental knowledge sees it neither rising nor disappearing.

38. Those who are always above discrimination, in conformity with truth, and removed from mind and its belongings, are in the celestial palace of Akanishṭha where all evils are discarded.

39. Such attain the powers, psychic faculties, and self-control, are thoroughly adept in the Samādhis, and are there [in the heaven] awakened to enlightenment; but the transformed ones are awakened here [on earth].

40. The Buddhas appear on earth in their innumerable transformation-bodies beyond calculation, and everywhere the ignorant following them listen to the Dharma.

41. [There is one thing which is] released from [such conditions of existence as] beginning, middle, and endling, removed from existence and non-existence, all-pervading, immovable, pure, and above multiplicity, and [yet] producing multiplicity.

42. There is an essence[2] entirely covered by thought-constructions and hidden inside all that has body; because of perversion there is Māyā; Māyā, [however], is not the cause of perversion.

43. Even because of the mind being deluded, there is a somewhat [perceived as real]; being bound up with the two Svabhāvas there is the transformation of the Ālaya-vijñāna.

(270) 44. The world is no more than thought-con-

---

[1] For the last quarter Wei has: "The honoured one of the world preaches these doings." T'ang: "The person who perceives this well will be honoured by the world."

[2] *Gotra* (真性) according to T'ang.

struction, and there rages an ocean of views as regards ego and things (*dharma*); when the world is clearly perceived as such and there takes place a revulsion[1] [in the mind], this [one] is my child who is devoted to the truth of perfect knowledge.

45. Things are discriminated by the ignorant as heat, fluidity, motility, and solidity; they are, however, unrealities asserted; there is neither signified nor signifying.

46. But this body, form (*saṁsthāna*) and senses are made of the eight substances; deluded in the cage of transmigration, the ignorant thus discriminate this phenomenal world (*rūpa*).

47. In the intermingling of causes and conditions, the ignorant imagine the birth [of all things]; but as they do not understand the truth, they go astray in this abode of the triple world.

48. (Chapter II, verse 146.)

(271) 49. What is known as multiplicity-seeds multiply in the mind (*citta*); in what is revealed, the ignorant imagine birth and are delighted with dualism.

50. Ignorance, desire, and karma—they are the causes of mind and its belongings;[2] as they evolve thus [relatively], they are [recognised] by me to be Paratantric.

51. When the field of mentation gets confused, they imagine that there is something [real] to take hold of; in this imagination there is no perfect knowledge, it is false imagination rising from delusion.

52. When bound in conditions there evolves a mind in all beings; when released from conditions, I say, I see no [mind rising].

53. When the mind, released from conditions and unsupported by thought of self, abides no longer in the body, to me there is no objective world.

54 and 55. (Chapter II, verses 147 and 148.)

56. (Chapter II, verse 99.)

(272) 57. So the flood of the Ālayavijñāna is always

---

[1] *Parāvṛitti*, turning-over, or turning-up, or turning-back.
[2] Read *cittacaittānaṁ kārakam*.

stirred by the winds of objectivity (*vishaya*), and goes on dancing with the various Vijñāna-waves.

58. Because there is that which is seized and that which seizes, mind rises in all beings; there are no such signs visible [in the world] as are imagined by the ignorant.

59. There is the highest Ālayavijñāna, and again there is the Ālaya as thought-construction (*vijñāpti*); I teach suchness (*tathatā*) that is above seized and seizing.

60. Neither an ego, nor a being, nor a person exists in the Skandhas; [there is birth when] the Vijñāna is born, and [cessation when] the Vijñāna ceases.

61. As a picture shows highness and lowness while [in reality] there is nothing of the sort in it; so in things existent there is thingness seen [as real] while there is nothing of the sort in them.

62. The visible world (*dṛiśyam*) has always the appearance of the city of the Gandharvas and that of fata morgana; it is to be regarded as such, but it does not thus exist to the transcendental wisdom [of the wise].

63 and 64. (Chapter III, verses 79 and 80.)

65. A proposition [is established] by means of conditions, reasons, and examples, (273) such as a dream, the Gandharva's [castle, fire-]wheel, mirage, the moon, the sun.

66. By such examples as flame, hair, etc., I teach that birth is something not to be recognised really as such;[1] the world is something imagined, empty like a dream, or Māyā, which is error.

67. The triple world has nowhere to place itself, either within nor without, it is thus [homeless]; seeing that all beings are unborn, there grows a full acceptance of the truth that nothing is ever born (*kshānti-anutpatti*).

68. He will then attain the Samādhi called Māyā-like, the will-body, the psychic faculties, the self-mastery, the various powers belonging to the Mind.

69. All things existent are unborn, empty, and without self-substance; and the delusion about them rises and ceases in accordance with conditions.

[1] Here I have followed T'ang.

70. Depending upon the Mind, there appears [within] a mind and, without a world of individual objects (*rūpiṇa*); this and no other is an external world which is imagined by the ignorant.

71. This heap of bones, the Buddha-image, the analysis of the elements—[these are subjects of meditation]; by means of mental images (*prajñapti*) good students handle the various aspects of the world.

72. Body, abode, and property are three representations (*vijñapti*) seized upon [as objects]; the will, [the desire] to hold, the discrimination of these representations are the seizing agents.

(274) 73. As long as those philosophers who get confused in their reasonings and who are unable to go beyond the realm of words, distinguish the discriminating from the discriminated—so long they do not see [the truth] of suchness.

74. When the Yogin by means of his transcendental wisdom understands that all things existent have no self-substance, he thus attains calmness and establishes himself in the state of no-form (*ānimitta*).

75. As an object painted black is taken by the unwise to be a cock, so by the ignorant who do not know, the triple vehicle is understood in like manner.

76. There are no Śrāvakas, no Pratyekabuddhas here; if, however, one recognises the form of a Buddha, of a Śrāvaka, this is a transformed manifestation of the Bodhisattva whose nature is compassion itself.

77. The triple world of existence is no more than thought-construction, which is discriminated by the twofold Svabhāva [of imagination and relative knowledge]; but when [within the mind] a turning-away from the course of sense-objects (*dharma*) and the ego-soul (*pudgala*) takes place, then we have [the truth of] suchness (*tathatā*).

78. The sun, the moon, the lamp-light, the elements, and the gems,—each functions in its own way without discrimination; and so does the Buddha's nature work on its own accord.

79. (Chapter II, verse 51.)

80. Things known as defiled or as pure are like hair-nets [that is, wrongly perceived by the dim-eyed]; they [really] have nothing to do with such notions as birth, abiding, and disappearance, or as eternity and non-eternity.

81. It is like a drugged man whoever he is, who sees the world in golden colours; though there is no gold, for him the earth has changed into gold.

82. The ignorant, thus defiled since beginningless time with the mind and what belongs to it, apprehend existing things to be really such as they appear to be; though in fact they owe their origin to Māyā or a mirage.

83. One seed and no-seed are of the same stamp, and one seed and all seed also; and in one mind you see multiplicity.

84. When one seed is made pure, there is a turning into a state of no-seed; the sameness comes from non-discrimination; from superabundance there is birth and general confusion from which there grows a multitude of seeds, hence the designation all-seed.[1]

85. (Chapter II, verse 140.)

86. (Chapter III, verse 52.)

87. When the self-nature of existence is understood there is no need of keeping off the delusion; no-birth is the self-nature of existence, seeing thus one is released.

88. (Chapter II, verse 170.)

89. (Chapter II, verse 144.)

90. (Chapter II, verse 141.)

91. (Chapter III, verse 48.)

92. (Chapter II, verse 136.)

93. When the mind is evolved, forms begin to manifest themselves; really [if] no minds, no forms; the mind is due to [the accumulation of] delusions since beginningless past; then the Yogin by his transcendental wisdom sees the world shorn of its appearances (*abhāsa*).[2]

---

[1] The two verses 83 and 84 on "seed" (*bīja*) require fuller explanation to make them more intelligible.

[2] The first line of verse 94 properly belongs to the preceding verse.

94. (Chapter III, verse 53.)

(277) 95. The Gandharva's air-castle, Māyā, a hair-circle, and a fata morgana,—they are non-entities yet they appear as if they were entities; the nature of an objective existence is thus to be regarded.

96. Nothing has ever been brought into existence, all that is seen before us is delusion; it is due to delusion that things are imagined to have come into existence, the ignorant are delighted with the dualism of discrimination.

97. As memory [or habit-energy, *vāsanā*] grows in various forms the Mind is evolved like the waves; when memory is cut off, there is no evolving of Mind.

98. The Mind is evolved dependent upon a variety of conditions, just as a painting depends upon the wall [on which it is painted]; if otherwise why is not the painting produced in the air?[1]

99. If Mind evolves at all depending on individual forms as conditions, then Mind is condition-born, and the doctrine of Mind-only will not be held true.

100. Mind is grasped by mind, it is not a something produced by a cause; Mind is by nature pure, memory (habit-energy) has no existence in [mind which is like] the sky.

101. An individual mind is evolved by clinging to Mind in itself; there is no visible world outside [Mind itself]; therefore, [it is declared that] Mind-only exists.

(278) 102. Mind (*citta*[2]) is the Ālayavijñāna, Manas is that which has reflection as its characteristic nature, it apprehends the various sense-fields, for which reason it is called a Vijñāna.

---

[1] The Sanskrit as it stands is unintelligible; I have followed the T'ang. This gāthā may be regarded as a question to which the following few verses are a reply.

[2] Citta which is generally translated "mind," either with the "m" capitalised or not, is used in this text in two different senses. When it stands in the series of Citta, Manas, and Vijñānas, it means the empirical mind. It is also used in a general sense meaning mentation. Besides this, *citta* has an absolute sense denoting something that goes beyond the realm of relativity and yet that lies at the foundation of this world of particulars. When the *Laṅkā* speaks of "Mind-only," it refers to this something defined here. It is important to keep this

103. Citta is always neutral; Manas functions in two ways; the functioning Vijñāna is either good or bad.

104. (Chapter II, verse 132.)

105–109. (Chapter IV, verses 1–5.)

(279) 110. In self-realisation itself there are no time [-limts]; it goes beyond all the realms belonging to the various stages; transcending the measure of thought, it establishes itself as the result [of discipline in the realm] of no-appearance.

111. That non-existence and existence is recognised, and multiplicity too, is due to erroneous attachment of the ignorant; the error [is to see] multiplicity.

112. If there is non-discriminative knowledge, it is not in accord with reason to say that [individual] realities (*vastu*) exist; because of Mind, there are no individual forms (*rūpāṇi*), and, therefore, we speak of non-discriminative [knowledge].

113. The sense-organs are to be known as Māyā, the sense-fields resemble a dream; actor, act, and acting—they do not at all [in reality] exist.[1]

114. (Chapter II, v. 133, v. 176.)

115. (Chapter II, v. 130, v. 177.)

116(280)–117. (Chapter II, vv. 9 and 10.)

118. (Chapter II, v. 174.)

119. (Chapter II, v. 173.)

120. According to worldly knowledge (*saṁvṛiti*) everything exists, but in ultimate truth (*paramārtha*) none exists; in ultimate truth, indeed, one sees that all things are devoid of self-substance. Although there is no self-substance, there rises something which one perceives [as objective reality]—this is called worldly knowledge.

121. If things are regarded as existing by themselves, they exist because of their being so designated in words; if there were no words to designate their existence, they are not.

---

distinction in mind. See also my *Studies in the Laṅkāvatāra*, p. 176 and elsewhere.

[1] This verse is missing in Wei.

122. That which exists only as word and not as reality—such is not to be found even in worldly knowledge; this comes from the nature of reality being erroneously understood, for no such perception is possible.

123. If such errors were granted, it would not be possible to talk about the non-existence of self-substance; (281) as the nature of reality is erroneously understood, there is something perceived where there is really no self-substance; all is indeed non-existent.

124. What is seen as multiplicity is the mind saturated with the forms of evil habits; because of mental delusions one clings to forms and appearances regarding them as objective [realities].

125. Discrimination is cut asunder by non-discriminating discrimination; the truth of emptiness is seen into by non-discriminating discrimination.

126. Like an elephant magically created, like golden leaves in a painting, the visible world is to the people whose minds are saturated with the forms of ignorance.

127-128. (Chapter II, vv. 168 and 169.)

129. As a man whose eye is affected with a cataract perceives a hair-circle because of his delusion, so the ignorant perceive an objective world rising with its various aspects.

130. (Chapter II, v. 150.)

(282) 131. Discrimination, that which is discriminated, and the setting up of discrimination; binding, that which is bound, and its cause: these six are conditions of liberation.

132. There are no stages [of Bodhisattvaship], no truths, no [Buddha-]lands, no bodies of transformation; Buddhas, Pratyekabuddhas, Śrāvakas are [products of] imagination.

133. (Chapter II, v. 139.)

134. Mind is all, it is found everywhere and in every body; it is by the evil-minded that multiplicity is recognised, there are no [recognisable] marks where Mind-only is.

135-137. (Chapter III, vv. 35, 36, 37.)

138. The constructing of appearances (*nimitta*) created

SAGATHAKAM

by delusion is the characteristic mark of Paratantra (dependence) knowledge; (283) the giving of names to these appearances [regarding them as real individual existences] is characteristic of the imagination.[1]

139. When the constructing of appearances and names, which come from the union of conditions and realities, no more takes place, we have the characteristic mark of perfected knowledge (*parinishpanna*).[2]

140. The world is everywhere filled with Buddhas of Maturity,[3] Buddhas of Transformation,[4] beings, Bodhisattvas, and [Buddha-]lands.

141. The Issuing[5][-Buddhas], Dharma[-Buddhas], Transformation[-Buddhas] and those that appear transformed—they all come forth from Amitābha's Land of Bliss.

142. What is uttered by Buddhas of Transformation and what is uttered by Buddhas of Maturity constitute the doctrine fully developed in the sutras, whose secret meaning you should know.

143. What is uttered by the Bodhisattvas and what is uttered by the teachers—they are both what is uttered by the Buddhas of Transformation and not by the Buddhas of Maturity.

144. All these individual objects (*dharmas*) have never been born, but they are not exactly non-existent either; they resemble the Gandharva's castle, a dream, and magical creations.

145. Mind is set in motion in various ways, and mind is liberated; mind rises in no other way, and mind thus ceases.

146. The mind of all beings is that which perceives something like objective reality, and this mind is the product of imagination; (284) in Mind-only there is no objective

---

[1] Generally *parikalpita*, but here *vikalpita*.
[2] This is the reading of T'ang, but I suggest the following: "When the constructing of names and appearances no more takes place in it, there are only causal signs indicative of reality—this is the characteristic mark of perfected knowledge." Both Wei and T'ang here understand *saṅketa* in the sense of "union."
[3] *Vaipākika*. [4] *Nairmāṇika*. [5] *Nisyanda*.

world; when one is released from discrimination there is liberation.

147. Brought together by the evil habit of erroneous reasoning, discrimination asserts itself; hence the evolution of this fallacious world.

148. [Relative] knowledge (*vijñāna*) takes place where there is something resembling an external world; [transcendental] knowledge (*jñāna*)[1] belongs to the realm of Suchness. When a turning-back (*parāvṛitta*) takes place, there is a state of imagelessness, which is the realm of the wise.

149. (Chapter II, v. 161.)

150. By reason of false imagination (*parikalpita*) all things existent are declared unborn; as people take refuge in relative knowledge (*paratantra*), they get confused in their discriminations.

151. When relative knowledge is purified by keeping itself aloof from discrimination, and detached from imagination, there is a turning-back to the abode of suchness.

152. Do not discriminate discrimination, there is no truth in discrimination; [this world of] delusion is discriminated as to that which is perceived and that which perceives, but in reality there is no such dualism in it; it is an error to recognise an external world, [the conception of] self-substance is due to imagination.

(285) 153. Imagining by this imagination, self-substance is conceived to rise by the conditions of origination (*pratyayodbhava*); an external world is recognised in distortion, there is [in fact] no such external world, but just the Mind.

154. To those who see [the world] clearly and properly, the separation between that which perceives and that which is perceived ceases; there is no such external world as is discriminated by the ignorant.

155. When the Mind is agitated by habit-energy (or memory) there rises what appears to be an external world; when the dualistic imagination ceases there grows [transcendental] knowledge (*jñāna*), the realm of suchness, the

[1] As to the distinction between Jñāna and Vijñāna see p. 135 et seq.

realm of the wise, which is free from appearances and beyond thought.[1]

156. (Chap. II, v. 134; Chap. VI, v. 3.)

157. From the union of mother and father, the Ālaya gets connected with Manas; like a rat in a pot of ghee, the red together with the white grows up.

158. Through the stages of Peśī, Ghanā, and Arbuda, the boil grows—an unclean mass bearing a variety of karma; nourished by the wind of karma and the four elements, it comes to maturity like a fruit.

159. The five, the five, and the five; and the sores are nine; (286) nails, teeth, and hair are supplied; when ready to spring forth it is born.

160. When [the baby] is just born, it is like a worm growing in the dung; like a man waking from sleep, the eye begins to distinguish forms, and discrimination goes on increasing.

161. With knowledge gained by discrimination, human speech is produced from the combination of the palate, lips, and cavity; and discrimination goes on like a parrot.

162. Philosophical doctrines are definite, but the Mahāyāna [or Great Vehicle] is not definite, it is set in motion by the thoughts of beings; it is not an abode for those who see wrongly. The vehicle realised within my own inner self is not the realm that can be reached by dialecticians.[2]

163–164. After the passing of the Teacher, pray tell me who will be the bearer [of the Mahāyāna]? O Mahāmati, thou shouldst know that there will be one who bears the Dharma, when sometime is past after the Sugata's entrance into Nirvana.

165. In Vedalī, in the southern part, a Bhikshu most illustrious and distinguished [will be born]; his name is Nāgāhvaya, he is the destroyer of the one-sided views based on being and non-being.

---

[1] The first line of verse 156 is a part of the preceding one. Cf. v. 148.

[2] The verses are wrongly divided here, for this line properly belongs to 162 and not to 163.

166. He will declare my Vehicle, the unsurpassed Mahāyāna, to the world; attaining the stage of Joy he will go to the Land of Bliss.

(287) 167. (Chapter II, v. 175.)

168. In the realm of conditional origination, "there is" and "there is not" do not take place; those who imagine something real in the midst of conditional origination say, "there is" and "there is not," but these philosophical views are far away from my teaching.

169. The giving names to all things existent has always been going on for hundreds of generations past; this has been repeated, is being repeated constantly; an endless mutual discrimination is thus taking place.

170. If this designating does not take place, the whole world falls into confusion; thus names are established in order to get rid of confusion.

171. Things existent are discriminated by the ignorant in the threefold form of discrimination; there is delusion from discriminating names, from conditional origination, and from the [the notion of] being born.

172. [The philosophers argue that] the primary elements are unborn and like the sky are imperishable; but [in reality] there are no individual self-substances and the notion [itself] belongs to discrimination.

173. [Individual existences are] appearances, images, like Māyā, like a mirage, a dream, a wheel made by a revolving fire-brand, the Gandharva's [castle], an echo—they are all born in the same manner.

(288) 174. Non-duality, suchness, emptiness, ultimate limit, essence (*dharmatā*), non-discrimination,—all these I teach as belonging to the aspect of perfected knowledge (*parinishpanna*).

175. Language belongs to the realm of thought, the truth becomes [thus] wrongly [represented]; transcendental knowledge (*prajñā*) being discriminated by thought falls into a duality; therefore, transcendental knowledge is something not imagined.

176–177. (Chap. III, vv. 9 and 10.)

178. The whole existence is not perceived by the ignorant as it is perceived by the wise; the whole existence as it is perceived by the wise, has no marks [of individuation].

179. As a spurious necklace, not of gold though looking like it, is imagined by the ignorant to be of [genuine] gold, so all things are imagined by those who reason wrongly.

180. (Chapter III, v. 11.)

181. Things have no beginning, no end; they are abiding in the aspect of reality; (**289**) there is no creator, nothing doing in the world, but the logicians do not understand.

182. Whatever things that are thought to have been in existence in the past, to come into existence in the future, or to be in existence at present,—all such are unborn.

183–184. (Chap. III, vv. 44 and 45.)

185. This [world] is just a sign[1] indicative of reality (*dharmatā*); apart from the sign, nothing is produced, nothing is destroyed.

186–187. (Chap. II, vv. 159 and 160.)

188–189. (Chap. III, vv. 1 and 2.)

(**290**) 190. Existence in its conditional relations cannot be [described] as unity or diversity; it is just in a general way of speaking that there is birth, cessation, and destruction.

191. Emptiness unborn is one thing, emptiness born is another; emptiness unborn is the better, [because] emptiness born leads to destruction.

192. Suchness, emptiness, the limit, Nirvana, and the Dharmadhātu, the various will-made bodies,—these I point out as synonymous.

193. Those who discriminate purity according to the Sutras, Vinayas, and Abhidharmas, follow books and not the inner meaning; they are not established in egolessness.

194–196. (Chap. III, vv. 12–14.)

(**291**) 197. The visible world is likened to the hare's horns as long as all beings go on discriminating; those who discriminate are deluded just like a deer running after a mirage.

---

[1] *Saṅketa*; see also verse 139.

198. By clinging to discrimination, [more] discrimination goes on; when the cause of discrimination is put away, one is disengaged therefrom.

199–200. (Chap. III, vv. 54 and 55.)

201. Transcendental knowledge is deep, exalted, far-reaching, and perceives all the Buddha-countries; this I teach for the sons of the Victorious One; for the Śrāvakas I teach transitoriness.

202. The triple existence is transitory, empty, devoid of the ego and what belongs to it; thus I teach the doctrine of generality to the Śrāvakas.

203. Not to be attached to anything existent, truly knowing what the truth of solitude is, is to walk all alone; the fruit of Pratyekabuddhahood which is above speculation is what I teach.

204. External objects are imagined, those endowed with corporeality are dependent on relative knowledge; being deluded they see not themselves, therefore a mind is evolved.

205 (**292**)–206. (Chap. IV, vv. 6 and 7.)

207 and 208. (Chapter III, verses 56 and 57.)

209. (Chapter II, verse 153.)

210. (Chapter II, verse 150.)

211. There are four psychic powers: that which comes from the maturing [of the disciplinary exercises], that which comes from the sustaining power of the Buddhas, that which rises from entering into the various paths of living beings, and that which is obtained in a dream.

212. The psychic power which is obtained in a dream, that which comes from the power of the Buddhas, and that which has its birth by entering the various paths of beings —these powers are not[1] born of the maturing [of the disciplinary exercises].

(**293**) 213. The mind being influenced by habit-energy, there rises a something resembling real existence (*bhāvābhāsa*); as the ignorant do not understand, it is said that there is the birth [of realities].

---

[1] Read after the Chinese and Tibetan versions. Not *vijñāna-vipākajaḥ*, but '*bhijñā na vipākajaḥ*.

SAGATHAKAM

214. As long as external objects (*bāhyam*)[1] are discriminated as possessing individual marks, the mind is confused (*vimuhyate*)[2] being unable to see its own delusion.

215. Why is birth spoken of? Why is not the perceived world spoken of? When the perceived world, which has no existence, is yet perceived as existing, what is that which is spoken of? To whom is it? and why?

216. The Citta in its essence is thoroughly pure, the Manas is defiled, and the Manas is with the Vijñānas, habit-energy is always casting out [its seeds].

217. The Ālaya is released from the body, the Manas solicits the [various] paths of existence; the Vijñāna is deluded with something resembling an objective world, and perceiving it is befooled.[3]

218. What is seen is one's own mind, an objective world exists not; when one thus perceives [that existence is] an error,[4] one even gets into suchness.

219. The [spiritual] realm attained by Dhyāna-devotees, karma, and the exalted state of the Buddhas—these three are beyond thought, they belong to the Vijñāna-[5] realm that surpasses thought.

(294) 220. The past and the future, Nirvana, a personal ego, [space[6]], words,—of these I talk because of worldly convention, but ultimate reality is beyond the letter.

221. The two vehicles[7] and the philosophers are one in their dependence on [wrong] views; they are confused in regard to Mind-only, and imagine an external existence.

222. The enlightenment attained by the Pratyeka-buddhas, Buddhahood, Arhatship, and the seeing of the Buddhas—these are the secret seeds that grow in enlightenment; but it is accomplished in a dream.[8]

---

[1] After the Chinese.   [2] After Wei.
[3] *Pralubhyate*, "greedily attached," according to Wei and T'ang.
[4] *Bhrānti*, "a delusion," "an external world."
[5] Should be *jñāna*, or does it refer to the Ālaya?
[6] According to the Chinese.
[7] *Naikāyikās*, literally, "they who belong to the Nikāya."
[8] What this verse purports to mean is difficult to gather from the contents of the *Laṅkāvatāra* as we have it here. The existence of such verses as this, and there are quite a number of them in the Sagāthakam,

223. Māyā, Citta (mind), intelligence,[1] tranquillity, the dualism of being and non-being—where are these teachings? for whom? whence? wherefore? and of what signification? Pray tell me.

224. I teach such things as Māyā, being and non-being, etc., to those who are confused in the teaching of Mind-only; when birth and death are linked together [as one], qualified and qualifying are removed.

225. Another name for Manas is discrimination (*vikalpa*), and it goes along with the five Vijñānas; mind seeds (*cittabīja*) take their rise in the way images [appear in a mirror] or [waves roll on] the ocean-waters.

226. When the Citta, Manas, Vijñāna cease to rise, (295) then there is the attainment of the will-body and of the Buddha-stage.

227. Causation, the Dhātus, Skandhas, and the self-nature of all things, thought-construction, a personal soul, and mind—they are all like a dream, like a hair-net.

228. Seeing the world as like Māyā and a dream, one abides with the truth; the truth, indeed, is free from individual marks, removed from speculative reasoning.

229. The inner realisation attained by the wise always abides in a state of no-memory[2]; it leads the world to the truth as it is not confused with speculative reasoning.

230. When all false speculation subsides, error no more rises; as long as there is discriminative knowledge,[3] error keeps on rising.

231. The world is empty and has no self-nature; to talk of permanency and impermanency is the view maintained by followers of birth and not by those of no-birth.

232. [The philosophers] imagine the world to be of oneness and otherness, of bothness [and not-bothness], and [to have risen] from Īśvara, or spontaneously, or from time, or from a supreme spirit, or other causal agency.

suggests in one way that this verse section has no organic relation with the main text.

[1] The Chinese read *gati* (path or course), and not *mati*.
[2] *Asmara*, T'ang.
[3] *Jñāna* for *prajñā*.

233. The Vijñāna which is the seed of transmigration is not evolved when this visible world is [truly] recognised; like a picture on a wall, it disappears when [its nature] is recognised.

(296) 234. Like figures in Māyā, people are born and die; in the same way the ignorant because of their stupidity [imagine] there really is bondage and release.

235. The duality of the world, inner and outer, and things subject to causation—by distinctly understanding what they are, one is established in imagelessness.

236. The mind (*citta*) is not separate from habit-energy, nor is it together with it; though enveloped with habit-energy the mind itself remains undifferentiated.

237. Habit-energy born of the Manovijñāna is like dirt wherewith the Citta, which is a perfectly white garment, is enveloped and fails to display itself.

238. As space is neither existent nor non-existent, so is the Ālaya in the body, I say; it is devoid of existence as well as of non-existence.

239. When the Manovijñāna is "turned over" (*vyāvṛitta*), the Citta frees itself from turbidity; by understanding [the nature of] all things, the mind (*citta*) becomes Buddha, I say.

240. Removed from the triple continuity, devoid of being and non-being, released from the four propositions, all things (*bhava*) are always like Māyā.

241. The [first] seven stages are mind-born and belong to the two Svabhābas; the remaining [two] stages and the Buddha-stage are the Nishpanna ("perfected knowledge").

(297) 242. The world of form, of no-form, and the world of desire, and Nirvana are in this body; all is told to belong to the realm of Mind.

243. As long as there is something attained, there is so much error rising; when the Mind itself is thoroughly understood, error neither rises nor ceases.

244. (Chapter II, verse 171.)

245. (Chapter II, verse 131.)

246. Two things are established by me; individual

objects and realisation; there are four principles which constitute the dogmas of logic.

247. The error [or the world] is discriminated when it is seen as characterised with varieties of forms and figures; when names and forms are removed self-nature becomes pure which is the realm of the wise.

248. As long as discrimination is carried on, the Parikalpita (false imagination) continues to take place; but as what is imagined by discrimination has no reality, self-nature is [truly understood in] the realm of the wise.

249. The mind emancipated is truth constant and everlasting; the essence making up the self-nature of things (298) and suchness is devoid of discrimination.

250. There is reality (*vastu*); it is not to be qualified as pure, nor is it to be said defiled; since a mind purified leaves traces of defilement, but reality is the truth that is [absolutely] pure, belonging to the realm of the wise.

251. The world is born of causation; when it is regarded as removed from discrimination and as resembling Māyā, a dream, etc., one is emancipated.

252. Varieties of habit-energy growing out of error are united with the mind; they are perceived by the ignorant as objects externally existing; and the essence of mind (*cittasya dharmatā*) is not perceived.

253. The essence of mind is pure but not the mind that is born of error; error rises from error, therefore Mind is not perceived.

254. Delusion itself is no more than truth, truth is neither in Saṁskāra nor anywhere else, but it is where Saṁskāra is observed [in its proper bearings].

255. When the Saṁskṛita is seen as devoid of qualified and qualifying, all predicates are discarded and thus the world is seen as of Mind itself.

256. When the [Yogin] enters upon Mind-only, he will cease discriminating an external world; establishing himself where suchness has its asylum he will pass on to Mind-only.[1]

---

[1] *Cittamātram* here and in the following verse is rendered in T'ang as 心量 (*hsin-liang*) and not the usual 唯心 (*wei-hsin*). *Hsin-*

257. By passing on to Mind-only, he passes on to the state of imagelessness; (299) when he establishes himself in the state of imagelessness, he sees not [even] the Mahāyāna.[1]

258. The state of non-striving (*anābhoga*) is quiescent and thoroughly purified with the [original] vows; the most excellent knowledge of egolessness sees no [duality in the world] because of imagelessness.

259. Let him review the realm of mind, let him review the realm of knowledge, let him review the realm, with transcendental knowledge (*prajñā*), and he will not be confounded with individual signs.

260. Pain belongs to mind, accumulation is the realm of knowledge (*jñāna*); the [remaining] two truths[2] and the Buddha-stage are where transcendental knowledge functions.

261. The attainment of the fruits, Nirvana, and the eightfold path—when all these truths are thus understood, there is Buddha-knowledge thoroughly purified.

262. The eye, form, light, space, and attention (*manas*) —out of this [combination] there is the birth of consciousness (*vijñāna*) in people; consciousness is indeed born of the Ālaya.

263. There is nothing grasped, nor grasping, nor one who grasps; there are no names, no objects; those who carry on their groundless discriminative way of thinking lack intelligence.

264. Name is not born of meaning, nor is meaning born of name; (300) whether things are born of cause or of nocause, such is discrimination; have no discrimination!

265. (Chapter II, verse 145.)

266. Imagining himself to be standing on a truth, he

liang means "mind-measurement," the term used in Sung throughout for *cittamātram*, for in the days of Sung *wei-shin* had not been thought of. But why does T'ang use *hsin-liang* for *wei-shin* in this particular case while *wei-shin* is used in the preceding line? Does *cittamātram* mean here simply "mental or intellectual measurement" and is not used in the technical sense in which the term is found elsewhere in this sutra?

[1] "Not" (*na*) is replaced by "he" (*sa*) in one MS. May this be a better reading?

[2] Referring to the Four Noble Truths.

discourses on thought-construction; oneness is not attained in five ways, and thus the truth is abandoned.[1]

267. Delusion (*prapañca*) is the evil one who is to be broken down; being and non-being is to be transcended; as one sees into [the truth of] egolessness, he has no longing for, no evil thought of, the world.

268. [The philosophers imagine] a permanently existing creator engaged in mere verbalism; highest truth is beyond words, the Dharma is seen when cessation takes place.

269. Leanig on the Ālaya for support the Manas is evolved; depending on the Citta and Manas the Vijñāna-system is evolved.

270. What is established by a proposition (*samāropa*) is a proposition; suchness is the essence of mind; when this is clearly perceived, the Yogin attains the knowledge of Mind-only.

271. Let one not think of the Manas, individual signs, and reality from the point of view of permanency and impermanency; nor let him think in his meditation of birth and no-birth.

272. They do not discriminate duality; the Vijñāna rises from Ālaya; (301) the oneness of meaning thus taking place is not to be known by a dually operating mind.

273. There is neither a speaker nor speaking nor emptiness, since the Mind is seen; but when the Mind is not seen there rises a net of philosophical doctrines.

274. There is no rising of the causation[-chain], nor are there any sense-organs; no Dhātus, no Skandhas, no greed, no Sanskrita.

275. There is no primarily working fire;[2] no working done, no effects produced, no final limit, no power, no deliverance, no bondage.

276. There is no state of being to be called neutral [or inexplicable] (*avyākṛita*); there is no duality of dharma

---

[1] The reference is not clear.
[2] T'ang has, "karma and its effects"; while Wei has, "karma in work."

and adharma; there is no time, no Nirvana, no dharma-essence.

277. And there are no Buddhas, no truths, no fruition, no causal agents, no perversion, no Nirvana, no passing away, no birth.

278. And then there are no twelve elements (*anga*), and no duality either, of limit and no-limit; because of the cessation of all the notions [that are cherished by the philosophers] I declare [there is] Mind-only.

279. The passions, path of karma, the body, creators, fruitions—they are like a fata morgana and a dream; they are like a city of the Gandharvas.

280. By maintaining the Mind-only, the idea of reality is removed; by establishing the Mind-only permanency and annihilation are seen [in their proper relationship].

281. There are no Skandhas in Nirvana, nor is there an ego-soul, nor any individual signs; (**302**) by entering into the Mind-only, one escapes from becoming attached to emancipation.

282. It is error (*dosha*) that causes the world to be externally perceived as it is manifested to people; Mind is not born of the visible world; therefore, Mind is not visible.

283. It is the habit-energy of people that brings out into view something resembling body, property, and abode; Mind is neither a being nor a non-being, it does not reveal itself because of habit-energy.

284. Dirt is revealed within purity but purity itself is not soiled; as when the sky is veiled with clouds, Mind is invisible [when defiled with error].

285. (Chapter III, verse 38.)
286. (,, II, ,, 182.)
287. (,, III, ,, 40.)
288. (,, III, ,, 41.)
289. (,, II, ,, 183.)

(**303**) 290. Mind is not born of the elements (*bhūta*), Mind is nowhere to be seen; it is the habit-energy of people that brings out into view body, property, and abode.[1]

[1] This is a repetition of the latter half of verse 282 and the first

291. All that is element-made is not form and form is not element-made; the city of the Gandharvas, a dream, Māyā, an image,—these are not element-made.

292.[1]

293.[2]

294. (Chapter III, verse 43.)

295. As reality and non-reality can be predicated of existence that originates from causation, the view of oneness and otherness definitely belongs to them.

296–302. (Chapter II, verses 184–190.)

(304) 303. There are three kinds of my Śrāvakas: the transformed, the born of the vows, and the Śrāvakas disengaged from greed and anger, and born of the Dharma.

304. There are three kinds, also, of the Bodhisattvas: those who have not yet reached Buddhahood, those who manifest themselves according to the thoughts of sentient beings, and those who are seen in the likeness of the Buddha.[3]

305–310. (Chapter II, verses 191–196.)

(305) 311. It is a man's mind that is perceived as something resembling (saṁnibham) the form of a star, a cloud, a moon, a sun; and what is thus perceived by them is born of habit-energy.

312. The elements are devoid of selfhood, there is neither qualified nor qualifying in them; if all element-made objects were the elements, form (rūpa) would be element-made.

313. The elements are uniform, there are no element-

half of 283. This is omitted in both T'ang and Wei, showing that the insertion is probably due to a clerical mistake.

[1] The first half of this corresponds to the first half of Chapter III, verse 42; while the second half of 292 and the first half of 293 are practically a repetition of 290, and also of the second half of 282 and the first half of 283. Nanjo's verse divisions are to be revised I think in some places, but fearing to cause greater confusion in the numbering of the whole "Sagāthakam" I have followed Nanjo.

[2] The first half of 292 and the second half of 293 correspond to Chapter III, verse 42.

[3] This is the T'ang reading. Another reading is: "There are three kinds of Bodhisattvas. As to the Buddhas, they have no [tangible] form, but something looking like a Buddha may be seen according to the thoughts of each sentient being."

made objects in the elements; the elements are the cause; the earth, water, etc. are the result.

314. Substances and forms of thought-construction are like things born of Māyā; **(306)** they appear like a dream and a city of the Gandharvas, they are a mirage and a fifth.[1]

315. There are five kinds of the Icchantika, so with the families which are five; there are five vehicles and no-vehicle, and six kinds of Nirvana.

316. The Skandhas are divided into twenty-five, and there are eight kinds of form, twenty-four Buddhas, and there are two kinds of Buddha-sons.

317. There are one hundred and eight doctrines, and three kinds of Śrāvakas; there is one land of the Buddhas, and so with the Buddha, there is one.

318. Likewise with emancipation; there are three forms, four kinds of mind-streams, six kinds of my egolessness, and also four kinds of knowledge.

319. Disjoined from causal agencies, removed from faulty theories, is the knowledge of self-realisation, which is the Mahāyāna, immovable and highest.

320. Of birth and no-birth there are eight and nine kinds; whether the attainment is instantaneous or successive, it is one realisation.

321. There are eight worlds of formlessness; Dhyāna is divided into six; and with the Pratyekabuddhas and Buddha-sons, there are seven forms of emancipation.

322. There are no such things as the past, present, and future; there is neither permanency nor impermanency; doing, work, and fruition—all is no more than a dream-event.

323. From beginning to end the Buddhas, Śrāvakas, and Buddha-sons have never been born; **(307)** the mind is removed from what is visible, being always a Māyā-like existence.

324. Thus the abode in the Tushita heaven, the conception, the birth, the leaving, the worldly life, the revolving

---

[1] The text gives no clue to this. Is *prajñaptirūpam* (form of thought-construction) the same as *vijñaptirūpam* of the *Abhidharmakośa*?

of the wheel, the wandering about in all the countries. [A Buddha] is seen [doing all these things], but he is not one born of the womb.

325. Thus, for the sake of sentient beings who are wandering and moving about from one place to another, emancipation is taught, the truth, the knowledge of the [Buddha-]land, and the rising of things by causation.

326 Worlds, forests, islands, egolessness, philosophers, wanderings, Dhyānas, the vehicles, the Ālaya, the attainments, the inconceivable realm of fruition,

327. Families of the moon and stars, families of kings, abodes of the gods, families of the Yakshas and Gandharvas. —they are all born of karma and are born of desire.

328. Inconceivable transformation-death is [still] in union with habit-energy; when interrupted, death is put a stop to, the net of passions is destroyed.

329. [The Bodhisattva] is not to keep[1] money, grain, gold, land, goods, kine and sheep, slaves, nor horses, elephants, etc.

330. He is not to sleep on a perforated couch, nor is he to smear the ground with mud;[2] he is not to have a bowl made of gold, silver, brass, or copper.

331. Let the Yogin have white cloth dyed in dark blue or brownish-red with cow-dung, or mud, or fruits, or leaves.

(308) 332. The Yogin is permitted to carry a bowl of full Magadha measure made of either stone, or clay, or iron, or shell, or quartz.

333. The Yogin whose final aim is to discipline himself may carry a curved knife four fingers long for cutting cloth; he who is intent on disciplining himself may not learn the science of mechanics.

334. The Yogin who disciplines himself in the exercises is not to be engaged in buying and selling; [if necessary] let the attendant see to it—these are the regulations I teach.

335. Thus, guarding his senses, let him have an exact

---

[1] According to the Chinese
[2] The source is unknown to the translator.

SAGATHAKAM

understanding in the meaning of the Sutras and the Vināya, and let him not associate with men of the world, such I call the Yogin.

336. Let the Yogin prepare his abode in an empty house, or a cemetery, or under a tree, or in a cavern, or among the straw, or in an open place.

337. Let [the Yogin] dress himself in three garments, whether in the cemetery or any other place; if anyone should voluntarily give him a garment—let him accept it.

338. When he goes about begging food, let him look ahead not more than the length of a yoke; let him conduct himself in the way bees treat flowers.

339. When the Yogin finds himself in a large company, in the confusion of a company, or with Bhikshunīs [women-mendicants], this is not a desirable relationship for Yogins; for it means to share a livelihood with them.

340. The Yogin, whose aim is to discipline himself in the exercise, (309) is not to approach for his food kings, princes, ministers of state, or persons of rank.

341. In houses where a death or a birth has taken place, or in the houses of friends and relatives, or where Bhikshus and Bhikshunīs are mixed together, it is not proper for the Yogins to take their food.

342. In the monasteries food is always regularly cooked, and when it is purposely prepared [somewhere else], it is not proper for the Yogins to take their food.

343. The Yogin should regard the world as removed from birth and death, as exempt from the alternation of being and non-being, though it is seen in the aspect of qualified and qualifying.

344. When birth [and death] is not discriminated, the Yogin before long will attain the Samādhi, the powers, the psychic faculties, and the self-mastery.

345. The Yogin should not cherish the thought that the world exists from such causal agents as atoms, time, or supreme soul; nor that it is born of causes and conditions.

346. From self-discrimination the world is imagined, which is born of varieties of habit-energy; let the Yogin

perceive existence as always like unto Māyā and a dream.

347. The [true] insight is always removed from assertions as well as from negations; let not [the Yogin] discriminate the triple world which appears as body, property, and abode.

348. Not thinking how to obtain food and drink, but holding his body upright, let him pay homage over and over again to the Buddhas and Bodhisattvas.

349. Gathering truth from the Vinaya, from the teachings in the Sutras, let the Yogin have a clear insight into the five Dharmas, Mind itself, and egolessness.

(310) 350. The Yogin should have a distinct understanding of the undefiled truth of self-realisation and as to what the stages [of Bodhisattvahood] and the Buddha-stage are and be anointed on the great lotus [seat].

351. Wandering through all the paths, he becomes averse to existence, and directing his steps toward some quiet cemetery he will begin various practices.

352–354. (Chapter II, verses 162–164.)

355. [According to the philosophers] there is a reality born of no-cause, neither permanent nor subject to annihilation, and removed from the alternatives of being and non-being, and this is imagined by them to be the Middle Path.

356. They imagine the theory of no-cause but their no-cause is nihilistic; as they fail to understand [the real nature of] external objects they destroy the Middle Path.

357. The attachment to existence is not abandoned for the fear of being nihilistic, and they try to teach the Middle Path by means of assertion and negation.

(311) 358. When Mind-only is understood, external objects are abandoned and discrimination no more takes place; here the Middle Path is reached.

359. There is Mind-only, there is no visible world; as there is no visible world, [Mind] is not risen;[1] this is taught by myself and other [Tathagatas] to be the Middle Path.

360. Birth and no-birth, being and non-being,—these

---

[1] After T'ang. Wei has: "Apart from Mind there is no rising." No rising of a visible world?

are all empty; there is no self-nature in all things; the duality is not to be cherished.

361. Where there is no possibility of discrimination taking its rise, the ignorant imagine there is emancipation; but as there is no understanding [in them] as to the rise of a mind, how can they destroy their attachment to duality?[1]

362. As it is understood that there is nothing but what is seen of the Mind, the attachment to duality is destroyed; knowledge, indeed, is the abandonment, not the destruction of the discriminated.

363. As it becomes thoroughly known that there is nothing but what is seen of the Mind, discrimination ceases; as discrimination ceases, suchness is removed from intellection (*citta*).[2]

364. If a man, seeing the rise [of all things], yet perceives that Nirvana is devoid of the faults of the philosophers, this is the Nirvana as held by the wise, because of its not being annihilation.

365. To realise this is said by myself and [other] Buddhas to be [the attainment of] Buddhahood; if there is any other discrimination one is committed to the philosophers' views.

366. Nothing is born, and yet things are being born; nothing dies and yet things are passing away; (312) all over millions of worlds what is seen simultaneously is like a lunar reflection in water.

367. Unity being transformed into plurality, rain falls and fire burns; as a mind is changed into [many] thoughts, they declare that there is Mind-only.

368. Mind is of Mind-only, no-mind is also born of Mind; when understood varieties of forms and appearances are of Mind-only.

369. By assuming Buddha[-forms], Śrāvaka-forms, Pratyekabuddha-appearances, and varieties of other forms, they declare Mind-only.

370. For the sake of beings [the Buddhas] show forms

---

[1] The text as it stands is difficult to understand. I follow T'ang.
[2] Cf. Chapter III, verses 25, and the "Sagāthakam," verse 651.

by means of no-form, from the world of no-form and of form down to the hells where hell-dwellers are; and all this originates from Mind-only.

371. When a [spiritual] revulsion [takes place in them], they will attain the Samādhi called Māyā-like, the will-body, the ten stages, the self-mastery.

372. On account of self-discrimination which causes errors and sets false reasonings in motion, the ignorant are bound up with ideas in what they see, hear, think, or understand.

373. (Chapter II, verse 197.)
374. (Chapter II, verse 198.)
(313) 375–378. (Chapter II, verses 199–202.)
379. The Buddhas in [every] land are those of transformation, where [the doctrine of] the one vehicle and the triple vehicle is taught; I never enter into Nirvana, for all things are empty being devoid of birth [and death].

380. There are thirty-six different Buddhas, and in each ten different ones; in accordance with the thought of all beings they share their lands.

381. When existence is discriminated there are varieties of appearances; in like manner the Dharma-Buddha's world may appear in its multiplicity, which in reality exists not.

382. The Dharma-Buddha is the true Buddha and the rest are his transformations; according to a continuous flow of their own seeds, sentient beings see their Buddha-forms.[1]

383. When [the mind is] bound up with error and appearance, discrimination is set in motion; (314) suchness is no other than discrimination and discrimination is no other than appearance.

384. The Self-nature Buddha, the Enjoyment Buddha, the Transformation Buddha, the five Transformation Buddhas, and a group of thirty-six Buddhas—they are all of the Self-nature Buddha.[2]

---

[1] After T'ang and Wei.
[2] The five transformation bodies (*pañcanirmita*) may mean those transformation Buddhas who manifest themselves in the five (sometimes six) paths of existence in order to save the sentient beings that are suffering there in the endless wheel of transformation. According

385-(315–316)-406. (Chapter II, verses 101–123, with verse-divisions occasionally varying.)

407. Owing to seeds of habit-energy [that grow from the recognition] of an outer world, discrimination takes place; and thereby the relativity aspect[1] is grasped, and that which is grasped is variously imagined.[2]

(317) 408. When one depending upon the mind recognises an external world, error is produced; error takes place from these two [causes], and there is no third cause.

409. Depending on that and from that cause error is produced; the six (*indryas*), the twelve (*āyatanas*), the eighteen (*dhātus*), are thus said by me to be of the Mind.

410. [When it is understood that things are because of] the combination of self-seeds and an external world (*grāhya*), the ego-attachment is abandoned.

411. Because of the Ālayavijñāna the Vijñāna [-system] is evolved; because of inner support there is something externally appearing.

412. The unintelligent imagine the Saṁskṛita and Asaṁskṛita to be permanent, while they are not, as they are like the stars, a hair-net, an echo, or things seen in a dream.

413. [As they are] like the city of the Gandharvas, a mirage, or Māyā; they are not, yet they are perceived [as if they were real]; so is the relativity aspect of existence (*paratantra*).

414. By means of a triple mentality I teach the self, senses, and their behaviour; but the Citta, Manas, and Vijñāna are devoid of self-nature.

to the Shingon doctrine of the fourfold Dharmakāya, this last transformation or manifestation is distinguished from the generally accepted transformation-Buddha and is given a special position by itself. The fourth one thus in the Shingon is known as the Nishyandakāya, distinguishing it from the third which is Nirmāṇa- or Nirmita-kāya. This verse is quoted by Amoghavajra (704–774), one of the Indian Shingon Fathers, who settled in China, in one of his works called 略述金剛頂瑜伽分別聖位修證法門經 (the Taisho Tripitaka, No. 870; Nanjo Catalogue, No. 1433). I owe this information to Professor Shōun Toganowo, of Kōya Buddhist College.

[1] *Tantram = paratantram.* [2] *Kalpitam = parikalpitam.*

415. The Citta, Manas, and Vijñāna, the twofold egolessness, the five Dharmas, the [three] Svabhāvas,— these belong to the realm of the Buddhas.

416. Habit-energy as cause is one, but as far as form (*lakshana*) goes it is triple; (**318**) this is the way in which a picture of one colour appears variously on the wall.

417. The twofold egolessness, the Citta, Manas, and Vijñāna, the five Dharmas, the [three] Svabhāvas—they do not belong to my essence.[1]

418. When the Citta-form is put aside, the Manas and Vijñāna removed, and the [five] Dharmas, and the [three] Svabhāvas abandoned, then one attains the essence of Tathagatahood.

419. The pure [essence of Tathagatahood] is not obtained by body, speech, and thought; the essence of Tathagatahood (*gotram tāthāgatam*) being pure is devoid of doings.

420. To be pure by means of the psychic faculties, and the self-mastery, to be embellished with the Samādhis and the powers, to be provided with varieties of the will-body—these belong to the pure essence of Tathagatahood.

421. To be undefiled in inner realisation, to be released from cause and form (*hetulakshana*), to attain the eighth stage and the Buddha-stage—this is the essence of Tathagatahood.

422. The Far-Going, the Good-Wisdom, the Law-Cloud, and the Tathagata-stage—they belong to the essence of Buddhahood, while the rest are taken up by the two vehicles.

423. Since sentient beings are differentiated as to their mentality and individuality, the Buddhas who have achieved self-mastery over their minds teach the ignorant the seven stages.

424. At the seventh stage no faults arise as to body, speech, and thought; at the eighth, the final abode [of consciousness], it seems to him like having crossed a great river in a dream.

(**319**) 425. At the fifth and the eighth stage the

---

[1] *Gotra*, lit. "family."

Bodhisattvas acquire proficiency in mechanical arts and philosophy and attain kingship in the triple world.

426. Birth and no-birth, emptiness and no-emptiness, self-nature and no-self-nature,—these are not discriminated [by the knowing one]; in Mind-only [no such things] obtain.

427. To discriminate, saying "This is true, this is true, this is false," is teaching meant for the Śrāvakas and Pratyekabuddhas, and not for the sons of the Buddha.

428. There is neither being-and-non-being, nor the aspect of momentariness, there are neither thought-constructions (*prajñapti*) nor substances (*dravya*); nothing obtains in Mind-only.

429. According to conventional truth (*saṁvṛiti*), things are, but not in the highest truth; to be confused in things not having self-nature—this belongs to conventional truth.

430. I establish thought-constructions where all things are non-existent; whatever expressions and experiences that belong to the ignorant are not of the truth as it is (*tattva*).

431. Things born of words seem to belong to an objective realm; but when it is perceived that they are born of words, they become non-existent.

432. As no pictures are separable from the wall, no shadow from the post, so are no [Vijñāna-] waves stirred when the Ālaya[-ocean] is pure [and quiet].

433. (Chapter VI, verse 4.)

(320) 434. It is taught that from the Dharma [-Buddha] comes the Nishyanda, and from the Nishyanda the Nirmita;[1] these are the original Buddhas, the rest are transformed bodies.

435–436. (Chapter II, verses 125–126.)

437. (Chapter II, verses 123 and 129.)

438–439. (Chapter II, verses 127–128.)

440. Do not discriminate, saying "Here is emptiness," or saying again, "Here is no emptiness"; both being and non-being are merely imagined, for there is no reality corresponding to the imagined.

[1] After T'ang.

441. The ignorant imagine that things originate from the accumulation of qualities, or atoms, or substances; but there is not a single atom in existence, and, therefore, there is no external world.

442. Forms seen as external are due to the imagination of people, they are nothing but the Mind itself; (**321**) there is nothing to be seen externally, and, therefore, there is no external world.

443–444. (Chapter III, verses 157–158.)
445–447. (Chapter II, verses 205–207.)
448. (Chapter II, verse 209.)
449. (Chapter II, verse 208.)
450. (Chapter II, verse 210.)

(**322**). 451. As the elephant who is immersed in deep mud is unable to move about, so the Śrāvakas, who are deeply intoxicated with the liquor of Samādhi, stand still.

452. (Chapter II, verse 135.)

453. Space, the hare's horns, and a barren woman's child are unrealities, and yet they are spoken of [as if real]; so are all things imagined.

454. The world originates from habit-energy, there is nothing whatever to be designated as being and non-being, nor is there its negation; those who see into this are emancipated, as they understand the egolessness of things.

455. [Of the three Svabhāvas] one is Parikalpita, mutuality is Paritantra, and suchness is Parinishpanna; this is always taught by me in the sutra.

456. (Chapter II, verse 172.)
457–458. (Chapter II, verses 203–204.)

459. The Citta, discrimination, thought-construction, Manas, Vijñāna, (**323**) the Ālaya, all that which sets the triple world in motion, are synonyms of Mind.

460. Life, warmth, the Vijñāna, the Ālaya, the vital principle, Manas, Manovijñāna,—these are the names for discrimination.

461. The body is maintained by the Citta, the Manas always cognitates, the [Mano-]vijñāna together with the Vijñānas cuts the world in pieces as objects of Citta.

462–464. (Chapter II, verses 3–5.)
465–469 (324). (Chapter II, verses 15–19.)
470–471. (Chapter III, verses 7–8.)

472. [Some say that] an ego-soul really is, which is separate from the Skandha-appearance, or that the Skandhas really exist; [but] there is after all no ego-soul in them.

473. When one's doings, together with the passions primary and secondary, are brought to light, one perceives the world to be the Mind itself and is released from all sufferings.

474–487 (325–326). (Chapter II, verses 20–33.)

488. The extinction-knowledge attained by the Śrāvakas, the birth of the Buddhas, and [that] of the Pratyekabuddhas and Bodhisattvas—all takes place by getting rid of the passions.

489. No external forms are in existence, what is external is what is seen of the Mind itself; as the ignorant fail to understand as regards the Mind itself, they imagine the Saṁskṛita [as real].

490. The insight that pluralities are of the Mind itself is withheld from the bewildered who, not knowing what the nature of the external world is, are under bondage to [the idea] of causation, and the fourfold proposition.

491. There are no reasons, no statements, no illustrations, no syllogistic members to the intelligent who know that the external world is the reflection of their own Mind.

492. Do not discriminate by discrimination, to discriminate is characteristic of the Parikalpita (imagination); depending on the imagination, discrimination is evolved.

493. One's habit-energy is the origin [of all things] which are mutually and uninterruptedly knitted together; (327) as dualism is [primarily] external to people's minds, there is no rising of it.

494. Because of mind and what belongs to it, there is discrimination, [the ignorant] are comfortably established in the triple world; that an external world of appearances is evolved is due to the discrimination of self-nature.

495. Because of the combination of appearances and

seeds there are the twelve Āyatanas; because of the combination of subject and object,[1] I talk of doings.

496. Like images in a mirror, like a hair-net, to the dim-eyed, the mind to the ignorant is seen enveloped in habit-energy.

497. Discrimination goes on in the world imagined by self-discrimination; but there is no external world as it is discriminated by the philosophers.

498. Like the ignorant who not recognising the rope take it for a snake, people imagine an external world, not knowing that it is of Mind itself.

499. Thus the rope in its own nature is neither the one nor the other; but owing to the fault of not recognising Mind itself, people go on with their discrimination over the rope.

500–501. (Chapter III, verses 82–83.)

(328) 502. While the imagined is being imagined, the imagination itself has no reality; seeing that discrimination has no reality, how does it [really] take place?

503. Form (*rūpam*, or matter) has no reality of its own, as is the case with a jar, a garment, etc.; in the world, however, which has no real existence, discrimination is carried on.

504. If people discriminate erroneously regarding the Saṁskṛita since the beginningless past, how is the self-nature of beings an error? Pray tell me, O Muni.

505. The nature of all beings is non-existent, and what is seen [as external] is nothing but the Mind; when the Mind itself is not perceived discrimination is evolved.

506. When it is said that there are no such things imagined as the ignorant imagine, it means that there is something which is not recognised by the intellect.

507. If it is said that something exists with the wise, this is not what is discriminated by the ignorant; if the wise and the ignorant walk the same way, that which [is real] with the wise must be a falsehood.

508. To the wise there is nothing erroneous, therefore

[1] *Āśraya* and *ālambana*, depended and depending.

their mind is undefiled; the ignorant whose mind is uninterruptedly defiled goes on imagining the imagined.

509. It is like the mother who fetches for her child a fruit from the air, saying, "O son, don't cry, pick the fruit, there are so many of them."

510. In like manner I make all beings covet varieties of imagined fruit (329) whereby I [lead them to] the truth that goes beyond the antithesis of being and non-being.

511. The being [which is realised by the wise] having never been in existence is not united with causation; it is primarily unborn and yet born, while its essence is not obtainable.[1]

512. The unobtainable essence (*alabdhātmaka*) is indeed unborn, and yet it is nowhere separated from causation; nor are things as they are for this moment anywhere separated from causation.

513. When the visible world is thus approached, it is anywhere neither existent nor non-existent, nor is it not-existent-and-non-existent; putting itself under causation, reality is not the subject of discrimination to the wise.

514. The philosophers cherishing wrong ideas and the ignorant have theories of oneness and otherness; they understand not that the world, subject to causation, is like Māyā and a dream.

515. The supreme Mahāyāna is beyond the realm of words, its meaning is well elucidated by me, but the ignorant do not comprehend.

516. [The doctrines] thus advanced by the Śrāvakas and philosophers are tainted with jealousy; they go astray from reality, because their doctrines are false theorisings.

517. Appearance, self-nature, form (*saṁsthānam*), and name,—depending on these four conditions all kinds of imagination are carried on.

518. Those who believe in the oneness or the manyness

---

[1] The meaning of this and what follow is this: there is an absolute being which precludes all form of qualification, but without which this world of cause and effect is impossible; the absolute is thus in one sense unobtainable, and yet in another sense it is the reason of this existence subject to causation.

[of cause], those who imagine Brahma god or the authority of Iśvara, (330) those who take the sun and the moon for an element—they are not my sons.[1]

519. Those who are equipped with a noble insight and are thoroughly conversant with the suchness of reality, know well how to turn over ideas and reach the other shore of the Vijñāna.

520. This is the seal of emancipation belonging to those sons who [have embraced] my teaching; it is released from existence and non-existence, removed from coming and going.

521. If karma disappears by causing a transformation in the world of matter (*rūpa*) and the Vijñānas, permanence and impermanence no more obtain, and transmigration ceases.

522. When this transformation takes place, the idea of matter is shaken off, space-relations are banished, but karma released from the fault of being and non-being abides with the Ālaya.

523. While matter and Vijñānas pass into annihilation, karma abides with the being of the Ālaya which is not destroyed, whereby there is the union of matter and Vijñānas.

524. If people's karma which is in combination with them is destroyed, karma-succession being thus destroyed, there will be no transmigration, no attainment of Nirvana.

525. If karma is destroyed together with matter and Vijñānas, and yet is subject to transmigration, matter will then subsist as it differs in no way from karma.

526. Mind (*citta*) and matter are neither different nor not-different from discrimination; there is no distinction of all things as they are removed from being and non-being.

(331) 527. The Parikalpita and the Paratantra are mutually dependent and are not to be differentiated; thus with matter and impermanency, they are mutually conditioning.

528. Apart from oneness and otherness the [Pari-]

---

[1] The whole verse is not at all clear.

kalpita is not knowable; so with matter and impermanency; how can one speak of their being and non-being?

529. When the Parikalpita is thoroughly understood [as to its nature], the Paratantra is not born; when the Paratantra is understood, the Parikalpita becomes suchness.

530. When the Parikalpita is destroyed my Dharma-eye (*netrī*)[1] is destroyed; and there takes place within my teaching [the controversy of] assertion and negation.

531. In this way, then, and at that time, there will rise disparagers of the Dharma, none of whom are worth talking with as they are destroyers of my Dharma-eye.

532. As they are not taken into the company of the intelligent, they abandon the life of the Bhikshu; and as they destroy the Parikalpita, they are engaged in controversies asserting and negating.

533. As their insight is bound up with being and non-being, what appears to their imagination resembles a hair-net, Māyā, a dream, the Gandharva's city, a mirage, etc.

534. He who studies under the Buddhas may not live together with those who cherish dualism and are destroyers of others.

535. But if there are Yogins who see a being separated from the imagination (332) and released from existence and non-existence, he [i. e. a Buddhist] may associate with them [i. e. such Yogins].

536. It is like a mine in the earth producing gold and precious stones; it harbours no cause of strife in it, and yet it furnishes people with various means of subsistence.

537. Likewise, though the essence (*gotra*)[2] of all beings appears various, it has nothing to do with karma; as the visible world is non-existent, there is no karma, nor is the path born of karma.

538. As is understood by the wise, all things have no self-being, but according to the discriminations of the ignorant things appear to exist.

539. If things are not existent as discriminated by the

---

[1] T'ang, 法眼; Wei, 法輪 or 我法.
[2] 性, read after Wei.

ignorant, all things being non-existent, there are no defilements for any one.

540. Because of varieties of defilement cherished by beings there is transmigration, and the sense-organs are completed; being bound up by ignorance and desire there is the evolution of beings possessed of a body.

541. If beings are not existent as discriminated by the ignorant, there will be no evolving of the sense-organs in these beings, which is not the Yogin's [view].

542. If beings themselves are not and yet they become the cause of transmigration, then there will be an emancipation which is independent of people's strivings.

543. If beings are non-existent to you, how can there be any distinction between the wise and the ignorant? Nor will there be anything characterising the wise who are disciplining themselves for the triple emancipation.

(333) 544. The Skandhas, personal soul, doctrines, individuality and generality, no-signs, causation, and senses —of these I talk for the sake of the Śrāvakas.

545. No-cause, Mind-only, the powers (*vibhūti*), the stages [of Bodhisattvahood], the inner realisation, pure suchness—of these I talk for the sake of the Bodhisattvas.

546. In the time to come there will be disparagers of my teaching who, putting on the Kāshāya robe, will talk about being-and-non-being and its works.

547. Things born of causation are non-existent—this is the realm of the wise; a thing imagined has no reality, yet things are imagined by the theorisers.

548. In the time to come there will be [a class of ignorant people headed by] Kaṇabhuj; they will talk about the non-existence of work, and will ruin the people with their evil theories.

549. The world is originated from atoms, atoms are causeless, and there are nine permanent substances—such evil theories they teach.

550. [They say that] substances are produced by substances, and so qualities by qualities; and they destroy the self-being of all things [saying that] it is another being.

SAGATHAKAM

551. If it is said that originally the world was not and then evolved, it must have had a beginning; but my statement is that there is no primary limit to transmigration.

(334) 552. If all the innumerable things in the triple world were not and then evolved, nobody would doubt if horns grow on a bitch, or a she-camel, or a donkey.

553. If the eye, form (*rupa*), and Vijñāna were not and now they are, straw-mats, crowns, cloth, etc. would be produced from lumps of clay.

554. A straw-mat is not found in cloth, nor cloth in a straw matting; why is it that by some combination anything is not produced from any other thing?

555. That life and the body so called were not and then evolved; all such controversies as this have been declared by me [as untrue].

556. The statement has been made first [against the philosophers] and their views are warded off; their views being warded off, I will make my own statement.

557. While I [first] make a statement in behalf of the philosophical systems, let not my disciples be disturbed by [my] drawing on the dualism of being and non-being.

558. That the world is born of a supreme soul and that changes are due to the qualities,—this is what the school of Kapita teaches its disciples; but it is not the right way of thinking.

559. There is no reality, no non-reality, nor is there any [world of] causation conditioned by causation; as there is nothing to be characterised as causation, non-reality never has its rise.

560. My statement is free from the alternatives of being and non-being, is removed from cause and condition, has nothing to do with birth and destruction, and is removed from qualified [and qualifying].

561. When the world is regarded as like Māyā and a dream, exempt from cause and condition, (335) and eternally causeless, there is no rising of imagination.

562. When existence is always regarded as resembling the Gandharva's [city], a mirage, a hair-net, and as free

from the alternatives of being and non-being, removed from cause and condition, and causeless, then the mind flows clear of defilements.

563. [The philosophers may say that] if there is no external reality, Mind-only too will be non-existent; how can Mind exist without objective reality? The [doctrine of] Mind-only[1] [therefore] is untenable.

564. [Further they may say that] on account of an objective world of realities, people's minds are aroused; how can there be a mind without a cause? [The doctrine of] Mind-only[1] is [therefore] untenable.

565. But suchness and Mind-only[1] are realities belonging to the teaching of the wise; neither those who deny nor those who affirm comprehend my teachings.

566. If a mind is said to evolve on account of perceived and perceiving, this is the mind that is of the world; then the Mind-only obtains not.

567. When it is said that there is something resembling body, property, and abode produced in a dream-like manner, a mind, indeed, is seen under the aspect of duality; but Mind itself is not dualistic.

568. As a sword cannot cut itself, or as a finger cannot touch its own tip, Mind cannot see itself.

569. In the state of imagelessness there is no reality, no Parikalpita, no Paratantra, no five Dharmas, no twofold mind.[2]

(**336**) 570. The dualism of giving-birth and being-born belongs to the nature of things; when I speak of the giving-birth of things that have no self-nature, it is on account of a hidden meaning.

571. If multiplicities of forms are born of imagination, there will be something of objectivity in [the notion of] space, in [that of] a hare's horns.

572. When an objective reality is of mind, this reality

---

[1] For these *cittamātra*, T'ang has 唯識 instead of 唯心. Ordinarily 唯識 is for *vijñānamātra* or *vijñaptimātra*, and not for *cittamātra*. In this respect Wei is consistent, for it has 唯心 throughout.

[2] After T'ang.

does not belong to imagination; but reality born of imagination is something other than mind and is unobtainable.

573. In a transmigration that has no beginning, an objective world nowhere obtains; when there is no nourishing mind, where can an objective semblance take its rise?

574. If there is any growth from nothingness, horns will grow on a hare; let no discrimination take place, thinking that something grows out of nothing.

575. As there is nothing existing now, so there was nothing existing previously; where there is no objective world, how can a mind which is bound up with an objective world take its rise?

576. Suchness, emptiness, [reality-]limit, Nirvana, the Dharmadhātu, no-birth of all things, self-being—these characterise the highest truth.

577. The ignorant, who cherish [the notion of] being and non-being, by imagining causes and conditions, are unable to understand that all things are causeless and unborn.

578. The Mind is manifested; there is no objective world of pluralities whose cause is in the beginningless past; (337) if there is no objective world since the beginningless past, how does individualisation[1] ever come to exist?

579. If anything grows from nothingness, the poor will become rich; when there is no objective world, how can a mind be born? Pray tell me, O Muni.

580. As all this is causeless, there is neither mind nor objective world; as the mind is not born, the triple world is devoid of doings.

581–613 (338–341). (Chapter III, verses 86–117.)

614. The statement that a hare has no horns is made out of the reasonings concerning a jar, a garment, a crown, and a horn; where there is no complete cause, there is no [real] existence; thus you should know.

615. There is non-existence when proof of existence [is produced]; non-existence does not prove non-existence;

[1] According to T'ang, *viśesha* here is evidently *citta*.

existence, indeed, looks for non-existence, they look for each other and are mutually conditioned.

616. If it is thought, again, that something appears depending on something else, the something thus depended upon must be causeless, but there is nothing that is causeless.

617. If [it is said that] there is another reality which is depended on, then this must have still another [reality to depend on]; this is commiting the fault of non-finality; may it not end in reaching nowhere?

618. Depending on leaves, pieces of wood, etc., the magical charm is effected; in like manner, pluralities of objects depending on some [other] objects are manifested to the people.

619. The magical net is neither the leaves nor the pieces of wood, nor the pebbles; (342) it is owing to the magician that the magic scene is perceived by the people.

620. Thus when something [of magic] depending on some objects is destroyed, dualism ceases at the moment of seeing; how will there be anything of discrimination?

621. The discriminated by discrimination exist not, and discrimination itself does not obtain; discrimination being thus unobtainable, there is neither transmigration nor Nirvana.

622. Discrimination now being unobtainable, it is not aroused; discrimination not being aroused, how can a mind rise? Mind-only then is not tenable.

623. When thought is divided into many, the teaching lacks in validity; and owing to the absence of validity, there is no emancipation, nor is there multitudinousness of objects.

624. There is no such objective world as is discriminated by the ignorant; when the Mind goes astray on account of habit-energy, it manifests itself like images.

625. All things are unborn and have nothing to do with being and non-being: all is nothing but Mind and is delivered from discrimination.

626. For the ignorant things are said to be causal, but not for the wise; when the self-nature of Mind is liberated, it becomes pure where the wise have their abode.

627. Thus, the Samkhya, the Vaiśeshika, the naked philosophers, the Brahmin theologians, followers of Śiva, (343) cherishing views based on being and non-being, are destitute of the truth of solitude.

628. Having no self-nature, being unborn, being empty, being like Māyā, being free from defilements—to whom is this taught by the Buddhas as well as by yourself?

629. For the sake of the Yogins who are pure in mind, spiritual discipline (*yoga*) is taught by the Buddhas who are free from theories and speculations, and such is also proclaimed by me.

630. If all this is the Mind, where does the world stand? Why are men seen coming and going on earth?

631. As a bird moves in the air according to its fancy without abiding anywhere, without depending on anything, as if moving on earth;

632. So people with all their discrimination move along, walk about in the Mind itself like a bird moving in the air.[1]

633. Tell me how something looking like body, property, and abode rises from the Mind. How does appearance take its rise? Why is Mind-only? Pray tell me.

634. Body, property, and abode are appearances and their rise is due to habit-energy; appearances are born of irrationality (*ayukta*), their rise is due to discrimination.

635. Objectivity discriminated makes the world, a mind takes its rise from [recognising] objectivity; when it is clearly perceived that what is seen is the Mind itself, discrimination ceases.

(344) 636. When discrimination is seen [as to its true nature, it is noticed that] name and sense are to be disjoined (*visaṁyukta*),[2] then both knowledge and knower will be discarded, and one is released of the Saṁskṛita.

---

[1] This means that in spite of our discriminations and imaginings we cannot get away from the control of Mind-only, which is, religiously expressed, Amitābha Buddha pursues sentient beings, as is taught in Shin Buddhism, in spite of their struggle to run away from his all-embracing love. Thus interpreted, this verse gives us a new outlook in the philosophy of the *Laṅkāvatāra*.

[2] This is the reading of T'ang.

637. To abandon both name and sense, this is the way of all the Buddhas;[1] those who wish to get enlightened in any other way will not attain enlightenment for themselves, nor for others.

638. (Chapter VI, verse 5.)

639. When the world is seen detatched from knowledge and knowability, there is no meaning to it, and discrimination ceases to go forth.

640. By seeing into [the nature of] Mind there is the cessation of discrimination as regards works and words; by not seeing into [the true nature of] Self-mind, discrimination evolves.

641. Four of the Skandhas are formless (*arūpiṇa*), they cannot be numbered; the elements differ from one another, how can they produce such pluralities of forms (*rūpa*)?

642. When [the notion of] individuality is abandoned, we have no elements, primary and secondary; if [we say that] form is produced by other qualities, why not by the Skandhas?[2]

643. When one is emancipated from the Āyatanas and Skandhas, seeing them as free of individual signs, then the mind is liberated because of seeing the egolessness of things.

(345) 644. From the differentiation of an objective world and the senses, the Vijñāna is set in motion in eight ways; thus the aspects [of self-nature][3] are three, but when imagelessness obtains they all cease.

645. When dualism is cherished, the Ālaya sets up in the Manas the consciousness of an ego and its belongings, and the Vijñānas; when this is penetratingly perceived, they all subside.

646. When the immovable is seen, oneness and otherness being discarded, then there will be no more discriminating of the two, ego and its belongings.

647. Nothing evolving, there is no growth, nor is there

---

[1] Read after T'ang. The Sanskrit text is too obscure for intelligent reading.
[2] Not clear.
[3] That is, Svabhāvalakshaṇa.

any cause to set the Vijñānas in action; work and cause being removed, there is cessation and nothing is aroused.

648. Pray tell me the why of discrimination, of Mind-only, and of the world. Why is the world said to be disjoined from causes, discarding qualified and qualifying?

649. The Mind is seen as manifold when visible forms are discriminated; as it is not clearly perceived that what is seen is of the Mind, there is something other than the Mind, because [the dualism of] a mind and an external world is clung to.

650. When [the world] is not understood with intelligence there is nihilism; [but] the Mind being asserted, how is it that this does not give rise to realism (*astitvadrishṭi*)?

651. Discrimination is neither existent nor non-existent, therefore, realism does not arise; as it is clearly understood that what is seen is of Mind-only, no discrimination is set to work.

652. Discrimination not rising, there is a turning-back (*parāvṛitti*), and there is no dependence on anything; (**346**) when things are regarded as subject to causation, the fourfold proposition obstructs [the way of truth].

653. Different expressions are distinguished but none is verifiable; in all these there is a necessary implication which rises from the notion of a primary causal agency.[1]

654. By maintaining the combination of causes and conditions, a primary causal agency is warded off; when a chain of causes is held to be impermanent, the fault of permanency is avoided.

655. There is neither birth nor destruction where the ignorant see impermanency; nothing is ever destroyed, what is seen [as real] is due to [the idea of] a causal agency.[2] How is the unseen [born]? By what does the impermanent world come into existence?

656. (Second line only, Chapter III, verse 62.)

---

[1] Not quite clear.
[2] In the Sanskrit text this line is made to belong to the next verse, which is wrong.

657–662 (**347**). (Chapter III, verses 62–68.)

663. The gods, the Asuras, mankind, the animals, hungry ghosts, and Yama's abode—these six paths of existence are enumerated, where sentient beings are born.

664. According to one's karma, be it superior, inferior, or middling, one is born in these [six] paths; guarding all that is good, [one will attain] an excellent emancipation.

665. The company of the Bhikshus is taught by you that there is birth and death at every moment; pray tell me its meaning.

666. As one form changes into another, so is the mind born and broken up; thence I tell my disciples how uninterruptedly and momentarily birth-[and-death] takes place.

667. In like manner discrimination also rises and disappears with every single form; where there is discrimination, there are living beings; outside of it there are no living beings.

668. At every moment there is a disjunction, this is called causation; (**348**) when one is liberated from the notion of form (*rūpa*), there is neither birth nor death.

669. When dualism is upheld, there rise causation-born and no-causation-born, ignorance and suchness, etc.; not to be dualistic is suchness.

670. When causation [-born] and no-causation-born [are distinguished], things are differentiated, there are permanency, etc., there are effect, cause, and causation.

671. As long as the notion of cause and effect is upheld, there is no difference between the philosophers; this is your teaching as well as that of [other] Buddhas; O Mahāmuni, such are not the wise ones.

672. Within the body, measuring one vyāna,[1] there is a world; the cause of its rising, the attaining of cessation, and the path (*pratipad*)—this I teach to sons of the Victor.

673. By clinging to the three Svabhāvas, perceived [or grasped] and perceiving [or grasping] are manifested; the simple-minded discriminate objects as belonging to the world and to the super-world.

---

[1] The measure of two extended arms.

674. From the viewpoint of relativity the notion of Svabhāva has been upheld, but in order to ward off one-sided views the Svabhāva is not to be discriminated.

675. As faults and defects are sought, the principle is not established, nor is the mind [properly] set to work; this is due to the rising of dualistic notions; non-duality is suchness.

(349) 676. [If one should think that] the Vijñāna, etc. are originated by ignorance, desire, and karma, this is wrong, for the fault of non-finality is committed; this being committed, the rise of the world becomes impossible.

677. The fourfold destruction of things is told by the unenlightened; discrimination is said to rise in two ways; [in fact,] there is no existence, no non-existence. When one is released from the fourfold proposition, one abandons dualism.

678. Discrimination may rise in two ways, but when it is seen [in its true nature], it will never rise [again]; for in all things not being born there is the awakening of intelligence; but[1] where there is the birth of things, this is owing to discrimination; let one not discriminate.

679.[2] Pray tell me, O Lord, about the truth in order to check dualistic views, [so that] I and others may not cherish the [dualism of] being and non-being.

680. And [thus] we may keep ourselves away from the philosophers' teachings and also from the Śrāvakas and Pratyekabuddhas; for it behoves the Bodhisattvas not to lose the life of enlightenment as realised by the Buddhas.

681. To be delivered from [the notion of] cause and no-cause, not to be born, and being one—these are synonyms; [the ignorant] are bewildered by them, but the wise always rise above them.

682. All things appear like a cloud, a multitude of clouds, a rainbow; they are like a vision, a hair-net, Māyā,

---

[1] That which follows forms the first half of verse 678 in the Sanskrit text.

[2] The verse 679 here is composed of the second half of 679 and the first line of 680 in the Sanskrit text.

etc., they are born of self-discrimination; and yet the philosophers discriminate the world as born of a self-creating agency.

683. Not being born, suchness, reality, limit, and emptiness,—these are other names for form (*rūpa*); one should not imagine it to mean a nothing.

(350) 684. In the world [another name of] *hasta* (hand) is *kara*; Indra [is also called] Śakra and Purandara; in the same way [there are many synonyms] for this existence; and one should not imagine it to mean a nothing.

685. Emptiness is no other than form, so is no-birth; one should not imagine anything different from this; if one does, faulty views will follow.

686. Because of objective appearances being asserted, there is general discrimination (*samkalpa*) and particular distrimination (*vikalpa*); because of imagination (*parikalpa*) there are long and short, square and round, etc.

687. General discrimination belongs to the Citta, imagination to the Manas, and particular discrimination to the Manovijñāna; [but reality] is neither the qualified nor the qualifying.

688. What is regarded by the philosophers as unborn is my own teaching wrongly viewed, and [the latter is] imagined to be indistinguishable [from theirs], but this is submitting a faulty argument.

689. Those who have acquired the knowledge of proper reasoning by making use of [the idea of] no-birth and its meaning, are said to have an understanding of my doctrine.

690. In order to crush the philosophical views, not being born is said to mean not having any abode; knowing what dualism means, I teach the doctrine of no-birth.

691. Are all things to be regarded as unborn, or not? Pray tell, O Mahāmuni. The doctrine of causelessness, no-birth, the rising of existence,—all these are held by the philosophers.

(351) 692.[1] I teach Mind-only which is removed from [the dualism of] being and non-being. One should discard

[1] The first half of this verse numbered 692 in the Sanskrit text

[the view of] birth and no-birth which causes various philosophical theories.

693. In the doctrine of causelessness, of no-birth, of birth, the notion of a causal agency [is involved] on which they depend. Effortless deeds come from nothingness, and deeds [as ordinarily performed] are mixed with motives.

694. Tell me the [right] view that goes with skilful means, original vows, etc.; how does the society [of the holy ones] come into existence when all things are not?

695. By separating oneself from [the dualism of] perceived and perceiving, there is neither evolution nor cessation; the mind is born as views are cherished as regards one existence or another.

696. Things are said to be unborn, how is this? Pray tell me. Sentient beings do not understand it, so it ought to be explained.

697. Pray explain to me, O Mahāmuni, all the contradictions [involved in the statements made] before and after, to escape the errors of the philosophers and to be released from the perverted theory of causation.

698. Pray tell me, O Most Excellent of Teachers, regarding cessation and coming back into existence, in order to be released from being and non-being, and yet not to destroy cause and effect.

699. Pray tell me as to the graded succession of the stages, O Lotus-eyed One;[1] for the world cherishes dualism and is bewildered with wrong views.

(352) 700. For on account of [the wrong views concerning] birth, no-birth, etc., the cause of serenity is not recognised, there is no society [of the holy ones] for me, and I have no chance to discourse on the nature of being.

701. There is error where dualism is maintained, but the Buddhas are thoroughly free from dualism; all things are empty, momentary, have no self-nature, and have never been born.

is evidently inserted here by mistake, and is not translated; and the first half of the following verse is brought over here to complete 691. The numbering, therefore, from 692 to 694 is altered in this translation.

[1] *Padma īkshaṇa!* according to T'ang.

702. Discriminations are carried on by those who are enveloped by evil theories and doctrines, but not by the Tathagatas; pray tell me about the rise and cessation of discrimination.

703. Accumulated by false reasonings, there is a combination of varieties of appearances [and Vijñānas], whereby [each Vijñāna] takes in an objective field according to its class.

704. Recognising external forms, discrimination is set in motion; as this is understood and the meaning of reality is seen as it is, the mind conforms itself to the nature of the wise and is no more set in motion.

705. The elements being rejected, there is no birth of things, but as the elements as appearances are always the Mind, one understands what is meant by no-birth.

706. Do not discriminate discrimination, the wise are those who are free from discrimination; when discrimination is carried on, there is dualism which does not lead to Nirvana.

707. By the statement of no-birth, Māyā is seen and destroyed; when Māyā is made to be born of no-causation, this injures the truth of the statement.

(353) 708. The mind is to be regarded as a reflected image originating in the beginningless past; it is something of reality but not reality itself; one should realise it truly as it is in itself.

709. The nature of birth [or existence] is like an image appearing in a mirror, which, while it is devoid of oneness and otherness, is not altogether non-existent.

710. Like the Gandharvas' city, Māyā, etc., which appear depending upon causes and conditions, the birth of all things is not no-birth [in a relative sense].

711. It is on account of general usage that a dualistic discrimination is set up as regards persons and things; but this is not clearly understood by the ignorant so that [the thought of] an ego-soul and individual objects is cherished.

712. There are five [classes of] Śrāvakas, the Śrāvakas [that is, hearers] generally, those who are attached to the doctrine of causation, those who are Arhats, those who are

dependent upon their own power, and those who are dependent upon [the power of] the Buddha.

713. Time-interruption, destruction, the highest reality, and mutuality—these four are imagined as involved in the idea of impermanency by the ignorant who are not endowed with intelligence.

714. The ignorant addicted to dualism cherish [such thoughts as] dualities, atoms, original matter, and primary cause, and fail to understand the means of emancipation, because they adhere to the alternatives of being and non-being.

715. (Chapter VI, verse 3.)

(354) 716. The primary elements are of different qualities, and how can they produce[1] this world of matter (*rūpa*)? [Each of] the elements has its own seat; what are [regarded as] secondary elements are not made by them.

717. Fire burns matter (*rūpa*), the nature of water is to wet, the wind scatters matter; how can matter be produced by the elements [when they are of such contradicting natures]?

718. The Rūpa-skandha (matter) and the Vijñāna (-Skandha)—there are these two Skandhas and not five; they are different names for the Skandhas; of this I have talked in a hundred ways.

719. By the separation of mind from what belongs to it, the present world evolves; [various] forms [of matter] are inseparably conjoined with one another; matter is mind [-made], and is not element-made.

720. Blue, etc., are to be referred to white, and white to blue; cause and effect being produced [in the same mutual way], both being and non-being are emptiness.

721. Effect and effecting and effected, cold and heat, qualified and qualifying,—such-like and all [other things] are not to be explained away by theories.

722. The Citta, Manas and the six Vijñānas are by nature united and removed from oneness and otherness; they are evolved from the Ālaya.

[1] After T'ang.

723. The Saṁkhya and the Vaiśeshika followers, the naked philosophers, and the advocates of Īśvara the creator, are addicted to the dualism of being and non-being, and do not know what solitary reality is.[1]

(**355**) 724. Varieties of forms (*sansthāna*) and figures (*ākriti*) are not produced by the primary elements; but the philosophers declare them to originate from the elements primary and secondary.

725. As the philosophers imagine causes other than the unborn, they do not understand, and because of stupidity they uphold the dualism of being and non-being.

726. There is a truth (*tattva*) characterised by purity; it is united with the Citta but disunited with the Manas, etc.; it abides with knowledge.

727. If karma is form (*rūpa*), it will be the cause of the Skandhas and the objective world; beings without attachment will not be abiding [even] in the world of formlessness.

728. That egolessness is the true doctrine follows from the non-existence of beings; the advocate of non-ego is a destroyer,[2] causing even the cessation of the Vijñāna.

729. There are four abodes of it, how does it arise from the non-existence of form? As there is nothing existent innerly or outwardly, no Vijñānas arise.

730. The theorisers wish to see the Skandhas in the middle existence; likewise, [they wish,] a being born in the world of formlessness is of no-form; what else is there?

731. [If one says that] emancipation is attained without exerting oneself, as there are no beings, no Vijñānas, this is no doubt a philosopher's theory; the theorisers do not understand.

732. If form is to be found in the world of formlessness, it is not visible; (**356**) its non-existence contradicts the truth, there is neither a vehicle nor a driver.[3]

733. The Vijñāna, born of habit-energy, is united with

---

[1] A repetition of verse 627.
[2] Literally, cutting off (*chela*).
[3] The statements about form here are not quite intelligible.

the senses; there are eight kinds of it, they do not grasp one field all at once.[1]

734. When form is not evolved, the senses are not the senses; therefore, the Blessed One declares that the senses, etc. are characterised with momentariness.

735. How without determining form (*rūpa*) can the Vijñāna take its rise? How without the rising of knowledge can transmigration take place?

736. To pass away instantly after birth,—this is not the teaching of the Buddhas; nor is there the uninterruptedness of all things; as discrimination moves about, one is born in the various paths.

737. The senses and their objective worlds are meant for the stupid but not for the wise; the ignorant grasp after names, the wise comprehend the meaning.

738. The sixth [Vijñāna] is not to be understood as non-attachment, or as attachment; the wise who are devoid of the fault of being are not committed to a definite theory.

739. Those theorisers who are without knowledge are frightened at eternalism and nihilism; (**357**) the ignorant are unable to distinguish between the Saṁskṛita, the Asaṁskṛita, and the ego-soul.

740. [Some imagine the ego-soul] to be one with the Citta, [others] to be different from the Manas, etc., attachment[2] exists in oneness as well as in otherness.[3]

741. If attachment is determined and mind and what belongs to it are designated, how is it that on account of the attachment there is the determination by oneness?[4]

742. By reason of attachment, attainment, karma,

---

[1] Not clear.

[2] *Dāna* evidently stands here for *upadāna*, as is understood by T'ang. However, this and the following two or three stanzas are difficult to understand very clearly as there are no references in the text to the ideas discussed here. Probably they contain allusions to the Abhidharma doctrines.

[3] Read after T'ang.

[4] This is not clear. A number of verses in these pages that give no sense as far as we can see in their several connections are not at all in cognation with the general thoughts of the *Laṅkā*. Are they later additions taken from somewhere else?

birth, effect, etc., they are brought to the goal like fire; there is resemblance and non-resemblance in the principle.[1]

743. As when fire burns, the burned and the burning are simultaneously there, so is attachment to an ego-soul; what is it that is not seized by the theorisers?

744. Whether there is birth or no-birth, the mind shines forth all the time; what illustrations will the theorisers produce to prove their notion of an ego-soul?

745. Those theorisers who are destitute of the principle are lost in the forest of Vijñānas; seeking to establish the theory of an ego-soul, they wander about here and there.

746. The ego (*ātma*) characterised with purity is the state of self-realisation; this is the Tathagata's womb (*garbha*) which does not belong to the realm of the theorisers.

747. When one thus knows what are the characteristics of attached and attaching by the analysis of the Skandhas, there rises the knowledge of the principle.

(358) 748. The Ālaya where the Garbha(womb) is stationed is declared by the philosophers to be [the seat of] thought in union with the ego; but this is not the doctrine approved [by the Buddhas].

749. By distinctly understanding it [i.e. the doctrine] there is emancipation and insight into the truth, and purification from the passions which are abandoned by means of contemplation and insight.

750. The Mind primarily pure is the Tathagata's Garbha which is good but is attached to [as an ego-soul] by sentient beings; it is free from limitation and non-limitation.

751. As the beautiful colour of gold and gold among pebbles become visible by purification, so is the Ālaya among the Skandhas of a being.

752. The Buddha is neither a soul nor the Skandhas, he is knowledge free from evil outflows; clearly perceiving him to be eternally serene, I take my refuge in him.

753. The Mind, primarily pure, is with the secondary passions, with the Manas, etc., and in union with the ego-soul—this is what is taught by the best of speakers.

Is this correct?

754. The Mind is primarily pure, but the Manas, etc., are other than that; varieties of karma are accumulated by them, and thus there are defilements giving rise to dualism.

755. The ego [primarily] pure has been defiled on account of the external passions since the beginningless past, (359) and what has been added from outside is like a [soiled] garment to be washed off.

756. As when a garment is cleansed of its dirt, or when gold is removed from its impurities, they are not destroyed but remain as they are; so is the ego freed from its defilements.

757. Imagining that a melodious sound obtains in a lute, a conch-shell, or in a kettle-drum, the unintelligent thus seek something of an ego-soul within the Skandhas.

758. As one tries to find precious stones in the treasure-house, or in water, or underneath the ground, where they are invisible, so do [they seek] a soul in the Skandhas.

759. As the unintelligent cannot take hold of a mind and what belongs to it as a group, and their functions which are connected with the Skandhas, so [they cannot find] an ego-soul in the Skandhas.

760. As the womb is not visible to the woman herself who has it, so the ego-soul is not visible within the Skandhas to those who have no wisdom.

761. Like the essence of the medicinal herb, or like fire in the kindling, those who have no wisdom do not see the ego-soul within the Skandhas.

762. Trying to find permanency and emptiness in all things, the unenlightened cannot see them; so with the ego-soul within the Skandhas.

763. When there is no true ego-soul, there are no stages, no self-mastery, no psychic faculties, no highest anointing, no excellent Samādhis.

(360) 764. If a destroyer should come around and say, "If there is an ego, show it to me;" a sage would declare, "Show me your own discrimination."[1]

---

[1] The statements so far made here regarding an ego-soul (*ātman* or *pudgala*) as they stand seem to contradict one another, and some

765. Those who hold the theory of non-ego are injurers of the Buddhist doctrines, they are given up to the dualistic views of being and non-being; they are to be ejected by the convocation of the Bhikshus and are never to be spoken to.[1]

766. The doctrine of an ego-soul shines brilliantly like the rising of the world-end fire, wiping away the faults of the philosophers, burning up the forest of egolessness.

767. Molasses, sugar-cane, sugar, and honey; sour milk, sesame oil, and ghee,—each has its own taste; but one who has not tasted it will not know what it is.

768. Trying to seek in five ways for an ego-soul in the accumulation of the Skandhas, the unintelligent fail to see it, but the wise seeing it are liberated.

769. By means of illustrations furnished by the sciences, etc., the mind is not accurately determined; as to the meaning contained in it, how can one accurately determine it?

770. Things are differentiated but the Mind is one—this is not perceived; the theorisers [imagine it] to be causeless and not-functioning, which is a mistake.

771. When the Yogin reflects upon the mind, he does not see the Mind in the mind; an insight comes forth from the perceived [i.e. the world]; whence is the rising of this perceived [world]?

(361) 772. I belong to the Katyāyana family, descending from the Śuddhāvāsa; I teach the Dharma in order to lead sentient beings to the city of Nirvana.

773. This is the course of the past; I and those Tathagatas have generally disclosed the meaning of Nirvana in three thousands of the sutras.

774. Not in the world of desire nor in [the world of] no-form is Buddhahood attained; but at the Akaniṣṭha in

really violate the Buddhist doctrine of Non-ātman as far as we know.

[1] This and the following verse again seem to contradict the Buddhist doctrine of non-ego. It is not easy to determine the purport of these verses as they stand all by themselves without any explanatory prose. In fact these verses in the Sagāthakam which have no direct connection with the main text, except those that are quite obvious in meaning, are mostly difficult to know precisely what they intend to signify.

the world of form one is awakened to Buddhahood by getting rid of greed.

775. The objective world is not the cause of bondage; the cause is bound up in the objective world; the passions are destroyed by knowledge, which is a sharp sword gained by discipline.

776. How is non-ego possible? How are things like Māyā, etc.? How about being and non-being? If suchness reveals itself to the ignorant, how is non-ego non-existent?[1]

777. Because of things done and of things not done, the cause is not the producer; all is unborn, and this is not clearly recognised by the ignorant.

778. The creating agencies are unborn; both the created and the conditions of causality are unborn; why is imagination carried on as regards creating agencies?

779. The theorisers explain a cause to consist in the simultaneity of antecedent and consequent; the birth of all things is told by means of a light, a jar, a disciple, etc.

780. The Buddhas are not Saṁskṛita-made, but are endowed with the marks [of excellence]; (362) they belong to the nature of a Cakravartin; the Buddhas are not so named because of these [marks].

781. What characterises the Buddhas is knowledge (*jñāna*); it is devoid of the defects of intellection (*dṛishti-dosha*); it is an insight attained by self-realisation, it is removed from all defects.

782. The religious life (*brahmacarya*) is not found in those especially, who are deaf, blind, one-eyed, dumb, aged, young, nor in those who are given up to the feeling of enmity.

783. The world-ruler is endowed with the celestial marks and the secondary characteristics though not manifested. They become, however, manifested in some of the homeless monks and not in anybody else—so it is declared.

784. After the passing of the Leader of the Śākyas, these will follow me: Vyāsa, Kaṇāda, Rishabha, Kapila, and others.

785. Then one hundred years after my passing, Vyāsa's

---

[1] Is this correct reading?

Bhārata will appear, the Pāṇḍavas, the Kauravas, Rāma, and then the Maurya.

786. The Maurya, the Nanda, the Gupta, and then the Mleccha who are bad kings; after the Mleccha will rage a warfare, and then the age of vice; (363) and after this age of vice, the good Dharma will no more prevail in the world.

787. After passing through these ages the world will be thrown into confusion like a wheel; fire and the sun being united, the world of desire will be consumed.

788. The heavens will again be restituted and therein the world will take its rise, together with its four castes, kings, Rishis, and the Dharma.

789. The Vedas, worship, and charity will again prevail with the revival of the Dharma; by narratives,[1] histories, prose-compositions, commentaries, annotations, thus-I-have-heard's, etc., the world will [again] fall into confusion.

790. Preparing properly-coloured cloth, have it further cleaned, have the cloth dyed with bluish mud and cow-dung making it nondescript in colour, so that the body may be covered with robes in every way different from the appearance of the philosophers.

791. Let the Yogin preach the doctrine, which is the badge of the Buddhas; let him drink water filtered through a cloth and carry the hip-string; in due time let him go about begging and keep away from things vile.

(364) 792. He will be born in a heaven filled with light, and the other two will appear among mankind; decorated with precious stones he will be born as a god and a world-lord.

793. In the abode of light he enjoys the four worlds by means of the teaching based on the Dharma; but after a long reign over the worlds he will retrograde on account of desire.

794. Thus there are the golden age, the age of triads, the age of two, and the age of vice; the Lion of the Śākyas will appear in the age of vice, I and others in the golden age.

795. Siddhartha of the Śākya family, Vishṇu, Vyāsa,

[1] Literally, "So indeed it was."

SAGATHAKAM

Maheśvara—such other philosophers will appear after my passing.

796. There will be the teaching of the Lion of the Śākyas told in the thus-I-have-heard's, and that of Vyāsa in the narratives (so-indeed-it-was), and the past events.

797. Vishṇu and Maheśvara will teach about the creation of the world; things like this will take place after my passing.

798. My mother is Vasumati, my father is the wise Prajāpati; I belong to the Kātyāyana family, and my name is Viraja the Victor.

799. I was born in Campā, and as my father and grandfather, being descendants of the lunar race (*somavaṁśa*), [my family name] is "The Moon-Protected" (*somagupta*).

(365) 800. Making vows, I shall become a homeless mendicant and teach the doctrine in a thousand ways; Mahāmati being given assurance and anointed, I shall enter into Nirvana.

801. Mati will hand [the doctrine] over to Dharma and Dharma to Mekhala; but Mekhala and his disciple being too weak [the doctrine] will disappear at the end of the Kalpa.

802. Kāśyapa, Krakucchanda, and Kanaka, who are the removers, and I, Viraja, and others—these Buddhas all belong to the golden age.

803. After the golden age there will appear a leader by the name of Mati, who is a great hero (*mahāvīra*) well acquainted with the five forms of knowledge.

804. Not in the age of two, not in the age of triads, not in the age of vice, which will come after, but in the golden age world-teachers will appear, and attain Buddhahood.

805. Without removing the marks, without cutting it into tens,[1] have the upper garment patched with spots like the eyes in the tail of a peacock.

806. Let the space between the eyes be two or three fingers apart; if the patches are otherwise distributed it will excite in the ignorant a desire to possess.

[1] Is this right?

807. Let the Yogin always keep the fire of greed under control, be bathed in the water of knowledge, and practise the triple refuge, and exert himself diligently throughout the three periods.

(366) 808. When an arrow, or a stone, or a piece of wood, is sent forth by means of a bow or sling, one hits and another falls; so it is with good and bad.

809. The one cannot be the many, for then nowhere would diversities be seen. Let all receivers be like the wind, and donors be like the land.

810. If the one were the many, all would be without a causal agency; this is the destruction of a causal agency, which is the teaching of the theorisers.

811. [Their teaching] will be like a lamp, like a seed, because of similitude; but where are the many? If the one becomes the many, this is the teaching of the theorisers.

812. From sesame no beans grow, rice is not the cause of barley, wheat does not produce corn; how can the one be the many?

813. There will be Pāṇini, author of the Śabdanetṛi, Akshapāda, Vṛihaspati; Praṇetṛi the Lokāyata will be found in Brahma-garbha.

814. Kātyāyana will be the author of a sutra, and Yajñavalka will be like him; Bhuḍhuka will write astronomical works; they will appear in the age of vice.

(367) 815. Balin will appear to promote the welfare of the world, the happiness of mankind, he will be the protector of all that is good; Balin the king will be a great ruler.

816. Vālmīka, Masurāksha, Kauṭilya, and Āśvalāyana, who are highly virtuous Rishis, will appear in the future.

817. Siddhartha of the Śākya family, Bhūtānta, Pañcacūḍaka, Vāgbaliratha, Medhāvin will appear in the times that follow.

818. When I take my abode in the forest-ground, Brahma, chief of the gods, will give me the hairy skin of a deer, a staff made of wood, a girdle, and a discus.

819. The great Yogin will be called Viraja the Muni,

the teacher and pointer of emancipation; he is the badge of all the Munis.

820. Brahma with his retinues and many gods will give me an antelope's skin from the sky, and then the ruler will vanish.

821. When I am in the forest-ground, Indra and Virūḍhaka and others, accompanied by the celestial beings, will give me most exquisite garments and a begging bowl.

(368) 822. Seeking for a cause in the doctrine of no-birth, [one may say that] that which is unborn is born, too, [and imagine that] the no-birth [theory] is [thereby] established; but this is done in words only.

823–828. (Chapter VI, verses 12–17.)[1]

829. That the mind is set in motion by ignorance which has been accumulated by thought since beginningless past, that it is bound to birth and destruction—this is the imagination of the theorisers.

830. The Sāṁkhya philosophy is twofold. There is transformation owing to primary matter; (369) in primary matter there is action, and action is self-originating.

831. Primary matter is with all existing beings, and qualities are regarded as differentiated, various are effects and causes, no transformation takes place.

832. As quicksilver is pure and not soiled dy dirt, so is the Ālaya pure, being the seat of all sentient beings.

833. The onion-odour of onion, the womb of a pregnant woman, the saltiness of salt, etc.—does not [each] evolve like the seed?

834. Otherness is not otherness, so is bothness not bothness; to be is not to be attached to, there is neither non-being nor the Saṁskṛita.

835. [To say that] an ego is found in the Skandhas is like saying that the horse-nature is in the cow-nature, which has nothing to do with it; we may speak of the Saṁskṛita and the Asaṁskṛita, but there is no self-nature.

---

[1] It is noteworthy that the repetitions grow less as we approach the end and that the subjects referred to are less congruous with those of the text. The Sagāthakam may be an independent collection.

836. Defiled by logic, by the traditional teachings (*āgama*),[1] by wrong views, by speculation, they are not able to ascertain definitely about the ego, which they say is; but it does not exist in any way other than clinging.

837. It is certainly their mistake to think that the ego is perceivable along with the Skandhas by reason of oneness and otherness; the theorisers are not enlightened.

838. As an image is seen in a mirror, in water, or in an eye, (370) so is the soul in the Skandhas devoid of oneness and otherness.

839. Let it be known that those who reflect and practise meditation can be released from the evil theories by training themselves in the three things: the path (*mārga*), the truth (*satya*), and the insight (*darśana*).

840. As a flash of lightning is seen and unseen as the sun passes through a slit of a door, so is the transformation of all things; it is not as it is imagined by the ignorant.

841. Being confused in mind the ignorant view Nirvana as the disappearance of the existent; but since the wise see into reality (*sadbhava*) as it abides in itself, they have a truer insight.

842. Transformation [which is the actual state of existence] is to be ascertained as removed from birth and destruction, devoid of existence and non-existence, released from qualified and qualifying.

843. Transformation is to be ascertained as having nothing to do with the philosophical doctrines, with names and forms, and giving an abode[2] to views of an inner ego.

844. With the [pleasant] touches of the gods and the harassings of the hells, if it were not for the middle existence, no Vijñānas would ever evolve.[3]

845. It should be known that the womb-born, the egg-born, the moisture-born, and other various bodies of sentient beings are born of the middle existence and descend into the [six] paths of existence.

---

[1] After T'ang.
[2] "Destroying", according to T'ang.
[3] Read after T'ang.

846. To say that the passions are quieted and destroyed apart from right reasoning and scriptural teaching, (371) is the view and discourse of the philosophers, which is not to be practised by the intelligent.

847. One should first examine into the nature of an ego-soul and keep oneself away from attachment; to try to go beyond without an examination is of no more worth than a barren-woman's child.

848. I observe with a divine eye which is of transcendental wisdom and is removed from the flesh, [with this I observe] sentient beings, the physical bodies of all living creatures as devoid of the Saṁskāra and Skandhas.[1]

849. It is seen that [beings] are distinguished as ugly-coloured and beautifully-coloured, as emancipated and unemancipated, as heavenly and free from the Saṁskāra, and as abiding with the Saṁskāra.

850. I have the body that goes about in the [six] paths of existence; this does not belong to the realm of the theorisers; it goes beyond the human world and is not the possession of the theorisers.

851. The ego-soul is not, and the mind is born; how does this evolving come about? Is it not said that its appearing is like a river, a lamp, and a seed?

852. The Vijñāna not being born there is no ignorance; ignorance being absent, there is no Vijñāna, and how can succession take place?

853. The three divisions of time and no-time, and the fifth is beyond description; this is what is known to the Buddhas [only, though] mentioned by the theorisers.

(372) 854. Knowledge that is the cause of the Saṁskāra is not to be described by the Saṁskāra; knowledge that is known as the Saṁskāra seizes the Saṁskāra-path.[2]

855. That being so, this is; causal conditions [everywhere] but no causes; because of this absence there are no causal agencies; they are [only] symbolically pointed out.

856. The wind, indeed, makes fire burn, but it only

[1] Read after T'ang.
[2] Is this the right reading?

incites and does not produce; further, incited by it the fire goes out; how can [the ego of] a sentient being be established?

857. The Saṁskṛita and the Asaṁskṛita are spoken of as devoid of attachment; how is fire imagined by the ignorant for the establishment [of their ego]?

858. Fire comes to exist in this world supported by the strength of mutuality; if it is imagined to be like fire, whence is the rising of a sentient ing [i.e. an ego-soul]?

859. By reason of the Manas, etc., there is the accumulation of the Skandhas and Āyatanas; non-ego like a wealthy merchant moves on with mentation (*citta*).

860. These two like the sun are always removed from effect and cause; fire does not establish them, and the theorisers fail to understand.

861. The mind, sentient beings, and Nirvana—these are primarily pure, but defiled by faults of the beginningless past; they are not differentiated, they are like space.

(373) 862. Defiled by the bad theories of the philosophers, Hastiśayya, etc., are wrapped and enveloped with [the false discriminations of] the Manovijñāna, they imagine fire, etc., are purifying.

863. Those who see [reality] as it is in itself will see their passions burst asunder; leaving the forest of bad analogies behind, they reach the realm of the wise.

864. Thus [reality] is imagined to be something other than itself by the differentiation of knower and known; the dull-witted do not understand it, and what is beyond description is talked about.

865. As the ignorant make a sandal-wood drum by taking something else which appears like sandal-wood and aloe wood, so is [true] knowledge [to be distinguished] from that of the theorisers.

866. Having eaten he will rise holding the bowl empty; he will have his mouth well cleansed of offensive and injurious matter; he is to conduct himself thus towards food.

867. He who reflects rationally on this truth will attain serenity of mind, accomplish the most excellent discipline,

SAGATHAKAM

and be above imagination; he will be released from attachment and realise the highest meaning; and thus he will light up the golden path of the Dharma.

868. When he who is possessed of stupidity and imagination rising from his views of being and non-being is freed from the net of bad theories tainted thereby, and from greed, vice, and anger, he is washed of the pigment and besprinkled by the Buddhas [with their own] hands.

869. Some philosophers are confused about the direction [of truth] because of their theory of causation; others are perturbed over conditions of causality; (374) others who are not wise abide in nihilism because of their negation of causation and reality.

870. There are transformations maturing from [the activities of] the Manas and the Vijñānas; the Manas is born of the Ālaya, and the Vijñāna comes from the Manas.

871. From the Ālaya all mental activities take their rise like the waves; with habit-energy as cause all things are born in accordance with conditions of causation.

872. [All things] momentarily divided but bound up in a continuous chain, are taken hold of as real while they are of Mind itself; they appear in varieties of forms and characters, but are the product of Manas and the eye-Vijñāna, etc.

873. Bound up by the faults [of speculation] since beginningless past, there is the growth of habit-energy which gives rise to something like an external world; it is Mind which is seen as manifoldness when it is hindered by wrong philosophical theories.

874. With that as cause and with that other as condition, [the Vijñāna system] is evolved; when these philosophical views are born, transformations take place.

875. All things are like Māyā and a dream and the Gandharvas' city; they appear as a mirage, as a lunar reflection in water; be it known that it is all due to self-discrimination.

876. From the splitting-up of moral conduct, there is suchness and the right knowledge dependent on it; such

Samādhis of superior grade as the Māyā-like, the Śūraṅgama, etc. [are attained].

877. By entering into the [various] stages, the psychic powers, and the self-masteries, the knowledge of the Māyā-likeness of existence and the [will-]body [are obtained], and there is anointment by the Buddhas.

(375) 878. When the world is seen as quiescent, the mind ceases and the [first] stage of Joy is attained, and [finally] they will reach Buddhahood.

879. A revulsion taking place at the seat [of consciousness, a man becomes] like a multicoloured gem; he performs deeds [of beneficence] for sentient beings in the same way as the moon reflects itself in water.

880. When the dualism of being and non-being is abandoned, there is neither bothness nor not-bothness; and going beyond Śrāvakahood and Pratyekabuddhahood, one will even pass over the seventh stage.

881. [As he goes up through the stages] his insight into the truth of self-realisation will be purified at every stage, and releasing himself from externality as well as from the philosophers, he will discourse on the Mahāyāna.

882. When there is a revulsion (parāvṛitti) from discrimination, one is removed from death and destruction; let him discourse on the truth of the emancipated ones, which is like a hare's horns,[1] and a [multicoloured] gem.

883. As the text [is completed] by reason, so is reason [revealed] by the text; therefore, let there be reason [and the text]; let there be no other discrimination than reason.[2]

---

[1] After Wei and T'ang. The text has "hare's hair" which in this connection yields no sense. The truth of emptiness may be in a manner compared to a hare's horns and not to its hair.

[2] This is the reading of T'ang. By "text" (教, grantha) is meant any literary production in which a principle or reason, 理, (yukti) is expounded. Grantha is here contrasted to yukti as deśanā or deśanā-pātha is to siddhānta or pratyātmagati, or as ruta is to artha. This contrasting the letter to spirit or meaning has been one of the main topics of the Laṅkāvatāra. Wei has 精 for grantha and 相應 for yukti, which does not yield any sense in this connection. The two versions, Wei and T'ang, are quoted in full:

Wei—如依精相應. 依法亦如是. 依相應相應. 莫分別於異.
T'ang—教由理故成. 理由教故顯. 當依此教理. 勿更餘分別.

SAGATHAKAM

884. Such are the eye, karma, desire, ignorance, and the Yogins; such is the Manas in relation to the eye[-consciousness] and form, such is the Mānas in relation to the defiled.[1]

Here Ends "The Mahāyāna Sūtra Called the *Ārya-Saddharma-Laṅkāvatāra*, Together with the Verses."

(376)   All things are born of causation,
        And their cause has been told by the Tathagata;
        And the Great Muni tells
        That their cessation takes place thus.

---

[1] This is missing in T'ang. Wei further adds: "When the Buddha preached this exquisite Sutra, the Holy Mahāmati the Bodhisattva-Mahāsattva, Rāvaṇa the King, Śuka, Sāraṇa, Kumbakarṇa, and other Rākshasas, the Devas, the Nāgas, the Yakshas, the Gandharvas, the Asuras, the gods, the Bhikshus were all delighted and accepted [the teaching]." This addition shows that Wei as a whole may be a much later production even than T'ang, for such a passage is ordinarily regarded as the regular conclusion for a sutra; nd when this was found missing in the earlier copy of the *Laṅkāvatāra*, the writer of the Wei original added it to complete the form.

APPENDIX

APPENDIX

APPENDIX

In order to show how varied are the three Chinese and one Tibetan translations, due to whatever causes textual or personal, I have herewith appended a comparative table of these versions which are accompanied with their respective English translations. The passage chosen for this purpose is one of the most difficult and at the same time most important sections (§ LXIX) in the *Laṅkā,* chiefly from the point of doctrinal interpretation. In the reading of the Tibetan version I have entirely relied upon Professor Yenga Teramoto, of Otani Buddhist College.

One thing in this section, which is most striking, is that the *Laṅkā* asserts the existence of a reality which is perceivable only by the eye of transcendental knowledge, which is in the possession of a wise man. The reality is here designated as Āryabhāvavastu or Āryavastubhāvasvabhāva. It is the exalted ultimate self-nature of all things, and as it can be recognised only when our spiritual eye looks beyond the realm of discriminations which is ruled by laws of being and non-being, it is also to be called the truth of Solitude, Viviktadharma, that is, the Absolute.

For *āryabhāvavastu,* Sung has 聖性事, Wei 聖人境界, and T'ang 諸聖法, while for *āryavastubhāvasvabhāva* Sung has 聖事性自性, Wei 聖人境界如實法體, and T'ang 聖人所見法. The Sung and the Nanjo text must have been the same as far as these two terms go, but Wei evidently had *vishaya* for *vastu* and *bhūta*(?) for *bhāva,* while T'ang has one 法 probably for both *vastu* and *bhāva,* though it has generally 事 for *vastu* and 法 for *bhāva.* For T'ang's 所見 (*driśya*) there is nothing corresponding in the Sanskrit.

The Tibetan for *āryabhāvavastu* and *āryavastubhāvasvabhāva* is respectively འཕགས་པའི་ངོ་བོའི་དངོས་པོ་ and འཕགས་པའི་དངོས་བོའི་ངོ་བོ་རང་བཞིན, whereas *āryajñānasvabhāvavastu* is འདགས་པའི་ཡེ་ཤེས་ཀྱི་དངོས་པོ. Evidently in this case the Tibetan equivalent for *vastu* is ངོ་བོ, and this is missing in the last combination. Generally in the *Laṅkā* the Tibetan has དངོས་པོ་རང་བཞིན for *bhāvasvabhāva*, and དངོས་པོ and ངོ་བོ are synonymously used as is sometimes the case with the Chinese.

In paragraph 5, towards the end, there is another reference to Āryajñānasvabhāvavastu for which both Sung and T'ang have quite literally 聖智自性事, whereas Wei gives 聖智法體. Ordinarily, *vastu* and *bhāva* are used both to designate particular objects of discrmination, thus making them interchangeable. But *vastu* is used in another sense in the *Laṅkā*, that is, in the sense of absolute reality. We have on p. 147, line 6 (Nanjo): *Vidyate tathatāvastu āryāṇāṁ gocaro yathā*, for which Sung has: 有事悉如如・如賢聖境界; Wei: 如眞如本有・彼見聖境界; and T'ang: 有眞如妙物・如諸聖所行. A Vastu to be characterised as suchness and the realm where the wise have their abode, cannot be a particular object of discriminating knowledge.

The following comparison will be I hope of some interest to Chinese and Sanskrit students of Buddhism.